ISBN 0-8373-5012-3

12 ADMISSION TEST SERIES

 *New* **RUDMAN'S QUESTIONS AND ANSWERS ON THE...**

DAT

DENTAL ADMISSION TEST

How to qualify for admission to the Dental Schools of...

PENNSYLVANIA	**ILLINOIS**
TUFTS	**N.Y.U.**
FLORIDA	**TORONTO**

...and hundreds of others.

Intensive preparation for all parts of the examination including...

- Survey of Natural Sciences
  - Biology
  - Inorganic Chemistry
  - Organic Chemistry
- Science Reading Comprehension
- Quantitative Ability
- Perceptual-Motor Ability
  (Abstract Reasoning)

NATIONAL LEARNING CORPORATION

Copyright © 1995 by

National Learning Corporation

212 Michael Drive, Syosset, New York 11791
(516) 921-8888

PRINTED IN THE UNITED STATES OF AMERICA

PASSBOOK®

NOTICE

This book is *SOLELY* intended for, is sold *ONLY* to, and its use is *RESTRICTED* to *individual*, bona fide applicants or candidates who qualify by virtue of having seriously filed applications for appropriate license, certificate, professional and/or promotional advancement, higher school matriculation, scholarship, or other legitimate requirements of educational and/or governmental authorities.

This book is *NOT* intended for use, class instruction, tutoring, training, duplication, copying, reprinting, excerption, or adaptation, etc., by:

    (1) Other Publishers

    (2) Proprietors and/or Instructors of "Coaching" and/or Preparatory Courses

    (3) Personnel and/or Training Divisions of commercial, industrial, and governmental organizations

    (4) Schools, colleges, or universities and/or their departments and staffs, including teachers and other personnel

    (5) Testing Agencies or Bureaus

    (6) Study groups which seek by the purchase of a single volume to copy and/or duplicate and/or adapt this material for use by the group as a whole without having purchased individual volumes for each of the members of the group

    (7) Et al.

Such persons would be in violation of appropriate Federal and State statutes.

PROVISION OF LICENSING AGREEMENTS. — Recognized educational commercial, industrial, and governmental institutions and organizations, and others legitimately engaged in educational pursuits, including training, testing, and measurement activities, may address a request for a licensing agreement to the copyright owners, who will determine whether, and under what conditions, including fees and charges, the materials in this book may be used by them. In other words, a licensing facility *exists* for the legitimate use of the material in this book on other than an individual basis. However, it is asseverated and affirmed here that the materials in this book *CANNOT* be used without the receipt of the express permission of such a licensing agreement from the Publishers.

NATIONAL LEARNING CORPORATION
212 Michael Drive
Syosset, New York 11791

Inquiries re licensing agreements should be addressed to:
The President
National Learning Corporation
212 Michael Drive
Syosset, New York 11791

PASSBOOK SERIES®

THE *PASSBOOK SERIES*® has been created to prepare applicants and candidates for the ultimate academic battlefield—the examination room.

At some time in our lives, each and every one of us may be required to take an examination—for validation, matriculation, admission, qualification, registration, certification, or licensure.

Based on the assumption that every applicant or candidate has met the basic formal educational standards, has taken the required number of courses, and read the necessary texts, the *PASSBOOK SERIES*® furnishes the one special preparation which may assure passing with confidence, instead of failing with insecurity. Examination questions—together with answers—are furnished as the basic vehicle for study so that the mysteries of the examination and its compounding difficulties may be eliminated or diminished by a sure method.

This book is meant to help you pass your examination provided that you qualify and are serious in your objective.

The entire field is reviewed through the huge store of content information which is succinctly presented through a provocative and challenging approach—the question-and-answer method.

A climate of success is established by furnishing the correct answers at the end of each test.

You soon learn to recognize types of questions, forms of questions, and patterns of questioning. You may even begin to anticipate expected outcomes.

You perceive that many questions are repeated or adapted so that you gain acute insights, which may enable you to score many sure points.

You learn how to confront new questions, or types of questions, and to attack them confidently and work out the correct answers.

You note objectives and emphases, and recognize pitfalls and dangers, so that you may make positive educational adjustments.

Moreover, you are kept fully informed in relation to new concepts, methods, practices, and directions in the field.

You discover that you are actually taking the examination all the time: you are preparing for the examination by "taking" an examination, not by reading extraneous and/or supererogatory textbooks.

In short, this PASSBOOK®, used directedly, should be an important factor in helping you to pass your test.

DENTAL ADMISSION TEST

1. WHAT IS THE DENTAL ADMISSION TEST (short name for the DENTAL ADMISSION TESTING PROGRAM)?

All applicants seeking admission to member dental schools of the American Association of Dental Schools, which, in turn, is affiliated with the American Dental Association, are required to take the DENTAL ADMISSION TESTING PROGRAM, a battery of tests requiring a full day for administration. This admission test program is conducted by the Council on Dental Education of the American Dental Association, in cooperation with the American Association of Dental Schools.

The tests are designed to measure general academic ability, comprehension of scientific information, and perceptual ability.

Four (4) examinations are included in the Dental Admission Testing Program. These are:

1. Survey of Natural Sciences (Biology, Inorganic, Organic Chemistry)
2. Reading Comprehension (Natural and Basic Sciences)
3. Quantitative Ability
4. Test of Perceptual-Motor Ability (Two and three dimensional problem solving)

The sections covered in Part I, Survey of Natural Sciences, are as follows:

BIOLOGY

Cell structure and function	Human anatomy and physiology
Life and its characteristics	Reproduction and development
The animal kingdom	Genetics
Evolution and ecology	

INORGANIC CHEMISTRY

Nature of Matter and Measurement	Rates of Reaction and Kinetics
Stoichiometry	Thermodynamics and Thermochemistry
Gases	
Atomic Structure	Solutions
Liquids and Solids	Oxidation-Reduction reactions
Chemical Equilibrium	Quantum Mechanics
Periodic Properties	Nuclear Reactions

ORGANIC CHEMISTRY

Bonding	Nomenclature
Mechanisms	Reactions & reaction mechanisms
Chemical and physical properties	Acids
Organic analysis	Aromatics
Stereo-chemistry	Electronic effects
Synthesis	

2. WHEN IS THE DENTAL ADMISSION TEST GIVEN?

The DENTAL ADMISSION TEST is given two (2) times a year, usually during October, and April. This program is predicated on the admission of freshmen in the fall term of the year.

In general, because of the significant increase in the number of applicants applying to dental school, candidates are encouraged to participate in this admission testing program well in advance of intended dental school enrollment. It is suggested that applicants participate during the October administration of the examination, one year prior to entering dental school. However, some dental schools may require an earlier examination.

3. HOW DOES THE CANDIDATE APPLY TO DENTAL SCHOOL?

To apply to a dental school, obtain directly from the school or schools in which you are interested their admissions application. You are then to complete the application, including all the requirements and details therein outlined, and return this material directly to the school(s). One of the basic requirements on the application forms of all dental schools is to apply for and to take the DENTAL ADMISSION TESTING PROGRAM.

4. HOW DOES THE CANDIDATE APPLY FOR THE DENTAL ADMISSION TEST?

All dental schools without exception, require the candidate to take the DENTAL ADMISSION TESTING PROGRAM (or DENTAL ADMISSION TEST). You may obtain the application form or blank for this test battery either from the school or from the American Dental Association. The *completed application* to take the DAT, with fee, must then be returned to this address only: Division of Educational Measurements, American Dental Association, 211 East Chicago Avenue, Chicago, Illinois 60611.

It is suggested that the applicant first obtain from the school to which he wishes to apply full information about that school's policies in regard to the timing of the Dental Admission Test. Each school has its own admission schedule and will, accordingly, advise the applicant of the testing period which will permit his record to be sent to them in time for processing. It will then be the applicant's responsibility to file his application with the American Dental Association in sufficient time to be assigned to the testing period and testing center that he prefers -- that is, at least two weeks before the testing period.

At the time the applicant submits his application, he carefully indicates the choice of testing city and testing date since it is difficult and requires a great deal of time to make changes after an assignment has been made. *The testing program requires one full day's attendance at the testing center.*

Applicants are allowed to repeat the examination during the next regularly scheduled test. There are no special makeup examination dates. Candidates are required to submit a new application and fee. Partial examinations are *not* allowed nor will the results of partial tests be scored and submitted to dental schools. Candidates repeating the examination must participate in all sections of the test.

5. HOW ARE SCORES ON THE DENTAL ADMISSION TEST REPORTED?

Approximately six (6) weeks (from the date of the test) are required for the test results to be reported to the dental schools which the candidate has designated. The reports on the applicant's test scores will be sent to the five (5) dental schools which the applicant has indicated on the dental admission test application form. In addition to the basic $35 fee that accompanies the application, there will be additional payments for each school in excess of the five (5) permitted.

6. WHAT IS THE IMPORTANCE OF THE SCORES ON THE DENTAL ADMISSION TEST?
    It can be said without equivocation that the scores on the DENTAL ADMISSION TEST are vital for the candidate's acceptance. It can be equally firmly stated that perhaps no other professional program of this type places so high a value on the scores achieved on a single aptitude test. This is for the reason that the Admission Test is considered to be the *one common denominator* by which applicants from *all* institutions may be compared.
    However, this does not mean that the results on the DAT are of greater importance than, or exclude attention from, the other -- more general and more usual -- factors for selection, such as previous college and university records, letters of recommendation, reports of committees that have interviewed the applicant, the high school record, and similar data concerning the ability, character, and personality of the applicant. Stated in another way, the results of the aptitude test battery will never constitute the sole basis for considering the application for admission. However, it is an important factor to be considered with the others. An interesting fact in this connection is that most dental schools have established certain minimum patterns of predental grade-point averages and aptitude test scores which must be met to be considered for admission.

7. WHAT UNDERGRADUATE PREPARATION IS PREFERRED BY DENTAL SCHOOLS?
    All of the dental schools require a minimum of two (2) academic years of liberal arts study. This means that the applicant must have completed at least sixty (60) semester hours or two (2) full academic years of work, which is the equivalent of 1/2 of the requirement for a Bachelor's Degree. Attendance at an accredited junior college will therefore satisfy this minimum requirement. However, the student who offers only two (2) years of college work must have completed therein one (1) year each of English, biology, physics, and inorganic chemistry, and one-half (1/2) year of organic chemistry. All science courses must include both class and laboratory instruction.
    These, it must be emphasized, are minimal requirements *only* prescribed by the Council on Dental Education. Although the usual pre-professional education requirement for admission to dental school stipulates at least two academic years of liberal arts study, many of the dental schools in the United States require three (3) years of collegiate education and most prefer baccalaureate degree candidates. Applicants should be aware that more than 90% of the first year dental class completed three or more years of pre-professional education and that the majority of students received a baccalaureate degree prior to dental school enrollment.
    Thus, the two-year student is not encouraged, and it is the

three-or four-year applicant who is preferred, since he is considered better prepared for a professional career.

The applicant should also keep in mind that many applicants for admission to dental school offer more than the minimum requirements and are, in effect, competing with him for the same place.

Finally, it is incumbent upon the applicant to ascertain the requirements of the individual schools to which he may apply so that he may be able to better plan his predental work since there are certain basic pre-dental education courses which must be completed prior to enrollment in dental school. Since the dental schools vary with regard to the required pre-dental education courses, it is essential that the applicant contact the appropriate schools to determine the specific admission requirements. The Council on Dental Education supports the trend in admission policies which encourages the acquisition of a baccalaureate degree prior to dental school enrollment.

8. HOW DOES THE CANDIDATE CHOOSE A PREDENTAL COLLEGE?

Most colleges fulfill the specific course requirements for entrance to dental school. A nationally approved predental list does not exist. Thus the student has a wide range of choices in the way of a predental college.

Guidance in this matter is best secured from your high school counselor, from the colleges to which you have referred, by correspondence with dental schools, by referring to accrediting agencies such as the Middle States Association of Colleges and Secondary Schools, and by consulting various publications and college catalogues.

9. HOW DOES THE DENTAL SCHOOL SELECT ITS APPLICANTS FOR ADMISSION?

The importance of the Dental Admission Test has been emphasized above. Let us now consider some of the "more general and usual" factors influencing the admission of applicants.
1. Scholastic record

The quality and quantity of predental education is of prime importance to an Admissions Committee in considering an application. All dental schools place a heavy emphasis on the grade-point standing. Generally, a student must have a C(2.0) average even to be *considered* for acceptance by any dental school. This, of course, is a minimal standard and very rarely does such an average gain admission.
2. Residence of the applicant

The State in which the applicant resides forms a very important consideration in the selection of students. Generally speaking, most dental schools give preference to students from their own general locality or region.

It is well to point out that one does not establish residence in a State merely by attending a college in that State. An out-of-State student is regarded as a non-resident even though he may have completed four years of undergraduate study in a college in that State.

3. Letters of recommendation
    Usually several letters of recommendation are called for in support of each application. One letter is always requested from the predental committee or predental advisor, as the case may be. In addition, the student is usually required to obtain letters from a non-science professor and from a member of the dental profession. It is a fact that the letter from the predental committee or predental advisor receives the greatest attention from the Admissions Committee.

4. Interviews
    This requirement varies from dental school to dental school. However, in many cases, it is required that the student visit the school. At this time, the applicant's appearance, personality, maturity, and ability to communicate are evaluated. Much useful information and many interesting facts are gleaned during these visits and, as a result, many dental schools consider the exchange between faculty members and applicants an integral part of their admission procedures.

5. Financial status
    The financial status of a student is carefully considered by an Admissions Committee. A professional education is a very expensive matter.
    Dental schools feel strongly that a student should not attempt to hold an outside job while attending dental school. The student should make every effort to obtain the necessary funds for a dental education *before* he enters upon attendance. Admittedly, the number of scholarships and loans available is inadequate. Therefore, the question of financing on the dental school application form is an important item to be answered -- carefully and honestly.

10. WHAT IS THE COURSE OF STUDY IN THE DENTAL SCHOOLS?
    After you have completed the predental requirements and have gained admission to a dental school, you must expect to spend four (4) academic years in dental study. Fortunately for the profession, there is no sub-standard dental school in the United States. All schools observe the minimum predental and professional requirements prescribed by the Council on Dental Education.
    The courses presented during the four-year program are divided between classroom instruction on the one hand, and laboratory and clinical experience and practice on the other. Roughly, about one-fourth of the student's time is taken up with classroom instruction and about three-fourths in the laboratory and clinic.
    The Council prescribes the subjects it expects to find in the curriculum of the school but leaves the time allotment in the several fields to the discretion and judgment of the individual school. The subjects included in the curricula are:

Anatomy-Macroscopic and Microscopic   Biochemistry
Anesthesia - General and Local   Dental Materials
Bacteriology   Diagnosis

Endodontics	Pathology - General and Oral
Ethics	Pedondontics
Histology and Embryology	Periodontics
History of Dentistry	Pharmacology and Materia Medica
Hygiene	Physiology
Jurisprudence	Practice Management
Medicine	Principles of Medicine
Operative Dentistry	Prosthodontics - Fixed & Removable
Oral Anatomy	Prosthesis
Oral Surgery	Public Health
Orthodontics	Roentgenology

Questions are frequently asked by prospective dental students and by guidance officers about scholarships in dental schools, the opportunities for students to find work, the cost of the entire course, the degrees conferred and the term system employed. Information should be sought on all of these matters directly from the individual dental schools.

11. HOW SHOULD THE APPLICANT PREPARE FOR THE DENTAL ADMISSION TEST?

This volume, QUESTIONS AND ANSWERS ON THE DENTAL ADMISSION TEST, is specifically designed to prepare students for the DAT. The book contains the appropriate general and background information, and follows in sequential form the format of the Examination.

The four (4) major areas of the Examination, viz., Natural Sciences, Reading Comprehension, and Quantitative Ability, and Test of Perceptual-Motor Ability, are fully delineated and exhaustively treated. The practice work exercises in the form of "Tests" help the candidate review important educational principles, practices, procedures, problems, and content in the form of varied concrete applications.

12. QUESTIONS AND ANSWERS APPEARING IN THIS PUBLICATION

The Dental Admission Test is prepared and administered by the American Dental Association, Chicago, Illinois 60611. Since copies of past examinations have not been made available, we have used in this book equivalent materials, including questions and answers, which are highly recommended by us as an appropriate means of preparing for the DENTAL ADMISSION TEST.

13. HOW TO APPLY

To initiate your application to any of the schools participating in AADSAS, you must obtain an official Application Request Card from your pre-dental advisor, a participating dental school, or from AADSAS, P.O. Box 4000, Iowa City, Iowa 52240.

If you decide to apply to any of the dental schools participating in AADSAS, you must file your application through AADSAS.

The American Association of Dental Schools and the American Dental Association are separate associations. All inquiries concerning the application service should be directed to:
American Association of Dental Schools
Application Service
1619 Massachusetts Avenue, N.W.
Washington, D.C. 20036

DENTISTRY CAREERS

CONTENTS

———

DENTISTRY CAREERS

Dentistry, as a branch of the health profession, emphasizes not only treatment but also prevention of problems associated with the hard and soft tissues of the mouth. Dentists and other trained personnel work in cooperation with physicians, school health services, nursing homes, and health-maintenance organizations to safeguard public health. Education of the public in good oral hygiene and nutrition contributes to the prevention and cure of oral-health problems.

As standards of living and education have risen along with the availability of prepaid dental plans, the demand for dental care has also risen. Dentistry, both in general and specialty practice, is a field offering lifetime opportunity for well-qualified, professional people.

The dental profession has tried to increase availability of services with the use of a large number of trained personnel. The trend is also toward the expansion of the role of dental auxiliaries (dental hygienists and dental assistants) by delegating to them specific tasks requiring greater skill and responsibility, in order to increase the dentist's productive capacity. These tasks, classified as "expanded functions," vary from State to State, but in all instances are performed under the dentist's supervision.

I. Dental Assistant

Today's busy dentist, in either general or specialized practice, needs one or more dental assistants.

It is the assistant's job to greet patients, make them comfortable, and prepare them for examination, treatment, or surgery. The assistant helps chairside—arranging instruments, materials, and medication; handing them to the dentist, as requested; preparing solutions, mixing materials, keeping accurate patient-treatment records, taking and processing X-rays; and sterilizing instruments. In addition, clerical work, which involves answering telephones, receiving payment for dental services, bookkeeping, and ordering supplies, is also usually part of the job.

As a dental auxiliary, the assistant may, in addition, perform expanded functions which vary from State to State and which may include applying materials to teeth to make them more resistant to decay, making models of patients' mouths as well as the impression trays to hold the materials used for the models. Cleaning, polishing, and making uncomplicated repairs on removable partial or complete dentures are other tasks which may be delegated to the dental assistant in States where this is legal.

Dental assistants do not specialize but may be employed by dentists in any of the specialties of dentistry such as oral surgery, orthodontics (straightening of teeth), or pedodontics (care and treatment of children's teeth). They may also be employed by hospital dental services, dental schools, dental products manufacturers and suppliers, health maintenance organizations, and insurance companies. Other employers are governmental agencies or organizations engaged in dental research.

Patience, understanding, and the ability to get along well with people are necessary qualities, since the assistant must be able to make the patient feel at ease. Good eyesight and hearing and the ability to use hands and fingers skillfully are needed, as well.

Job Requirements

American Dental Association (ADA) accredited courses for dental assistants are offered in dental schools, community colleges, vocational-technical schools, and privately owned and managed schools. Depending upon the curriculum, a program can be from 9 months to 2 years in length and lead to a certificate or associate degree in applied science. Admission requirements vary from school to school but generally will include a high school diploma, above average grades in science and English, a high school average of C or better, and a personal interview. Some programs require applicants to take a college entrance examination; for example, the School and College Ability Test (SCAT), the American College Test (ACT) and/or the Dental Assisting Aptitude Test (DAAT). The DAAT is administered by the Certifying Board of the American Dental Assistants Association.

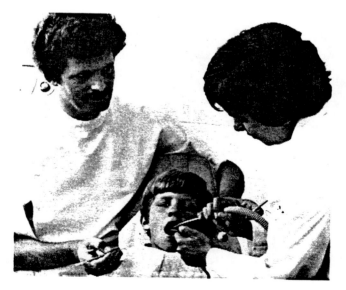

Certification is optional and not usually a requirement for employment, although it may occasionally result in higher wages. Continuing education is also optional but is required in order to maintain current certification.

Eligibility for certification is based upon graduation from an A.D.A. accredited program, and certification is issued by the Certifying Board of the American Dental Assistants Association.

Two States—Minnesota and California—currently have registration for performance of expanded functions and are both governed by their State board of dentistry. Qualifications vary and their relationship to employment would vary depending on the type of dental practice.

Opportunities

Dental assistants may advance to dental assisting educator by completing college-level courses leading to a baccalaureate degree.

Currently, the job outlook for dental assistants is excellent. As more and more dentists make use of expanded functions which these dental auxiliaries may now perform, the need for dental assistants will continue. Greater use of prepaid dental care plans by many persons will also increase the need for these workers.

For further information, contact:
American Dental Assistants Association

II. Dental Hygienist

Registered dental hygienist

The majority of dental hygienists are employed in dental office practice; others are employed in public schools, State and local health clinics, hospitals, industry, and voluntary health agencies. Duties vary according to the type of employment.

The hygienist, working in private practice under the dentist's direction, removes scale from teeth; applies materials to make teeth more resistant to decay; takes X-rays; and performs various laboratory tests, as well as other patient services related to health care of the mouth. Professional instruction in selection and use of toothbrushes and other devices, as well as instruction to patients about the relationship between diet and oral health, are also part of the job.

The practice of dental hygiene is governed by State laws and in some areas, hygienists may now perform expanded functions to aid the dentist. Administering local anesthetics, performing curettage (scraping under gums), placing dressings on open wounds after gum surgery, and placement and removal of temporary tooth restorations constitute some of these duties.

When working in a school system, dental hygienists provide dental health education to students and teachers. They may also provide counseling, instruct students on proper dental care, and plan programs on oral hygiene, as well as other duties.

When employed in the area of community dental health, hygienists assist dentists in determining the need for dental care and identifying resources for dental care. They may also develop and conduct organized dental-health-education programs designed to meet the needs of the community.

Some hygienists are engaged in dental research projects. Responsibilities can include interpreting data, writing reports on all studies, and preparing and presenting papers and publications on the research conducted.

Advanced training provides opportunities for teaching and/or administrative responsibilities in a dental-hygiene educational program. As a faculty member, the dental hygienist may teach a particular part of the curriculum which includes patient education, sciences, office practice, clinical techniques, and services to the community.

Dental hygienists also serve as consultants in an advisory capacity for State public health offices. Here, they provide in-service training for dental hygienists in local health departments; work cooperatively with other public health personnel, schools, and civic groups; and assist in field training for graduate dental hygiene students in public health. Responsibilities may also include the collection, development, and evaluation of dental-health-education materials as well as other duties.

Some hygienists work in nursing or convalescent homes or hospitals where they may act as consultants in developing dental-care procedures. They are primarily concerned with the special oral health problems of patients who are very ill, bedridden, and physically or mentally handicapped.

Although there are no recognized specialties in dental hygiene, many dental hygienists work in specialty areas, such as periodontics (treatment of tissues supporting the teeth), orthodontics (straightening of teeth), and pedodontics (care and treatment of children's teeth).

Job Requirements

Before entering practice in the field of dental hygiene, graduation from an accredited program and a license to practice are required. A high school diploma with a college preparatory course is basic to entry into such a program.

Two-year dental hygiene programs are offered by many community colleges, technical institutes, some 4-year colleges and universities, as well as schools of dentistry. Most will accept students for the 2-year program directly after their graduation from high school. On completing the 2-year program, the graduate receives a certificate or an associate degree. This type of degree prepares the graduate for office practice, work in a clinic, and work on some local public health projects.

There is an increasing emphasis on college-level work before entering a dental hygiene program. This is particularly true in 4-year colleges and universities and programs affiliated with dental schools, even though students are not working toward a bachelor's degree. Some junior colleges recommend previous work, usually in the sciences, before enrollment in the dental hygiene curriculum.

Prior to entering college, applicants take one or more of the standard college entrance examinations, and some schools recommend or require the Dental Hygiene Aptitude Test (DHAT) as well. The DHAT is designed to measure skills and knowledge in the biological, physical, chemical, and social sciences and the ability to read, analyze, and remember new information.

Other requirements may include physical and dental examinations and personal interviews. State and community-supported colleges usually give preference to residents of the State or area.

Post-certificate bachelor's degrees are offered by a number of 4-year colleges and universities. These

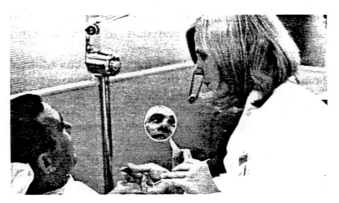

programs allow the hygienist who has completed a 2-year program to acquire clinical experience as well as to earn a bachelor of science degree with only 2 additional years of academic work. Usually, hygienists in these programs are preparing for a teaching career.

Some dental schools also offer bachelor of science degrees requiring 4 years of college work. In addition to office practice, graduates are prepared for positions requiring some supervisory and administrative responsibilities in health departments, hospitals, and educational institutions.

Graduate work leading to a master's degree in dental hygiene or a related field of public health is offered in several schools. Programs are designed for dental hygientists interested in teaching or administrative positions.

All States require a license to practice dental hygiene. A license is obtained by successfully completing both clinical and written examinations. Most States accept the National Board Dental Hygiene Examination at all accredited dental hygiene programs instead of the State written examination.

Clinical or practical examinations are given at least once a year by all State boards of dentistry and by several regional testing agencies. The dental hygiene license is issued by the State. Information, specific requirements, and testing dates can be obtained from individual State boards of dentistry or the Council on the National Boards of Dental Examiners of the American Dental Association.

Continuing education courses are available in some States for hygienists who want to keep up with the latest techniques and materials. They may be regularly scheduled evening classes in local schools or "refresher" courses running from a few days to several weeks and sponsored by professional associations or educational institutions.

In several States, continuing education is required to maintain licensure.

When licensed, the dental hygienist is ready to start working. The average week runs 35 to 40 hours with an occasional Saturday or evening included in the schedule.

The work itself involves contact with patients, patients' families, dentists, and other members of the oral health care team. In private practice, a considerable amount of time is spent working next to the patient in the dental chair. Physical stamina, good eyesight, and manual skills are important to success.

Opportunities

The overall employment outlook for dental hygienists is excellent due, in part, to growth of dental prepayment plans and also to increasing public demand for oral-health care. Opportunities are also good for hygienists willing to work in areas which do not have enough dental services and for those seeking part-time employment, as well as for dental hygiene health educators who benefit from increases in the number of health-education programs.

Advancement in this field is usually dependent upon additional education. Graduates of 2- or 3-year certificate or associate degree programs are generally limited to dental office practice and some public health positions. However, these graduates may decide to continue their education to the baccalaureate or master's degree level. Hygienists with baccalaureate degrees may work in a private practice and, with office experience, are eligible for positions requiring some supervisory and administrative responsibilities in health departments, hospitals, and educational institutions. Education to the master's level prepares the dental hygienist for advanced positions in teaching, administration, and public health.

For further information, contact:
American Dental Hygienists Association

III. Dental Laboratory Technician

Dental laboratory technicians make and repair orthodontic-tooth straightening devices, dental restorations, such as full or partial dentures, inlays, and crowns, using plastics, ceramics, and metals. The technician, a skilled craftsworker, produces dental appliances under the direction, or according to the prescription, of a licensed dentist by means of a procedure which must be performed with painstaking accuracy in order to insure perfect fit in the patient's mouth. An impression of the tooth or teeth is taken in the dentist's office and sent to the dental technician along with the prescription or work order. (To make full or partial dentures, the technician uses wax and plaster models, electric grinders and polishers, as well as instruments to hold models or casts so teeth can be arranged properly or to check casts for fit of the clasps which will hold partial dentures in the patient's mouth.) Bending, soldering, and casting are necessary techniques.

Dental laboratories, which are usually small, privately owned businesses located mostly in large cities,

employ the majority of technicians, although some technicians work in dentists' offices and a small number are employed by the Federal Government.

The work of the technician is not strenuous. Though there may be some pressure to meet time schedules, the dental laboratory is usually quiet and calm.

Good vision, ability to recognize very fine color shadings, finger and manual dexterity to work with delicate tools and materials are essential attributes which must be combined with the ability to follow instructions and work with absolute accuracy.

There are five areas of specialization available to dental technicians: complete dentures, partial dentures, crown and bridge, ceramics, and orthodontics. Ceramics is concerned with creating crowns of porcelain by building up layers of mineral powders which are then fused in an oven. Orthodontic devices require laying out designs of metal frameworks and clasps or constructing and repairing appliances used to straighten teeth.

Job Requirements

The single educational requirement for most jobs as dental technician is a high school diploma. These courses are particularly helpful—chemistry, physiology, art, ceramics, mechanical drawing, and shopwork. If possible, the student should acquire basic knowledge of the chemistry of plastics and simple metallurgy.

Many dental technicians learn the craft by on-the-job training lasting 3 to 4 years in a dental laboratory. Another way to prepare for this career is to enroll in an

approved training program offered by an accredited school. There are about 30 dental laboratory training programs in various schools throughout the country offering academic courses and laboratory instruction. These are 2-year programs leading to an associate degree in applied science.

Some technicians acquire their training in the armed services.

Certification exists for applicants who successfully complete the certified dental technician program examination after meeting the following qualifications: 5 years of experience in the field (time spent in an approved supervised training in a dental laboratory school may be substituted for part of this experience). For example, if a candidate is a graduate of an accredited 2-year school of dental laboratory technology, the 2 years plus 3 years of actual experience would qualify the individual to take the examination. Certified technicians are required to renew certification each year. They must meet continuing education requirements set by the National Board for Certification, National Association of Certified Dental Laboratories. The basic written examination covers history, law, and ethics. A second examination is concerned with 1 of the 5 laboratory specialties. Candidates then must pass a practical examination in the specialty or specialties for which they seek certification.

Opportunities

Although a career in dental laboratory technology may begin with on-the-job training in a commercial dental laboratory, additional education in an accredited school program leading to an associate degree is desirable. Dental technicians, depending upon their skill, experience, and education, may advance to managerial positions. Most of today's commercial dental laboratory owners came up "from the bench" to own their own business.

There are many factors which point to a greatly increased demand for dental technicians. First is the growth in the national population and the increasing numbers of older age groups which frequently require comprehensive dental health care. Second, there is a rising level of personal income and a growing public awareness of the importance of preventive dentistry. Third, it is estimated that a large number of Americans will be covered by dental prepayment insurance plans in the next 10 years.

For further information, contact: National Association of Dental Laboratories

IV.

Dentist

Dental surgeon
Doctor of dental medicine
Doctor of dental surgery

The majority of dentists are self-employed, work in their own offices in general practice, and provide a wide range of general care. This includes treating problems associated with the gums and teeth and also trying to prevent their occurrence or reccurrence. Their duties also include locating and filling cavities, straightening crooked teeth, performing extractions, treating gum and mouth diseases, as well as providing artifical teeth when necessary. The patient's general health is also of concern to the dentist. Symptoms may be detected which call for a physical checkup and require the dentist to work closely with the family doctor to correct the trouble. Cooperation with school nurses and health departments in prevention programs is often also involved.

Instead of entering private practice, a dentist may choose to take a salaried position. For those who do, there are opportunities in industry, hospitals, any branch of the armed forces, the Veterans Administration, public health facilities, dental research, health-maintenance organizations, and nursing homes.

Dentists can also find teaching opportunities in dental schools, and those interested in research will want to become associated with a teaching center. Teaching and research are often combined on a part-time basis with either private or salaried practice.

Although most dentists provide a wide range of general care, many take additional professional training in a specialty and then limit practice to that area of dentistry. In order to become a diplomate of a specialty board, the candidate must have at least 2 years of advanced training (3 years for oral surgery), meet certain other specific requirements, and pass a comprehensive examination given by the nationally recognized examining board assigned to the chosen specialty.

There are eight recognized dental specialties, and each specialty is concerned with a different aspect of oral health care. They are as follows:

The endodontist diagnoses and treats problems affecting teeth roots.

An oral pathologist examines specimens form patients' mouths, using a microscope and other laboratory equipment to diagnose tumors and other abnormal changes, both in the mouth and nearby areas.

Oral surgeons perform surgery on the mouth and jaws. Difficult extractions; removal of tumors; and surgical treatment of diseases, injuries, and defects in the oral region are some of the procedures involved in this specialty.

Orthodontists prevent, diagnose, and correct poor positioning of teeth and related structures.

Pedodontists treat childrens' teeth from birth through adolescence.

Periodontists treat tissues supporting and surrounding the teeth.

Prosthodontists restore patients' natural teeth and replace missing teeth with artificial substitutes so as to improve appearance, mastication, and speech.

Public health dentists are involved in preventing and controlling dental diseases and promoting good dental health in a community through planning, organizing, and maintaining the dental-health program of a public health agency.

Job Requirements

A career in dentistry requires early planning on the part of the student interested in this field. After graduation from high school, 6 to 7 years of school are required to complete the training necessary to become a D.M.D. (Doctor of Dental Medicine) or D.D.S. (Doctor of Dental Surgery)—equal titles.

While all dental schools are on a 4-year academic program, the college curriculum may vary from 3 to 4 years. Applicants must have a minimum of 2 years at an approved liberal arts college. Many schools require 3 or 4 years of study. Currently, the majority of students have completed 4 years of preprofessional education prior to enrollment in dental schools. Preprofessional (predental) education should emphasize courses in English, physics, inorganic and organic chemistry, as well as various biological sciences.

In recent years, dental schools have shown an increasing willingness to waive traditional prerequisites in order to admit students of high potential ability. As a result, the entire admissions scene is a changing one, and individual schools must be consulted for current requirements. Nevertheless, applicants should be aware of the stiff competition for admission to dental school. The prerequisites for dentistry are better than average grades, especially in the sciences, good eyesight, and skillful hands. Since dentists work closely with patients who are often in pain and under stresss, good health and a genuine liking for people are also necessary. Dental schools also look for a high degree of motivation and good scores on the Dental Admissions Test (an examination designed to show potential for dentistry).

Prospective dental students should seek guidance from faculty members and write for advice to the ad-

missions office of the dental school they plan to attend.

Students who have been admitted to dental school work in three broad academic areas. One area is the basic health sciences which include anatomy, biochemistry, history, microbiology, pathology, pharmacology, and physiology, each with emphasis on the special concerns of dentistry. A second area is application of the health sciences to delivery of oral health services, with emphasis on diagnosis, treatment planning, and the performance of all aspects of clinical dentistry. Among the subjects covered are patient psychology, business management, professional ethics, community health, and the use of dental auxiliaries (dental hygienist, dental assistant, and dental technician). The basic laboratory courses were formerly concentrated in the first and second years, with the third and fourth years reserved for clinical training. There is a growing tendency today to combine theory with practice as soon as possible. Dental schools are responding by designing curriculums which focus on the student as an individual and permit each student to gain professional knowledge and proficiency in ways best suited to individual needs.

After completion of dental school, a licensing examination must be taken by all new dentists in order to be able to practice. The examination is given by the dental licensure board of the State where the person

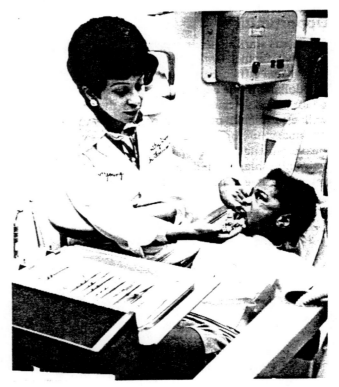

wishes to practice. Annual registration is required by some States. A number of States have agreements recognizing licenses issued in other States. Some States may also require a practical examination.

The American Dental Association conducts the National Board of Dental Examiners. This board gives written examinations which are accepted in lieu of written State tests in all States except Delaware and Florida. All clinical and practical examinations are administered by State boards.

Dentists who plan to specialize, teach, or do research may continue their education with postgraduate courses, or may enter a hospital as dental interns or residents. There is a nationally recognized examining board for each of the dental specialties.

Those who look forward to a career in the administration of dental health programs will need to supplement dental training and basic experience with an additional year of study leading to the degree of Master of Public Health.

All dentists, whether they specialize or not, are strongly encouraged to continue their education annually through special courses which are offered at hospitals, dental schools, and other places throughout the country. Continuing education requirements vary from State to State depending upon the State law regarding licensure.

Opportunities

Dentists starting out in private practice must face the fact that financial problems may be difficult the first few years. Office equipment may cost several thousand dollars. In the beginning, office hours will probably be long and irregular. Even when their practices are well established, many dentists work more than the customary 40-hour week. Being one's own employer means shouldering responsibility for office rent, assistants' salaries, and so on. However, private practice offers good income and other long-term satisfactions.

A staff post in a health agency may not offer the potential earnings of private practice but does bring economic security as well as the opportunity for promoting good dental health through community service.

Dentists advance by expansion of their practice. When employed in the education and administration fields, the dentist can advance from assistant to full professor or from assistant administrator at a public health agency to director.

The demand for dental services and the overall outlook for dentists is expected to be good despite the increased number of dental school graduates and a leveling off of population. However, areas of employment and need for specific types of dentists are changing. Rural and inner-city areas will continue to have the greatest demand for practicing dentists. As dentists, especially those in specialty practices, locate in large numbers in major urban areas, the job market in these areas will tighten. Medical advances and improvements in dental technology will lead to greater delegation of specific dental tasks to auxiliary personnel whose services extend the dentists' productive capacity.

For further information, contact:
American Dental Association
American Association of Dental Schools
American Association of Orthodontists
National Dental Association (Professional organization of Minority Dentists)

How to Take a Test

You have studied hard, long, and conscientiously.

With your official admission card in hand, and your heart pounding, you have been admitted to the examination room.

You note that there are several hundred other applicants in the examination room waiting to take the same test.

They all appear to be equally well prepared.

You know that nothing but your best effort will suffice. The "moment of truth" is at hand: you now have to demonstrate objectively, in writing, your knowledge of content and your understanding of subject matter.

You are fighting the most important battle of your life—to pass and/or score high on an examination which will determine your career and provide the economic basis for your livelihood.

What extra, special things should you know and should you do in taking the examination?

BEFORE THE TEST

Your Physical Condition Is Important

If you are not well, you can't do your best work on tests. If you are half asleep, you can't do your best either. Here are some tips:

1. Get about the same amount of sleep you usually get. Don't stay up all night before the test, either partying or worrying—DON'T DO IT.

2. If you wear glasses, be sure to wear them when you go to take the test. This goes for hearing aids, too.

3. If you have any physical problems that may keep you from doing your best, be sure to tell the person giving the test. If you are sick or in poor health, you really cannot do your best on any test. You can always come back and take the test some other time.

AT THE TEST

Examination Techniques

1. Read the *general* instructions carefully. These are usually printed on the first page of the examination booklet. As a rule, these instructions refer to the timing of the examination; the fact that you should not start work until the signal and must stop work at a signal, etc. If there are any *special* instructions, such as a choice of questions to be answered, make sure that you note this instruction carefully.

2. When you are ready to start work on the examination, that is as soon as the signal has been given, read the instructions to each question booklet, underline any key words or phrases, such as *least, best, outline, describe,* and the like. In this way you will tend to answer as requested rather than discover on reviewing your paper that you *listed without describing,* that you selected the *worst* choice rather than the *best* choice, etc.

3. If the examination is of the objective or so-called multiple-choice type, that is, each question will also give a series of possible answers: A, B, C, or D, and you are called upon to select the best answer and write the letter next to that answer on your answer paper, it is advisable to start answering each question in turn. There may be anywhere from 50 to 100 such questions in the three or four hours allotted and you can see how much time would be taken if you read through all the questions before beginning to answer any. Furthermore, if you come across a question or a group of questions which you know would be difficult to answer, it would undoubtedly affect your handling of all the other questions.

4. If the examination is of the essay-type and contains but a few questions, it is a moot point as to whether you should read all the questions before starting to answer any one. Of course if you are given a choice, say five out of seven and the like, then it is essential to read all the questions so you can eliminate the two which are most difficult. If, however, you are asked to answer all the questions, there may be danger in trying to answer the easiest one first because you may find that you will spend too much time on it. The best technique is to answer the first question, then proceed to the second, etc.

5. Time your answers. Before the examination begins, write down the time it started, then add the time allowed for the examination and write down the time it must be completed, then divide the time available somewhat as follows:

    a. If 3 ½ hours are allowed, that would be 210 minutes. If you have 80 objective-type questions, that would be an average of about 2 ½ minutes per question. Allow yourself no more than 2 minutes per question, or a total of 160 minutes, which will permit about 50 minutes to review.

    b. If for the time allotment of 210 minutes, there are 7 essay questions to answer, that would average about 30 minutes a question. Give yourself only 25 minutes per question so that you have about 35 minutes to review.

6. The most important instruction is *to read each question* and make sure you know what is wanted. The second most important instruction is to *time yourself properly* so that you answer every question. The third most important instruction is to *answer every question*. Guess if you have to but include something for each question, Remember that you will receive no credit for a blank and will probably receive some credit if you write something in answer to an essay question. If you guess a letter, say "B" for a multiple-choice question, you may have guessed right. If you leave a blank as the answer to a multiple-choice question, the examiners may respect your feelings but it will not add a point to your score. Some exams may penalize you for wrong answers, so in such cases *only*, you may not want to guess unless you have some basis for your answer.

7. Suggestions

    a. Objective-Type Questions

        (1) Examine the question booklet for proper sequence of pages and questions.

        (2) Read all instructions carefully.

        (3) Skip any question which seems too difficult; return to it after all other questions have been answered.

        (4) Apportion your time properly; do not spend too much time on any single question or group of questions.

        (5) Note and underline key words — *all, most, fewest, least, best, worst, same, opposite.*

        (6) Pay particular attention to negatives.

        (7) Note unusual option, e.g., unduly long, short, complex, different or similar in content to the body of the question.

        (8) Observe the use of "hedging" words — *probably, may, most likely, etc.*

        (9) Make sure that your answer is put next to the same number as the question.

      (10) Do not second guess unless you have good reason to believe the second answer is definitely more correct.

      (11) Cross out original answer if you decide another answer is more accurate; do not erase, *until* you are ready to hand your paper in.

      (12) Answer all questions; guess unless instructed otherwise.

      (13) Leave time for review.

b. Essay-Type Questions

    (1) Read each question carefully.

    (2) Determine exactly what is wanted. Underline key words or phrases.

    (3) Decide on outline or paragraph answer.

    (4) Include many different points and elements unless asked to develop any one or two points or elements.

    (5) Show impartiality by giving pros and cons unless directed to select one side only.

    (6) Make and write down any assumptions you find necessary to answer the question.

    (7) Watch your English, grammar, punctuation, choice of words.

    (8) Time your answers; don't crowd material.

8. Answering the Essay Question

Most essay questions can be answered by framing the specific response around several key words or ideas. Here are a few such key words or ideas:

M's: manpower, materials, methods, money, management

P's: purpose, program, policy, plan, procedure, practice, problems, pitfalls, personnel, public relations

a. Six basic steps in handling problems:

    (1) preliminary plan and background development

    (2) collect information, data and facts

    (3) analyze and interpret information, data and facts

    (4) analyze and develop solutions as well as make recommendations

    (5) prepare report and sell recommendations

    (6) install recommendations and follow up effectiveness

b. Pitfalls to Avoid

    (1) *Taking Things for Granted*
A statement of the situation does not necessarily imply that each of the elements is necessarily true; for example, a complaint may be invalid and biased so that all that can be taken for granted is that a complaint has been registered

    (2) *Considering only one side of a situation*
Wherever possible, indicate several alternatives and then point out the reasons you selected the best one.

    (3) *Failing to indicate follow up*
Whenever your answer indicates action on your part, make certain that you will take proper follow-up action to see how successful your recommendations, procedures, or actions turn out to be.

    (4) *Taking too long in answering any single question*
Remember to time your answers properly.

EXAMINATION SECTION

EXAMINATION SECTION

TEST 1

1. A characteristic of all known living organisms is that they   1.___
   A. require oxygen for respiration
   B. originate from pre-existing life
   C. have complex nervous systems
   D. carry on heterotrophic nutrition

2. Control of all physiological activities of an organism is   2.___
   necessary to maintain that organism's stability in its
   environment.
   This life activity is known as
   A. nutrition   B. respiration
   C. transport   D. regulation

3. Which cell organelles are the sites of aerobic cellular   3.___
   respiration in both plant and animal cells?
   A. Mitochondria   B. Centrosomes
   C. Chloroplasts   D. Nuclei

4. The diameter of the field of vision of a compound light   4.___
   microscope is 1.5 millimeters.
   This may also be expressed as _____ microns.
   A. 15   B. 150   C. 1,500   D. 15,000

5. An organic compound that has hydrogen and oxygen in a 2:1   5.___
   ratio would belong to the group of compounds known as
   A. lipids   B. fatty acids
   C. proteins   D. carbohydrates

6. Which inorganic substance found in living matter aids in   6.___
   the diffusion of gases through a cell membrane?
   A. Water   B. Salt   C. Phosphorus D. Iron

7. An earthworm that has partially entered its burrow can be   7.___
   surprisingly difficult to pull from the ground.
   This is due PRIMARILY to the earthworm's
   A. chitinous outer covering and legs
   B. bristle-like setae and muscles
   C. powerful ventral suckers and claws
   D. grasping mouth parts and scales

8. Because they aid in the regulation of body processes,   8.___
   neurohumors are MOST similar to
   A. hormones   B. chitin   C. urine   D. pigments

9. Wastes that may be excreted from human liver cells include 9.___
    A. water, oxygen, and mineral salts
    B. water, carbon dioxide, and urea
    C. hormones, urea, and carbon dioxide
    D. hormones, oxygen, and water

10. Carbon dioxide released from the interior cells of a grass- 10.___
    hopper is transported to the atmosphere through the
    A. Malpighian tubules   B. tracheae
    C. contractile vacuoles   D. lungs

11. Vigorous activity of human voluntary muscle tissues may 11.___
    result in the production of lactic acid.
    Insufficient amounts of which gas would result in the
    buildup of lactic acid in muscle cells?
    A. Carbon dioxide   B. Nitrogen
    C. Oxygen   D. Hydrogen

12. In animal cells, the energy to convert ADP to ATP comes 12.___
    directly from
    A. hormones   B. sunlight
    C. organic molecules   D. inorganic molecules

13. Which organism has an internal, closed circulatory system 13.___
    which brings materials from the external environment into
    contact with its cells?
    A. Ameba   B. Paramecium
    C. Hydra   D. Earthworm

14. There is a higher concentration of mineral salts within 14.___
    the body of a Paramecium than in its external water
    environment.
    This higher concentration is maintained as a result of
    the action of
    A. pinocytosis   B. cyclosis
    C. CO_2 D. ATP

15. Which are produced as a result of the mechanical digestion 15.___
    of a piece of meat?
    A. Amino acids   B. Fatty acids
    C. Smaller meat particles   D. Larger glycerol molecules

16. The complete hydrolysis of carbohydrates results directly 16.___
    in the production of
    A. glycogen   B. urea molecules
    C. carbon dioxide   D. simple sugars

17. Nutrients are reduced to soluble form within the food 17.___
    vacuoles of the
    A. grasshopper and earthworm
    B. Ameba and Paramecium
    C. earthworm and human
    D. Hydra and grasshopper

18. Which locomotive structures are found in some protozoa?   18.____
    A. Muscles   B. Tentacles C. Cilia   D. Setae

19. Which animal has a ventral nerve cord?   19.____
    A. Grasshopper   B. Ameba
    C. Hydra   D. Human

20. The two systems that directly control homeostasis in most   20.____
animals are the ____ systems.
    A. nervous and endocrine   B. endocrine and excretory
    C. nervous and locomotive   D. excretory and locomotive

21. Ribosomes supply the cell with complex proteins needed for   21.____
maintenance and repair by the process of
    A. oxidation   B. digestion
    C. dehydration synthesis   D. enzymatic hydrolysis

22. Which part of a plant is specialized for anchorage and   22.____
absorption?
    A. Leaf   B. Flower   C. Stem   D. Root

23. Removing the tip of the stem of a young plant will MOST   23.____
directly interfere with the production of
    A. sugars   B. auxins
    C. carbon dioxide   D. oxygen

24. Rose oil pressed from petals is used to make perfume.   24.____
The rose oil is present in plant cells as a result of
    A. absorption from the sun
    B. absorption from the soil
    C. synthesis from simpler compounds
    D. synthesis from chlorophyll molecules

25. Nitrogenous compounds may be used by plants in the   25.____
synthesis of
    A. glucose   B. waxes   C. proteins   D. starch

26. In plants, the molecular oxygen concentration of a leaf   26.____
cell USUALLY increases during the process of
    A. aerobic respiration   B. photosynthesis
    C. transpiration   D. capillary action

27. Which structures transport food downward in a geranium   27.____
plant?
    A. Phloem vessels   B. Xylem tubes
    C. Root hairs   D. Chloroplasts

28. In a maple tree, the enzymatic hydrolysis of starches,   28.____
lipids, and proteins occurs
    A. extracellularly *only*
    B. intracellularly *only*
    C. both extracellularly and intracellularly
    D. neither extracellularly nor intracellularly

29. A characteristic of animals that makes them similar to   29.___
    heterotrophic plants is that animals
    A. obtain preformed organic molecules from other organisms
    B. need to live in a sunny environment
    C. are sessile for most of their lives
    D. use energy to manufacture organic compounds from
       inorganic compounds

30. One bean plant is illuminated with green light and another   30.___
    bean plant of similar size and leaf area is illuminated
    with blue light.
    If all other conditions are identical, how will the photo-
    synthetic rates of the plants MOST probably compare?
    A. Neither plant will carry on photosynthesis.
    B. Photosynthesis will occur at the same rate in both
       plants.
    C. The plant under green light will carry on photosynthe-
       sis at a greater rate than the one under blue light.
    D. The plant under blue light will carry on photosynthesis
       at a greater rate than the one under green light.

KEY (CORRECT ANSWERS)

1. B	11. C	21. C
2. D	12. C	22. D
3. A	13. D	23. B
4. C	14. D	24. C
5. D	15. C	25. C
6. A	16. D	26. B
7. B	17. B	27. A
8. A	18. C	28. B
9. B	19. A	29. A
10. B	20. A	30. D

TEST 2

DIRECTIONS: Each question or incomplete statement is followed by several suggested answers or completions. Select the one that BEST answers the question or completes the statement. *PRINT THE LETTER OF THE CORRECT ANSWER IN THE SPACE AT THE RIGHT.*

1.

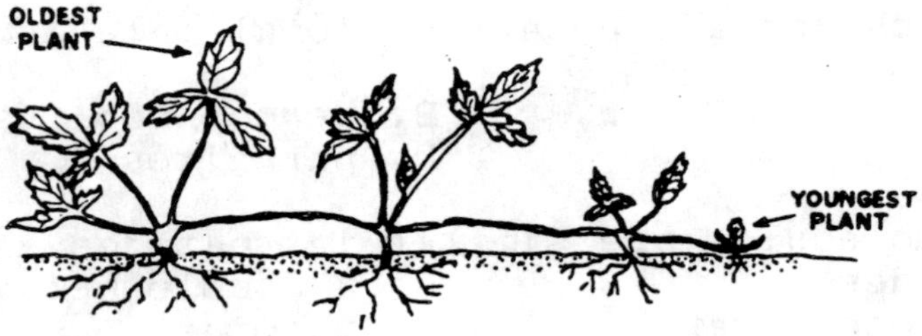

The above diagram illustrates which type of reproduction?
A. Cleavage   B. Fission
C. Zygote formation   D. Vegetative propagation

1.___

2. Only one member of each pair of homologous chromosomes is NORMALLY found in a
A. zygote   B. multicellular embryo
C. gamete   D. cheek cell

2.___

3. The production of sperm nuclei in plants occurs in cells from the
A. anther   B. stigma   C. pistil   D. ovary

3.___

4. In human males, the MAXIMUM number of functional sperm cells that is normally produced from each primary sex cell is
A. one   B. two   C. three   D. four

4.___

5.

primary sex cell   egg cell   growth of male bee

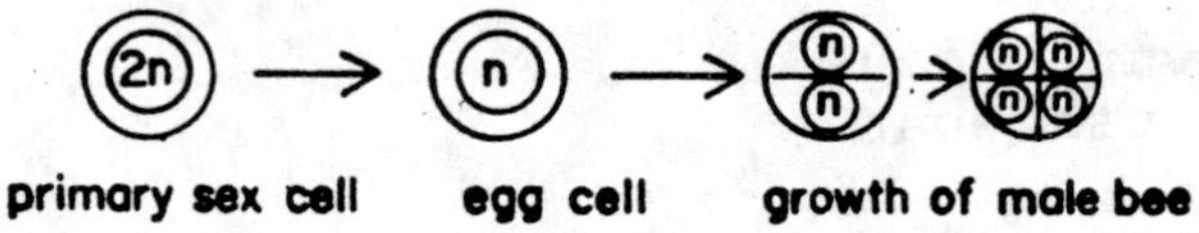

The above diagram represents processes in the reproduction of a honeybee.
As indicated in this diagram, which processes produce a male honeybee?
A. Meiosis and budding
B. Meiosis and parthenogenesis
C. Fertilization and cleavage
D. Fertilization and parthenogenesis

5.___

6. Each strand of a double-stranded chromosome is known as a
A. centromere   B. homologue
C. chromatid   D. tetrad

6.___

7. Which event occurs in the cytoplasmic division of plant cells but NOT in the cytoplasmic division of animal cells?
   A. Cell plate formation   B. Centromere replication
   C. Chromosome replication   D. Centriole formation

7.____

8. When a cell with 24 chromosomes divides by mitotic cell division, the resulting daughter cells will each have a MAXIMUM chromosome number of
   A. 6   B. 12   C. 24   D. 48

8.____

9. Organisms which contain both functional male and female gonads are known as
   A. hybrids   B. hermaphrodites
   C. phagocytes   D. parasites

9.____

10. DNA and RNA molecules are similar in that they both contain
    A. nucleotides   B. a double helix
    C. deoxyribose sugars   D. thymine

10.____

11. Which is a form of vegetative reproduction used to propagate desirable varieties of plants quickly?
    A. Hybridization   B. Pollination
    C. Fertilization   D. Grafting

11.____

12. In many humans, exposing the skin to sunlight over prolonged periods of time results in the production of more pigment by the skin cells (tanning).
    This change in skin color provides evidence that
    A. ultraviolet light can cause mutations
    B. gene action can be influenced by the environment
    C. the inheritance of skin color is an acquired characteristic
    D. albinism is a recessive characteristic

12.____

13. Which terms BEST describe MOST mutations?
    _____ and _____ to the organism.
    A. Dominant; disadvantageous
    B. Recessive; disadvantageous
    C. Recessive; advantageous
    D. Dominant; advantageous

13.____

14. A pair of chromosomes fail to separate during meiosis, producing a gamete with an extra chromosome.
    This process is known as
    A. crossing-over   B. polyploidy
    C. nondisjunction   D. recombination

14.____

15. Three brothers have blood types A, B, and O.
    What are the chances that the parents of these three will produce a fourth child whose blood type is AB?
    A. 0%   B. 25%   C. 50%   D. 100%

15.____

16. A colorblind woman marries a man who has normal color vision.
    What are their chances of having a colorblind daughter?
    A. 0%   B. 25%   C. 75%   D. 100%

16.____

17. A student crossed wrinkled-seeded (rr) pea plants with round-seeded (RR) pea plants. Only round seeds were produced in the resulting plants.
    This illustrates the principle of
    A. independent assortment   B. segregation
    C. dominance   D. incomplete dominance

17.____

18. The modern classification system is based on structural similarities and
    A. evolutionary relationships
    B. habitat similarities
    C. geographic distribution
    D. Mendelian principles

18.____

19. In peas, flowers located along the stem (axial) are dominant to flowers located at the end of the stem (terminal). Let A represent the allele for axial flowers and a represent the allele for terminal flowers. When plants with axial flowers are crossed with plants having terminal flowers, all of the offspring have axial flowers. In this cross, the genotypes of the parent plants are MOST likely
    A. aa x aa   B. Aa x Aa   C. AA x Aa   D. AA x aa

19.____

20. In an ecological succession in New York State, lichens growing on bare rock are considered to be
    A. climax organisms   B. pioneer organisms
    C. primary consumers   D. decomposers

20.____

21. The pig has four toes on each foot. Two of the toes are very small and do not have a major function in walking. Lamarck PROBABLY would have explained the reduced size of the two small toes by his evolutionary theory of
    A. natural selection   B. mutation
    C. use and disuse   D. synapsis

21.____

22. The study of mutations is important to the modern theory of evolution because it helps to explain
    A. differentiation in embryonic development
    B. stability of gene pool frequencies
    C. the extinction of the dinosaurs
    D. the appearance of variations in organisms

22.____

23. Many related organisms are found to have the same enzymes and hormones.
    This suggests that
    A. enzymes work only on specific substrates
    B. enzymes act as catalysts in biochemical reactions
    C. organisms living in the same environment require identical enzymes
    D. these organisms may share a common ancestry

23.____

24. The fossil record may be used as evidence for organic   24.___
    evolution if it is assumed that
        A. in undisturbed rock, the oldest fossils are in the
           lowest layers
        B. fossils in different layers existed at the same time
        C. all fossils have homologous structures
        D. all fossils filled the same niche

25. At times, hyenas will feed on the remains of animals they   25.___
    themselves have not killed. At other times, they will kill
    other animals for food.
    Based on their feeding habits, hyenas are BEST described as
        A. herbivores and parasites B. herbivores and predators
        C. scavengers and parasites D. scavengers and predators

26. Which is TRUE of MOST producer organisms?   26.___
    They
        A. are parasitic
        B. contain chlorophyll
        C. are eaten by carnivores
        D. liberate nitrogen

27. Which is an abiotic factor in the environment?   27.___
        A. Water   B. Earthworm
        C. Fungus   D. Human

Questions 28-30.

DIRECTIONS: Questions 28 through 30 are to be answered on the basis
             of the following food chain and on your knowledge of
             biology.

   rosebush → aphid → ladybird beetle → spider → toad → snake

28. Which organism in the food chain can transform light   28.___
    energy into chemical energy?
        A. Spider   B. Ladybird beetle
        C. Rosebush   D. Snake

29. At which stage in the food chain will the population with   29.___
    the SMALLEST number of animals probably be found?
        A. Spider   B. Aphid
        C. Ladybird beetle   D. Snake

30. Which organism in this food chain is herbivorous?   30.___
        A. Rosebush   B. Aphid
        C. Ladybird beetle   D. Toad

KEY (CORRECT ANSWERS)

1. D	11. D	21. C
2. C	12. B	22. D
3. A	13. B	23. D
4. D	14. C	24. A
5. B	15. B	25. D
6. C	16. A	26. B
7. A	17. C	27. A
8. C	18. A	28. C
9. B	19. D	29. D
10. A	20. B	30. B

TEST 3

DIRECTIONS: Each question or incomplete statement is followed by several suggested answers or completions. Select the one that BEST answers the question or completes the statement. *PRINT THE LETTER OF THE CORRECT ANSWER IN THE SPACE AT THE RIGHT.*

Questions 1-4.

DIRECTIONS: For each of Questions 1 through 4, select the structural formula, chosen from those below, which BEST answers the question.

A

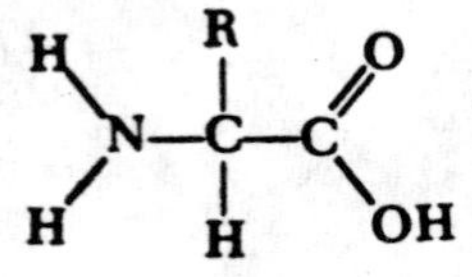

B

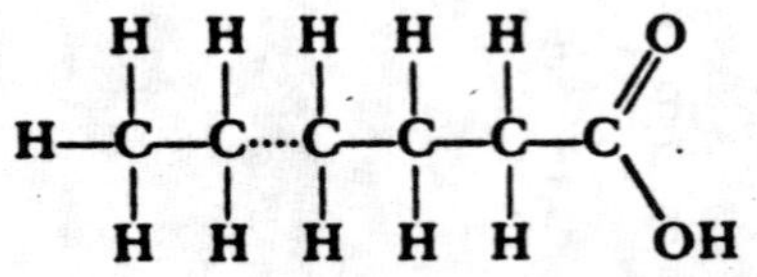

C $O=C=O$

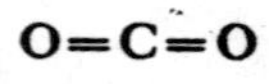

D

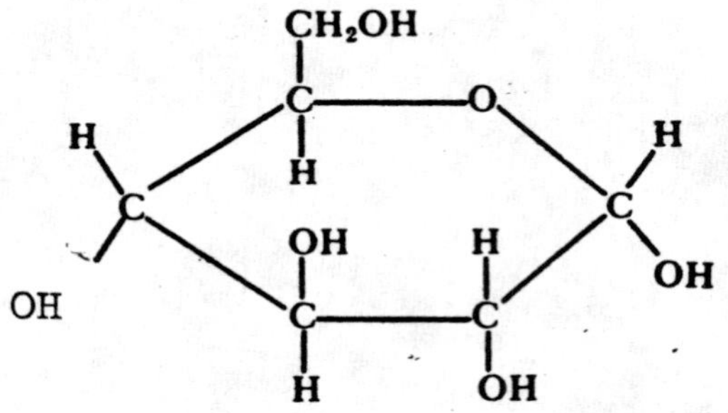

E

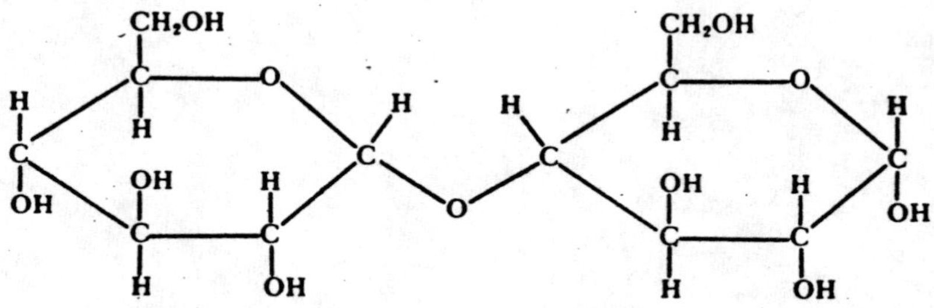

1. Which is a structural formula for a component of a fat?   1.___

2. Which formula represents a substance formed as a direct result of a dehydration synthesis?   2.___

3. Which formula represents a component of all proteins?   3.___

4. Which formula represents a monosaccharide?   4.___

5. An organic compound formed in the dark reactions of photo-   5.___
   synthesis is
      A. chlorophyll   B. oxygen
      C. H_2O D. PGAL

6. Digestive enzymes which hydrolyze molecules of fat into   6.___
   fatty acid and glycerol molecules are known as
      A. proteases   B. lipases   C. maltases   D. vitamins

7. In certain bacteria and yeasts, under anaerobic conditions,   7.___
   the oxidation of glucose leads to the production of
      A. ethyl alcohol   B. complex sugars
      C. oxygen   D. starches

Questions 8-10.

DIRECTIONS: Questions 8 through 10 are to be answered on the basis
                    of the graph below and on your knowledge of biology.
                    The graph represents the rate of enzyme action when
                    different concentrations of enzyme are added to a system
                    with a fixed amount of substrate.

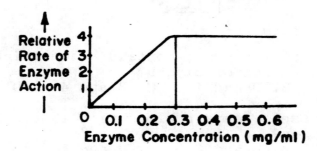

8. At which enzyme concentration does all of the available   8.___
   substrate react with the enzyme?
     ____ mg/ml.
      A. 0.1   B. 0.2   C. 0.3   D. 0.05

9. When the enzyme concentration is increased from 0.5 mg/ml   9.___
   to 0.6 mg/ml, the rate of enzyme action
      A. decreases   B. increases
      C. remains the same   D. increases then decreases

10. If more substrate is added to the system at an enzyme   10.___
    concentration of 0.4 mg/ml, the rate of the reaction would
    MOST likely
       A. decrease   B. increase
       C. remain the same   D. increases then decreases

Questions 11-13.

DIRECTIONS: Questions 11 through 13 are to be answered on the basis
             of the schematic diagram below of blood flow throughout
             the human body and on your knowledge of biology.

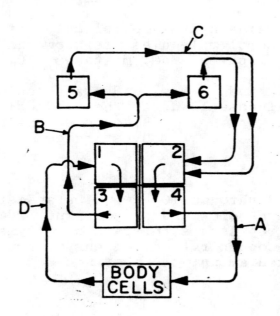

11. Which chambers of the heart contain blood which has the   11.____
     HIGHEST concentration of oxygen?
     A. 1 and 2   B. 2 and 4   C. 3 and 4   D. 1 and 3

12. Which blood vessels contain blood with the LOWEST concen-   12.____
     tration of oxygen?
     A. A and D   B. B and C   C. C and A   D. D and B

13. Microscopic structural units known as alveoli are located   13.____
     in structures
     A. 1 and 3   B. B and C   C. 5 and 6   D. D and B

14. Which BEST illustrates the pathway of an impulse in a   14.____
     reflex arc?
     A. Effector → motor neuron → associative neuron → sensory
        neuron → receptor
     B. Receptor → motor neuron → associative neuron → sensory
        neuron → effector
     C. Receptor → sensory neuron → associative neuron → motor
        neuron → effector
     D. Effector → sensory neuron → associative neuron → motor
        neuron → receptor

15. A person was admitted to the hospital with abnormally high   15.____
     blood sugar and an abnormally high sugar content in his
     urine.
     Which gland MOST likely caused this condition by secreting
     lower than normal amounts of its hormone?
     A. Pancreas   B. Parathyroid
     C. Salivary   D. Thyroid

16. In the human elbow joint, the bone of the upper arm is   16.___
    connected to the bones of the lower arm by flexible
    connective tissue known as
       A. tendons   B. ligaments   C. muscles   D. neurons

Questions 17-20.

DIRECTIONS: For each phrase in Questions 17 through 20, select the
              organ, chosen from the drawing below, which is MOST
              closely related to that phrase. (A letter may be used
              more than once or not at all.)

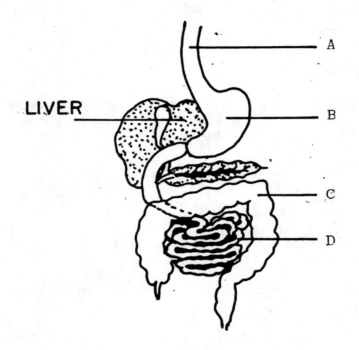

17. Where feces are formed.   17.___

18. Where protein digestion begins.   18.___

19. Where lipid digestion is completed.   19.___

20. Contains gastric glands.   20.___

21. In plants, which is a function of the seed parts known as   21.___
    cotyledons?
       A. Formation of flowers   B. Development of stems
       C. Production of roots   D. Storage of food

22. The factors necessary for maple seed germination are   22.___
    moisture, proper temperature, and
       A. oxygen   B. soil
       C. chlorophyll   D. darkness

23. The human male's testes are located in an outpocketing of   23.____
    the body wall known as the scrotum.
    An advantage of this adaptation is that
       A. the testes are better protected in the scrotum than
          in the body cavity
       B. sperm production requires contact with atmospheric air
       C. a temperature lower than body temperature is best for
          sperm production and storage
       D. the sperm cells can enter the urethra directly from
          the testes

24. In a developing embryo, the process MOST closely associated   24.____
    with the differentiation of cells is
       A. gastrulation   B. menstruation
       C. ovulation   D. fertilization

Questions 25-27.

DIRECTIONS: For each of Questions 25 through 27, select the structure
               in a developing chicken egg, chosen from the list below,
               that BEST answers the question.

               Developing Egg Structures

                  A. Amnion
                  B. Allantois
                  C. Chorion
                  D. Yolk sac

25. Which structure MOST directly protects the embryo from   25.____
    shocks?

26. Which structure lines the shell and surrounds the other   26.____
    membranes?

27. In which structure are embryonic wastes stored?   27.____

Questions 28-30.

DIRECTIONS: Questions 28 through 30 are to be answered on the basis
               of the diagram below, which represents a cross-section
               of a part of the human female reproduction system, and
               on your knowledge of biology.

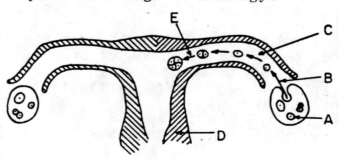

28. Which structure is prepared for implantation of a fertilized   28.___
    egg as a result of the action of reproductive hormones?
    A. A   B. B   C. C   D. D

29. Within which structure does fertilization NORMALLY occur?   29.___
    A. A   B. B   C. C   D. D

30. Which represents the process of ovulation?   30.___
    A. A   B. B   C. C   D. E

————

KEY (CORRECT ANSWERS)

1. B	11. B	21. D
2. E	12. D	22. A
3. A	13. C	23. C
4. D	14. C	24. A
5. D	15. A	25. A
6. B	16. B	26. C
7. A	17. C	27. B
8. C	18. B	28. D
9. C	19. D	29. C
10. B	20. B	30. B

————

TEST 4

DIRECTIONS: Each question or incomplete statement is followed by
             several suggested answers or completions. Select the
             one that BEST answers the question or completes the
             statement. *PRINT THE LETTER OF THE CORRECT ANSWER IN
             THE SPACE AT THE RIGHT.*

1. A change which affects the base sequence in an organism's   1.___
    DNA by the addition, deletion, or substitution of a single
    base is known as
       A. DNA replication   B. gene mutation
       C. chromosomal mutation   D. independent assortment

2. The replication of a double-stranded DNA molecule begins   2.___
    when the strands separate at the
       A. phosphate bonds   B. ribose molecules
       C. deoxyribose molecules   D. hydrogen bonds

3. Which nitrogenous bases tend to pair with each other in a   3.___
    double-stranded molecule of DNA?
       A. Adenine-uracil   B. Thymine-adenine
       C. Cytosine-thymine   D. Guanine-adenine

4. Within which organelles have genes been found?   4.___
       A. Food vacuoles   B. Contractile vacuoles
       C. Mitochondria   D. Cell walls

5. The function of transfer RNA molecules is to   5.___
       A. transport amino acids to messenger RNA
       B. transport amino acids to DNA in the nucleus
       C. synthesize more transfer RNA molecules
       D. provide a template for the synthesis of messenger RNA

Questions 6-10.

DIRECTIONS: Questions 6 through 10 are to be answered on the basis
             of the diagram below, which represents a portion of a
             messenger RNA molecule associated with a ribosome, and
             on your knowledge of biology.

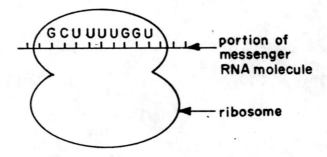

6. The presence of which nitrogen base indicates that the molecule associated with the ribosome is RNA?   6.___
   A. Guanine   B. Cytosine   C. Uracil   D. Adenine

7. The sequence of nucleotides on the RNA molecule was deter-   7.___
   mined by the
   A. sequence of nucleotides on transfer RNA molecules
   B. base sequence of the original DNA molecule that served
      as the template
   C. sequence of amino acids that will be linked together
      to form a polypeptide chain
   D. base sequence of the original messenger RNA molecule
      that served as a template

8. The messenger RNA genetic codes for 3 different amino acids   8.___
   are:
                    U-U-U = phenylalanine
                    G-C-U = alanine
                    G-G-U = glycine
   Using this information, the strip of messenger RNA shown
   in the illustration would result in an amino acid sequence
   consisting of
   A. phenylalanine-alanine-glycine
   B. alanine-glycine-glycine
   C. alanine-glycine-phenylalanine
   D. alanine-phenylalanine-glycine

9. The association between the ribosome and the messenger RNA   9.___
   molecule occurs in the
   A. cytoplasm   B. centrosome
   C. nucleolus   D. nucleus

10. The substance being synthesized in the cell is MOST likely   10.___
    a
    A. fat   B. vitamin
    C. polypeptide   D. carbohydrate

11. Which statement concerning living organisms is LEAST in   11.___
    agreement with the modern concept of evolution?
    They
    A. have nucleic acids as their genetic material
    B. have similar chemical reactions controlled by enzymes
    C. consist of one or more cells
    D. are grouped into species which are unchanging

12. According to the heterotroph hypothesis, the FIRST   12.___
    organisms were probably
    A. aerobic heterotrophs   B. anaerobic heterotrophs
    C. aerobic autotrophs   D. anaerobic autotrophs

13. All the genes in a given population which can be inherited   13.___
    constitute a
    A. gene pool   B. genotype
    C. gene frequency   D. phenotype

14. Several species of milkweed are growing in the same area.   14.___
    All are capable of hybridization but none ever do because
    the surface of the stigma of each species accepts only a
    certain shape pollen grain.
    This paragraph BEST describes an evolutionary process
    known as
        A. artificial selection   B. reproductive isolation
        C. survival of the fittest   D. overproduction

15. In a large population located in a constant environment,   15.___
    the following conditions exist: random mating, no migration,
    and no mutations.
    Which will MOST probably occur within the population?
        A. The gene frequencies will remain stable.
        B. The dominant gene frequencies will increase.
        C. The recessive gene frequencies will increase.
        D. All gene frequencies will decrease.

Questions 16-17.

DIRECTIONS: Questions 16 and 17 are to be answered on the basis of
             the graph and information below and on your knowledge
             of biology.

    Scientists studying a moth population in a woods recorded the
distribution of moth wing color as shown in the graph below. The
woods contained trees whose bark color was predominantly brown.

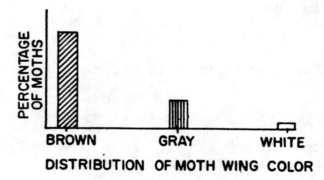

DISTRIBUTION OF MOTH WING COLOR

16. A fungus infection affected nearly all trees in the woods   16.___
    so that the coloration of the tree bark was changed to a
    gray-white color.
    Which graph shows the MOST probable results that would
    occur in the distribution of wing coloration in this moth
    population after a long period of time?

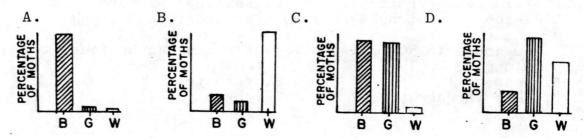

17. As a result of the fungus infection, the change in the   17.___
    moth wing color distribution would MOST probably occur by
    the
    A. inheritance of an acquired characteristic
    B. natural selection of favorable variations
    C. ingestion of pigmentation from fungus spores
    D. production of fungus-induced gene mutations

Questions 18-20.

DIRECTIONS: Questions 18 through 20 are to be answered on the basis
              of the information below and on your knowledge of the
              Hardy-Weinberg principle of gene frequencies.

    In a certain population of rabbits, two alleles for coat color
exist, tan and white. Tan is the dominant allele. The frequency of
the gene for white coat color is .30.

    Foxes are also present in the area, and rabbits constitute a major
portion of their diet. Foxes recognize prey by the degree to which the
prey contrast with their background.

18. What is the frequency of the gene for tan coat color?   18.___
    A. .09   B. .21   C. .49   D. .70

19. In the entire population, the percentage of rabbits hybrid 19.___
    for tan coat color is
    A. 42%   B. 2%   C. 3%   D. 49%

20. If the climate where the rabbits live were to change so   20.___
    that snow covered the ground for much of the year, what
    change might be expected in the rabbit population?
    The frequency of
    A. the tan allele would increase
    B. rabbits homozygous for the white allele would probably
       increase
    C. rabbits homozygous for the tan coat color would
       increase
    D. the white allele would decrease

21. In which of the following biomes does MOST of the photo-   21.___
    synthesis taking place on the Earth occur?
    A. Deciduous forests   B. Oceans
    C. Deserts   D. Coniferous forests

22. The rate of photosynthesis carried on by plants living in   22.___
    a body of water depends CHIEFLY upon the _____ the water.
    A. amount of molecular oxygen in
    B. number of decomposers in
    C. amount of light that penetrates
    D. number of saprophytes in

23. Recent studies have found traces of the insecticide DDT   23.____
    accumulated in human fat tissue.
    A CORRECT explanation for this accumulation is that
       A. DDT is needed for proper metabolic functioning
       B. DDT is passed along food chains
       C. fat tissue absorbs DDT directly from the air
       D. fat tissue cells secrete DDT

24. Which statement describes an ecological importance of   24.____
    insects?
       A. Insects are humans' chief competitor for available
          food.
       B. The destruction of all insects will maintain the
          balance of nature.
       C. The destruction of all insects would help maintain
          proper food webs.
       D. Insects are causing the bird population to decrease.

25. The MOST serious consequence of cutting down forests and   25.____
    overgrazing land is
       A. the prevention of flooding
       B. an increase in the chance of fire
       C. an increase in the number of predators
       D. the loss of topsoil cover

Questions 26-30.

DIRECTIONS: For each description in Questions 26 through 30, select
              the biome, chosen from the list below, that is MOST closely
              associated with that description. (A letter may be used
              more than once or not at all.)

              Biomes

              A. Grassland
              B. Tundra
              C. Temperate deciduous forest
              D. Tropical rain forest
              E. Taiga
              F. Desert

26. This biome is found in the foothills of the Adirondack and   26.____
    Catskill Mountains of New York State and supports the
    growth of dominant vegetation including maples, oaks, and
    beeches.

27. The characteristic climax vegetation in this biome consists   27.____
    of coniferous trees composed mainly of spruce and fir.

28. This biome receives less than 10 inches of rainfall per   28.____
    year. Extreme temperature variations exist throughout the
    area over a 24-hour period. Water-conserving plants such
    as cacti, sagebrush, and mesquite are found.

29. This biome receives the least amount of solar energy. The   29.___
    ground is permanently frozen (permafrost) throughout the
    year. During the summer season, plants quickly grow,
    reproduce, and form seeds during their short life cycle.
    Lichens and mosses grow abundantly on the surface of rocks.

30. A moderate, well-distributed supply of rain in this biome   30.___
    supports the growth of broad-leaved trees, which shed
    their leaves as winter approaches.

KEY (CORRECT ANSWERS)

1. B	11. D	21. B
2. D	12. B	22. C
3. B	13. A	23. B
4. C	14. B	24. A
5. A	15. A	25. D
6. C	16. D	26. C
7. B	17. B	27. E
8. D	18. D	28. F
9. A	19. A	29. B
10. C	20. B	30. C

EXAMINATION SECTION

TEST 1

DIRECTIONS: Each question or incomplete statement is followed by several suggested answers or completions. Select the one that BEST answers the question or completes the statement. *PRINT THE LETTER OF THE CORRECT ANSWER IN THE SPACE AT THE RIGHT.*

1. Small molecules combine chemically and form large, complex molecules by a process known as
   A. hydrolysis
   B. digestion
   C. synthesis
   D. nutrition

   1.___

2. Which group of organisms in the animal kingdom is characterized by jointed appendages and exoskeletons?
   A. Arthropods
   B. Chordates
   C. Annelids
   D. Coelenterates

   2.___

3. The internal structure of a mitochondrion and a chloroplast can BEST be observed by using
   A. an ultracentrifuge
   B. a compound light microscope
   C. microdissection instruments
   D. an electron microscope

   2.___

4. Which organelle is PRIMARILY concerned with the conversion of potential energy of organic compounds into a suitable form for immediate use by the cell?
   A. Mitochondria
   B. Centrosomes
   C. Ribosomes
   D. Vacuoles

   4.___

5. Within a cell, which of the following elements is found in the GREATEST amount?
   A. Carbon   B. Calcium   C. Iron   D. Iodine

   5.___

6. When the end-products of protein hydrolysis enter the cytoplasm of a cell, they may become building blocks for the synthesis of
   A. glycogen   B. starches   C. enzymes   D. lipids

   6.___

7. Which is characteristic of an enzyme?
   It
   A. is an inorganic catalyst
   B. is destroyed after each chemical reaction
   C. provides energy for any chemical reaction
   D. regulates the rate of a specific chemical reaction

   7.___

Questions 8-9.

DIRECTIONS: Questions 8 and 9 are to be answered on the basis of the diagram of a cell below.

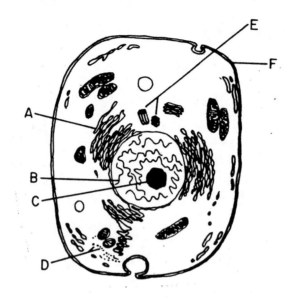

8. Which structures function MAINLY in reproduction?   8.___
    A. A and B   B. B and E   C. C and D   D. A and D

9. Which structures function MAINLY in transport?   9.___
    A. A and F   B. B and D   C. C and F   D. C and D

10. Which organisms add more oxygen to the atmosphere than   10.___
    they remove?
        A. Grasshoppers   B. Bread molds
        C. Corn plants   D. Mushrooms

11. As seeds germinate, the starch contained within the seeds   11.___
    is converted into glucose molecules.
    This conversion is necessary because
        A. starch is toxic to a germinating seed
        B. starch contains no energy
        C. cell membranes are more permeable to glucose than to
           starch
        D. glucose is excreted from all seeds as a metabolic
           waste

12. Animals which ingest organic materials are classified as   12.___
        A. heterotrophic   B. photosynthetic
        C. autotrophic   D. chemosynthetic

13. A student filled a bag of dialysis tubing   13.___
    with a milky-white starch solution and
    placed the bag in a beaker of iodine-water
    as shown in the diagram at the right.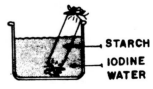
    An hour later, the student observed that
    the starch solution had turned blue-black
    (positive test for starch).

What is the MOST probable explanation for the change?
The
    A. iodine diffused into the bag
    B. starch was changed to sugar
    C. iodine was changed to starch
    D. starch diffused out of the bag

14. The dissolved sugars produced in the leaves of a maple tree move to the tree's roots through the
    A. xylem   B. phloem
    C. epidermis   D. guard cells

14.___

15. Which organism contains an open circulatory system and excretes its nitrogenous waste in the form of uric acid?
    A. Earthworm   B. Grasshopper
    C. Hydra   D. Ameba

15.___

16. Alcohol fermentation and aerobic respiration are similar in that both processes
    A. utilize light   B. produce ethyl alcohol
    C. require free oxygen   D. release carbon dioxide

16.___

17. glucose $\xrightarrow{\text{enzymes}}$ 2 lactic acid + 2 ATP

In the summary equation above, which process produces the lactic acid?
    A. Dehydration synthesis   B. Enzymatic hydrolysis
    C. Fermentation   D. Aerobic respiration

17.___

18. In the earthworm, the exchange of gases with the external environment occurs through the
    A. skin   B. lungs   C. nephridia   D. pharynx

18.___

19. Oxygen molecules absorbed by moist respiratory surfaces in humans diffuse immediately into
    A. endocrine glands   B. blood capillaries
    C. external tubules   D. skin pores

19.___

20. Nitrogenous wastes result from the metabolism of
    A. amino acids   B. glucose molecules
    C. fatty acids   D. water molecules

20.___

21. The diagram at the right represents some epidermal cells from the lower surface of a leaf. The arrow shows the direction of the movement of water vapor molecules.
Which process is indicated by the arrow?
    A. Osmosis
    B. Active transport
    C. Transpiration
    D. Anaerobic respiration

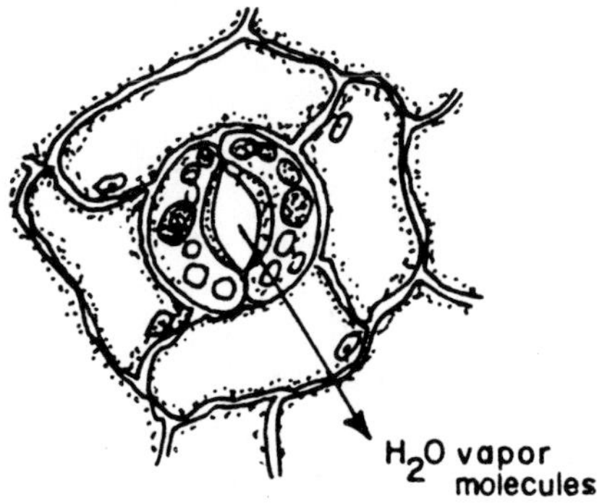

21.___

H_2O vapor molecules

22. A Hydra can function without an organized excretory   22.___
system because its cells
   A. do not produce wastes
   B. change all wastes to useful substances
   C. remove only solid wastes
   D. are in direct contact with a water environment

23. What is the role of sensory organs in the body?   23.___
The
   A. transmission of impulses directly to effectors
   B. detection of environmental stimuli
   C. conduction of impulses from the spinal cord
   D. interpretation of impulses from motor neurons

24. A student viewing a sample of pond water   24.___
through a microscope observed and drew a
protist as shown at the right.
Which organism has locomotive structures
MOST similar to this organism?
   A. Earthworm
   B. Ameba
   C. Paramecium
   D. Hydra

25. The removal of a human gallbladder interferes MOST directly   25.___
with the
   A. production of gastric juice
   B. production of saliva
   C. storage of pancreatic juice
   D. storage of bile

KEY (CORRECT ANSWERS)

1. C		11. C
2. A		12. A
3. D		13. A
4. A		14. B
5. A		15. B
6. C		16. D
7. D		17. C
8. B		18. A
9. A		19. B
10. C		20. A

21. C
22. D
23. B
24. C
25. D

TEST 2

DIRECTIONS: Each question or incomplete statement is followed by several suggested answers or completions. Select the one that BEST answers the question or completes the statement. *PRINT THE LETTER OF THE CORRECT ANSWER IN THE SPACE AT THE RIGHT.*

1. In the human body, which blood components engulf foreign   1.____
   bacteria?
      A. Red blood cells   B. White blood cells
      C. Antibodies   D. Platelets

2. In humans, the exchange of materials between blood and   2.____
   intercellular fluid directly involves blood vessels known as
      A. capillaries   B. arterioles
      C. venules   D. arteries

3. In the diagram at the right, which   3.____
   structure is indicated by the arrow?
      A. Bronchus
      B. Nasal cavity
      C. Trachea
      D. Lung

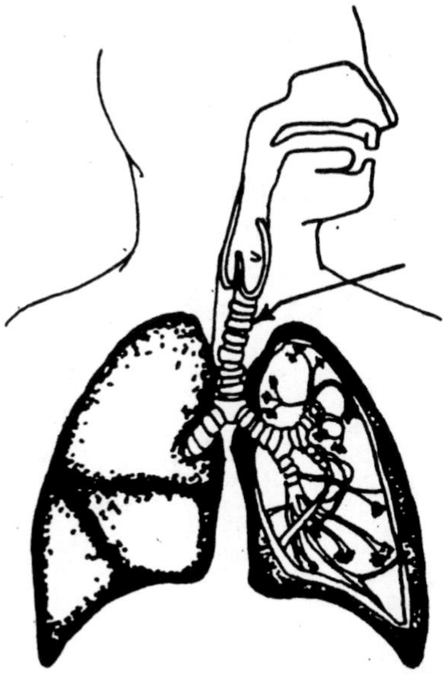

4. What is the PRINCIPAL nitrogenous waste in humans?   4.____
      A. Salt   B. Urea
      C. Uric acid   D. Carbon dioxide

5. In humans, the organ that breaks down red blood cells and   5.____
   deaminates amino acids is the
      A. kidney   B. liver
      C. gallbladder   D. small intestine

6. Impulses from the spinal cord to the muscle fibers in the   6.____
   human leg are transmitted through structures known as
   _____ neurons.
      A. sensory   B. inter-
      C. motor   D. connective

7. Which type of connective tissue makes up the GREATEST proportion of the skeleton of a human embryo?
   A. Ligaments B. Cartilage C. Tendons D. Bone

7.___

8. Which structure contains pairs of opposing skeletal muscles?
   A. Stomach   B. Small intestine
   C. Heart   D. Hand

8.___

9. The diagram at the right represents a cell that will undergo mitosis.
   Which diagrams below BEST illustrate the nuclei of the daughter cells that result from a normal mitotic cell division of the parent cell shown?

9.___

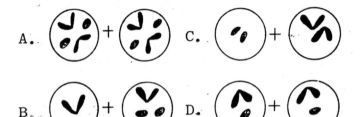

10. Double-stranded chromosomes are produced as a direct result of the
    A. synapsis of homologous chromosomes
    B. formation of spindle fibers
    C. replication of chromosomes
    D. formation of cell plates

10.___

11. The diagram at the right represents reproduction in a Paramecium.
    Which specific process is represented by the diagram?
    A. Sporulation
    B. Binary fission
    C. Budding
    D. Regeneration

11.___

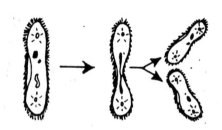

12. Compared to vertebrates, invertebrate animals exhibit a higher degree of regenerative ability because they
    A. produce larger numbers of gametes
    B. produce larger numbers of spindle fibers
    C. possess more chromosomes in their nuclei
    D. possess more undifferentiated cells

12.___

13. One apple tree can bear such varieties as Delicious,   13.___
    McIntosh, and Cortland apples on its branches.
    These three varieties of apples grown on the same tree
    as a result of a type of vegetative propagation known as
        A. cross-pollination   B. fertilization
        C. grafting   D. binary fission

14. Which equation BEST represents the change in chromosome   14.___
    number in the process of normal fertilization in animals?
        A. $n + 2n \rightarrow 3n$ B. $n + n \rightarrow 2n$
        C. $n \rightarrow n$ D. $2n + 2n \rightarrow 4n$

15. Meiotic cell division in animals is DIRECTLY responsible   15.___
    for the
        A. formation of gametes
        B. fertilization of an egg
        C. growth of a cell
        D. production of muscle cells

16. Which are examples of male reproductive organs?   16.___
        A. Stamens and pistils   B. Pistils and ovaries
        C. Pistils and testes   D. Stamens and testes

17. Heavy use of insecticides in springtime may lead to a   17.___
    decrease in apple production.
    This decreased apple production is MOST probably due to
    interference with the process of
        A. pollination   B. cleavage
        C. absorption   D. transpiration

18. One reason for Mendel's success with genetic studies of   18.___
    garden peas was that he
        A. used only hybrid pea plants
        B. used peas with large chromosomes
        C. studied large numbers of offspring
        D. discovered the sources of variations in peas

19. In pea plants, the gene for tallness (T) is dominant over   19.___
    the gene for shortness (t).
    If 100% of the F_1 generation offspring are heterozygous
    tall, what were the MOST probable genotypes of the parent
    plants?
        A. Tt × Tt   B. Tt × tt   C. TT × Tt   D. TT × tt

20. In a certain species of meadowmouse, dark coat color is   20.___
    dominant over cream coat color.
    If heterozygous dark-coated male mice are mated with
    cream-coated female mice, what would be the expected
    percentage of phenotypes in their offspring?
        A. 25% dark-coated, 75% cream-coated
        B. 50% dark-coated, 50% cream-coated
        C. 75% dark-coated, 25% cream-coated
        D. 100% dark-coated

21. A trait which is not visible in either parent appears in   21.___
several of their offspring.
Which genetic concept does this demonstrate?
   A. Linked genes   B. Replication
   C. Segregation   D. Sex determination

22. A pea plant which produces green pods is crossed with a   22.___
pea plant which produces yellow pods. The resulting offspring had green pods.
With respect to pod color, the genotype of the offspring
is MOST likely
   A. heterozygous dominant   B. pure recessive
   C. homozygous dominant   D. homozygous recessive

23. Rabbits of a certain species produce yellow fat when on a   23.___
diet of carrots and leafy vegetables. However, when their
diet does not include carrots and leafy vegetables, they
develop white fat.
Which is the BEST explanation for these results?
   A. Colchicine can alter genotypes and phenotypes.
   B. Carrots cause mutations in rabbits.
   C. Polyploidy produces 2n gametes.
   D. Environmental factors influence gene expression.

24. A strand of DNA consists of thousands of smaller, repeating 24.___
units known as
   A. lipids   B. amino acids
   C. nucleotides   D. polysaccharides

25. In molecules of DNA, which nitrogenous base bonds with   25.___
adenine?
   A. Adenine   B. Uracil   C. Guanine   D. Thymine

KEY (CORRECT ANSWERS)

1. B		11. B	
2. A		12. D	
3. C		13. C	
4. B		14. B	
5. B		15. A	
6. C		16. D	
7. B		17. A	
8. D		18. C	
9. A		19. D	
10. C		20. B	

21. C
22. A
23. D
24. C
25. D

TEST 3

DIRECTIONS: Each question or incomplete statement is followed by several suggested answers or completions. Select the one that BEST answers the question or completes the statement. *PRINT THE LETTER OF THE CORRECT ANSWER IN THE SPACE AT THE RIGHT.*

1. The diagram at the right represents a cross-section of undisturbed rock layers. A scientist discovers bones of a complex vertebrate species in layers B and C. In which layer would an earlier, less complex form of this vertebrate MOST likely first appear?
    A. A
    B. E
    C. C
    D. D

1.___

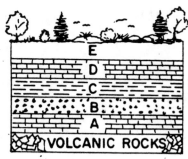

SEDIMENTARY ROCK LAYERS

2. It is thought that all citrus fruit trees evolved from a common ancestor because of their common ability to synthesize citric acid.
    This type of evidence of evolution is known as
    A. comparative embryology   B. comparative biochemistry
    C. geographical distribution D. anatomical similarity

2.___

3. In areas of heavy use of the insecticide DDT, fly populations may show marked resistance to the DDT over a period of time.
    Someone who accepts the evolutionary theory of Lamarck would MOST likely explain this observation using the concept of
    A. natural selection
    B. inheritance of acquired characteristics
    C. overproduction of a species
    D. a change in the gene frequencies

3.___

4. Which concept is part of the modern evolutionary theory, but NOT Darwin's original theory?
    A. Variations in traits are caused by mutation and recombination.
    B. Species tend to produce more offspring than can survive.
    C. Better adapted individuals survive to produce offspring.
    D. The environment is responsible for eliminating less fit individuals.

4.___

5. According to the heterotroph hypothesis, the first living   5.___
   things PROBABLY were anaerobic because their environment
   had no available
      A. food   B. energy   C. water   D. oxygen

6. All the cottontail rabbits in a county would represent a(n)   6.___
      A. community   B. biome
      C. population   D. ecosystem

7. Contamination of the soil, atmosphere, and water by humans   7.___
   is partially the result of the use of
      A. wildlife management   B. reforestation programs
      C. chemical biocides   D. pollution controls

8. Erosion resulting from loss of topsoil due to poor farming   8.___
   techniques may be prevented by
      A. overgrazing pasturelands
      B. removing trees, shrubs, and herbs
      C. overcropping farm fields
      D. covercropping plowed fields

Questions 9-11.

DIRECTIONS: Questions 9 through 11 are to be answered on the basis
                of the diagram below, which represents the distribution
                and variation in two similar species of plants.

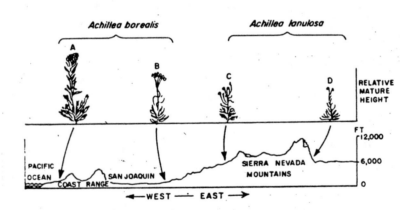

9. Groups C and D are considered biologically to be of the   9.___
   same species because they
      A. have stems which grow to similar lengths
      B. both exist at an altitude of 6000 ft. above sea level
      C. contain identical genetic makeup
      D. may mate with each other and produce fertile offspring

10. Although they are members of the same species and exist at   10.___
    similar altitudes, groups A and B vary from each other in
    many ways.
    These variations are MOST likely a result of
       A. geographic isolation of group A from group B
       B. asexual reproduction in group A and group B
       C. lack of mutations in both group A and group B
       D. lack of migration in both group A and group B

11. If groups C and D remain isolated from each other by the   11.___
    Sierra Nevada Mountains for a long period of time, what
    will MOST probably occur?
    A. D will become extinct within its native range.
    B. C will become more similar to D.
    C. Accumulated variations will prevent successful inter-
       breeding between C and D.
    D. C will gradually evolve into a marine species.

Questions 12-15.

DIRECTIONS: Questions 12 through 15 are to be answered on the basis
              of the diagram below, which represents four possible
              pathways for the transfer of energy stored by green plants.

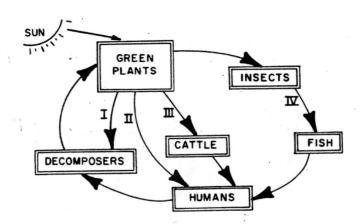

12. The pathway labeled IV represents a(n)   12.___
    A. food chain   B. population
    C. ecosystem   D. abiotic factor

13. Through which pathway would the sun's energy be MOST   13.___
    directly available to humans?
    A. I   B. II   C. III   D. IV

14. In this diagram, humans are shown to be   14.___
    A. herbivores *only*   B. carnivores *only*
    C. omnivores   D. parasites

15. The cattle in the diagram represent   15.___
    A. primary consumers   B. secondary consumers
    C. producers   D. autotrophs

4 (#3)

Questions 16-20.

DIRECTIONS: Questions 16 through 20 are to be answered on the basis of the structural formulas below, which represent certain organic compounds found in living cells.

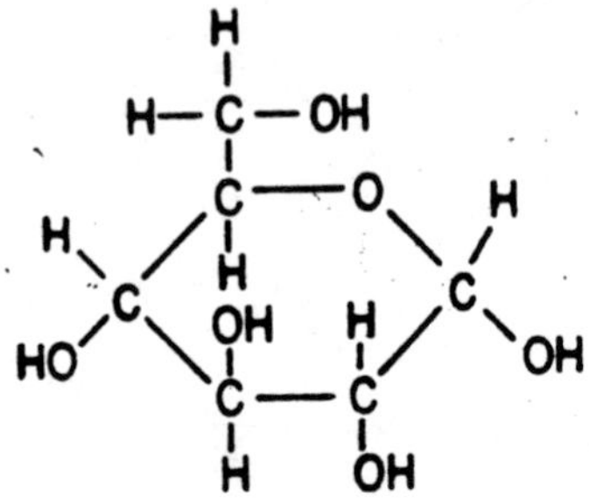

(1)

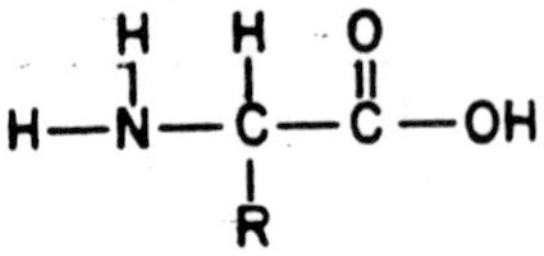

(2)

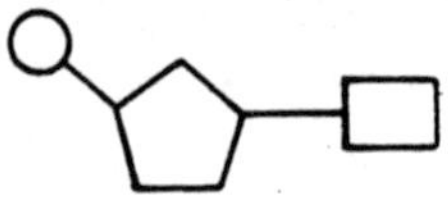

(3)

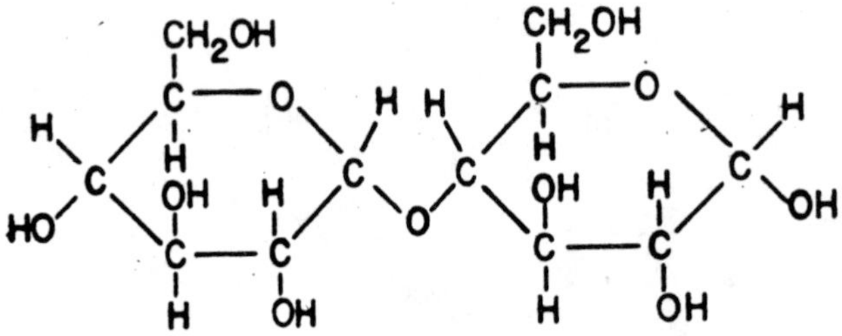

(4)

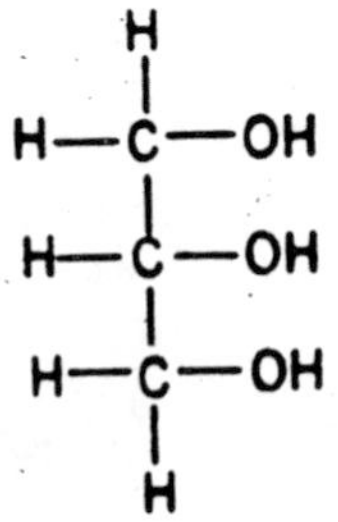

(5)

16. A strand of RNA is a polymer made up of many repeating units of the compound represented by
    A. 1   B. 5   C. 3   D. 4
    16.___

17. The hydrolysis of a protein would produce molecules represented by
    A. 1   B. 2   C. 3   D. 4
    17.___

18. Which formula represents a monosaccharide?
    A. 1   B. 2   C. 3   D. 5
    18.___

19. Which formula represents a molecule of glycerol?
    A. 1   B. 2   C. 3   D. 5
    19.___

20. Which molecule results from the bonding together of two glucose molecules?
    A. 5   B. 2   C. 3   D. 4
    20.___

Questions 21-25.

DIRECTIONS: Questions 21 through 25 are to be answered on the basis of the word equation below, which represents a summary of the two major sets of reactions occurring during photosynthesis.

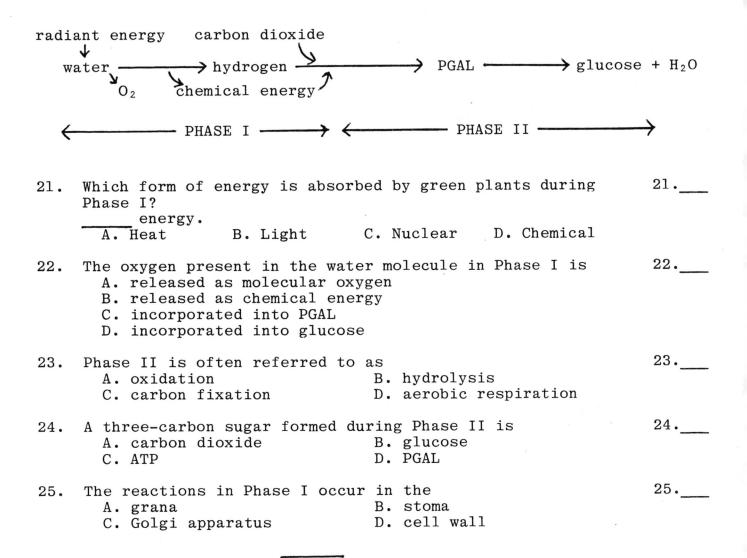

21. Which form of energy is absorbed by green plants during   21.___
    Phase I?
    _____ energy.
    A. Heat   B. Light   C. Nuclear   D. Chemical

22. The oxygen present in the water molecule in Phase I is   22.___
    A. released as molecular oxygen
    B. released as chemical energy
    C. incorporated into PGAL
    D. incorporated into glucose

23. Phase II is often referred to as   23.___
    A. oxidation   B. hydrolysis
    C. carbon fixation   D. aerobic respiration

24. A three-carbon sugar formed during Phase II is   24.___
    A. carbon dioxide   B. glucose
    C. ATP   D. PGAL

25. The reactions in Phase I occur in the   25.___
    A. grana   B. stoma
    C. Golgi apparatus   D. cell wall

_____

KEY (CORRECT ANSWERS)

1. A	6. C	11. C	16. C	21. B
2. B	7. C	12. A	17. B	22. A
3. B	8. D	13. B	18. A	23. C
4. A	9. D	14. C	19. D	24. D
5. D	10. A	15. A	20. D	25. A

_____

TEST 4

DIRECTIONS: Each question or incomplete statement is followed by several suggested answers or completions. Select the one that BEST answers the question or completes the statement. *PRINT THE LETTER OF THE CORRECT ANSWER IN THE SPACE AT THE RIGHT.*

Questions 1-5.

DIRECTIONS: For each phrase in Questions 1 through 5, select the endocrine gland, chosen from the list below, which is BEST described by that phrase. (A letter may be used more than once or not at all.)

Endocrine Glands

A. Thyroid
B. Adrenal
C. Pancreas
D. Pituitary
E. Ovary
F. Parathyroid

1. Is located on top of the kidney and influences the heart-beat and breathing rates.   1.___

2. Produces FSH, which influences a phase of the human female menstrual cycle.   2.___

3. Produces insulin, which helps to regulate the blood sugar levels.   3.___

4. Produces thyroxin, which regulates the rate of metabolism.   4.___

5. Produces estrogen, which influences the development of secondary sex characteristics.   5.___

Questions 6-8.

DIRECTIONS: Questions 6 through 8 are to be answered on the basis of the graph below, which represents relative blood pressure in human circulatory structures A through D.

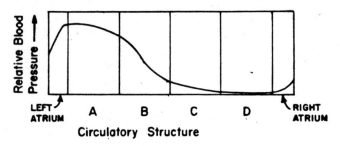

6. Blood pressure drops MOST drastically within structure   6.___
   A. A   B. B   C. C   D. D

7. What prevents the backflow of blood in structure D?   7.___
   A. Ganglia   B. Enzymes   C. Pumps   D. Valves

8. A heavy, muscular ventricle would be found as part of   8.___
   structure
   A. A   B. B   C. C   D. D

9. Which is an allergic reaction characterized by constriction   9.___
   of the bronchial tubes and reduced airflow to the lungs?
   A. Anemia   B. Arthritis C. Asthma   D. Angina

10. Which is a disease of the bone marrow characterized by   10.___
    uncontrolled production of nonfunctional white blood cells?
    A. An ulcer   B. Leukemia
    C. Anemia   D. Hemophilia

Questions 11-15.

DIRECTIONS: Questions 11 through 15 are to be answered on the basis
             of the diagram below of some anatomical organs of a
             human female and on your knowledge of biology.

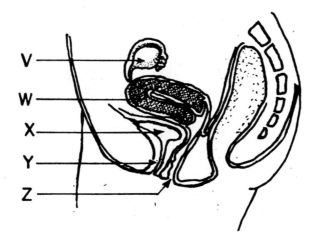

11. Some female sex hormones are produced and secreted by the   11.___
    structure represented by
    A. Z   B. X   C. W   D. V

12. Sperm cells are normally deposited in the structure   12.___
    represented by
    A. Z   B. Y   C. X   D. V

13. An ovum is produced in the structure represented by   13.___
    A. X   B. Y   C. V   D. W

14. During pregnancy, an embryo will normally develop in the structure represented by   14.____
   A. Z   B. X   C. V   D. W

15. The reproductive tube known as the oviduct would normally be located between structures   15.____
   A. Y and Z   B. X and Y   C. V and W   D. W and Z

Questions 16-18.

DIRECTIONS: Questions 16 through 18 are to be answered on the basis of the diagrams below, which represent the stages in the development of starfish eggs after fertilization.

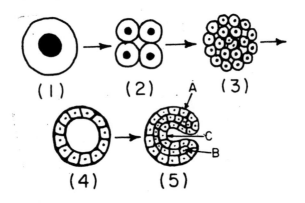

16. The structure numbered 4 is known as   16.____
   A. a blastula   B. a gastrula
   C. mesoderm   D. ectoderm

17. The structure numbered 1 is MOST likely a   17.____
   A. blastula   B. zygote   C. gastrula   D. gonad

18. From which of the embryonic layers shown in diagram 5 would the nervous system develop?   18.____
   A. A *only*   B. B and C   C. C *only*   D. A and B

19. If an allantois failed to develop in a bird egg, the MOST likely result would be that   19.____
   A. the embryo would not be protected from its environment
   B. a placenta could not develop
   C. the processes of gas exchange and excretion would be affected
   D. food could not be transported to the developing embryo

20. The structure in a bird egg which absorbs shock and provides a watery environment for an embryo is known as the   20.____
   A. placenta   B. yolk sac
   C. chorion   D. amniotic sac

21. Which combination of techniques can be used before birth   21.___
    to detect chromosomal abnormalities?
       A. Ultracentrifugation and chromatography
       B. Screening and vaccination
       C. Blood typing and vaccination
       D. Amniocentesis and karyotyping

Questions 22-25.

DIRECTIONS: Questions 22 through 25 are to be answered on the basis
               of the following pedigree chart and your knowledge of
               biology. The chart shows that Sally is a carrier for
               red-green color blindness.

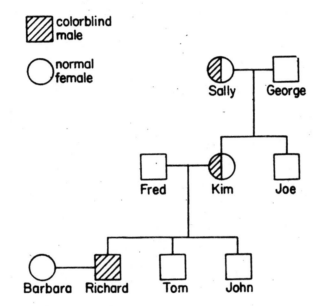

22. Which is MOST likely the chromosomal makeup of George's   22.___
    body cells?
       A. 11 pairs of autosomes and one X-chromosome
       B. 11 pairs of autosomes and one Y-chromosome
       C. 22 pairs of autosomes and two X-chromosomes
       D. 22 pairs of autosomes, an X-chromosome, and a
          Y-chromosome

23. What is the probability that Barbara, who has no genes   23.___
    for color blindness, will have a colorblind daughter?
       A. 0%   B. 25%   C. 50%   D. 100%

24. Which statement BEST describes Sally?   24.___
    She has
       A. no genes for colorblindness
       B. one gene for colorblindness located on an X-chromosome
       C. one gene for colorblindness located on a Y-chromosome
       D. two genes for colorblindness

25. Richard is colorblind because he inherited the trait from   25.____
    his
    A. father, Fred   B. grandfather, George
    C. mother, Kim   D. uncle, Joe

KEY (CORRECT ANSWERS)

1. B		11. D
2. D		12. A
3. C		13. C
4. A		14. D
5. E		15. C
6. B		16. A
7. D		17. B
8. A		18. A
9. C		19. C
10. B		20. D

21. D
22. D
23. A
24. B
25. C

TEST 5

DIRECTIONS: Each question or incomplete statement is followed by several suggested answers or completions. Select the one that BEST answers the question or completes the statement. *PRINT THE LETTER OF THE CORRECT ANSWER IN THE SPACE AT THE RIGHT.*

1. A human hereditary disorder that may result in mental retardation is
   A. phenylketonuria
   B. hemophilia
   C. sickle-cell anemia
   D. albinism

   1.___

2. Which nitrogenous base is NORMALLY present in DNA but absent from RNA?
   A. Adenine　　B. Cytosine　　C. Thymine　　D. Guanine

   2.___

3. A gene mutation is believed to involve
   A. replacing deoxyribose with glucose
   B. the substitution of a nitrogen base
   C. hydrolysis of strong hydrogen bonds
   D. replacing a phosphate with a nitrate

   3.___

4. Which level of biological organization is studied in the Hardy-Weinberg principle?
   A. Population
   B. Community
   C. Ecosystem
   D. Organism

   4.___

5. All the heritable genes found in a population constitute the population's
   A. recessive alleles
   B. chromosome mutations
   C. homologous structures
   D. gene pool

   5.___

Questions 6-8.

DIRECTIONS: Questions 6 through 8 are to be answered on the basis of the diagram below, which represents a cycle and on your knowledge of biology.

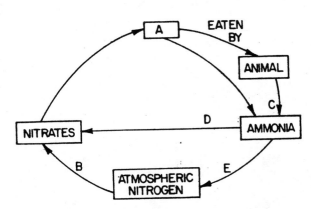

6. Nitrifying bacteria are represented by letter   6.___
      A. A   B. E   C. C   D. D

7. The letter B MOST likely represents   7.___
      A. bacteria of decay   B. denitrifying bacteria
      C. a leguminous plant   D. nitrogen-fixing bacteria

8. The cycle represented by the diagram is the ____ cycle.   8.___
      A. nitrogen   B. carbon   C. water   D. oxygen

9. Nitrogen-fixing bacteria enrich the soil by producing   9.___
   nitrates beneficial to green plants. The bacteria live in
   nodules located on the roots of legumes. These nodules
   provide a favorable environment for the bacteria to grow
   and reproduce.
   The relationship between these bacteria and the leguminous
   plant is an example of
      A. parasitism
      C. mutualism
                              B. commensalism
                              D. competition

Questions 10-12.

DIRECTIONS: Questions 10 through 12 are to be answered on the basis
               of the diagram below, which represents four biome regions
               of representative plant vegetation growing on a mountain.
               Each plant community is located in a different zone (A, B,
               C, or D), which provides the characteristic climate for
               each level.

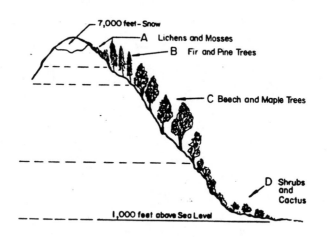

10. A person traveling from zone B into zone C could identify   10.___
    the type of biome he had just entered by
      A. measuring the nitrogen content of the air
      B. observing the type of rock substratum
      C. measuring the amount of water held by soil particles
      D. observing the climax vegetation of the area

11. Which zone contains many species of broad-leaved plants   11.___
    which shed their leaves as cold weather approaches?
        A. A   B. B   C. C   D. D

12. A taiga region contains climax vegetation similar to the   12.___
    plant growth located in the diagram of zone
        A. A   B. B   C. C   D. D

Questions 13-15.

DIRECTIONS: Questions 13 through 15 are to be answered on the basis
               of the diagrams below and on your knowledge of biology.
               The sequence A through E represents stages of ecological
               succession in a given area.

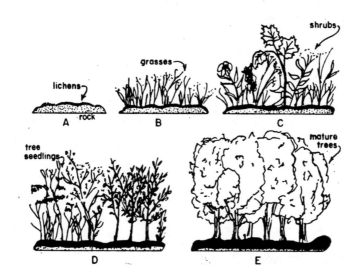

13. Which diagram shows the GREATEST number of pioneer   13.___
    organisms?
        A. A   B. E   C. C   D. D

14. In this sequence, which diagram represents a climax stage?   14.___
        A. E   B. B   C. C   D. D

15. What caused succession to occur in stages A through E?   15.___
        A. Importation of organisms that have no natural enemies
        B. Each community modifying the environment
        C. Urban development disrupting natural habitats
        D. Technological oversights leading to air pollution

16. While a student is heating a liquid in a test tube, the   16.___
    mouth of the tube should ALWAYS be
        A. corked with a rubber stopper
        B. pointed toward the student
        C. allowed to cool
        D. aimed away from everybody

Questions 17-20.

DIRECTIONS: Questions 17 through 20 are to be answered on the basis
of your knowledge of biology and on the diagrams which
represent fields of vision under the low power of the
same compound light microscope (100x). Diagram A shows
the millimeter divisions of a plastic ruler, and
diagram B shows a sample of stained onion epidermal cells.

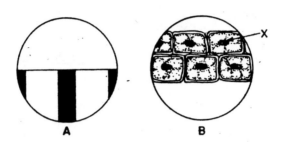

17.   Structure X in diagram B was MOST likely stained by adding   17.___
A. water   B. iodine solution
C. Benedict's solution   D. bromthymol blue

18.   Structure X in diagram B indicates a(the)   18.___
A. nucleus   B. mitochondrion
C. cell wall   D. cytoplasm

19.   The diameter of the field of vision in diagram A is APPROXI-   19.___
MATELY _____ µm.
A. 500   B. 1,000   C. 1,500   D. 2,000

20.   What is the APPROXIMATE length of each onion epidermal   20.___
cell in field B?
_____ µm.
A. 200   B. 660   C. 1,000   D. 2,500

Questions 21-25.

DIRECTIONS: Questions 21 through 25 are to be answered on the basis
of the following two charts and on your knowledge of
biology. Chart I shows the percentages of certain
materials in the blood entering the kidney and the
percentages of the same materials in the urine leaving
the body. Chart II shows the number of molecules in
the beginning and end of the kidney tubule for every 100
molecules of each substance entering the glomerulus.

Chart I

Substance	% in blood	% in urine
Protein	7.0	0.0
Water	91.5	96.0
Glucose	0.1	0.0
Sodium	0.33	0.29
Potassium	0.02	0.24
Urea	0.03	2.7

Chart II

Substance	Number of Molecules		
	in blood entering glomerulus	Beginning of Tubule	End of Tubule
Protein	100	0	0
Water	100	30	1
Glucose	100	20	0
Sodium	100	30	1
Potassium	100	23	12
Urea	100	50	90

21. According to Chart I, which substance is MORE highly concentrated in the urine than in the blood?   21.___
    A. Water   B. Sodium   C. Protein   D. Glucose

22. According to Charts I and II, which substance enters the tubules but does NOT appear in the urine leaving the body?   22.___
    A. Protein   B. Water   C. Glucose   D. Potassium

23. According to the data, which substance did NOT pass out of the blood into the tubule?   23.___
    A. Water   B. Urea   C. Glucose   D. Protein

24. The data in the charts would BEST aid a biologist in understanding the function of the   24.___
    A. heart of a frog
    B. nephron of a human
    C. nerve net of a Hydra
    D. contractile vacuole of a Paramecium

25. Which substances enter the tubule and then are reabsorbed back into the blood as they pass through the tubule?   25.___
    A. Urea and potassium   B. Water and sodium
    C. Urea and protein   D. Protein and glucose

KEY (CORRECT ANSWERS)

1. A		11. C
2. C		12. B
3. B		13. A
4. A		14. A
5. D		15. B
6. D		16. D
7. D		17. B
8. A		18. A
9. C		19. D
10. D		20. B

21. A
22. C
23. D
24. B
25. B

EXAMINATION SECTION

TEST 1

DIRECTIONS: Each question or incomplete statement is followed by
                several suggested answers or completions. Select the
                one that BEST answers the question or completes the
                statement. *PRINT THE LETTER OF THE CORRECT ANSWER IN
                THE SPACE AT THE RIGHT.*

1. If a protein contains 80 amino acids, its corresponding   1.___
    gene must contain AT LEAST how many nucleotides?
        A. 40   B. 120   C. 240   D. 360   E. 480

2. Which one of the following is characteristic ONLY of   2.___
    mitosis and NOT of meiosis?
        A. Synapsis occurs
        B. Cells with identical genotypes are produced
        C. Splitting of centromeres takes place
        D. Homologous chromosomes separate
        E. Spindle fibers are formed

3. The PRIMARY role of oxygen in respiration is to   3.___
        A. yield energy in the form of ATP as it is passed down
           the respiratory chain
        B. act as an acceptor for electrons and hydrogen ions
           to form water
        C. combine with carbon to form CO_2
        D. combine with lactic acid to form pyruvic acid
        E. catalyze the reactions of glycolysis

4. Fetal cells sloughed off into the amniotic fluid can be   4.___
    collected and cultured.
    The cultured cells CANNOT be used for prenatal diagnosis of
        A. identical twinning
        B. paternity
        C. genetic diseases whose metabolic basis is known
        D. the sex of the fetus
        E. aneuploidy

5. The function of the Loop of Henle is to   5.___
        A. rid the body of excess urea and ammonia
        B. rid the body of excess hydrogen ions
        C. return reusable nutrients to the blood
        D. produce a sugar gradient capable of concentrating urine
        E. produce a salt gradient capable of concentrating urine

6. The cells of the testis that are MOST like the follicle   6.___
    cells of the ovary in that they respond to the pituitary
    hormone LH by producing steroid hormones are
        A. spermatids   B. endometrial cells
        C. stem cells   D. interstitial cells
        E. germ cells

7. Bacteriophages are
   A. organelles   B. organisms   C. prokaryotes
   D. bacteria   E. viruses

7.___

8. When an aerobic organism is temporarily deprived of O_2, it obtains its chemical energy from
   A. the substrate level of ATP synthesis in glycolysis
   B. the oxidation of pyruvic acid to acetyl-CoA
   C. the respiratory electron transport chain
   D. chemiosmotic coupling
   E. metabolism of succinic acid in the TCA cycle

8.___

9. Examination of the eukaryotic cell surface by the electron microscope reveals that the plasma membrane
   A. is composed of a single layer of molecules approximately 75 Angstrom units in thickness
   B. is composed exclusively of phospholipids
   C. invaginates into the cellular cytoplasm to form canals and vesicles
   D. invaginates to form cristae on which are arranged the electron transport systems
   E. is composed exclusively of proteins

9.___

10. In a research project, a chemical was introduced to developing embryos that selectively destroyed the mesoderm germ layer.
    Which of the following structures would be absent in the fetus?
    A. Brain   B. Pectoralis muscle
    C. Epidermis   D. Intestinal mucosa
    E. Adrenal medulla

10.___

11. A restriction endonuclease produces a break in
    A. DNA at a specific base sequence
    B. tRNA at a specific base sequence
    C. any nucleic acid at the end of the molecule
    D. proteins at a specific amino acid sequence
    E. DNA at the 3' terminal end *only*

11.___

12. All chemosynthetic autotrophic prokaryotes belong to the
    A. bacteria   B. fungi   C. protozoa
    D. viruses   E. tracheophytes

12.___

13. The carbon dioxide carried in the blood from the tissues to the lungs is MOST commonly found in the form of
    A. carbaminohemoglobin
    B. free carbon dioxide
    C. carbonic acid
    D. bicarbonate ions
    E. membrane-bound carbon dioxide

13.___

14. The regulation of body temperature, water balance, and appetite are a function of the
    A. thalamus   B. hypothalamus
    C. medulla oblongata   D. anterior lobe of pituitary
    E. cerebrum

14.___

15. In sex-linkage   15.___
    A. the recessive autosomal characters of the father are
       expressed in the sons
    B. X-linked characters of the mother must be expressed
       in the daughters
    C. the X-linked characters of the mother are never
       expressed in the daughters
    D. the primary sexual characteristics are determined
       by the sex hormones
    E. normal male fruitflies and humans always have a
       Y-chromosome

16. Assuming Hardy-Weinberg conditions, when 16 percent of a   16.___
    population is homozygous recessive for a trait, the
    percent that is heterozygous is
    A. 30   B. 25   C. 48   D. 24   E. 36

17. One of the evolutionary adaptations of reptiles for a   17.___
    terrestrial environment was
    A. a thin, pliable skin
    B. a four-chambered heart
    C. air breathing lung
    D. a shelled egg with extraembryonic membranes
    E. legs for rapid locomotion

18. According to the theory of natural selection, the environ-   18.___
    ment *selects* ONLY those characteristics which
    A. fit the organism to future environmental change
    B. *increase* the life span of the individual
    C. *increase* the number of offspring which reach repro-
       ductive age
    D. result in stronger individuals
    E. affect social behavior

19. If acetylcholine were released at a synapse and acetyl-   19.___
    cholinesterase was inhibited, the
    A. postsynaptic neuron would not respond to the
       acetylcholine
    B. postsynaptic neuron would produce a single nerve
       impulse
    C. postsynaptic neuron would produce an abnormally
       long series of nerve impulses
    D. acetylcholine would not diffuse across the synapse
    E. acetylcholine would spontaneously decompose

20. Cystic fibrosis is inherited as a simple autosomal   20.___
    recessive. Suppose a woman who is heterozygous for this
    trait marries a man who is also heterozygous for it.
    What is the probability that they will have a child who
    is heterozygous for the trait?
    A. 0   B. 1/4   C. 1/2   D. 2/3   E. 3/4

KEY (CORRECT ANSWERS)

1.	C	11.	A
2.	B	12.	A
3.	B	13.	D
4.	A	14.	B
5.	E	15.	E
6.	D	16.	C
7.	E	17.	D
8.	A	18.	C
9.	C	19.	C
10.	B	20.	C

TEST 2

DIRECTIONS: Each question or incomplete statement is followed by several suggested answers or completions. Select the one that BEST answers the question or completes the statement. *PRINT THE LETTER OF THE CORRECT ANSWER IN THE SPACE AT THE RIGHT.*

1. Which of the following statements is TRUE of the archenteron?   1.___
   A. The cavity of the archenteron is called the blastocoel.
   B. The cavity of the archenteron represents the beginning of the primitive gut.
   C. The archenteron is formed during blastula formation.
   D. The cavity of the archenteron represents the first cavity of the developing heart.
   E. The archenteron is formed by a closing of the neural tube.

2. Which part of the cell is involved MOST directly with the synthesis of ribosomal subunits?   2.___
   A. Nucleolus   B. Microtubules
   C. Endoplasmic reticulum   D. Golgi apparatus
   E. Nuclear envelope

3. Which of the following substances is a nucleotide?   3.___
   A. Estrogen
   B. Growth hormone (somatotropin)
   C. Insulin
   D. Adenosine triphosphate (ATP)
   E. Amylose

4. Which of the following is NOT a function of microtubules?   4.___
   A. Maintaining or controlling the shape of the cell
   B. Movement of chromosomes during anaphase
   C. Temporary storage of proteins prior to secretion
   D. Forming the structural elements of the centrioles
   E. Activity of cells and flagella

5. The thymus gland is involved in   5.___
   A. the regulation of calcium metabolism
   B. the development of the immune response
   C. regulation of the activity of the thyroid gland
   D. endocrine and exocrine functions
   E. reproductive physiology

6. At different stages during the normal sequence of events   6.___
   in the menstrual cycle, there is an increase in progesterone, FSH, and estrogen.
   Which one of the following is the CORRECT sequence of *initial* increases in each substance, beginning with menstruation?
   A. Estrogen, FSH, progesterone
   B. FSH, estrogen, progesterone

C. Estrogen, progesterone, FSH
D. FSH, progesterone, estrogen
E. Progesterone, estrogen, FSH

7. Suppose an individual is heterozygous for ten different 7.___
   independently assorting genes.
   How many genetically different gametes will be possible
   from this individual?
   A. 10   B. 20   C. 10^2 D. 200   E. 2^{10}

8. Viruses may not be considered true living organisms 8.___
   because they
      A. are too small
      B. can only reproduce in the cells of another living
         organism
      C. are not eukaryotes
      D. are extremely primitive organisms
      E. can only replicate in an anaerobic environment

9. One of the MAJOR advantages in using scanning electron 9.___
   microscopy as opposed to transmission electron microscopy
   is that
      A. greater magnification can be obtained
      B. greater resolving power can be obtained
      C. the specimen does not have to be treated with chemicals
      D. a three-dimensional image can be obtained
      E. there is no advantage

10. The following gland is both endocrine and exocrine in 10.___
    function.
       A. Thyroid   B. Liver   C. Adrenal
       D. Pancreas   E. Pituitary

11. Sucrose is 11.___
       A. a disaccharide of glucose and fructose
       B. a trisaccharide of galactose, glucose, and fructose
       C. the technical term for blood sugar
       D. the major subunit of cellulose
       E. the major subunit of starch

12. The intracellular ion that is PRIMARILY responsible for 12.___
    triggering muscle contraction is
       A. sodium   B. potassium   C. phosphorus
       D. calcium   E. magnesium

13. In which two of the following phyla do most biologists 13.___
    place the MOST primitive bilaterally symmetrical animals?
       A. Chordata and Hemichordata
       B. Coelenterata (Cnidaria) and Ctenophora
       C. Onycophora and Arthropoda
       D. Echinodermata and Chaetognatha
       E. Platyhelminthes and Nemertina

14. A classic example of primary embryonic induction is the   14.___
    induction by the vertebrate chordamesoderm of the
      A. vertebrae   B. axial musculature
      C. neural tube   D. heart
      E. liver primordium

15. In which of the following organelles is water synthesized   15.___
    from oxygen and hydrogen?
      A. Nucleus   B. Mitochrondria
      C. Ribosomes   D. Lysosomes
      E. Golgi apparatus

16. The biological significance of the evolution of fleshy   16.___
    fruits such as the apple and the peach is that such
    fruits are
      A. necessary for seed transpiration
      B. to protect the seeds from being eaten by animals
      C. exposed to rigorous natural selection because the
         matured ovary wall is triploid
      D. important sources of vitamin C for the plant
      E. adaptations to securing seed dispersal by animals

17. In a simple food chain, animals with the SMALLEST popula-   17.___
    tion *probably*
      A. are least likely to be an endangered species
      B. have a very high biotic potential
      C. are physically smaller than the others in the food
         chain
      D. are herbivorous
      E. are carnivorous

18. Which of the following enzymes acts on carbohydrates?   18.___
      A. Carboxypeptidase   B. Trypsin
      C. Chymotrypsin   D. Lipase
      E. Amylase

19. All of the following processes require energy input   19.___
    EXCEPT
      A. active transport
      B. muscle contraction
      C. DNA synthesis
      D. maintenance of the resting potential of neurons
      E. osmosis

20. The movement of fluid from the arteriole end of a   20.___
    mammalian capillary bed into the interstitial spaces
    is PRIMARILY due to
      A. hydrostatic pressure
      B. osmotic pressure
      C. active transport by the capillary walls
      D. contraction of skeletal muscles
      E. contraction of smooth muscle of the capillary walls

KEY (CORRECT ANSWERS)

1.	B	11.	A
2.	A	12.	D
3.	D	13.	E
4.	C	14.	C
5.	B	15.	B
6.	B	16.	E
7.	E	17.	E
8.	B	18.	E
9.	D	19.	E
10.	D	20.	A

———

EXAMINATION SECTION

DIRECTIONS: Each question or incomplete statement is followed by several suggested answers or completions. Select the one that BEST answers the question or completes the statement. *PRINT THE LETTER OF THE CORRECT ANSWER IN THE SPACE AT THE RIGHT.*

1. According to the Second Law of Thermodynamics,   1.___
    A. energy can neither be created nor destroyed
    B. energy can be created or destroyed
    C. any system isolated from an energy source tends to decrease in entropy
    D. organisms could not evolve
    E. any system isolated from an energy source tends toward its least ordered state

2. The distinction between the anaerobic metabolism of   2.___
   glucose in muscle cells and in yeast cells is the
    A. formation of lactic acid (lactate) in muscle cells and the formation of ethanol in yeast cells
    B. formation of acetate in yeast cells and lactate in muscle cells
    C. synthesis of more ATP per glucose molecule in muscle than in yeast cells
    D. formation of carbon dioxide in muscle but not in yeast cells
    E. synthesis of less ATP per glucose molecule in muscle cells

3. Organisms that obtain their energy from light can be   3.___
   termed
    A. autotrophic   B. holotrophic   C. chemotrophic
    D. heterotrophic   E. heliotrophic

4. An investigator isolated small particles from cancer cells   4.___
   which hydrolyzed protein and concluded that these were
    A. ribosomes   B. lipid vacuoles
    C. lysosomes   D. food vacuoles
    E. mitochondria

5. The first enzyme-catalyzed reaction in the glycolysis of   5.___
   glucose is
    A. deamination   B. lipolysis   C. phosphorylation
    D. hydrolysis   E. carboxylation

6. The generation of ATP (adenosine triphosphate) by the   6.___
   electron transport system (respiratory chain) occurs
    A. on the inner membrane of mitochondria
    B. on the outer surface of the nuclear envelope
    C. in the cytoplasm
    D. in the Golgi apparatus
    E. on the endoplasmic reticulum

7. Messenger ribonucleic acid (mRNA) differs from   7.___
   deoxyribonucleic acid (DNA) in that RNA
      I. contains thymine instead of uracil
     II. contains a ribose sugar
    III. is single-stranded

   The CORRECT answer is:
      A. I *only*   B. II *only*   C. III *only*
      D. I and III   E. II and III

8. The so-called dark reactions (light-independent reactions)   8.___
   of photosynthesis
      A. do not occur during the daytime
      B. use the direct energy of light quanta
      C. occur in all plants cells
      D. do not require the products of the light reactions
      E. result in the assimilation (fixation) of carbon
         dioxide

9. If animal muscle cells are deprived of oxygen, anaerobic   9.___
   glycolysis will result and pyruvic acid will then be
   converted to
      A. alcohol   B. glucose
      C. lactic acid   D. phosphoric acid
      E. acetyl CoA

10. A sample of blood is added to a test tube containing a   10.___
    1.6% salt solution. A short while later, the red blood
    cells are observed to be smaller and wrinkled in shape
    due to water loss.
    This indicates that
       A. red blood cells are isotonic to the 1.6% salt solution
       B. red blood cells are hypertonic to the 1.6% salt
          solution
       C. red blood cells are hypotonic to the 1.6% salt solu-
          tion
       D. the 1.6% salt solution is hypotonic to the red blood
          cells
       E. the 1.6% salt solution is isotonic to the red blood
          cells

11. Which of the following is the key intermediate compound   11.___
    linking glycolysis to the Krebs cycle?
       A. NADH   B. ATP   C. Cytochrome b
       D. Succinic acid   E. Acetyl Co A

12. A plant kept in the dark will not be able to produce   12.___
    glucose because light is necessary
       A. for the oxidation of glucose
       B. to excite electrons in the CO_2 molecules
       C. for activating enzymes necessary for converting CO_2
          to glucose
       D. for sufficient ATP and reduced NADP to be available
          to synthesize glucose from CO_2
       E. for glucose phosphorylation

13. The First Law of Thermodynamics implies that living   13.___
    organisms cannot create their own energy but can only
    convert one form of energy into another.
    What, then, is the ULTIMATE source of energy for most
    living organisms?
    A. Chemical energy from the glucose molecule made by
       plants during photosynthesis
    B. The chemical energy released by the numerous hydro-
       lytic reactions in a cell
    C. Heat energy from the sun
    D. Light energy from the sun
    E. ATP made in the mitochondria of both plants and
       animals

14. Which of the following is NOT a function of any hormone?   14.___
    A. Affects membrane transport of substances
    B. Regulates water balance in the body
    C. Changes the amount of activity of enzymes
    D. Promotes transcription of messenger RNA
    E. Acts as a source of energy

15. Which of the following pairs of structures have similarity   15.___
    of function?
    _____ nervous system.
    A. Thyroid gland and sympathetic
    B. Adrenal cortex and sympathetic
    C. Adrenal cortex and parasympathetic
    D. Adrenal medulla and parasympathetic
    E. Adrenal medulla and sympathetic

16. In the nephron of the kidney, filtration occurs between   16.___
    A. Bowman's capsule and Henle's loop
    B. the glomerulus and Bowman's capsule
    C. the proximal tubule and Henle's loop
    D. Henle's loop and the vasa recta
    E. the peritubular network and the convoluted tubules

17. The stimulation of parasympathetic nerves would produce   17.___
    a(n)
    A. increase in peristaltic activity
    B. increase in perspiration
    C. decrease in salivary gland activity
    D. increase in blood pressure
    E. none of the above

18. Clotting of human blood   18.___
    A. requires that hemoglobin be present
    B. results from fibrin joining globulin
    C. is a result of platelets releasing fibrinogen
    D. depends on the formation of fibrin from fibrinogen
    E. is accelerated when Ca^{++} is removed

19. The muscle cells of the human heart are PRIMARILY   19.___
    nourished by
    A. blood within the four chambers of the heart
    B. fluid in the pericardial cavity
    C. the lymphatic system
    D. blood delivered by the coronary arteries
    E. blood delivered by the ductus arteriosus

20. Carbon dioxide passes from tissues to blood to lungs by   20.___
    A. diffusing from a region of high concentration to an
       area of lesser concentration
    B. diffusing from a region of lower to one of higher
       concentration
    C. active transport
    D. irreversibly binding to hemoglobin
    E. chemiosmosis

21. Products of digestion absorbed in the mammalian small   21.___
    intestine
    A. are carried directly to the heart by the posterior
       vena cava
    B. are carried to the spleen for processing
    C. must be further digested in the blood before they can
       be absorbed by the cells
    D. are processed by the cells of the small intestine,
       which then secrete ATP into the blood
    E. are carried to the liver by the hepatic portal vein

22. Which of the following are typically autotrophic?   22.___
    A. Protozoa   B. Plants   C. Animals
    D. Fungi   E. Bacteria

23. Of the following phyla, the one that contains more species 23.___
    than the others combined is
    A. Annelida   B. Arthropoda   C. Mollusca
    D. Echinodermata   E. Chordata

24. All chordates   24.___
    A. possess backbones
    B. possess a dorsal, tubular nerve cord at some stage
       of life
    C. lack larval forms
    D. have endoskeletons composed of cartilage
    E. have a water vascular system

25. In which of these kingdoms are the organisms entirely   25.___
    heterotrophic?
    A. Protista and Fungi   B. Plantae and Fungi
    C. Animalia and Fungi   D. Protista and Animalia
    E. Monera and Protista

26. Mendel's law of segregation reflects the fact that   26.___
    A. linkage never occurs in peas
    B. alleles segregate differently in males and females
    C. each member of an allelic pair of genes enters a
       separate cell during meiosis
    D. during the course of development, DNA becomes
       segregated in the nucleus, RNA in the cytoplasm
    E. increasing specialization in the course of evolution
       is characterized by a segregation of tissue types

27. A diploid cell (2N = 20) has how many tetrads at metaphase   27.___
    I?
    A. 0   B. 10   C. 20   D. 40   E. 80

28. For the human ABO blood typing system, which of the   28.___
    following is ALWAYS determined by a homozygous genotype?
    Type
    A. A   B. B
    C. AB   D. O
    E. all of the above

29. During the synthesis of a polypeptide at the ribosome   29.___
    site, the completed polypeptide is released when the
    A. ribosome reaches a termination codon
    B. ribosome reaches a termination anticodon
    C. tRNAs are depleted
    D. amino acids are depleted
    E. ribosome reaches the 5' end of the mRNA

30. A particular double-stranded DNA molecule was found to   30.___
    have 24% of its bases consist of adenine (A).
    What percentage of its bases would be expected to consist
    of guanine (G)?
    A. 24   B. 26   C. 48   D. 52   E. 76

31. In humans, a phenotype resulting from a homozygous auto-   31.___
    somal recessive pair of genes would be expected to appear
    A. in unequal numbers in the two sexes
    B. phenotypically in every generation as long as one
       of the original parents manifested the trait
    C. only in those individuals who had at least one parent
       with the gene
    D. in approximately one-fourth of the children produced
       by two heterozygotes
    E. none of the above

32. One form of colorblindness is caused by a gene c carried   32.___
    on the X chromosome in humans. The gene is recessive to
    its normal allele C. Far more men are colorblind than
    women.
    Geneticists explain this by pointing out that
    A. women possess no X chromosomes in their cells
    B. men carry no genes for color vision on their Y chromo-
       somes
    C. men carry more genes for colorblindness than women do

D. colorblindness is inhibited by female sex hormones
E. colorblindness is promoted by male sex hormones

33. Sexual reproduction as compared with asexual reproduction   33.___
ordinarily results in
A. more offspring
B. a greater inducement to reproduce
C. greater genetic diversity in the offspring
D. a higher frequency of well-adapted individual off-
spring
E. fewer individuals carrying recessive alleles

34. Gastrulation involves the   34.___
A. formation of the blastocoel
B. formation of germ layers
C. loss of the blastopore
D. formation of the blastula
E. final differentiation of the stomach

35. Of the germ layers comprising the early human embryo,   35.___
which one forms MOST of the central nervous system?
A. Ectoderm   B. Mesoderm   C. Endoderm
D. Notochord   E. Dermis

36. Embryonic induction is a process in which   36.___
A. embryonic tissues influence adjacent tissues to
differentiate
B. an unfertilized egg is induced to develop
C. genes are transferred from one developing tissue to
another
D. resting potentials are induced in neurons of embryos
E. the maternal parent induces expression of recessive
genes in embryos

37. One of the loveliest sounds in nature is bird song.   37.___
Such song is commonly associated with
A. hunger   B. pugnacity   C. territoriality
D. orientation   E. happiness

38. A deciduous forest biome differs from that of the grass-   38.___
land biome in that the forest biome receives more
A. sunlight
B. CO_2 for photosynthesis
C. fixed nitrogen from the soil
D. moisture
E. ultraviolet light

39. Which of the following situations is MOST likely to result   39.___
in genetic drift?
A. An increase in population size
B. A lack of gene mutation
C. A prevention of emigration
D. Random mating
E. Isolation of a small population from a larger one

40. Under Hardy-Weinberg conditions,   40.___
    A. dominant alleles eventually replace recessive alleles
    B. evolution occurs at a rapid rate
    C. the frequency of dominant alleles slowly increases
    D. gene frequencies remain constant
    E. a 50%-50% equilibrium is reached between dominant
       and recessive alleles

———

KEY (CORRECT ANSWERS)

1. E	11. E	21. E	31. D
2. A	12. D	22. B	32. B
3. A	13. D	23. B	33. C
4. C	14. E	24. B	34. B
5. C	15. E	25. C	35. A
6. A	16. B	26. C	36. A
7. E	17. A	27. B	37. C
8. E	18. D	28. D	38. D
9. C	19. D	29. A	39. E
10. C	20. A	30. B	40. D

———

EXAMINATION SECTION

DIRECTIONS: Each question or incomplete statement is followed by
several suggested answers or completions. Select the
one that BEST answers the question or completes the
statement. *PRINT THE LETTER OF THE CORRECT ANSWER IN
THE SPACE AT THE RIGHT.*

1. All of the following secrete digestive enzymes EXCEPT the   1.___
   A. pancreas   B. salivary glands
   C. stomach   D. small intestine
   E. liver

2. Soon after fertilization, the dividing zygote of the   2.___
   amphibian forms a hollow ball of cells surrounding a
   central cavity.
   This stage in development is called the
   A. morula   B. blastula
   C. gastrula   D. primitive streak
   E. fetus

3. The two products of the *light reactions* of photosynthesis   3.___
   that are required for the synthetic *dark reactions* are ATP
   and
   A. carbon dioxide
   B. the reduced form of coenzyme NADP
   C. oxygen
   D. glucose
   E. ribulose-1, 5-bisphosphate (RuBP)

4. Vertebrate skeletal muscle is able to contact as a result   4.___
   of muscle membrane depolarization due to the action of
   A. neurotransmitters   B. Ca^{2+} ions
   C. actin and myosin   D. phosphocreatine
   E. myoglobin

5. Assuming that all are of the same size, which of the   5.___
   following fishes would you expect to produce the *greatest*
   volume of urine per unit time?
   A. Bony fish living in freshwater
   B. Bony fish living in an estuary
   C. Bony fish living in the ocean
   D. Shark living in the ocean
   E. All about the same

6. One of the functions of light in the process of photo-   6.___
   synthesis is to
   A. raise the energy level of electrons
   B. cause the formation of water
   C. cause the formation of ribulose-diphosphate
   D. fix CO_2
   E. oxidize NADP (nicotinamide adenine dinucleotide
      phosphate)

7. In mammalian embryonic development, the embryo proper
develops from the
    A. trophoblast   B. amnion
    C. inner cell mass   D. primary yolk sac
    E. placenta

7.__

8. Hydrogen bonds
    A. have bond energy about equal to covalent bonds
    B. have bond energy much larger than covalent bonds
    C. are important in maintaining protein conformations
    D. are too weak to be of importance in biological
       molecules
    E. are any bonds between hydrogen and another atom

8.__

9. The MAIN function of the nucleolus is to
    A. direct the transcriptive activities of the nucleus
    B. coordinate the replication of chromosomal DNA
    C. synthesize components of the nuclear membrane
    D. synthesize ribosomal RNA
    E. regulate the condensation of chromosomes as the cell
       approaches metaphase

9.__

10. Which of the following would tend to shift a population
out of Hardy-Weinberg equilibrium?
    A. Barriers to migration
    B. Prevention of mutation
    C. Population size increase
    D. Prevention of genetic drift
    E. Preferential mating

10.__

11. In the modern understanding of the concept of natural
selection, the fittest individuals are those who
    A. produce the largest number of progeny
    B. are adapted to the widest diversity of environments
    C. produce most highly variable offspring
    D. survive for the largest number of years
    E. have the largest number of fertile offspring

11.__

12. Recombinant DNA technology uses which of the following
to cleave DNA molecules into polynucleotide fragments?
    A. Reverse transcriptases   B. DNA topoisomerases
    C. Restriction enzymes   D. Plasmids or episomes
    E. Recombinases

12.__

13. During the development of a typical vertebrate embryo,
the mesoderm germ layer produces the following series of
structures:
    A. Epidermis, nails, and hair
    B. Dermis, blood vessels, and vertebrae
    C. Neural tube, brain and cranial nerves
    D. Lining of the gut, liver, and pancreas
    E. All of the above

13.__

14. The stem length of pea plants is genetically determined   14.___
    by a pair of alleles, *T* for tall and *t* for short. *T* is
    completely dominant over *t*.
    If the gene frequency for *T* is 0.9 in a given population,
    what will be the frequency of short-stemmed pea plants in
    the population?
       A. 0.1   B. 0.01   C. 0.5   D. 0.05   E. 0.15

15. The pituitary gland is attached to and secretes its   15.___
    hormones in response to neurahormonal stimulation from the
       A. thalamus   B. hypothalamus
       C. cerebrum   D. medullaoblongata
       E. cerebellum

16. To say that the genetic code is *degenerate* means that   16.___
       A. a given codon may specify more than one amino acid
       B. a given amino acid may be specified by more than
          one codon
       C. some of the codons are nonsense codons
       D. the code is nonoverlapping
       E. nonsense suppressor mutations occur in tRNA genes

17. When mammalian eyes become accommodated for close vision,   17.___
    the
       A. ciliary muscles are contracted and the lens becomes
          more convex
       B. ciliary muscles are relaxed and the lens becomes
          more convex
       C. ciliary muscles are contracted and the lens becomes
          flattened
       D. ciliary muscles are relaxed and the lens becomes
          flattened
       E. eyeball undergoes auteroposterior shortening

18. The movement of materials across a cell membrane from a   18.___
    region of low concentration to a region of high concentra-
    tion
       A. is termed free diffusion
       B. occurs only in osmosis
       C. requires the expenditure of energy
       D. is termed faciliated diffusion
       E. none of the above

19. The liver of the mammal has many important functions.   19.___
    One function is the synthesis of a nitrogen waste product
    in the form of
       A. ammonia   B. urea   C. nitrates
       D. nitric acid   E. nitrous oxide

20. Which of the following organs plays a major role in the   20.___
    immune function?
       A. Thyroid   B. Pituitary   C. Pancreas
       D. Pineal   E. Thymus

21. The phylum chordata is usually judged to be *most closely*   21.____
    related to the
    A. Arthropoda   B. Annelida
    C. Echinodermata   D. Mollusca
    E. Coelenterata

22. The organelle MOST involved in the energy-producing   22.____
    functions of the cell is the
    A. nucleus   B. Golgi complex
    C. ER   D. mitochondrion
    E. ribosome

23. A feature common to the chromosomes of both prokaryotic   23.____
    and eukaryotic cells is the
    A. presence of DNA and histones in about equal amounts
    B. circularity of the DNA molecules
    C. involvement of DNA polymerase in chromosomal
       replication
    D. presence of the pyrimidines uracil and cytosine
    E. location of the chromosomes within a cell

24. Which of the following is homeothermic?   24.____
    A. Pisces   B. Amphibia   C. Aves
    D. Reptilia   E. Insects

25. Mammalian somatic motor neurons   25.____
    A. leave the spinal cord via the ventral root
    B. enter the spinal cord via the dorsal root
    C. innervate pressure receptors in muscle
    D. have their cell bodies outside the spinal cord
    E. innervate visceral organs

26. If a portion of a DNA base sequence is G-A-T, the   26.____
    complementary portion of a mRNA base sequence must be
    A. C-T-A   B. C-T-U   C. C-U-A
    D. G-A-T   E. C-U-U

27. The amylase present in saliva is *most likely* to be   27.____
    involved in the digestion of which component of a bacon,
    lettuce and tomato sandwich?
    A. Bacon   B. Lettuce   C. Tomato
    D. Bun   E. Butter

28.   28.____

INITIAL SOLUTION CONCENTRATIONS

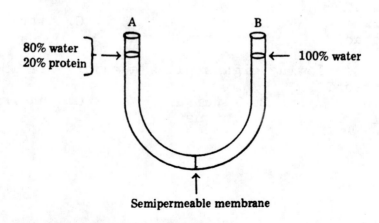

Semipermeable membrane

In the U-shaped tube with a semipermeable membrane
separating Solution A from Solution B in the diagram on
the preceding page, the water level will
   A. rise inside A, because water will pass from the area
      of greater concentration of water to the area of
      lesser concentration of water
   B. rise inside B, because water will pass from the area
      of lesser concentration of water to the area of
      greater concentration of water
   C. rise inside B as the protein concentration equalizes
      on both sides
   D. remain the same because atmospheric pressure is equal
      on both sides of the system
   E.

29. All of the solar energy that is converted by photosynthesis 29.___
    into the biomass of an ecosystem is ultimately lost from
    the ecosystem as
      A. exports of biomass
      B. organisms die
      C. more biomass is produced
      D. heat
      E. decreased entropy

30. The majority of the known species of multicellular   30.___
    animals in the animal kingdom are characterized by
      A. no skeleton
      B. bony exoskeleton
      C. chitinous endoskeleton
      D. bony endoskeleton
      E. chitinous exoskeleton

31. Which of the following is one of the morphogenetic move- 31.___
    ments that forms the gastrula of vertebrate embryos?
      A. Differentiation   B. Cleavage
      C. Metamorphosis   D. Induction
      E. Invagination

32. In adult mammals, a blood vessel that carries deoxygenated 32.___
    blood is the
      A. dorsal aorta   B. ventral aorta
      C. pulmonary vein   D. pulmonary artery
      E. coronary artery

33. Peptide linkages are found in   33.___
      A. enzymes   B. nucleic acids
      C. nucleosides   D. fatty acids
      E. carbohydrates

34. ATP is a chemical compound classified as a   34.___
      A. nucleoside   B. nucleotide
      C. nucleic acid   D. deoxyriboside
      E. nucleopeptide

35. When toxic nonbiodegradable fat-soluble organic chemicals, such as DDT, are introduced into an ecosystem, they become
    A. diluted and dispersed as they pass through the food chain
    B. harmless as organisms excrete them into the environment
    C. less toxic in higher trophic levels
    D. an energy source for tertiary consumers
    E. more concentrated in successive levels of the food chain

35.___

36. During contraction of vertebrate striated muscle cells,
    I. the thick filaments slide past the thin filaments in an energy-dependent process
    II. calcium ions are pumped rapidly into the sarcoplasmic reticulum
    III. the creatine phosphate concentration in the cell rises
    IV. the actin molecules of the thin filament contract
    V. the myosin molecules are replaced by tropomyosin

    The CORRECT answer is:
    A. I   B. I, III   C. I, IV
    D. I, II, III, IV   E. IV *only*

36.___

37. A *basic* difference between all prokaryotic and all eukaryotic cells is that prokaryotic cells lack a
    A. cell wall   B. plasma membrane
    C. centriole   D. chlorophyll
    E. nuclear envelope

37.___

38. All flowering plants are classified as
    A. bryophytes   B. phytoplankton
    C. gymnosperms   D. angiosperms
    E. sea anemones

38.___

39. Escherichia coli is a common intestinal bacterium. One would expect a typical E. coli cell to be about the size of a(n)
    A. human liver cell   B. polyribosome
    C. amoeba   D. mitochondrion
    E. microfilament

39.___

40. Hemophilia is a sex-linked disease characterized by the inability of blood to clot. Prince Frederick was a hemophiliac.
    Which statement must be TRUE of Frederick's family? His
    A. mother must have been a carrier
    B. father must have been a hemophiliac
    C. grandfather must have been a carrier
    D. sister must have been a hemophiliac
    E. uncle could have been a carrier

40.___

41. In the oxidation-reduction reaction
$$2MnO_4^- + 5C_2O_4^{2-} + 16H^+ \rightarrow 2Mn^{2+} + 10CO_2 + 8H_2O$$
the oxidation number of each carbon atom changes from
   A. +2 to +4   B. +3 to +6   C. +3 to +4
   D. +4 to +2   E. +3 to +2

41.___

42. Considering the nuclear reaction below, what is X?
    $$X + proton \rightarrow {}^{22}Mg + neutron$$

   A. ${}^{22}Na$ B. ${}^{23}Na$ C. ${}^{21}Mg$ D. ${}^{23}Mg$ E. ${}^{21}Ne$

42.___

43. Which trend in the halogen family occurs with increasing atomic number?
    A. *Decreasing* ionic radius
    B. *Decreasing* melting points
    C. *Increasing* covalent radius
    D. *Increasing* electronegativity
    E. *Increasing* first ionization potential

43.___

44. In which of the following species does phosphorus exhibit its *highest* oxidation number?
    A. PCl_3 B. P_4 C. H_3PO_3 D. PH_3 E. P_2O_5

44.___

45. In which of the following solutions would CaF_2 be LEAST soluble?
    A. 0.01M $CaCl_2$ B. 0.02M $CaCl_2$
    C. 0.01M NaF   D. 0.02M NaF
    E. 0.02M NaCl

45.___

46. A mixture of gases containing CO_2 and SO_2 is allowed to effuse from one container through a pinhole into a second container which has been evacuated.
    A. The rate of effusion for CO_2 is *faster* because the molecules of CO_2 are *lighter*.
    B. The rate of effusion for SO_2 is *faster* because the molecules of SO_2 are *lighter*.
    C. The rate of effusion for CO_2 is *slower* because the molecules of CO_2 are *lighter*.
    D. The rate of effusion for SO_2 is *faster* because the molecules of SO_2 are *heavier*.
    E. Both compounds will effuse at the same rate since they are both at the same temperature.

46.___

47. The numbers of protons and neutrons, respectively, in ${}^{17}_{8}O^{2-}$ are
    A. 8, 17   B. 8, 10   C. 9, 8   D. 6, 17   E. 8, 9

47.___

48. The percent composition, by weight, of nitrogen in the compound $(NH_4)_2Cr_2O_7$ is (Atomic weights: H = 1, N = 14, O = 16, Cr = 52)
    A. $\dfrac{14}{14 + 4(1) + 2(52) + 7(16)} \times 100$

    B. $\dfrac{2(14)}{2(14) + 8(1) + 2(52) + 7(16)} \times 100$

48.___

C. $\dfrac{14}{14 + 1 + 52 + 16} \times 100$

D. $\dfrac{2(14)}{2(14) + 4(1) + 2(52) + 7(16)} \times 100$

E. $\dfrac{2(14)}{8(1) + 2(52) + 7(16)} \times 100$

49. How many unpaired electrons are in the ground state of a selenium atom (Z=34)?
    A. One   B. Two   C. Three   D. Four   E. Zero

49.___

50. The PRINCIPAL attractive force contributing to lattice energy in an ionic solid is
    A. coulombic repulsion   B. electrostatic attraction
    C. London forces   D. Van der Waals forces
    E. hydrogen bonding

50.___

51. Which gives the MOST basic solution when dissolved in water?
    A. H_3PO_4 B. NaH_2PO_4
    C. P_2O_5 D. $NaNO_3$
    E. $P_2O_5Na_3PO_4$

51.___

52. How many liters of 5.0 molar ethyl alcohol (C_2H_5OH) can be prepared by dissolving 460 grams of ethyl alcohol in water? (C_2H_5OH M.W. = 46)
    A. 0.5   B. 10   C. 2.0   D. 50   E. 5.0

52.___

53. What is the molarity of a solution resulting from the addition of 200 ml of 0.6M H_2SO_4 to 500 ml of 0.4M H_2SO_4 solution?

A. $\dfrac{(0.6)(0.2) + (0.4)(0.5)}{0.7}$

B. $\dfrac{0.6 + 0.4}{2}$

C. $\dfrac{200/0.6 + 500/0.4}{700}$

D. $\dfrac{(0.6)(200) + (0.4)(500)}{1000}$

E. $(0.6)(200) + (0.4)(500)$

53.___

54. What is the geometry of SO_2 and the hybridization of the central atom?
    A. Linear, sp   B. Linear, sp^2
    C. Bent, sp   D. Bent, sp^2
    E. Triangular, sp^3

54.___

55. The data shown below were obtained for the reaction   55.____
    A + 2B → 2C + D

Experiment	Initial [A](M)	Initial [B](M)	Initial rate of appearance of D (M min^{-1})
1	1.0×10^{-4}	1.0×10^{-2}	0.65×10^{-6}
2	2.0×10^{-4}	1.0×10^{-2}	1.30×10^{-6}
3	2.0×10^{-4}	0.50×10^{-2}	0.65×10^{-6}
4	0.50×10^{-4}	2.0×10^{-2}	0.65×10^{-6}

According to these data, the rate law for this system is
rate =

A. $\dfrac{k[C]^2 [D]}{[A] [B]^2}$ B. $k[A][B]$ C. $k[A][B]^2$

D. $k[B]^2$ E. $k[A]$

56. The rate of most reactions tends to double with a 10°C   56.____
    increase in temperature. This is thought to be due to a(n)
    A. *decrease* in the activation energy
    B. *increase* in the activation energy
    C. *increase* in the equilibrium constant
    D. *increase* in the fraction of molecules possessing at
       least the activation energy
    E. *decrease* in the fraction of molecules possessing at
       least the activation energy

57. Which reaction has the MOST positive value of ΔS?   57.____
    A. $2NO_{2(g)} \rightarrow N_2O_{4(l)}$ B. $2NO_{2(g)} \rightarrow N_2O_{4(g)}$

    C. $N_2O_{4(l)} \rightarrow 2NO_{2(g)}$ D. $N_2O_{4(g)} \rightarrow 2NO_{2(g)}$

    E. $N_2O_{4(l)} \rightarrow 2NO_{2(l)}$

58. The trigonal planar BCl_3 molecule is nonpolar. What is   58.____
    the explanation for this?
    A. Boron and chlorine have the same electro-negativity.
    B. The net polarity is zero due to the symmetry of the
       molecule.
    C. The polarity of each boron-chlorine bond is zero.
    D. Boron and chlorine have the same electron affinity.
    E. The electron density around the boron is the same as
       around the chlorine.

59. Which of the following will produce a change in the value   59.____
    of the equilibrium constant for a reaction?
    A. *Increase* the concentration of reactant
    B. *Decrease* the concentration of product
    C. Addition of a suitable catalyst
    D. *Increase* the temperature of the reaction
    E. All of the above

60. When 1.00 g of liquid water (M.W. = 18.0) is produced from H_2 and O_2 at a constant temperature (25°C) and pressure (1 atm), 15.8 kilojoules are produced. What is the molar heat of formation of liquid water, in kilojoules?

   A. -15.8 x 18.0

   B. 15.8 x 18.0

   C. $\dfrac{15.8}{18.0}$

   D. $\dfrac{-15.8}{18.0}$

   E. $\dfrac{-18.0}{15.8}$

61. Consider Crystalline solids made from the following types of particles. Which type of particles gives the solid with the LOWEST melting point?

   A. Small non-polar molecules
   B. Small polar molecules
   C. Positive and negative ions
   D. Positive ions and mobile electrons
   E. Atoms covalently bonded in a continuous array

62. If the Group Numbers of elements x and z in the Periodic Table are VIA and VIIA, respectively, then what is the overall charge on the following Lewis dot formula?

$$:\overset{..}{Z} - \overset{..}{X} - \overset{..}{Z}:$$
$$|$$
$$:\overset{..}{Z}:$$

   A. +1   B. -1   C. +2   D. -2   E. +3

63. The equation for the Haber process for production of ammonia is $N_2 + 3H_2 \rightarrow 2NH_3$. What is the MAXIMUM number of moles of NH_3 which can be produced on reaction of a mixture containing 5 moles of N_2 and 6 moles of H_2?

   A. 9   B. 10   C. 6   D. 2   E. 4

64. A liter of solution contains 0.00001 moles of hydrochloric acid. What is the pH of this solution?

   A. 1.0   B. 4.0   C. -4.0   D. -5.0   E. 5.0

65. When solid NaOH is added to water, it dissolves and the solution becomes warm (sometimes even hot!). The signs of ΔG, ΔH, and ΔS, respectively, are

   A. +, +, +   B. +, -, +
   C. -, -, -   D. -, +, +
   E. -, -, +

66. The unbalanced equation for the oxidation of ammonia is:
$$NH_3 + O_2 \rightarrow NO + H_2O$$
After balancing the equation, which is the CORRECT set of coefficients for the substances from left to right?

   A. 2, 3, 2, 3   B. 3, 2, 3, 2
   C. 4, 5, 4, 6   D. 4, 6, 4, 6
   E. 2, 2, 2, 3

67. Which substance is oxidized in this reaction?   67.____
    $$3Cu + 8H^+ + 2NO_3^- \rightarrow 3Cu^{2+} + 2NO + 4H_2O$$

    A. NO   B. NO_3^- C. H^+ D. Cu   E. Cu^{2+}

68. Experimentally, it was found that 1.5×10^{-6} moles of   68.____
    $BaSO_4$ would dissolve in one liter of 0.001M Na_2SO_4
    solution.
    Assuming ideal solution behavior, what is the solubility
    product constant for $BaSO_4$?
    A. $(1.5 \times 10^{-6})^2$ B. $(1.5 \times 10^{-6})^2(10^{-3})$

    C. $\dfrac{(1.5 \times 10^{-6})^2}{10^{-3}}$ D. $(1.5 \times 10^{-6})(10^{-3})$

    E. $\dfrac{10^3}{1.5 \times 10^{-6}}$

69. Which one of the following concentration terms is   69.____
    temperature dependent?
    A. % by weight   B. Molality
    C. Molarity   D. Mole fraction
    E. None of the above

70. What is the molecular weight of an ideal gas if a 15.0 g   70.____
    sample occupies 25.5 liters at 100°C and 1 atmosphere of
    pressure?
    A. $\dfrac{(15)(0.082)(100)}{(1)(25.5)}$ B. $\dfrac{(15)(0.082)(373)}{(1)(25.5)}$

    C. $\dfrac{(15)(82.0)(100)}{(1)(25.5)}$ D. $\dfrac{(15)(82.0)(373)}{(760)(25.5)}$

    E. $\dfrac{(15)(0.082)(373)}{(760)(25.5)}$

71. Which compound gives the BEST yield of a *single* alkene   71.____
    on treatment with ethanolic KOH?

    A.   B.

    $CH_3 - \underset{\underset{OH}{|}}{\overset{\overset{CH_3}{|}}{C}} - CH_3$ $CH_3 - \underset{\underset{Br}{|}}{CH} - CH_2 - CH_3$

    C.   D.

    cyclohexane with CH_3 and Br substituents   cyclohexane with OH substituent

    E.   Br
                |
    $CH_3 - CH_2 - CH - CH_2 - CH_3$

72. Which of the following reactions would give   72.___

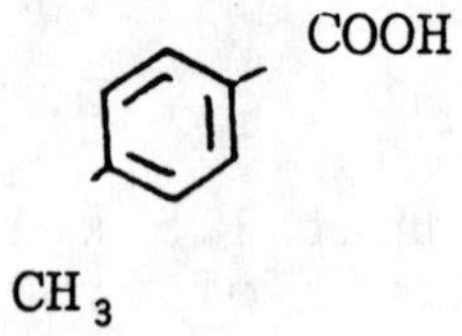

A. CH_3MgBr + $\xrightarrow{\Delta}$

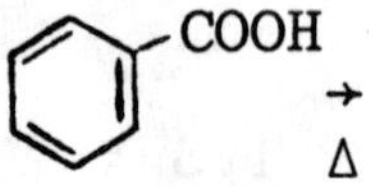

B. CH_3OH + 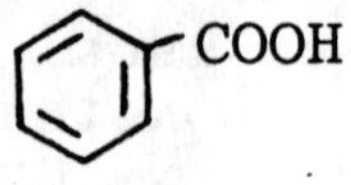 $\xrightarrow{H^+}$

C. 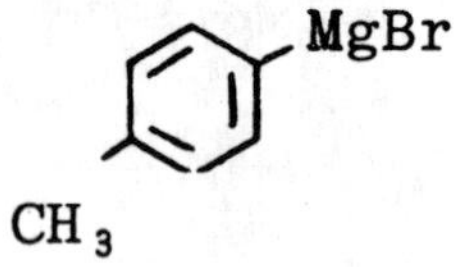 $\begin{array}{l}1)\ CO_2 \\ 2)\ H^+\end{array}$ →

D. $NaHCO_3$ + 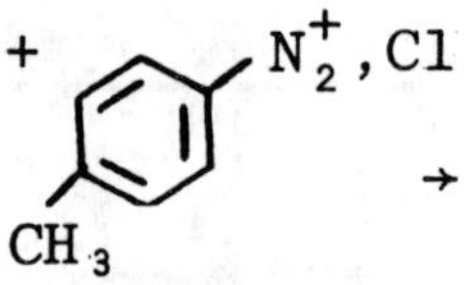 →

E. $LiAlH_4$ + 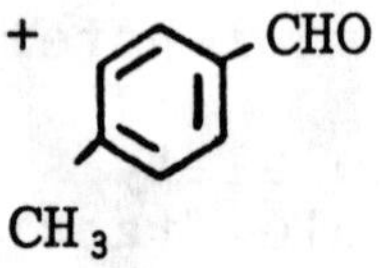 →

73. What is the product of the following reaction?   73.___

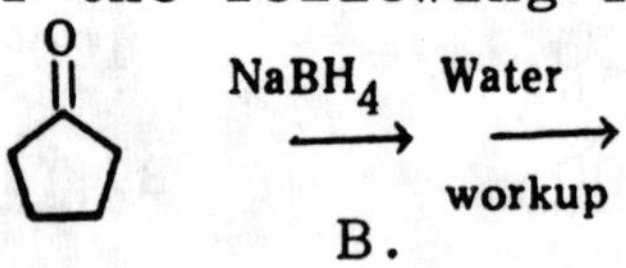

$\xrightarrow{NaBH_4}$ $\xrightarrow[\text{workup}]{\text{Water}}$

A.

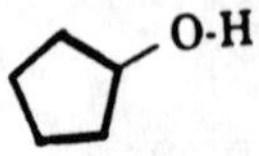

B.

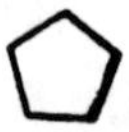

C. $HO_2C-CH_2CH_2CH_2CO_2H$

D.

E.

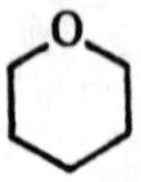

74. Which of the following is the STRONGEST acid?   74.___
    A. $ClCH_2CH_2CO_2H$ B. Cl_2CHCO_2H

    C. $CH_3CHClCO_2H$ D. $ClCH_2CHClCO_2H$

    E. $CH_3CH_2CO_2H$

75. Which of the following reactions will proceed by an   75.___
    S_N2 reaction mechanism?

    A. CH_3CH_2OH + $K_2Cr_2O_7$ → $CH_3-\overset{\text{O}}{\overset{\|}{C}}-OH$

    B. CH_4 + O_2 $\xrightarrow{\text{heat}}$ CO_2 + H_2O

C. $CH_3CH_2Br + NaNH_2 \rightarrow CH_2=CH_2 + NaBr + NH$

D. $CH_3CH_2Br + NaCN \rightarrow CH_3CH_2CN + NaBr$

E. $CH_3-CH=CH_2 + HBr \rightarrow CH_3-CH-CH_3$
$\quad\quad\quad\quad\quad\quad\quad\quad\quad\quad\quad\quad |$
$\quad\quad\quad\quad\quad\quad\quad\quad\quad\quad\quad\quad Br$

76. Which of the following statements is TRUE for the S_N2 76.___
reaction shown below?

$$CH_3CH_2 \blacktriangleright C \blacktriangleleft Br + CN^- \xrightarrow{\text{acetone}} Product$$

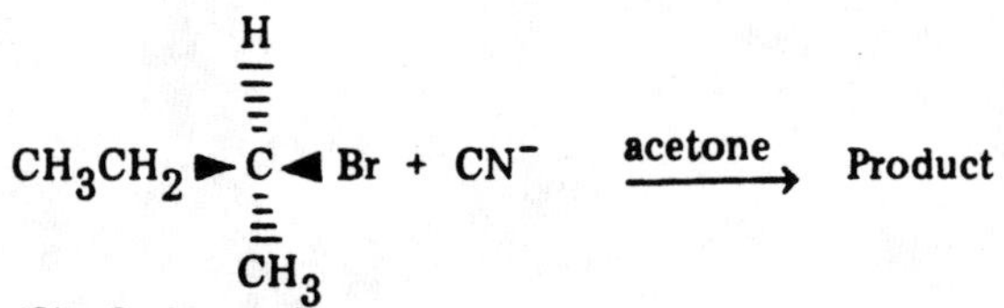

(S) - 2 - bromobutane

A. The product will be a racemate.
B. A change in the concentration of the cyanide ion
will not alter the rate of reaction.
C. A carbocation intermediate will be formed.
D. The reaction will occur with inversion of configuration.
E. The reaction will occur with retention of configuration.

77. What is the reagent and reaction condition that will bring   77.___
about the conversion of benzoic acid to benzoyl chloride?

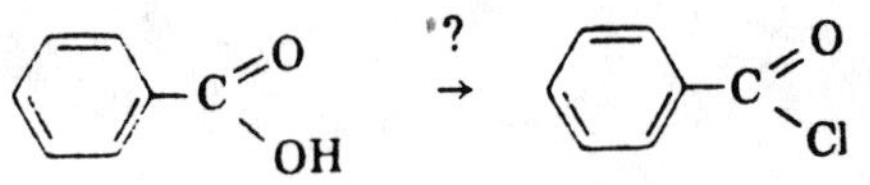

A. HCl (in CCl_4)   B. CH_3Cl (reflux)
C. Fe, Cl_2 D. $SOCl_2$ (reflux)
E. $AlCl_3$

78. Which alcohol undergoes acid-catalyzed dehydration MOST   78.___
readily when heated with concentrated sulfuric acid?

A. $CH_3CH_2CH_2CH_2CH_2OH$

B.
$\quad\quad OH$
$\quad\quad |$
$CH_3CHCH_2CH_2CH_3$

C. 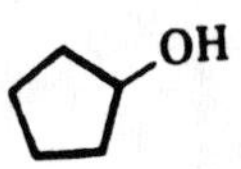   OH (cyclopentanol)

D. CH_3CH_2OH

E.
$\quad\quad CH_3$
$\quad\quad |$
CH_3CH_2COH
$\quad\quad |$
$\quad\quad CH_3$

14

79. D.(-)-Ribose shown below contains how
    many chiral centers?

    A. One

    B. Two

    C. Three

    D. Four

    E. None

79.___

```
        O
        ||
        C-H
        |
    H-C-OH
        |
    H-C-OH
        |
    H-C-OH
        |
    H-C-OH
        |
        H
```

D-(-)-Ribose

80. Which of the following phenols is the STRONGEST acid?

80.___

A.

B.

C.

D.

E.

81. Reaction of with a mixture of HNO_3 and H_2SO_4

81.___

would give predominately which of the following compounds?

    A. ⬡-COOH

    B. O_2N-⬡-COOH

    C. O_2N-⬡-OH

    D. ⬡-CH_3 , O_2N

    E. O_2N-⬡-CH_3

82. In the bromination of benzene ($Br_2/FeBr_3$), one of the reactive intermediates is:

82.____

A.

B.

C.

D.

E.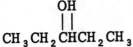

83. Which compound is *most likely* to have an infrared spectrum with a large peak between 1750-1700 cm^{-1} (5.77-5.88μ)?

83.____

A. CH_3-O-CH_3

B. $CH_3-\overset{\overset{\displaystyle O}{||}}{C}-CH_3$

C. $CH_3-CH_2-\overset{\overset{\displaystyle -H}{|}}{N}-CH_2-CH_3$

D. CH_3-CH_2-OH

E. CH_3-CH_2-I

84. How many hydrogens in the compound below are exchangeable with the deuterium in D_2O under basic catalysis?

84.____

$CH_3-CH_2-O-\overset{\overset{\displaystyle O}{||}}{C}-CH_2-\overset{\overset{\displaystyle O}{||}}{C}-$ [cyclohexane ring with CH_3 groups] $\xrightarrow[D_2O]{NaOD}$

A. Two   B. Four   C. Five
D. Seven   E. Thirteen

85. Propionaldehyde, CH_3CH_2CHO, is allowed to react with ethyl magnesium bromide, CH_3CH_2MgBr. Upon hydrolysis, compound A is formed. Oxidation of A by potassium dichromate-sulfuric acid gives compound B. What is B?

85.____

A. $CH_3CH_2\overset{\overset{\displaystyle O}{||}}{C}CH_3$

B. $CH_3CH_2\overset{\overset{\displaystyle O}{||}}{C}CH_2CH_3$

C. $CH_3CH_2\overset{\overset{\displaystyle OH}{||}}{C}HCH_2CH_3$

D. $(CH_3CH_2)COH$

E. $CH_3CH_2CH_2OCH_2CH_3$

86. What is the product of the following sequence of
    reactions?

86.

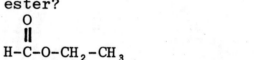

$$CH_3\text{-}CH_2\text{-}CH_2\text{-}\overset{\overset{\displaystyle O}{\|}}{C}\text{-OH} \xrightarrow{SOCl_2} A \xrightarrow[\text{excess}]{NH_3} B$$

A.
$$CH_3\text{-}CH_2\text{-}\overset{\overset{\displaystyle NH_2}{|}}{CH}\text{-}\overset{\overset{\displaystyle O}{\|}}{C}\text{-OH}$$

B. $CH_3\text{-}CH_2\text{-}CH_2\text{-}CH_2\text{-}NH_2$

C. $CH_3\text{-}CH_2\text{-}CH_2\text{-}CH_2\text{-}Cl$

D.
$$CH_3\text{-}CH_2\text{-}CH_2\text{-}\overset{\overset{\displaystyle O}{\|}}{C}\text{-}NH_2$$

E.

87. Which of the following is NOT an ester?

87. ___

A.
$$CH_3\text{-}\overset{\overset{\displaystyle O}{\|}}{C}\text{-}O\text{-}CH_3$$

B.
$$H\text{-}\overset{\overset{\displaystyle O}{\|}}{C}\text{-}O\text{-}CH_2\text{-}CH_3$$

C.
$$CH_3\text{-}\overset{\overset{\displaystyle O\text{-}CH_3}{|}}{\underset{\underset{\displaystyle H}{|}}{C}}\text{-}O\text{-}CH_3$$

D.
$$CH_3\text{-}O\text{-}\overset{\overset{\displaystyle O}{\|}}{C}\text{-}H$$

E.

88. The correct hybridization state of the central carbon
    in neopentane,

88. ___

$$CH_3\text{--}\overset{\overset{\displaystyle CH_3}{|}}{\underset{\underset{\displaystyle CH_3}{|}}{C}}\text{--}CH_3$$

and the approximate angles between the C-C bonds is
    A. sp^2 and 120°   B. sp^3 and 90°
    C. sp and 180°   D. sp^3 and 109°
    E. sp and 109°

89. What is the product of the following reaction?

89. ___

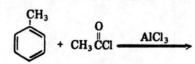

$$+ \; CH_3\overset{\overset{\displaystyle O}{\|}}{C}Cl \xrightarrow{AlCl_3}$$

A.

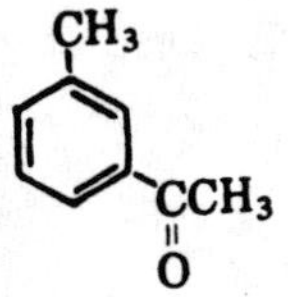

CH_3 ... CCH_3 ... O

B.

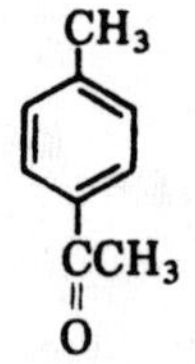

CH_3 ... CH_3 ... O

C.

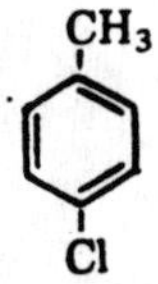

CH_3 ... Cl

D.

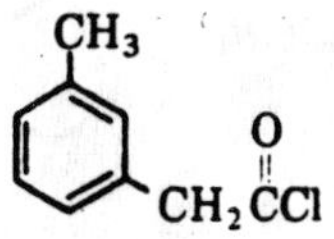

CH_3 ... $CH_2\overset{O}{\overset{\|}{C}}Cl$

E.

$CH_2\overset{O}{\overset{\|}{C}}CH_3$

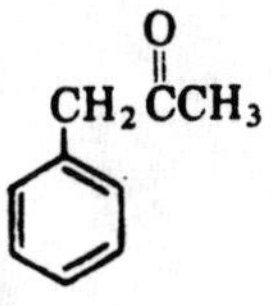

90. Aniline ($C_6H_5NH_2$) will react *most rapidly* with

A.

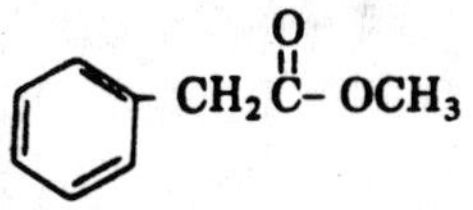

$CH_2\overset{O}{\overset{\|}{C}}- OCH_3$

B.

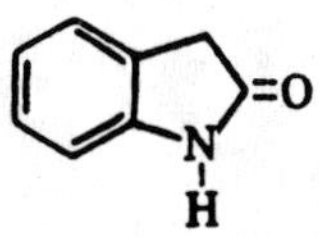

... $=O$ ... N H

C.

$(CH_3)_2CH-\overset{O}{\overset{\|}{C}}-Cl$

D.

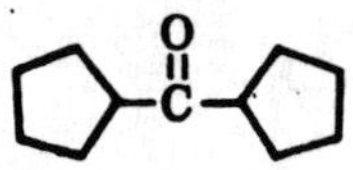

... $\overset{O}{\overset{\|}{C}}$ ...

E.

Cl ...

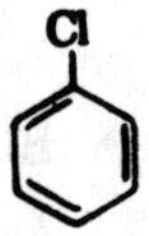

91. In the reaction sequence

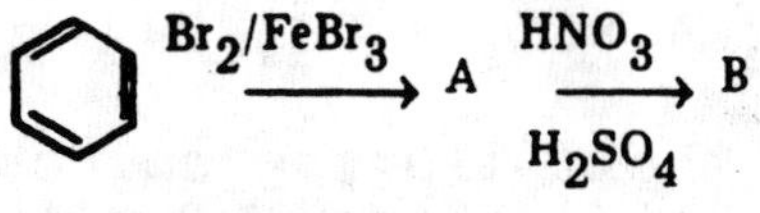

... $\xrightarrow{Br_2/FeBr_3}$ A $\xrightarrow[H_2SO_4]{HNO_3}$ B

the MAJOR product is:

A.

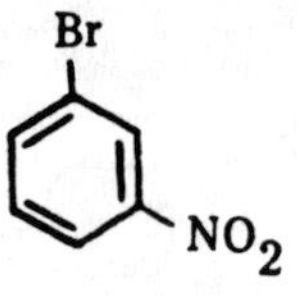

Br ... NO_2

B.

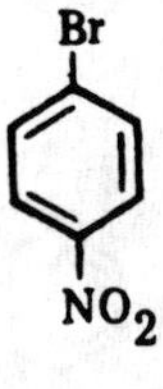

Br ... NO_2

C.

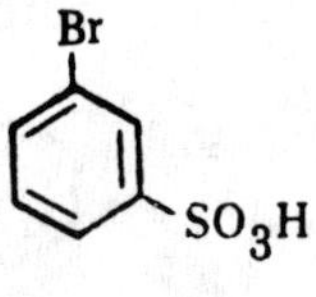

Br ... SO_3H

D.

Br ... NH_2

E.

Br ... Br ... Br ... NO_2

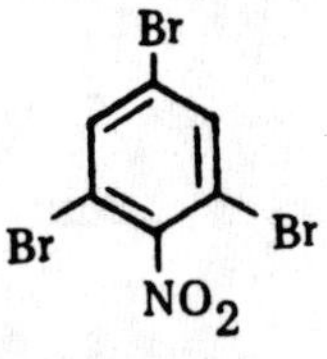

92. From the following compounds (which have similar molecular weights), select the one which has the *highest* boiling point.

A. $CH_3CH_2CCH_3$ with $\overset{\|}{O}$

B. $CH_3CH_2OCH_2CH_3$

C. $CH_3CH_2CO_2H$ D. $CH_3CH_2CH_2CH_2OH$

E. $CH_3CH_2CH_2CH_2CH_3$

93. Which of the following is a product of   93._____

$CH_3\text{-}CH_2\text{-}ONa$ + [cyclohexyl-CH_2-Br] $\longrightarrow$?

A. [cyclohexyl-$CH_2\text{-}O\text{-}CH_2\text{-}CH_3$]

B. [cyclohexane with CH_3 and OCH_2CH_3]

C. [cyclohexyl-$CH_2\text{-}CH_2\text{-}CH_2\text{-}OH$]

D. [cyclohexene with CH_3] + $CH_3\text{-}CH_2OH$

E. [cyclohexane with $=CH_2$ and $O\text{-}CH_2\text{-}CH_3$]

94. Which of the following reactions listed below would have   94._____
the *lowest* energy of activation (E act.)?

A. $Cl\text{-}Cl \rightarrow Cl\cdot + Cl\cdot$ B. $Cl\cdot + CH_3\text{-}H \rightarrow HCl + \cdot CH_3$

C. $CH_3\text{-}CH_3 \rightarrow \cdot CH_3 + \cdot CH_3$ D. $\cdot CH_3 + Cl\text{-}Cl \rightarrow CH_3\text{-}Cl + Cl\cdot$

E. $\cdot CH_3 + \cdot CH_3 \rightarrow CH_3\text{-}CH_3$

95. Which of the following compounds will undergo nitration   95._____
the *fastest* when treated with a mixture of concentrated
H_2SO_4 and HNO_3?

A. [benzene]   B. [toluene, CH_3]   C. [acetophenone, $\overset{O}{\overset{\|}{C}}\text{-}CH_3$]

D. [nitrobenzene, NO_2]   E. [phenol, OH]

96. Which of the following compounds is capable of intra-   96._____
molecular (internal) hydrogen bonding?
A.   B.   C.

D.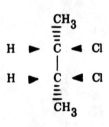

E. (structure with OH, benzene ring, CH₂OH)

97. Select the IUPAC name for

$$CH_3CHCH-C-CH_3$$
(with OH and O substituents, and CH₃ branch)

97.___

A. 3-hydroxy-2-hexanone
B. 3-hydroxy-4-hexanone
C. 3-hydroxy-2-methyl-4-pentanoate
D. 3-hydroxy-4-methyl-2-pentanal
E. 3-hydroxy-4-methyl-2-pentanone

98. Which of the following is achiral and, therefore, will NOT rotate plane polarized light?

98.___

A.

$$CH_3$$
$$H \blacktriangleright C \blacktriangleleft Cl$$
$$CH_2CH_3$$

B. an equimolar mixture of

$$CH_3$$
$$H \blacktriangleright C \blacktriangleleft Cl$$
$$H \blacktriangleright C \blacktriangleleft Cl$$
$$CH_3$$

and

$$CH_3$$
$$H \blacktriangleright C \blacktriangleleft Cl$$
$$Cl \blacktriangleright C \blacktriangleleft H$$
$$CH_3$$

C.

$$CH_3$$
$$H \blacktriangleright C \blacktriangleleft Cl$$
$$H \blacktriangleright C \blacktriangleleft Cl$$
$$CH_3$$

D.

$$CH_3$$
$$H \blacktriangleright C \blacktriangleleft Cl$$
$$Cl \blacktriangleright C \blacktriangleleft H$$
$$CH_3$$

E.

$$CH_3$$
$$H \blacktriangleright C \blacktriangleleft Cl$$
$$CCl_2CH_3$$

99. Which compound is chiral and, therefore, has a nonsuper-imposable mirror image?

99.___

A. $CH_3-CH-CH_2-CH_3$
     |
     NH_2

B. $CH_3-CH_2-CH_2-CH_2-NH_2$

20

C. $CH_3-CH-CH_2-NH_2$
          |
         CH_3

D. $CH_3-CH_2-CH-CH_2-CH_3$
               |
              NH_2

E.

     NH_2

100. The fact that the allyl carbocation $(CH_2=CH-\overset{+}{C}H_2)$ is more stable than primary carbocations such as $CH_3CH_2\overset{+}{C}H_2$ can BEST be accounted for on the basis of

    A. lack of steric hindrance in the allyl carbocation
    B. tautomerism in the allyl carbocation
    C. the electron withdrawing characteristic of the double bond in the allyl carbocation
    D. resonance stabilization of the allyl carbocation
    E. hydrogen bonding in the allyl carbocation

100. _____

KEY (CORRECT ANSWERS)

1. E	21. C	41. C	61. A	81. E
2. B	22. D	42. A	62. A	82. A
3. B	23. C	43. C	63. E	83. B
4. A	24. C	44. E	64. E	84. A
5. A	25. A	45. D	65. E	85. B
6. A	26. C	46. A	66. C	86. D
7. C	27. D	47. E	67. D	87. C
8. C	28. A	48. B	68. D	88. D
9. D	29. D	49. B	69. C	89. B
10. E	30. E	50. B	70. B	90. C
11. E	31. E	51. E	71. E	91. B
12. C	32. D	52. C	72. C	92. C
13. B	33. A	53. A	73. A	93. A
14. B	34. B	54. D	74. B	94. E
15. B	35. E	55. B	75. D	95. E
16. B	36. A	56. D	76. D	96. A
17. A	37. E	57. C	77. D	97. E
18. C	38. D	58. B	78. E	98. C
19. B	39. D	59. D	79. C	99. A
20. E	40. A	60. A	80. B	100. D

EXAMINATION SECTION

DIRECTIONS: Each question or incomplete statement is followed by several suggested answers or completions. Select the one that BEST answers the question or completes the statement. *PRINT THE LETTER OF THE CORRECT ANSWER IN THE SPACE AT THE RIGHT.*

1. Vaporization is an example of a process for which ____   1.___
   at all temperatures.
   A. ΔH and ΔG are positive   B. ΔH and ΔS are positive
   C. ΔS and ΔG are positive   D. ΔH and ΔS are negative
   E. ΔH and ΔG are negative

2. Which of the following elements is MOST electronegative?   2.___
   A. Li   B. K   C. C   D. Ge   E. N

3. What is the percentage of oxygen by weight in $Ba(HCO_3)_2$
   (259g/mol)?
   A. 9.6%   B. 18.5%   C. 24.2%   D. 37.1%   E. 49.0%

4. What species is missing in the following nuclear equation?   4.___

   $$_{92}^{235}U + _{0}^{1}n \rightarrow _{42}^{103}Mo + 2_{0}^{1}n + ?$$

   A. $_{50}^{131}Sn$ B. $_{50}^{132}Sn$ C. $_{52}^{131}Te$ D. $_{52}^{132}Te$ E. $_{51}^{132}Sb$

5. Two tanks of gas with identical volumes are filled at one   5.___
   atmosphere pressure and at the same temperature.
   If one tank contains H_2 and the other contains O_2, then
   A. both tanks contain the same mass of gas
   B. both tanks contain the same number of gas molecules
   C. both gases have the same density
   D. the molecules in both tanks are traveling at the same
      average speed
   E. the average kinetic energy in the H_2 tank is greater
      than in the O_2 tank

6. A solution of potassium acetate ($KC_2H_3O_2$) in water is   6.___
   A. basic because acetic acid molecules are formed
   B. basic because KOH molecules are formed
   C. acidic because acetic acid molecules are formed
   D. acidic because KOH molecules are formed
   E. neutral because potassium acetate is a salt

7. In an aqueous solution, the following equilibrium reactions   7.___
   are present:

   $$Ag(NH_3)_2^+ \rightleftharpoons Ag^+ + 2NH_3$$

   $$NH_3 + H_2O \rightleftharpoons NH_4^+ + OH^-$$

If the soluble salt, AgNO , is added to the solution, the following changes in concentration take place:

A. $[NH_3]$, $[NH_4^+]$, and $[OH^-]$ decrease

B. $[NH_3]$ increases; $[NH_4^+]$ and $[OH^-]$ decrease

C. $[NH_4^+]$ increases; $[NH_3]$ and $[OH^-]$ decrease

D. $[NH_4^+]$ and $[OH^-]$ increase; $[NH_3]$ decreases

E. $[NH_3]$ and $[OH^-]$ increase; $[NH_4^+]$ decreases

8. If an isotope of an element has an atomic number of 45 and   8.__
a mass number of 103, another isotope of the element could
have
A. 58 neutrons   B. fewer than 45 protons
C. more than 45 protons   D. 57 neutrons
E.

9. The conjugate acid of HPO_4^{2-} in water solution is   9.__

A. H^+ B. H_3PO_4 C. $H_4PO_4^+$ D. PO_4^{3-} E. $H_2PO_4^-$

10. Calculate the heat of reaction, $\Delta H°$, for the reaction   10.__

$$C_3H_8(g) + 5O_2(g) \rightarrow 3CO_2(g) + 4H_2O(l)$$

The necessary values for $\Delta H_f^°$, in Kcal/mole, are

$$H_2O(l) = -68.3, \quad CO_2(g) = -94.0, \quad C_3H_8(g) = -24.8$$

A. $1(-24.8) - 3(-94.0) - 4(-68.3)$
B. $-94.0 - 68.3 + 24.8$
C. $-24.8 - 94.0 - 68.3$
D. $3(-94.0) + 4(-68.3) - 1(-24.8)$
E. $3(-94.0) + 4(-68.3) + 1(-24.8)$

11. If a solution which is initially 1.00M in compound X   11.__
undergoes a decomposition reaction for 20.0 sec at an
average rate of 0.020 mol/l. sec, the new concentration
of X will be ___ M.
A. 0.10   B. 0.40   C. 0.60   D. 1.0   E. 1.4

12. A gaseous mixture of 10 mole % nitrous oxide (N_2O), 20   12.__
mole % oxygen (O_2), and 70 mole % nitrogen (N_2) has a
total pressure of 800 mm.
What is the partial pressure, in mm, of the nitrous oxide?

A. 800×0.10 B. $\dfrac{800}{0.10}$ C. $\dfrac{0.10}{800}$

D. 800×0.90 E. $\dfrac{800}{0.90}$

13. The simplest empirical formula for a compound was determined to be CH_2O, and its molecular weight was found to be 60g/mol.
How many atoms of hydrogen are in a molecule of this compound?
   A. 2　　　　B. 3　　　　C. 4　　　　D. 5　　　　E. 6

13.___

14. In the following reaction, identify the oxidizing agent and the reducing agent:

$$4 Zn + NO_3^- + 7 OH^- \rightarrow NH_3 + 4ZnO_2^{2-} + 2H_2O$$

The oxidizing agent is ____; the reducing agent is ____.
   A. Zn; NO_3^-　　　　B. NO_3^-; Zn　　　　C. OH^-; Zn^-

   D. Zn; OH^-　　　　E. NO_3^-; OH^-

14.___

15. What is the ionization constant of a weak acid whose hydronium ion concentration is 3.0×10^{-5} in an 0.02M solution?
   A. 1.8×10^{-11}　　　　B. 3.0×10^{-10}　　　　C. 3.0×10^{-3}

   D. 4.5×10^{-12}　　　　E. 4.5×10^{-8}

15.___

16. Which one of the following 0.15m aqueous solutions has the LOWEST freezing point?
   A. KCL　　　　B. $Al_2(SO_4)_3$　　　　C. CH_3OH
   D. C_2H_5OH　　　　E. NaOH

16.___

17. The boiling point of any liquid is
   A. 100°C
   B. the temperature at which as many molecules leave the liquid as return to it
   C. the temperature at which the vapor pressure is equal to the external pressure
   D. the temperature at which no molecules can return to the bulk of the liquid
   E. the temperature at which the intermolecular forces are at their maximum

17.___

18. A gaseous sample contains 0.02000 moles of N_2.
How many atoms of nitrogen are in this sample?
   A. 0.02000　　　　B. 0.04000　　　　C. 6.02×10^{23}
   D. 12.04×10^{25}　　　　E. 24.08×10^{21}

18.___

19. In which of the following compounds does sulfur have an oxidation number of +2?
   A. Na_2S　　　　B. Na_2S_2　　　　C. $Na_2S_2O_3$
   D. Na_2SO_3　　　　E. Na_2SO_4

19.___

20. In which solvent should NaCl be MOST soluble?
   A. CH_3OH (methyl alcohol)
   B. C_8H_{18} (octane)
   C. $(C_2H_5)_2O$ (diethyl ether)
   D. CCl_4 (carbon tetrachloride)
   E. C_6H_6 (benzene)

20.___

21. A common oxidation number of +2 exists for most period four transition metals because
    A. the elements are filling in the d orbitals
    B. of a d orbital screening effect
    C. the +2 oxidation state is always the most stable
    D. the 4s orbital fills before the 3d orbitals in these elements
    E. the 4s electrons are more easily removed than 3d electrons during ionization

21.___

22. If the rate of a reaction is second order with respect to component A, how will the rate change if the concentration of A is tripled?
It will
    A. double
    B. triple
    C. be six times as great
    D. be nine times as great
    E. be reduced to one-third its original value

22.___

23. An element has the electron configuration as follows:
$$1s^2 2s^2 2p^6 3s^2 3p^6 3d^{10} 4s^2 4p^3$$
This element
    A. is a transition element
    B. belongs to the halogen family
    C. has 33 neutrons
    D. belongs to Group V
    E. is an alkaline earth metal

23.___

24. When the following oxidation-reduction reaction is balanced, what is the correct stoichiometric coefficient for Sn^+? $Sn^{2+} + H^+ + Cr_2O_7^{2-} \rightarrow Sn^{4+} + Cr^{3+} + H_2O$

    A. 1   B. 2   C. 3   D. 4   E. 6

24.___

25. Which one of the following is the CORRECT chemical symbol for a particle containing 6 protons, 8 neutrons, and 7 electrons?
    A. N   B. C^+ C. C^- D. O^+ E. O^-

25.___

26. Select the one element below with a partially filled d-orbital subshell.
    A. Pb   B. Mg   C. Se   D. Cr   E. Al

26.___

27. What mass of NaOH (40.0g/mol) should be weighted out to make 2.50 liters of 1.50M NaOH?
    A. 40g   B. 60g   C. 100g   D. 120g   E. 150g

27.___

28. The solubility of Ag_2CrO_4 in water is x mol/L. Its solubility product constant, Ksp., is
    A. $4x^3$ B. $4x^2$ C. $2x^2$ D. $2x^3$ E. x^2

28.___

29. The amount of heat it takes to raise the temperature of   29.____
    1 gram of any substance by 1 degree celsius is ALWAYS
    A. the entropy of the substance
    B. the exothermic capacity of the substance
    C. the free energy of the substance
    D. the specific heat of the substance
    E. one (1) calorie

30. If 200 mL of 1.60M NaOH are diluted with water to a   30.____
    volume of 350 mL, the new concentration of the solution is

    A. $(\frac{200}{350})(\frac{1}{1.60})$ B. $(\frac{200}{350})(\frac{1.60}{1})$ C. $(\frac{1.60}{1})(\frac{200}{550})$

    D. $(\frac{350}{200})(\frac{1.60}{1})$ E. $(\frac{350}{200})(\frac{1}{1.60})$

———

KEY (CORRECT ANSWERS)

1. B	11. C	21. E
2. E	12. A	22. D
3. D	13. C	23. D
4. A	14. B	24. C
5. B	15. E	25. C
6. A	16. B	26. D
7. A	17. C	27. E
8. D	18. E	28. A
9. E	19. C	29. D
10. D	20. A	30. B

———

EXAMINATION SECTION

DIRECTIONS: Each question or incomplete statement is followed by several suggested answers or completions. Select the one that BEST answers the question or completes the statement. *PRINT THE LETTER OF THE CORRECT ANSWER IN THE SPACE AT THE RIGHT.*

1. The density of graphite (carbon) is 2.2 g/cm^3. Accordingly, which of the following graphite samples is the LARGEST?
   A. 12 g
   B. 12 cm^3
   C. 12 moles
   D. 12 atoms
   E. All are the same size

   1.___

2. How many grams of copper are produced when 1.5 g of aluminum are reacted with excess $Cu(NO_3)_2$ according to the following equation:
   $$2Al + 3Cu(NO_3)_2 \rightarrow 2Al(NO_3)_3 + 3Cu.$$
   (The atomic masses of copper and aluminum are 63.5 and 27.0 a.m.u., respectively.)
   1.5 ×
   A. $(2/3) \times (27.0/63.5)$
   B. $(3/2 \times (27.0/63.5)$
   C. $(2/3) \times (63.5/27.0)$
   D. $(3/2) \times (63.5/27.0)$
   E. $(63.5/27.0)$

   2.___

3. For the reaction between A and B to form C, it is found that when one combines 0.6 moles of A with 0.6 moles of B, all of the B reacts, 0.2 moles of A remain unreacted, and 0.4 moles of C are produced.
   What is the balanced equation for this reaction?
   A. $A + 2B \rightarrow C$
   B. $A + 3B \rightarrow 2C$
   C. $3A + 3B \rightarrow 2C$
   D. $3A + 2B \rightarrow 3C$
   E. $2A + 3B \rightarrow 2C$

   3.___

4. If 3.00 g of a nitrogen-oxygen compound is found to contain 2.22 g of oxygen, what is the percentage of nitrogen in the compound?
   A. $(3.00/2.22)(100/1)$
   B. $((3.00 + 2.22)/3.00)(100/1)$
   C. $((3.00 - 2.22)/2.22)(100/1)$
   D. $((3.00 - 2.22)/3.00)(100/1)$

   4.___

5. A 10.0 liter sample of oxygen at 100°C and 1 atm is cooled to 27°C and expanded until the pressure is 0.5 atm. Find the final volume of the oxygen.
   A. $(10.0)(1/5)(27/100)$
   B. $(10.0)(1/.5)(373/300)$
   C. $(10.0)(.5/1)(373/300)$
   D. $(10.0)(1/.5)(300/373)$
   E. $(10.0)(.5/1)(300/373)$

   5.___

6. When the volume of a gas is decreased at constant temperature, the pressure increases because the molecules
   A. move faster
   B. move slower
   C. become heavier
   D. become lighter
   E. strike a unit area of the container more often

6.___

7. Which of the following types of bonding is found in diamond?
   A. Covalent   B. Hydrogen
   C. Van der Waal's   D. Metallic
   E. Ionic

7.___

8. The molar volume of copper (63.5 g/mole) at 25°C is 7.09 cm^3 $mole^{-1}$.
   Which of the following is the density of copper at 25°C in g cm^{-3}?
   A. (63.5)/(7.09)   B. (63.5)(7.09)
   C. (7.09)/(63.5)   D. 7.09
   E. ((63.5)/(7.09))(25)

8.___

9. A strong acid can be distinguished from a weak acid of the same concentration by the fact that the strong acid
   A. neutralizes a base
   B. is a better conductor of electricity
   C. turns blue litmus paper red
   D. reacts with a metal to liberate hydrogen
   E. none of the above

9.___

10. Which of the following is NOT a colligative property (a property based on the number of particles present)?
    A. Boiling point elevation
    B. Sublimation energy
    C. Vapor pressure lowering
    D. Freezing point depression
    E. Osmotic pressure

10.___

11. Which of the following will be the final volume in mL when 400 mL of 0.6 M HCl is diluted to 0.5 M HCl?
    A. (400/1)(0.5/0.6)
    B. (400/1)(0.6/0.5)
    C. ((0.6 - 0.5)/1)(400/1)
    D. ((1,000 - 400)/1)(0.5/0.6)
    E. (0.6/0.5)((1,000 - 400)/1)

11.___

12. Chlorine bleaches are solutions that contain approximately 5% $NaClO$.
    These solutions are
    A. slightly acidic   B. strongly acidic
    C. neutral   D. slightly basic
    E. strongly basic

12.___

13. What is the hydroxide ion concentration $[OH^-]$ of a
    solution having a pH of 5.0?　　　　　　　　　　　　　　　13.___
    A. 5×10^{-5} M   B. 5×10 M
    C. 1×10^{-5} M   D. 1×10^{-9} M
    E. 5×10^{-9} M

14. The solubility product of CuI is 5.1×10^{-12}. 14.___
    How many moles of Cu^+ will be in equilibrium with CuI
    in 1.0 liter of a 0.01 M KI solution?
    A. 5.1×10^{-6} B. 2.3×10^{-6} C. 5.1×10^{-12}
    D. 2.3×10^{-5} E. 5.1×10^{-10}

15. For the reaction: 15.___
    $$AgCl_{(s)} + 2NH_{3(aq)} \rightleftarrows Ag(NH_3)_2^+ + Cl^-,$$
    the equilibrium constant $K = 4 \times 10^{-3}$, which of the
    following statements is TRUE? [K_{sp} for AgCl is 1.0×10^{-10}]

    A. The addition of NH_3 decreases the solubility of AgCl.
    B. AgCl is more soluble in aqueous NH_3 than in water.
    C. AgCl is more soluble in an aqueous solution contain-
       ing Cl^- than in water.
    D. AgCl is less soluble in aqueous NH_3 than in water.
    E. None of the above

16. What is the equilibrium constant expression, K, for the 16.___
    gaseous reaction: $O_2 + 4HCl \rightleftarrows 2H_2O + 2Cl_2$?
    K =

    A. $\dfrac{[H_2O]^2[Cl_2]^2}{[O_2][HCl]^4}$ B. $\dfrac{[H_2O][Cl_2]}{[O_2][HCl]}$

    C. $\dfrac{[O_2][HCl]^4}{[H_2O]^2[Cl_2]^2}$ D. $\dfrac{2[H_2O]2[Cl_2]}{[O_2]4[HCl]}$

    E. $\dfrac{2[H_2O]^2 2[Cl_2]^2}{[O_2]4[HCl]^4}$

17. What would be the heat of formation, ΔH_f, for NO_2 gas if 17.___
    one considers the equations for the following reactions
    where all substances are gases?
    $\frac{1}{2}N_2 + \frac{1}{2}O_2 \rightarrow NO$ $\Delta H_f^\circ = +21.6$ kcal

    $NO_2 \rightarrow NO + \frac{1}{2}O_2$ $\Delta H^\circ = +13.5$ kcal

    A. -28.7 kcal   B. -8.1 kcal   C. 35.1 kcal
    D. 28.7 kcal   E. 8.1 kcal

18. Which one of the following processes is accompanied by 18.___
    a decrease in entropy?
    A. Freezing of water
    B. Evaporation of water
    C. Sublimation of carbon dioxide
    D. Shuffling a deck of cards
    E. Heating a balloon filled with a gas

19. Rates of reactions are USUALLY studied by
    A. measuring the concentration of the reactants or products as a function of time
    B. calculating the free energy change for the reaction
    C. measuring the heat evolved under different conditions
    D. measuring the amount of each reactant in the reaction
    E. calculating the entropy change for the reaction

    19.___

20. Suppose a solution, which is initially 0.6 M in compound X, undergoes a decomposition reaction. After 10 seconds, the concentration of X is 0.40 M.
    Which of the following is the average rate of decomposition of X in mol/L sec?
    A. 0.020   B. 0.040   C. 0.10   D. 0.20   E. 0.50

    20.___

21. Which of the following is the number of hydrogen ions in the balanced reaction: $H_2SO_3(aq) + IO_3^-(aq) \rightarrow SO_4^{2-}(aq) + I^-(aq) + H^+(aq)$?
    A. 2   B. 4   C. 6   D. 8   E. 10

    21.___

22. Given the following half-cell reactions:
    $Cl_2(g) + 2e^- \rightarrow 2Cl^-(aq)$ $E° = 1.36v$
    $Cu^{2+}(aq) + 2e^- \rightarrow Cu(s)$ $E° = 0.34v$
    what is the value of E° for the following reaction:
    $Cu^{2+}(aq) + 2Cl^-(aq) \rightarrow Cu(s) + Cl_2(g)$?

    A. -2.38v   B. -1.70v   C. -1.02v   D. +1.02v   E. +1.70v

    22.___

23. Which of the following represents the change in oxidation state of nitrogen during the chemical reaction:
    $2NO + 3S + 4H_2O \rightarrow 2HNO_3 + 3H_2S$?
    A. 1   B. 2   C. 3   D. 4   E. 5

    23.___

24. The ion $_4^9Be^{2+}$ has _____ protons, _____ neutrons, and _____ electrons.
    A. 4; 5; 4   B. 4; 5; 2
    C. 5; 4; 2   D. 5; 4; 4
    E. none of the above

    24.___

25. The correct Lewis formula for a nitrate ion (NO_3^-) is

    Which of the following are the oxygen-nitrogen-oxygen bond angles in this ion closest to?
    A. 90°   B. 109°   C. 120°   D. 150°   E. 180°

    25.___

26. Which of the following is the ground state electron configuration for $_{12}^{24}Mg^{2+}$?
    A. $1s^22s^22p^63s^2$ B. $1s^22s^22p^6$
    C. $1s^22s^22p^63s^23p^2$ D. $1s^22s^22p^43s$
    E. $1s^22s^22p^63s^23p^63d^44s^2$

    26.___

27. Antimony (Sb) has a smaller atomic radius than strontium   27.___
    (Sr) because of
    A. increased electron shielding
    B. the lanthanide contraction
    C. increased metallic character
    D. increased nuclear to electron attraction
    E. the difference in number of neutrons in their nucleus

28. Which of the following compounds would have the MOST   28.___
    polar bonds?
    A. BH_3 B. CH_4 C. NH_3 D. H_2O E. PH_3

29. The LEAST electronegative element can be found in the   29.___
    _____ corner of the periodic table.
    A. upper left   B. upper right
    C. lower left   D. lower right
    E.

30. In the nuclear reaction: $^{14}_{7}N + ^{4}_{2}He \rightarrow ^{17}_{8}O + X$, the symbol   30.___
    X represents which of the following?
    A. $^{4}_{2}He$ B. $^{1}_{0}n$ C. $^{0}_{-1}e$ D. $^{0}_{+1}e$ E. $^{1}_{1}H$

KEY (CORRECT ANSWERS)

1. C	11. B	21. C
2. D	12. D	22. C
3. E	13. D	23. C
4. E	14. E	24. B
5. D	15. B	25. C
6. E	16. A	26. B
7. A	17. E	27. D
8. A	18. A	28. D
9. B	19. A	29. C
10. B	20. A	30. E

EXAMINATION SECTION

DIRECTIONS: Each question or incomplete statement is followed by several suggested answers or completions. Select the one that BEST answers the question or completes the statement. *PRINT THE LETTER OF THE CORRECT ANSWER IN THE SPACE AT THE RIGHT.*

1.

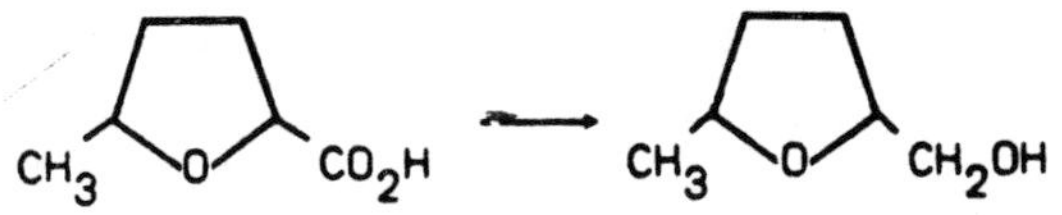

1.____

Which reagent could be used to accomplish the above conversion?
A. Aqueous $KMnO_4$
B. KOH in ethanol
C. H_2O_2 in aqueous acetone
D. CrO_3
E. $LiAlH_4$ followed by H_2O

2. Cyclopentadiene is an unusually acidic hydrocarbon and readily undergoes the following reaction:

2.____

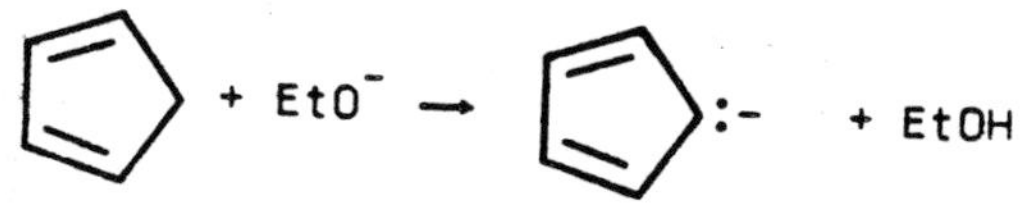

An explanation for this observation is:
A. Cyclopentadiene contains four sp^2 hybridized carbons
B. The ethoxide ion readily reacts with unsaturated hydrocarbons
C. Cyclopentadiene is an aromatic hydrocarbon
D. The reaction yields an aromatic carbocation
E. The reaction yields an aromatic carbanion

3.

3.____

$$\begin{array}{ccccc} & O & & O & \\ a & \| & b & \| & c & d & e \\ CH_3-C-CH_2-C-CH_2-CH-CH_3 \\ & & & & | \\ & & & & CH_3 \end{array}$$

The hydrogen at which position in the above compound is MOST acidic?
A. a   B. b   C. c   D. d   E. e

4. Which of the following compounds will undergo elimination MOST readily by the E1 mechanism?

4.____

A. CH_3CH_2Br B. 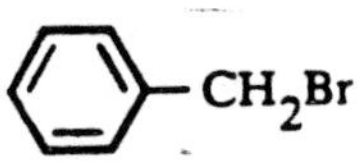 ⬡—CH_2Br C. 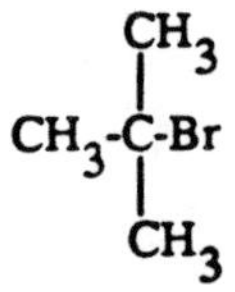 CH_3—$\overset{CH_3}{\underset{CH_3}{C}}$-Br

D. 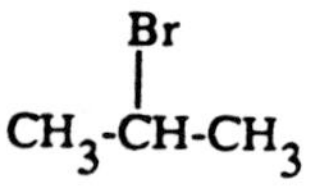 $CH_3-\overset{\overset{\displaystyle Br}{|}}{CH}-CH_3$

E. 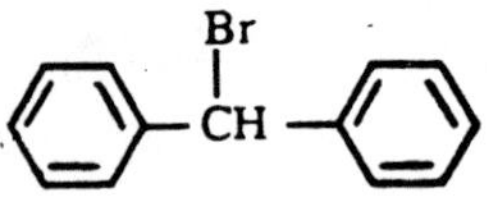 (benzene)$-\overset{\overset{\displaystyle Br}{|}}{CH}-$(benzene)

5. The benzyl carbanion (benzene)$-\overset{..}{\overset{-}{CH}}_2$ is an unusually stable   5.___

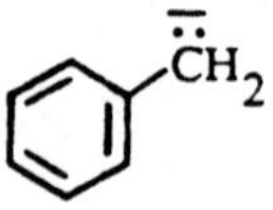

carbanion. This stability arises from
   A. the inductive effect of electron release by the phenyl group
   B. resonance stabilization of the benzyl carbanion
   C. steric hindrance by the large phenyl group
   D. the conformation present in the benzyl carbanion
   E. the hybridization of the charged carbon

6. How many PRIMARY hydrogens are present in the compound at the right?   6.___

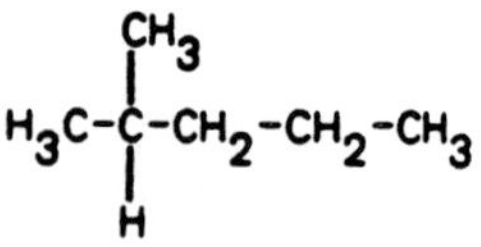

   A. 1
   B. 3
   C. 4
   D. 9
   E. 14

$H_3C-\overset{\overset{\displaystyle CH_3}{|}}{\underset{\underset{\displaystyle H}{|}}{C}}-CH_2-CH_2-CH_3$

7. Which of the structures below is an IMPORTANT resonance form of   7.___
   $CH_3\overset{-}{\overset{..}{C}H}-\overset{\overset{\displaystyle O}{||}}{C}-CH_3$?

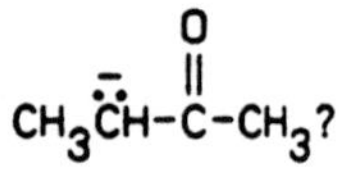

   A. $CH_3\overset{..}{C}H-\overset{\overset{\displaystyle O^-}{|}}{\underset{\underset{\displaystyle +}{}}{C}}-CH_3$

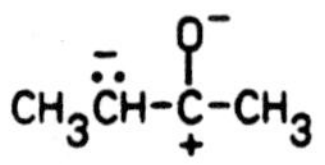

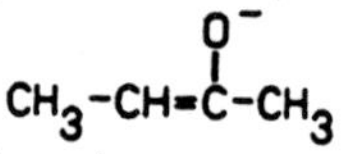

   B. $CH_3-CH=\overset{\overset{\displaystyle O^-}{|}}{C}-CH_3$

   C. $CH_2=CH-\overset{\overset{\displaystyle OH}{|}}{\overset{}{\underset{..}{C}}}-CH_3$

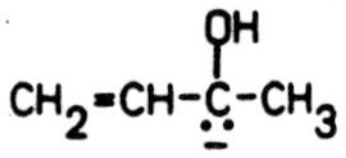

   D. 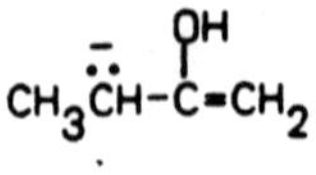 $CH_3\overset{..}{\overset{-}{C}H}-\overset{\overset{\displaystyle OH}{|}}{C}=CH_2$

   E. 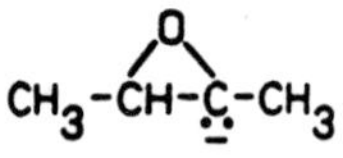 $CH_3-\overset{O}{\overset{\triangle}{CH-C}}-CH_3$

8. Identical molecules are capable of weakly bonding to one   8.___
   another through forces such as hydrogen bonding, dipolar
   interactions, and van der Waals forces.
   From the following sets, select the molecules showing
   the WEAKEST self-association.
   A. HF, HF   B. H_2O, H_2O
   C. NH_3, NH_3 D. CH_4, CH_4
   E. CH_3OH, CH_3OH

9. Which of the following combinations of reagents will yield the compound at the right after hydrolisis and work up? 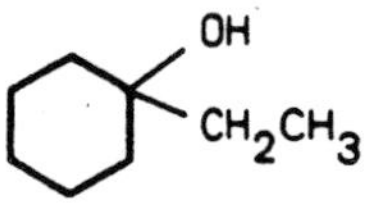 9.____

A. 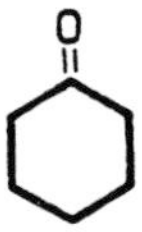 + $BrCH_2CH_3$

B. 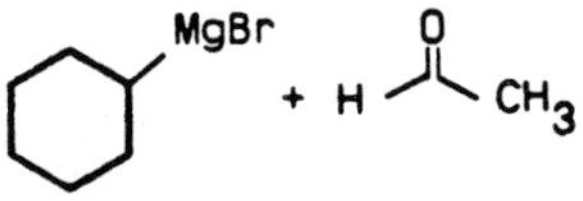

C. 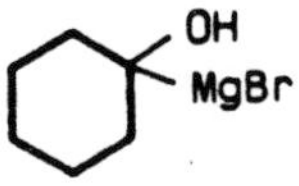 + $BrCH_2CH_3$

D. 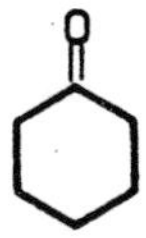 + $BrMgCH_2CH_3$

E. 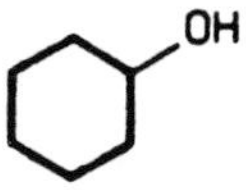 + $BrMgCH_2CH_3$

10. Which of the following is the MOST stable? 10.____

A. 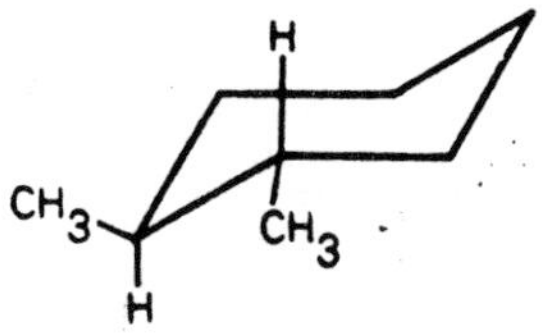

B. 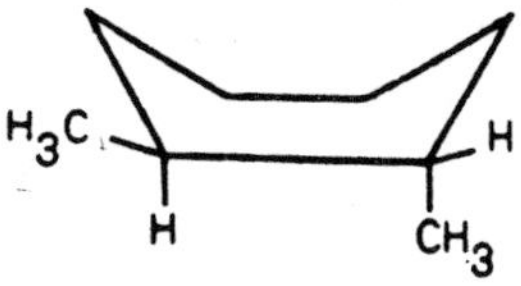

C. 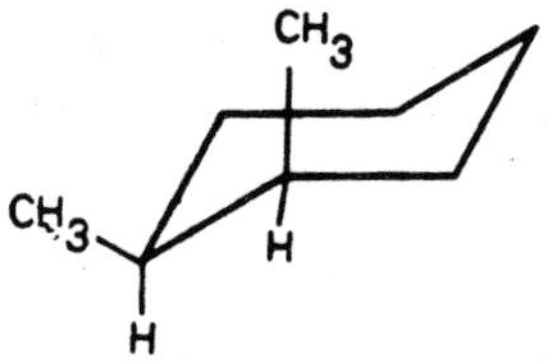

D. 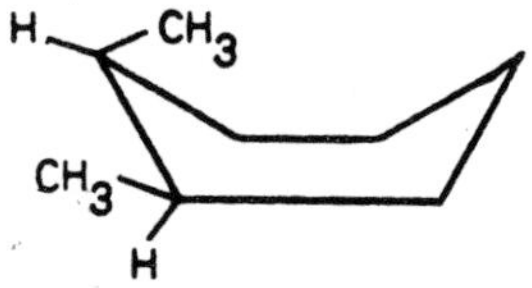

E. 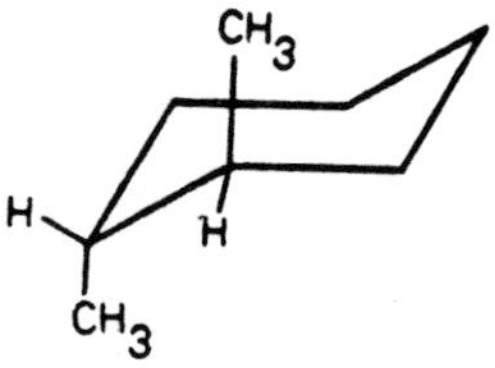

11. What is the product of the following reaction? 11.____

$$CH_3C \equiv CCO_2H + \text{excess } H_2 \xrightarrow{Pd}$$

A. 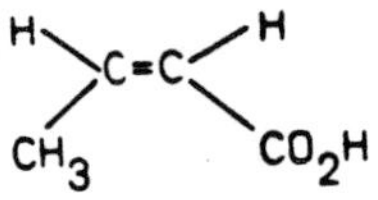

B. 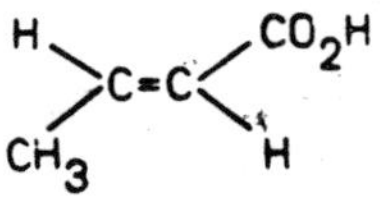

C. $CH_3C \equiv CCHO$

D. $CH_3C \equiv CH_2OH$

E. $CH_3CH_2CH_2CO_2H$

12. Which statement below is TRUE when comparing cis-2-hexene
    and trans-2-hexene?
    These compounds
    A. have the same boiling point at atmospheric pressure
    B. liberate the same amount of heat when hydrogenated
    C. are nonsuperimposable mirror images
    D. will rotate the plane of polarized light
    E. produce the same alkane product upon catalytic
       hydrogenation

12.____

13. Although the molecular weights of acetic acid (60) and
    propionaldehyde (58) are quite similar, the former boils
    at a temperature of 69°C higher than the latter.
    This phenomenon is due to
    A. effective hydrogen bonding in propionaldehyde
    B. effective hydrogen bonding in acetic acid
    C. ion-dipole interactions in propionaldehyde
    D. ion-dipole interactions in acetic acid
    E. dipole-dipole interactions in propionaldehyde

13.____

14. Which compound would NOT yield any $CH_3CH_2CH=O$ on
    ozonolysis?
    A. $CH_3CH_2CH=CHCH_2CH_3$ B. $CH_3CH=CHCH_2CH_3$

    C.  (hexagon) $=CHCH_2CH_3$ D. $CH_2=CHCH_2CH=CH_2$

    E. $O=CHCH_2CH=CHCH_2CH_3$

14.____

15. Which of the following reactions MOST likely proceeds
    by the S_N2 mechanism?

    A. $CH_3CH_2Cl + {}^-OH \rightarrow CH_3CH_2OH + Cl^-$

    B. 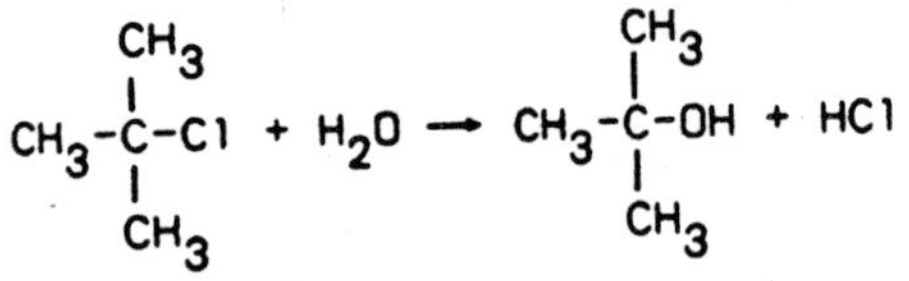 $CH_3-\overset{CH_3}{\underset{CH_3}{C}}-Cl + H_2O \rightarrow CH_3-\overset{CH_3}{\underset{CH_3}{C}}-OH + HCl$

    C. $CH_3-\overset{CH_3}{\underset{CH_3}{C}}-Cl + {}^-OH \rightarrow CH_3-\overset{CH_2}{\underset{CH_3}{C}} + H_2O + Cl^-$

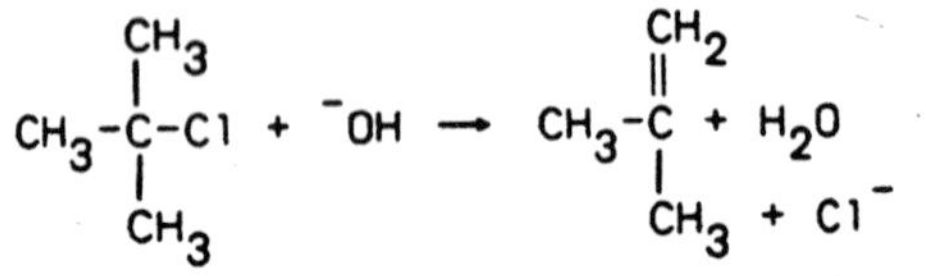

    D. 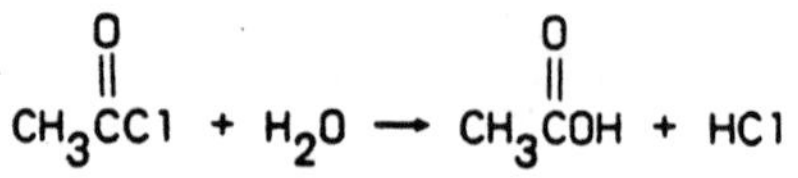 $CH_3\overset{O}{C}Cl + H_2O \rightarrow CH_3\overset{O}{C}OH + HCl$

    E. 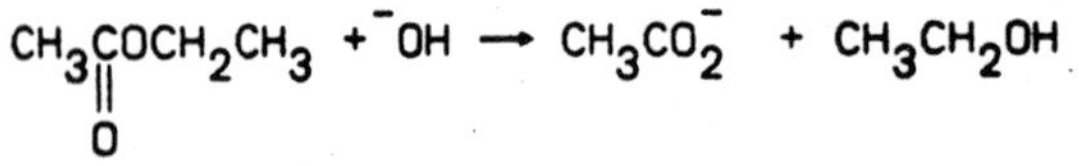 $CH_3\underset{O}{C}OCH_2CH_3 + {}^-OH \rightarrow CH_3CO_2^- + CH_3CH_2OH$

15.____

16. What is the PRINCIPAL organic product of this reaction
    sequence?

    $$CH_3CH_2CH_2Br \xrightarrow[\text{Ether}]{Mg} \xrightarrow{D_2O}$$

    A. $CH_3CH_2CH_2D$ B. $CH_3CH_2CH_2OD$ C. $CH_3CD=CH_2$

    D. $CH_3CH_2CD=O$ E. CH_3CH_2COOD

16.____

17. Which compound is soluble in aqueous HCl but separates   17.___
    from solution when excess aqueous NaOH is added?

    A. 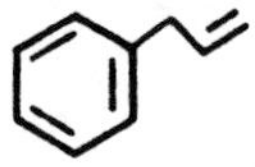   B. 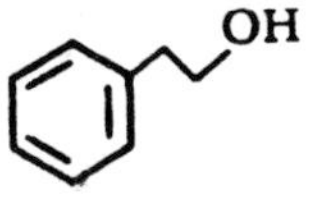   C.

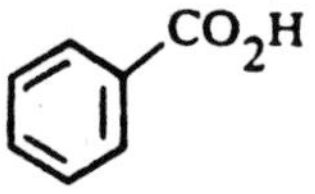

    D. 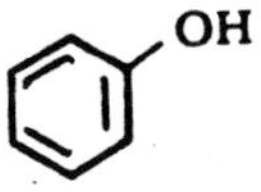   E.

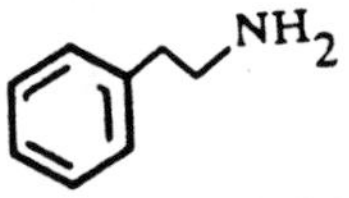

18. Which of the following would react MOST rapidly with   18.___
    aqueous NaOH?

    A. $CH_3COCH_2CH_3$ B. CH_3CCH_3 C. $CH_3CH_2OCH_2CH_3$
       (with O above C)   (with O above C)

    D. CH_3CCl E. CH_3CNH_2
       (with O above C)   (with O above C)

19. The reaction of 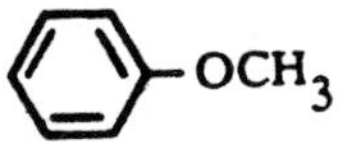 OCH_3 with HNO_3/H_2SO_4 will give   19.___
    ____ and will be ____ than nitration of benzene.

    A. 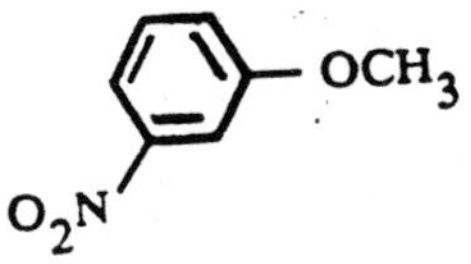   ; slower

    B. 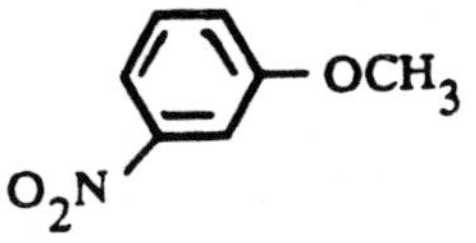   ; faster

    C. 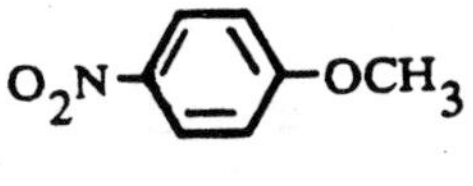 O_2N——OCH_3 ; slower

    D. 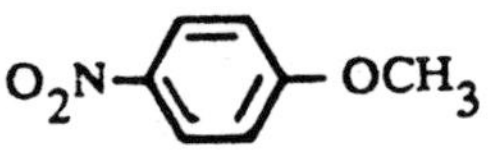 O_2N——OCH_3 ; faster

    E. 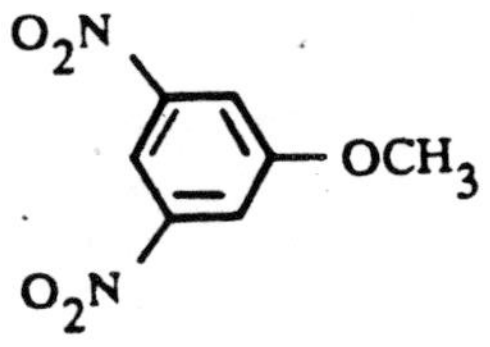   ; faster

20. Which of the following variations of experimental conditions has essentially no effect upon the position of the equilibrium of the hydrochloric acid catalyzed esterification of acetic acid, CH_3COOH, with ethyl alcohol, CH_3CH_2OH?

20.___

    A. Addition of more hydrochloric acid
    B. Removal of water as it is formed
    C. Removal of ester as it is formed
    D. Addition of excess ethyl alcohol
    E. Addition of excess acetic acid

21. According to the Cahn-Ingold-Prelog convention, what is the CORRECT designation of the stereoisomer shown at the right?

21.___

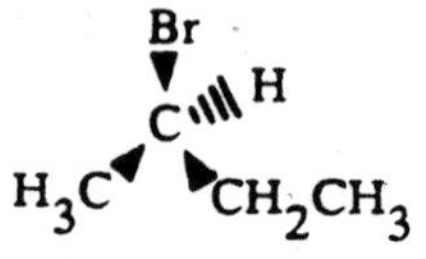

    A. (S)
    B. (R)
    C. (R,S)
    D. (Z)
    E. Meso

22. The acid catalyzed addition of H_2O to $CH_3-\overset{\overset{\displaystyle CH_3}{|}}{C}=CH-CH_3$ would yield predominantly

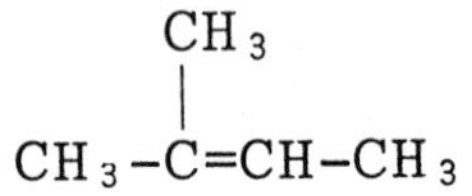

22.___

A. 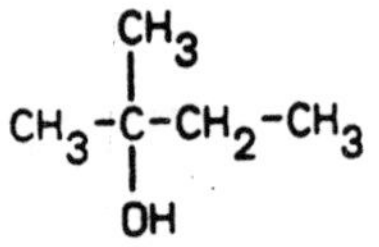 $CH_3-\overset{\overset{\displaystyle CH_3}{|}}{\underset{\underset{\displaystyle OH}{|}}{C}}-CH_2-CH_3$

B. $CH_3-\overset{\overset{\displaystyle CH_3}{|}}{\underset{\underset{\displaystyle H}{|}}{C}}-\overset{}{\underset{\underset{\displaystyle OH}{|}}{C}}H-CH_3$

C. $CH_3-\overset{\overset{\displaystyle CH_3}{|}}{C}-CH-CH_3 + 2H^+$ (epoxide O bridge)

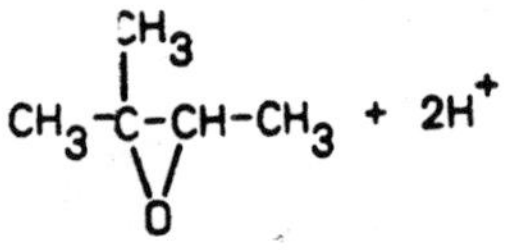

D. 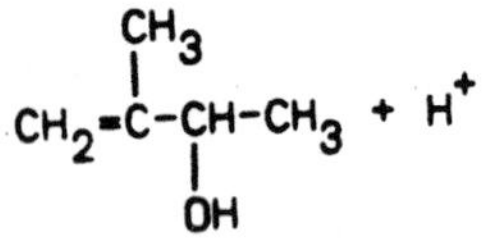 $CH_2=\overset{\overset{\displaystyle CH_3}{|}}{C}-\overset{\underset{\underset{\displaystyle OH}{|}}{}}{C}H-CH_3 + H^+$

E. 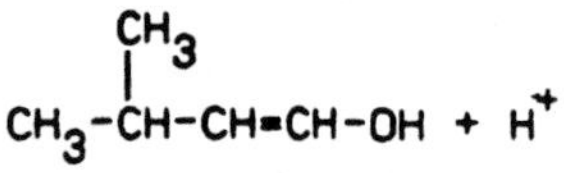 $CH_3-\overset{\overset{\displaystyle CH_3}{|}}{C}H-CH=CH-OH + H^+$

23. Which of the following is the MOST stable carbocation?

23.___

A. 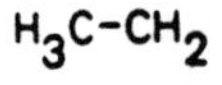 $H_3C-\overset{+}{C}H_2$

B. $CH_2=\bigcirc^+$

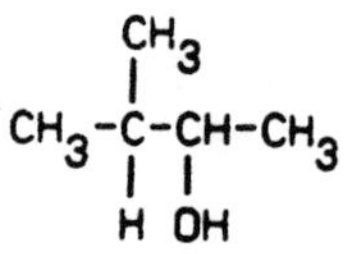

C. $CH_2=CH-\overset{+}{\underset{\underset{\displaystyle CH_3}{|}}{C}}-CH_3$

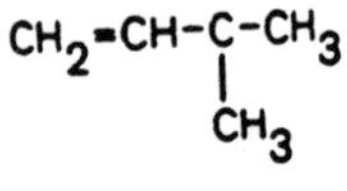

D. 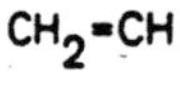 $CH_2=\overset{+}{C}H$

E. 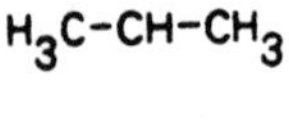 $H_3C-\overset{+}{C}H-CH_3$

24. Which of the structures below is a SECONDARY amine?

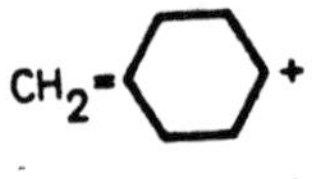

24.___

A. 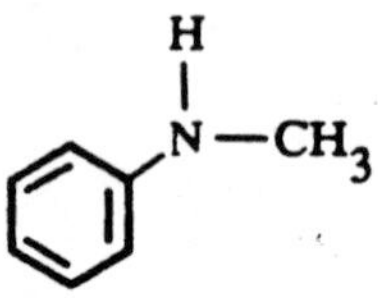 benzene ring $-\overset{\overset{\displaystyle H}{|}}{N}-CH_3$

B. 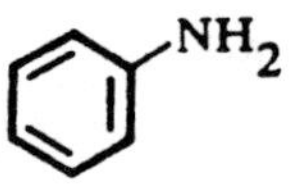 benzene ring $-NH_2$

C. 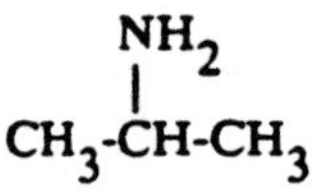 $CH_3-\overset{\overset{\displaystyle NH_2}{|}}{C}H-CH_3$

D. 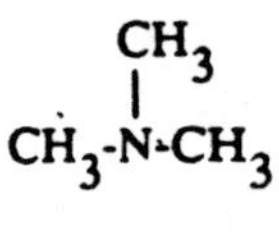 $CH_3-\overset{\overset{\displaystyle CH_3}{|}}{N}-CH_3$

E. 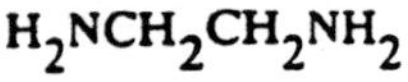 $H_2NCH_2CH_2NH_2$

25. Which of the following compounds is the STRONGEST acid?   25.___

A.
$$CH_3CH_2\overset{\displaystyle O}{\overset{\displaystyle \|}{C}}OH$$

B.
$$BrCH_2CH_2\overset{\displaystyle O}{\overset{\displaystyle \|}{C}}OH$$

C.
$$CH_3\underset{\displaystyle CH_2Br}{CH}CH_2\overset{\displaystyle O}{\overset{\displaystyle \|}{C}}OH$$

D.
$$CH_3\underset{\displaystyle Br}{CH}\overset{\displaystyle O}{\overset{\displaystyle \|}{C}}OH$$

E.
$$CH_3CH_2CH_2\overset{\displaystyle O}{\overset{\displaystyle \|}{C}}OH$$

26. The transformation shown at the right   26.___
is an example of
    A. dehydration
    B. reduction
    C. oxidation
    D. rearrangement
    E. mutarotation

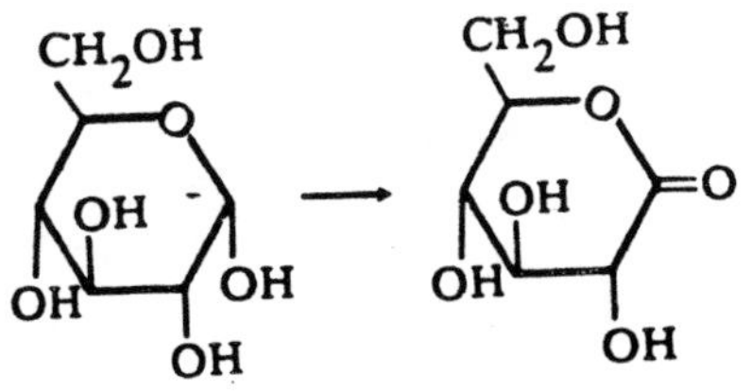

27. When ethyl benzene is brominated using iron as a catalyst,   27.___
the predominant product is

A. 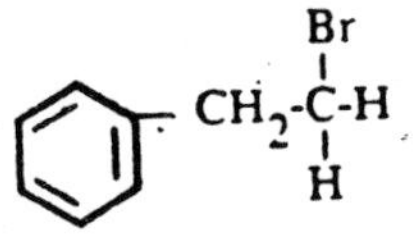 $\bigcirc$—CH_2-$\overset{\displaystyle Br}{\underset{\displaystyle H}{C}}$-H

B. $\bigcirc$—$\overset{\displaystyle Br}{\underset{\displaystyle H}{C}}$-$CH_3$

C. Br—$\bigcirc$—CH_2-CH_3

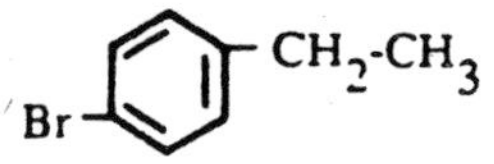

D. 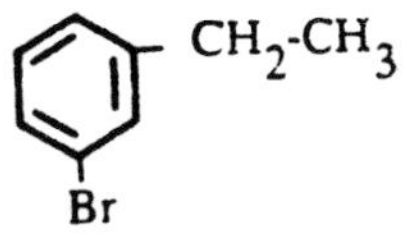 $\bigcirc$—CH_2-CH_3 with Br

E. None of the above

28. Which molecule has a nonlinear structure, i.e., nuclei   28.___
NOT in a straight line?
    A. H–C≡N   B. O=C=O   C. H–O–H

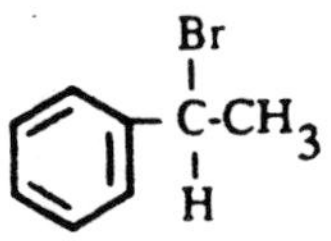

    D. H–Cl   E. H–C≡C–H

29. Which Fischer projection represents a meso isomer?   29.___

A. 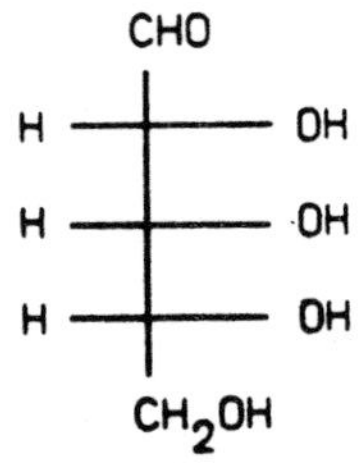
```
        CHO
  H ----+---- OH
  H ----+---- OH
  H ----+---- OH
       CH2OH
```

B. 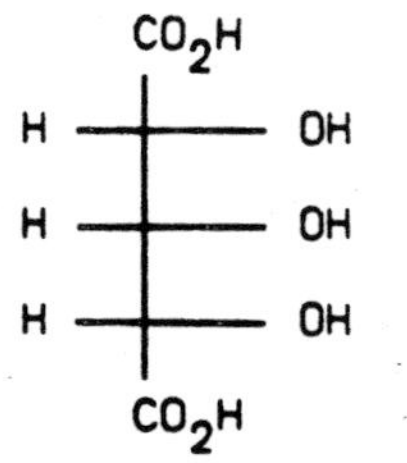
```
       CO2H
  H ----+---- OH
  H ----+---- OH
  H ----+---- OH
       CO2H
```

C. 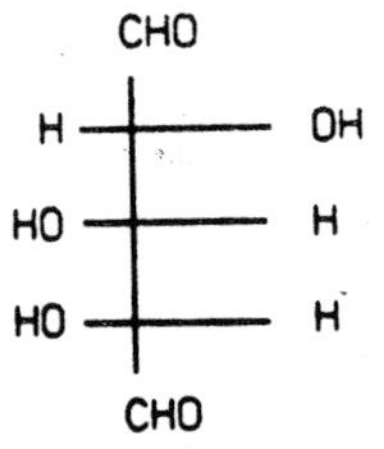
```
        CHO
  H ----+---- OH
 HO ----+---- H
 HO ----+---- H
        CHO
```

D. 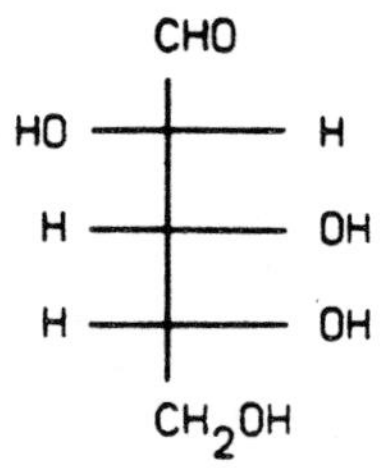
```
        CHO
 HO ----+---- H
  H ----+---- OH
  H ----+---- OH
       CH2OH
```

E. 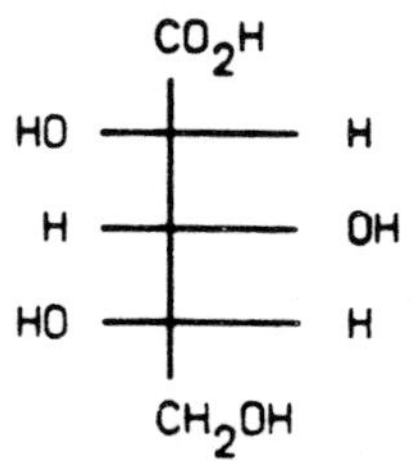
```
       CO2H
 HO ----+---- H
  H ----+---- OH
 HO ----+---- H
       CH2OH
```

30. What would be the principal final product, C, of the reaction sequence below?

$$\text{benzene} \xrightarrow[\text{AlCl}_3]{\text{CH}_3\text{Cl}} A \xrightarrow[\text{FeCl}_3]{\text{Cl}_2} B \xrightarrow[\substack{\text{U.V.} \\ \text{light}}]{\text{Br}_2} C$$

A.

(para-substituted benzene with Cl at top and Br at bottom)

B.

(para-substituted benzene with CH$_3$ at top and Br at bottom)

C.

(para-substituted benzene with CH$_2$Br at top and Cl at bottom)

D.

(benzene with CH$_3$, Br ortho, and Cl)

E.

(benzene with CH$_2$Cl and Br ortho)

30. ___

KEY (CORRECT ANSWERS)

1. E	11. E	21. B
2. E	12. E	22. A
3. B	13. B	23. C
4. C	14. D	24. A
5. B	15. A	25. D
6. D	16. A	26. C
7. B	17. E	27. C
8. D	18. D	28. C
9. D	19. D	29. B
10. A	20. A	30. C

EXAMINATION SECTION

DIRECTIONS: Each question or incomplete statement is followed by several suggested answers or completions. Select the one that BEST answers the question or completes the statement. *PRINT THE LETTER OF THE CORRECT ANSWER IN THE SPACE AT THE RIGHT.*

1. In the reaction A → E that has the following energy diagram, what is the intermediate?
   A. A
   B. B
   C. C
   D. D
   E. E

   1.___

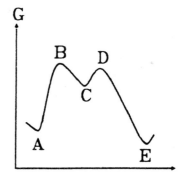

Progress of Reaction

2. A characteristic feature of the S_N2 reaction mechanism is that
   A. it follows first-order kinetics
   B. it produces stereochemical inversion of configuration
   C. there is no rate-determining step
   D. steric factors have little influence on the reaction rate constant
   E. collision of three or more particles is required

   2.___

3. Which of the following alkyl bromides would react MOST rapidly by an S_N2 mechanism?

   3.___

   A. $CH_3CH_2CH_2CH_2CH_2-Br$

   B. $CH_3CH_2CHCH_2CH_3$
      |
      Br

   C. $CH_3CH_2\overset{\displaystyle CH_3}{\underset{\displaystyle CH_3}{\overset{|}{\underset{|}{C}}}}-Br$

   D. $CH_3\overset{\displaystyle CH_3}{\underset{\displaystyle CH_3}{\overset{|}{\underset{|}{C}}}}CH_2-Br$

   E. $CH_3CH_2CH_2CHCH_3$
      |
      Br

4. Which statement MOST correctly describes the rate deter-   4.___
    mining step in the reaction below?

    A. Formation of a 3° carbocation
    B. Formation of a 2° carbocation
    C. Formation of a 3° radical
    D. Rearrangement of a 2° to 3° carbocation
    E. Addition of Cl⁻ to a carbocation

5. Which of the following carbocations is the MOST stable?   5.___

    A. $H_2C = \overset{+}{C}H$ B. $CH_3-\overset{+}{C}H_2$

    C. $H_3C-\overset{\overset{\displaystyle CH_3}{|}}{\underset{\underset{\displaystyle H}{|}}{C}}+$ D. $H_3C=\overset{\overset{\displaystyle CH_3}{|}}{\underset{\underset{\displaystyle CH_3}{|}}{C}}+$

    E. $H_3C-\overset{\overset{\displaystyle CH_3}{|}}{\underset{\underset{\displaystyle H}{|}}{C}}-CH_2-\overset{+}{C}H_2$

6. Nitration of toluene (Ph-CH_3) with HNO_3/H_2SO_4 occurs   6.___
    A. faster than nitration of benzene and produces mostly
       ortho and para products
    B. slower than nitration of benzene and produces mostly
       meta product
    C. faster than nitration of benzene and produces mostly
       meta product
    D. slower than nitration of benzene and produces mostly
       ortho and para products
    E. at the same rate as nitration of benzene and produces
       mostly meta product

7. Which of the following does a strong infrared absorption   7.___
    band between 1750 and 1700 cm⁻¹ (5.77 - 5.88μ) indicate
    the presence of?

    A. $-NH_2$ B. $-\overset{\overset{\displaystyle O}{||}}{C}-$ C. $-OH$

    D. $\diagup\!\!\!\!\diagdown C=C \diagdown\!\!\!\!\diagup$ E. $-C\equiv C-$

8. Which of the compounds below would be MOST soluble in   8.___
   water?

   A. $H_3C-CH_2-CH_2-CH_2-CH_3$ B. $Br-CH_2-Ch_2-CH_2-CH_3$

   C.   D.

   E.   H
           |
      $H_3C-C-CH_3$
           |
           OH

9. Which of the following pure liquids would be expected to   9.___
   show extensive intermolecular hydrogen bonding?

                         OH
                         |
   I. 2-butanol ($CH_3CHCH_2CH_3$)

   II. Ethyl ether ($CH_3CH_2OCH_2CH_3$)

                     O
                     ‖
   III. Acetone (CH_3CCH_3)

   IV. Butyric acid ($CH_3CH_2CH_2CO_2H$)

   The CORRECT answer is:
     A. I *only*   B. II *only*   C. IV *only*
     D. III *only*   E. I and IV

10. Which of the following BEST describes the relationship   10.___
    between the two compounds shown below?

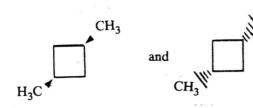

and

     A. Structural isomers   B. Enantiomers
     C. Diasteromers   D. Identical compounds
     E. Meso compounds

11. Which of the conformations of 1,3-dimethylcyclohexane   11.___
    is the LEAST stable?

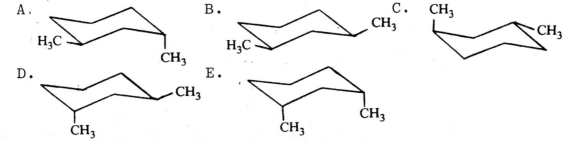

12. Which of the following compounds is NOT super-imposable   12.___
    on its mirror image?

A. $H_3C \overset{\displaystyle Br}{\underset{\displaystyle CH_2-CH_3}{-\!\!\!\!\!-\!\!\!\!\!-}} CH_3$

D. $C_6H_5 \overset{\displaystyle H}{\underset{\displaystyle Br}{-\!\!\!\!\!-\!\!\!\!\!-}} CH_3$

B.

E.

C. $H \overset{\displaystyle CH_3}{\underset{\displaystyle CH_3}{\underset{\displaystyle H-\!\!\!-OH}{-\!\!\!-OH}}}$

13. Which of the following compounds is a tertiary (3°) amine? 13.___

A.

B. $H_3C-\overset{\displaystyle CH_3}{\underset{\displaystyle CH_3}{C}}-NH_2$

D. $H_3C-CH_2-CH_2-\overset{\displaystyle CH_3}{\overset{|}{N}}-CH_2-CH_3$

C.

E.

14. Which structure represents a trans (E) isomer?   14.___

A.

C. $\underset{\displaystyle H}{\overset{\displaystyle H}{}} \!\! C \!\!=\!\! C \!\! \underset{\displaystyle CH_3}{\overset{\displaystyle CH_3}{}}$

E. $\underset{\displaystyle H}{\overset{\displaystyle F}{}} \!\! C \!\!=\!\! C \!\! \underset{\displaystyle Br}{\overset{\displaystyle H}{}}$

B.

D. $\underset{\displaystyle H}{\overset{\displaystyle CH_3}{}} \!\! C \!\!=\!\! C \!\! \underset{\displaystyle Br}{\overset{\displaystyle CH_3}{}}$

15. Which of the following will undergo a free radical bromination MOST rapidly?   15.___

    A. $CH_3-CH-CH_3$
                |
               CH_3

    B.
                  CH_3
                  |
          CH_3-C-CH_3
                  |
                  CH_3

    C. CH_4

    D. CH_3-CH_3

    E.

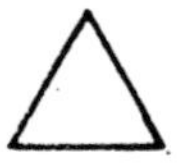

16. Which combination of reagents will produce   16.___

             OH
             |
$CH_3CH_2CCH_3$?
             |
             CN

    A. $CH_3CH_2CH_2CH_3$ + KOH + KCN

    B.
             O
             ||
      $CH_3CH_2CCH_3$ + HCN + KCN

    C.
             OH
             |
      $CH_3CH_2CHCH_3$ + KCN

    D.
             Cl
             |
      $CH_3CH_2CHCH_3$ + KCN

    E.
             CN
             |
      $CH_3CH_2CHCH_3$ + KOH

17. Which set of reactants could be used to prepare   17.___

            OH
            | ?
$CH_3CH_2CHCH_3$

    A.
                        O
                     / \
      CH_3CH_2MgBr + CH_2-CH_2

    B.
                        O
                        ||
      CH_3CH_2MgBr + CH_3CH

    C. CH_3CH_2Br + CH_3CH_2ONa

    D.
                        O
                        ||
      $CH_3CH_2CH_2MgBr$ + HCH

    E.
                      O
                      ||
      CH_3MgI + $CH_3CH_2COCH_3$

18. What is the product of the following sequence of reactions? 18.___

$$CH_3-CH_2-Br \xrightarrow{Mg} \xrightarrow{CO_2} \xrightarrow{H_3O^+}$$

A. CH_3-CH_2-OH

B.
$$CH_3-CH_2-\overset{\overset{\textstyle O}{\|}}{C}-H$$

C.
$$CH_3CH_2-\overset{\overset{\textstyle O}{\|}}{C}-OH$$

D. $CH_3-CH_2-CH_3$

E. $CH_3CH_2-CH_2-Br$

19. What is the MAJOR product of the following reaction? 19.___

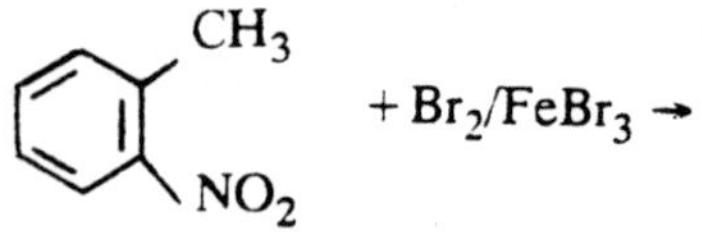

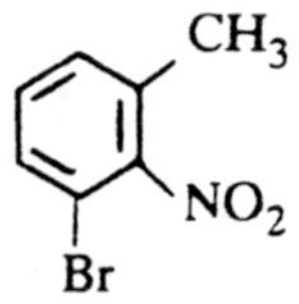

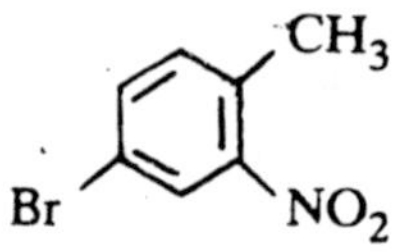

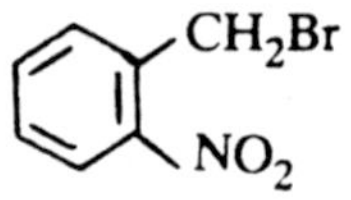

20. Which reagent, followed by the appropriate work-up procedure, could you use to effect the following conversion: 20.___

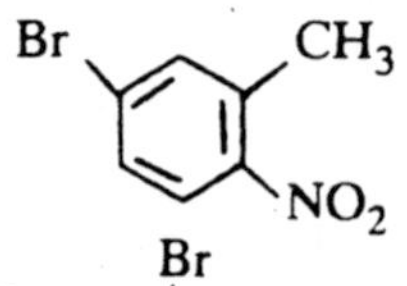

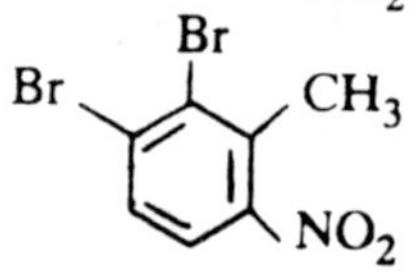

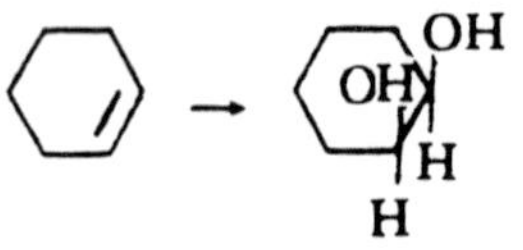

A. $H_2O/\ ^-OH$

B. H_2SO_4

C. $(BH_3)_2$

D.
$$CH_3\overset{\overset{\textstyle O}{\|}}{C}OH$$

E. $KMnO_4/OH^-$

21. Which compound would be the product of the reaction shown below? 21.___

$$CH_3-\underset{\underset{\textstyle CH_3}{|}}{CH}-CO_2H \xrightarrow{LiAlH_4} \xrightarrow{H_3O^+}$$

A. $CH_3-CH_2-CH-OH$
  $\quad\quad\quad\quad\quad\;\; |$
  $\quad\quad\quad\quad\quad\; CH_3$

B. $\quad\quad\quad CH_3$
  $\quad\quad\quad\quad |$
  $\quad CH_3-C-OH$
  $\quad\quad\quad\quad |$
  $\quad\quad\quad CH_3$

C. $CH_3-CH-CH_3$
  $\quad\quad\quad\; |$
  $\quad\quad\quad CH_3$

D. $CH_3-CH-CH_2-OH$
  $\quad\quad\quad\; |$
  $\quad\quad\quad CH_3$

E. $CH_3-CH-O-CH_3$
  $\quad\quad\quad\; |$
  $\quad\quad\quad CH_3$

22. What is the product of the following addition reaction? 22.___

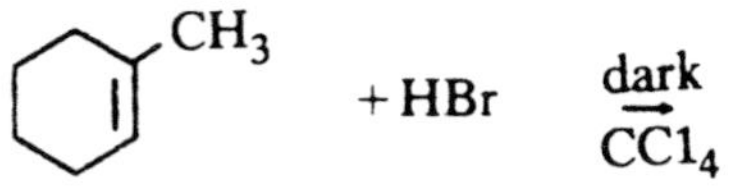

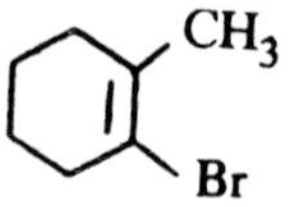

23. Which of the following are the two Brönsted-Lowry bases   23.___
    represented in the equilibrium below?
    HOAc + NaCN ⇄ HCN + NaOAc

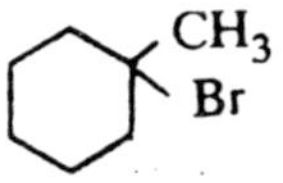

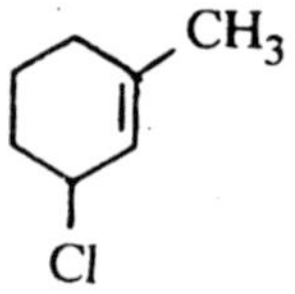

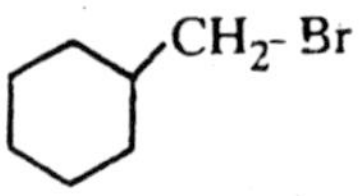

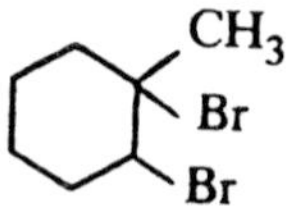

    A. HOAc + NaCN   B. HOAc + NaOAc   C. NaCn + NaOAc
    D. NaCn + HCN   E. HOAc + HCN

24. Which of the compounds below would be MOST acidic?   24.___

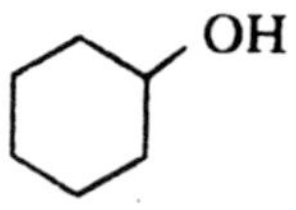

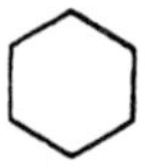

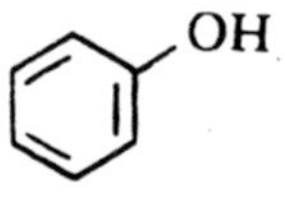

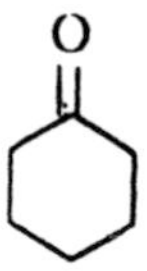

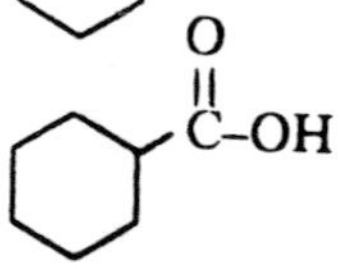

25. The MOST acidic hydrogen(s) in the following compound are   25.___
attached to which of the following carbons?

$$CH_3-CH_2-\overset{O}{\overset{||}{C}}-CH_2-\overset{O}{\overset{||}{C}}-CH_2-CH_2-\overset{O}{\overset{||}{C}}-O-CH_3$$
$$\underset{1}{\uparrow}\ \underset{2}{\uparrow}\quad\underset{3}{\uparrow}\qquad\qquad\underset{4}{\uparrow}\qquad\quad\underset{5}{\uparrow}$$

A. 1   B. 2   C. 3   D. 4   E. 5

26. Which of the following is a group that is both deactivat-   26.___
ing and ortho, para directing in the nitration reaction
of substituted benzenes?
A. -COOH   B. -CH$_3$ C. -Br   D. -NO$_2$ E. -OCH$_3$

27. Which of the following ions is stabilized by resonance?   27.___

A.   B.   C. O$^-$ D.   E.

28. How does the hybridization of carbon change during the   28.___
oxidation sequence: CH$_3$-OH → CH$_2$=O → HCO$_2$H → CO$_2$?

A. sp^2, sp^2, sp^2, sp   B. sp^3, sp^2, sp, sp
C. sp^2, sp^3, sp^3, sp^3 D. sp^3, sp^2, sp^2, sp
E. sp^3, sp^3, sp^3, sp^2

29. Treatment of benzoic acid with thionyl chloride followed   29.___
by addition of ethanol gives which of the following as
the MAJOR product?

30. What is the MAJOR product (B) of the following reaction sequence?   30. ___

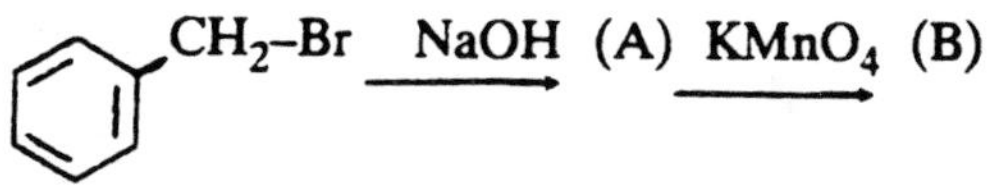

CH_2–Br $\xrightarrow{NaOH}$ (A) 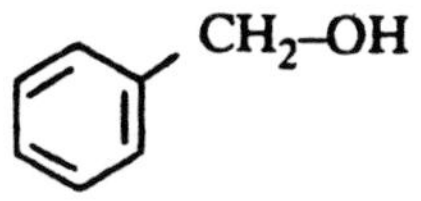 $\xrightarrow{KMnO_4}$ (B)

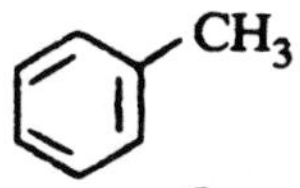

A. CH_2–OH (benzene ring)

B. CH_3 (benzene ring)

C. 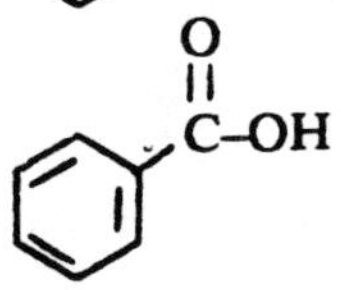 $\overset{O}{\overset{||}{C}}$–OH (benzene ring)

D. 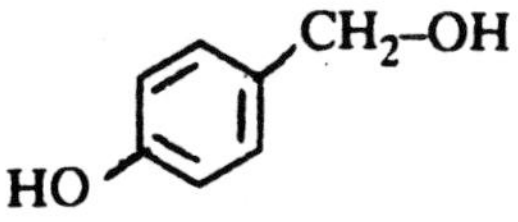 CH_2–OH, HO– (benzene ring)

E. 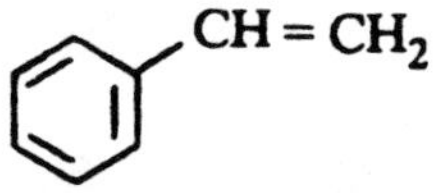 $CH=CH_2$ (benzene ring)

_____

KEY (CORRECT ANSWERS)

1. C	11. E	21. D
2. B	12. D	22. A
3. A	13. D	23. C
4. A	14. E	24. E
5. D	15. A	25. C
6. A	16. B	26. C
7. B	17. B	27. A
8. E	18. C	28. D
9. E	19. B	29. B
10. D	20. E	30. C

_____

EXAMINATION SECTION
TEST 1

DIRECTIONS: Each question or incomplete statement is followed by several suggested answers or completions. Select the one that BEST answers the question or completes the statement. *PRINT THE LETTER OF THE CORRECT ANSWER IN THE SPACE AT THE RIGHT.*

1. An Na^+ ion is similar to a K^+ ion in that both ions have the same   1.___
     A. nuclear charge   B. number of electrons
     C. atomic mass   D. oxidation number

2. Which formula represents a nonpolar molecule?   2.___

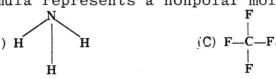

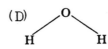

(B) H——F

3. Which compound is a network solid?   3.___
     A. CH_4 B. CO_2 C. CaH_2 D. SiO_2

4. A compound formed from potassium and chlorine will have   4.___
     A. a molecular crystal structure
     B. a high melting point
     C. good heat conductivity in the solid state
     D. poor electrical conductivity in solution

5. The compound _____ contains ionic bonds.   5.___
     A. $NaH(s)$ B. $C_6H_{12}O_6(s)$
     C. $CH_3OH(\ell)$ D. $H_2O(\ell)$

6. All elements whose atoms in the ground state have a total of 5 electrons in their outermost p sublevel are called   6.___
     A. noble gases   B. metalloids
     C. halogens   D. alkaline earth metals

7. The alkali metals are in Group   7.___
     A. IA   B. IB   C. IIA   D. IIB

8. Which solution contains colored ions?   8.___
     A. $KCl(aq)$ B. $HCl(aq)$ C. $NiCl_2(aq)$ D. $LiCl_2(aq)$

9. An element that has an ionic radius larger than its atomic radius is   9.___
     A. Al   B. Cl   C. Li   D. Ni

10. Which element may be prepared ONLY by the electrolysis of its fused compounds?   10.___
     A. F_2 B. I_2 C. Cl_2 D. Br_2

11. A compound contains 0.50 mole of carbon for each 1.0 mole   11.___
    of hydrogen.
    The empirical formula of this compound is
       A. CH   B. CH_2 C. C_2H D. C_2H_2

12. What is the molarity of a solution that contains 28 grams   12.___
    of KOH (formula mass = 56) in 2.0 liters of solution?
       A. 1.0 M   B. 2.0 M   C. 0.25 M   D. 0.50 M

13. Given the reaction: $S + O_2 \rightarrow SO_2$.   13.___
    The TOTAL number of grams of oxygen needed to react
    completely with 2.0 moles of sulfur is
       A. 20   B. 32   C. 64   D. 128

14. A 22.0 gram sample of a gas occupies 11.2 liters at STP.   14.___
    The gram molecular mass of the gas is _____ grams.
       A. 11.2   B. 22.4   C. 22.0   D. 44.0

15. A 38 gram sample of F_2 contains APPROXIMATELY the same   15.___
    number of molecules as
       A. 14 g of N_2 B. 2.0 g of H_2
       C. 36 g of H_2O D. 40 g of Ne

16. What is the equilibrium constant for the reaction   16.___
    $AgCl (s) \rightleftarrows Ag^+(aq) + Cl^-(aq)$ at 298°K?
       A. 4.2×10^{-7} B. 1.6×10^{-10}
       C. 1.0×10^{-14} D. 6.0×10^{-23}

17. Consider the reaction at equilibrium: 17.___
       $2AB(g) + heat \rightleftarrows A_2(g) + B_2(g)$.
    The equilibrium will shift to the right when the
       A. temperature increases   B. temperature decreases
       C. pressure increases   D. pressure decreases

18. Heat of reaction, ΔH, is equal to $H_{products}$ _____ $H_{reactants}$. 18.___
       A. +   B. -   C. ×   D. ÷

19. A chemical change MUST occur spontaneously if   19.___
       A. $T\Delta S$ is positive   B. $T\Delta S$ is negative
       C. ΔG is positive   D. ΔG is negative

20. Given the reaction: $H_2(g) + \frac{1}{2}O_2(g) = H_2O(g) + 57.8$ kcal.   20.___
    If the activation energy for the forward reaction is 40.0
    kilocalories per mole, the activation energy for the
    reverse reaction, in kilocalories per mole, will be
       A. 17.8   B. 30.0   C. 60.0   D. 97.8

21. What is the H_3O^+ ion concentration, in moles per liter, of   21.___
    a solution with a pH of 4?
       A. 1×10^{-4} B. 4×10^{-1}
       C. 1×10^4 D. 4×10^4

22. Which 0.1 molar aqueous solution contains the HIGHEST concentration of OH^- ions?
    A. CH_3OH B. NaOH   C. C_2H_5OH D. NH_3 22.___

23. Red litmus will turn blue when placed in an aqueous solution of   23.___
    A. HCl   B. CH_3COOH C. CH_3OH D. KOH

Questions 24-25.

DIRECTIONS: Questions 24 and 25 are to be answered on the basis of the following chart.

RELATIVE STRENGTHS OF ACIDS IN AQUEOUS SOLUTION at 1 atm AND 298 K		
Conjugate Pairs		
ACID	BASE	K_a
$HI \longrightarrow H^+ + I^-$		very large
$HBr \longrightarrow H^+ + Br^-$		very large
$HCl \longrightarrow H^+ + Cl^-$		very large
$HNO_3 \longrightarrow H^+ + NO_3^-$		very large
$H_2SO_4 \longrightarrow H^+ + HSO_4^-$		large
$H_2O + SO_2 \longrightarrow H^+ + HSO_3^-$		1.7×10^{-2}
$HSO_4^- \longrightarrow H^+ + SO_4^{2-}$		1.3×10^{-2}
$H_3PO_4 \longrightarrow H^+ + H_2PO_4^-$		7.1×10^{-3}
$Fe(H_2O)_6^{3+} \longrightarrow H^+ + Fe(H_2O)_5(OH)^{2+}$		6.0×10^{-3}
$HF \longrightarrow H^+ + F^-$		6.7×10^{-4}
$HNO_2 \longrightarrow H^+ + NO_2^-$		5.1×10^{-4}
$Cr(H_2O)_6^{3+} \longrightarrow H^+ + Cr(H_2O)_5(OH)^{2+}$		1.0×10^{-4}
$CH_3COOH \longrightarrow H^+ + CH_3COO^-$		1.8×10^{-5}
$Al(H_2O)_6^{3+} \longrightarrow H^+ + Al(H_2O)_5(OH)^{2+}$		1.0×10^{-5}
$H_2O + CO_2 \longrightarrow H^+ + HCO_3^-$		4.4×10^{-7}
$H_2S \longrightarrow H^+ + HS^-$		1.0×10^{-7}
$H_2PO_4^- \longrightarrow H^+ + HPO_4^{2-}$		6.3×10^{-8}
$HSO_3^- \longrightarrow H^+ + SO_3^{2-}$		6.2×10^{-8}
$NH_4^+ \longrightarrow H^+ + NH_3$		5.7×10^{-10}
$HCO_3^- \longrightarrow H^+ + CO_3^{2-}$		4.7×10^{-11}
$HPO_4^{2-} \longrightarrow H^+ + PO_4^{3-}$		4.4×10^{-13}
$HS^- \longrightarrow H^+ + S^{2-}$		1.3×10^{-13}
$OH^- \longrightarrow H^+ + O^{2-}$		$< 10^{-36}$
$NH_3 \longrightarrow H^+ + NH_2^-$		very small

24. Which 0.1 M aqueous solution would have the LOWEST freezing point?   24.___
    A. HI   B. HF   C. HNO_2 D. CH_3COOH

25. Which ion is amphiprotic?   25.___
    A. NH_4^+ B. HSO_4^- C. O^{2-} D. Cl^-

26. The element hydrogen will have a negative oxidation number when it forms a binary compound with   26.___
    A. sulfur   B. selenium   C. oxygen   D. potassium

27. Given the reaction: $Pb(s) + 2Ag^+ \rightarrow Pb^{2+}(aq) + 2Ag(s)$. The cell voltage ($E°$) for the overall reaction is _____ volt(s).   27.___
    A. 0.67   B. 0.93   C. 1.47   D. 1.73

28. In the half-reaction $Mg \rightarrow Mg^{2+} + 2e^-$, the magnesium   28.___
    A. gains electrons and is oxidized
    B. gains electrons and is reduced
    C. loses electrons and is oxidized
    D. loses electrons and is reduced

29. How many moles of electrons would be required to completely   29.___
    reduce 0.50 mole of Cu^{2+} ions to Cu?
    A. 1.0   B. 2.0   C. 0.25   D. 0.50

30. Given the cell reaction: $Zn(s) + Cu^{2+}(aq) \rightarrow Zn^{2+}(aq) + $ 30.___
    $Cu(s)$.
    The negative electrode in this cell is
    A. $Zn(s)$ B. $Cu^{2+}(aq)$ C. $Zn^{2+}(aq)$ D. $Cu(s)$

31. The reaction $C_3H_5(C_{17}H_{35}COO)_3 + 3NaOH \rightarrow 3C_{17}H_{35}COONa + $ 31.___
    $C_3H_5(OH)_3$ is an example of
    A. polymerization   B. fermentation
    C. esterification   D. saponification

32. What compound is a member of the homologous series with   32.___
    the general formula C_nH_{2n}?

    A. Acetylene B. Benzene   C. Propene   D. Toluene

33. A molecule of ethene is similar to a molecule of methane   33.___
    in that both have the same
    A. structural formula   B. molecular formula
    C. number of carbon atoms   D. number of hydrogen atoms

34. The formula for ethanoic acid is   34.___
    A. CH_3COOH B. CH_3CH_2OH
    C. CH_3CH_2COOH D. $CH_3CH_2CH_2OH$

35. The compound CH_3COOCH_3 is classified as a(n)   35.___
    A. acid   B. alcohol
    C. ester   D. hydrocarbon

———

KEY (CORRECT ANSWERS)

1. D	11. B	21. A	31. D
2. C	12. C	22. B	32. C
3. D	13. C	23. D	33. D
4. B	14. D	24. A	34. A
5. A	15. B	25. B	35. C
6. C	16. B	26. D	
7. A	17. A	27. B	
8. C	18. B	28. C	
9. B	19. D	29. A	
10. A	20. D	30. A	

———

TEST 2

DIRECTIONS: Each question or incomplete statement is followed by several suggested answers or completions. Select the one that BEST answers the question or completes the statement. *PRINT THE LETTER OF THE CORRECT ANSWER IN THE SPACE AT THE RIGHT.*

1. Given the reaction at equilibrium: 1.___
   $2SO_2(g) + O_2(g) \rightleftharpoons 2SO_3(g) + 47$ kcal.
   The amount of $SO_3(g)$ will increase if there is a(n)
   A. increase in temperature
   B. decrease in pressure
   C. increase in concentration of $SO_2(g)$
   D. decrease in concentration of $O_2(g)$

2. What is the equilibrium expression for the reaction   2.___
   $H_2(g) + I_2(g) \rightleftharpoons 2HI(g)$?
   $K =$

   A. $\dfrac{2[HI]}{[H_2][I_2]}$ B. $\dfrac{[H_2][I_2]}{2[HI]}$

   C. $\dfrac{[H_2][I_2]}{[HI]^2}$ D. $\dfrac{[HI]^2}{[H_2][I_2]}$

Questions 3-4.

DIRECTIONS: Questions 3 and 4 are to be answered on the basis of the following chart.

RELATIVE STRENGTHS OF ACIDS IN AQUEOUS SOLUTION at 1 atm AND 298 K		
Conjugate Pairs		
ACID	*BASE*	K_a
$HI \rightarrow H^+ + I^-$		very large
$HBr \rightarrow H^+ + Br^-$		very large
$HCl \rightarrow H^+ + Cl^-$		very large
$HNO_3 \rightarrow H^+ + NO_3^-$		very large
$H_2SO_4 \rightarrow H^+ + HSO_4^-$		large
$H_2O + SO_2 \rightarrow H^+ + HSO_3^-$		1.7×10^{-2}
$HSO_4^- \rightarrow H^+ + SO_4^{2-}$		1.3×10^{-2}
$H_3PO_4 \rightarrow H^+ + H_2PO_4^-$		7.1×10^{-3}
$Fe(H_2O)_6^{3+} \rightarrow H^+ + Fe(H_2O)_5(OH)^{2+}$		6.0×10^{-3}
$HF \rightarrow H^+ + F^-$		6.7×10^{-4}
$HNO_2 \rightarrow H^+ + NO_2^-$		5.1×10^{-4}
$Cr(H_2O)_6^{3+} \rightarrow H^+ + Cr(H_2O)_5(OH)^{2+}$		1.0×10^{-4}
$CH_3COOH \rightarrow H^+ + CH_3COO^-$		1.8×10^{-5}
$Al(H_2O)_6^{3+} \rightarrow H^+ + Al(H_2O)_5(OH)^{2+}$		1.0×10^{-5}
$H_2O + CO_2 \rightarrow H^+ + HCO_3^-$		4.4×10^{-7}
$H_2S \rightarrow H^+ + HS^-$		1.0×10^{-7}
$H_2PO_4^- \rightarrow H^+ + HPO_4^{2-}$		6.3×10^{-8}
$HSO_3^- \rightarrow H^+ + SO_3^{2-}$		6.2×10^{-8}
$NH_4^+ \rightarrow H^+ + NH_3$		5.7×10^{-10}
$HCO_3^- \rightarrow H^+ + CO_3^{2-}$		4.7×10^{-11}
$HPO_4^{2-} \rightarrow H^+ + PO_4^{3-}$		4.4×10^{-13}
$HS^- \rightarrow H^+ + S^{2-}$		1.3×10^{-13}
$OH^- \rightarrow H^+ + O^{2-}$		$< 10^{-36}$
$NH_3 \rightarrow H^+ + NH_2^-$		very small

3. Which compound is the WEAKEST electrolyte?   3.___
   A. HCl   B. HNO_3 C. H_2S D. H_2SO_4

4. The strongest acid and the strongest base are   4.___
   A. NH_3 and I^- B. NH_3 and NH^-
   C. HI and I^- D. HI and NH_2^-

5. Which hydrogen ion concentration indicates the MOST acidic   5.___
   solution?
   $1 \times$ _____ M.
   A. 10^{-11} B. 10^{-9} C. 10^{-7} D. 10^{-5}

6. Indicate which compound is CORRECTLY classified as a salt.   6.___
   A. KNO_3 B. HNO_3 C. CH_3COOH D. C_2H_5OH

7. How many milliliters of 2.0 M NaOH are needed to exactly   7.___
   neutralize 50 milliliters of 2.0 M HCl?
   A. 25   B. 50   C. 100   D. 200

8. In the reaction $H_2O + H_2O \rightleftharpoons H_3O^+ + HO^-$, water is acting as   8.___
   A. a Bronsted acid *only*
   B. a Bronsted base *only*
   C. neither a Bronsted acid nor base
   D. both a Bronsted acid and base

9. The conjugate base of the HSO_4^- ion is   9.___
   A. H_2SO_4 B. H_3O^+ C. SO_4^{2-} D. OH^-

10. What is the oxidation number of chlorine in $KClO_3$?   10.___
    A. +1   B. +5   C. +3   D. +7

11. The potential ($E°$) for the standard hydrogen half-cell   11.___
    reaction is _____ volt(s).
    A. -0.41   B. -0.83   C. 0.00   D. 0.78

12. In the reaction $3Cu + 8HNO_3 \rightarrow 3Cu(NO_3)_2 + 2NO + 4H_2O$,   12.___
    what change in oxidation state does nitrogen undergo?
    A. +5 to -2   B. +5 to +2   C. -2 to -5   D. -2 to +5

13. Based on the chart at the right, which metal will react spontaneously with $Co^{2+}(aq)$?
    A. Ag(s)
    B. Au(s)
    C. Zn(s)
    D. Pb(s)

13.___

STANDARD ELECTRODE POTENTIALS

Ionic Concentrations 1 M Water at 298 K, 1 atm

Half-Reaction	E° (volts)
$F_2(g) + 2e^- \longrightarrow 2F^-$	+2.87
$MnO_4^- + 8H^+ + 5e^- \longrightarrow Mn^{2+} + 4H_2O$	+1.52
$Au^{3+} + 3e^- \longrightarrow Au(s)$	+1.50
$Cl_2(g) + 2e^- \longrightarrow 2Cl^-$	+1.36
$Cr_2O_7^{2-} + 14H^+ + 6e^- \longrightarrow 2Cr^{3+} + 7H_2O$	+1.33
$MnO_2(s) + 4H^+ + 2e^- \longrightarrow Mn^{2+} + 2H_2O$	+1.28
$\frac{1}{2}O_2(g) + 2H^+ + 2e^- \longrightarrow H_2O$	+1.23
$Br_2(\ell) + 2e^- \longrightarrow 2Br^-$	+1.06
$NO_3^- + 4H^+ + 3e^- \longrightarrow NO(g) + 2H_2O$	+0.96
$\frac{1}{2}O_2(g) + 2H^+(10^{-7}M) + 2e^- \longrightarrow H_2O$	+0.82
$Ag^+ + e^- \longrightarrow Ag(s)$	+0.80
$\frac{1}{2}Hg_2^{2+} + e^- \longrightarrow Hg(\ell)$	+0.79
$Hg^{2+} + 2e^- \longrightarrow Hg(\ell)$	+0.78
$NO_3^- + 2H^+ + e^- \longrightarrow NO_2(g) + H_2O$	+0.78
$Fe^{3+} + e^- \longrightarrow Fe^{2+}$	+0.77
$I_2(s) + 2e^- \longrightarrow 2I^-$	+0.53
$Cu^+ + e^- \longrightarrow Cu(s)$	+0.52
$Cu^{2+} + 2e^- \longrightarrow Cu(s)$	+0.34
$SO_4^{2-} + 4H^+ + 2e^- \longrightarrow SO_2(g) + 2H_2O$	+0.17
$Sn^{4+} + 2e^- \longrightarrow Sn^{2+}$	+0.15
$2H^+ + 2e^- \longrightarrow H_2(g)$	0.00
$Pb^{2+} + 2e^- \longrightarrow Pb(s)$	−0.13
$Sn^{2+} + 2e^- \longrightarrow Sn(s)$	−0.14
$Ni^{2+} + 2e^- \longrightarrow Ni(s)$	−0.25
$Co^{2+} + 2e^- \longrightarrow Co(s)$	−0.28
$2H^+(10^{-7}M) + 2e^- \longrightarrow H_2(g)$	−0.41
$Fe^{2+} + 2e^- \longrightarrow Fe(s)$	−0.44
$Cr^{3+} + 3e^- \longrightarrow Cr(s)$	−0.74
$Zn^{2+} + 2e^- \longrightarrow Zn(s)$	−0.76
$2H_2O + 2e^- \longrightarrow 2OH^- + H_2(g)$	−0.83
$Mn^{2+} + 2e^- \longrightarrow Mn(s)$	−1.18
$Al^{3+} + 3e^- \longrightarrow Al(s)$	−1.66
$Mg^{2+} + 2e^- \longrightarrow Mg(s)$	−2.37
$Na^+ + e^- \longrightarrow Na(s)$	−2.71
$Ca^{2+} + 2e^- \longrightarrow Ca(s)$	−2.87
$Sr^{2+} + 2e^- \longrightarrow Sr(s)$	−2.89
$Ba^{2+} + 2e^- \longrightarrow Ba(s)$	−2.90
$Cs^+ + e^- \longrightarrow Cs(s)$	−2.92
$K^+ + e^- \longrightarrow K(s)$	−2.92
$Rb^+ + e^- \longrightarrow Rb(s)$	−2.93
$Li^+ + e^- \longrightarrow Li(s)$	−3.00

14. Which half-cell reaction CORRECTLY represents reduction?
    A. $Sn^0 \rightarrow Sn^{2+} + 2e^-$ B. $Sn^{2+} \rightarrow Sn^0 + 2e^-$
    C. $Sn^0 + 2e^- \rightarrow Sn^{2+}$ D. $Sn^{2+} + 2e^- \rightarrow Sn^0$

14.___

15. Which is a redox reaction?
    A. $Cu(NO_3)_2 + H_2S \rightarrow CuS + 2HNO_3$
    B. $CuCl_2 + 2AgNO_3 \rightarrow Cu(NO_3)_2 + 2AgCl$
    C. $Cu(OH)_2 + 2HNO_3 \rightarrow Cu(NO_3)_2 + 2H_2O$
    D. $Cu + 2AgNO_3 \rightarrow Cu(NO_3)_2 + 2Ag$

15.___

16. In the following reaction, $Cl_2(aq) + 2KBr(aq) \rightarrow 2KCl(aq) + Br_2(aq)$, which is the oxidizing agent?
    A. Cl_2 B. KCl   C. KBr   D. Br_2

16.___

17. The fermentation of $C_6H_{12}O_6$ will produce carbon dioxide and a(n)
    A. polymer   B. soap   C. ester   D. alcohol

17.___

18. Compounds which have the same molecular formula but different molecular structures are called
    A. isomers   B. isotopes
    C. allotropes   D. homologs

18.___

19. A saturated hydrocarbon is represented by the formula 19.___
    A. C_2H_2 B. C_2H_4 C. C_5H_8 D. C_5H_{12}

20. Which is the structural formula of methanol? 20.___

    A. $H-C=O$ B. $H-\overset{\displaystyle H}{\underset{\displaystyle H}{C}}-OH$ C. $H-\overset{\displaystyle H}{\underset{\displaystyle H}{C}}-\overset{\displaystyle H}{\underset{\displaystyle H}{C}}-OH$ D. $H-\overset{\displaystyle H}{\underset{\displaystyle H}{C}}-\overset{\displaystyle }{\underset{\displaystyle O}{C}}=O$
        $\underset{\displaystyle H}{\overset{\displaystyle |}{O}}$ $\underset{\displaystyle H}{}$

21. Which is the structural formula of 1,1-dichloropropane? 21.___

    (A) $Cl-\overset{H}{\underset{Cl}{C}}-\overset{H}{\underset{H-H}{C}}-\overset{H}{C}-H$ (C) $H-\overset{H}{\underset{Cl}{C}}-\overset{H}{\underset{H}{C}}-\overset{H}{\underset{Cl}{C}}-H$

    (B) $H-\overset{H}{\underset{H}{C}}-\overset{H}{\underset{Cl}{C}}-\overset{H}{\underset{Cl}{C}}-H$ (D) $H-\overset{H}{\underset{H}{C}}-\overset{Cl}{\underset{Cl}{C}}-\overset{H}{\underset{H}{C}}-H$

22. As a substance changes from a liquid to a gas, the average 22.___
    distance between molecules
       A. decreases   B. increases
       C. remains the same   D. cannot be determined

23. As the distance between two iodine molecules INCREASES, the 23.___
    attraction of the van der Waals forces between them
       A. decreases   B. increases
       C. remains the same   D. fluctuates

24. As the concentration of a reactant in a chemical reaction 24.___
    increases, the rate of the reaction GENERALLY
       A. decreases   B. increases
       C. remains the same   D. cannot be determined

25. As the elements of Group VA are considered in order of 25.___
    INCREASING atomic radius, their tendency to lose electrons
       A. decreases   B. increases
       C. remains the same   D. varies

26. When heat is added to a substance at a constant rate, the temperature of the substance remains the same. This substance is a
    A. solid melting at its melting point
    B. solid below its melting point
    C. liquid freezing at its freezing point
    D. liquid above its freezing point

26.___

27. The difference between the boiling point and the freezing point of pure water at standard pressure is _____ K.
    A. 32   B. 100   C. 273   D. 373

27.___

28. If water is boiling in an open container, then its
    A. temperature must equal 100°C
    B. vapor pressure must equal 760 torr
    C. temperature must equal atmospheric temperature
    D. vapor pressure must equal atmospheric pressure

28.___

29. Which 1 liter sample contains the same number of molecules as 1 liter of $O_2(g)$ at STP?
    A. $H_2O(\ell)$ at 0°C and 1 atm   B. $Hg(\ell)$ at 0°C and 2 atm
    C. $NO_2(g)$ at 0°C and 1 atm   D. $Ne(g)$ at 0°C and 2 atm

29.___

30. The temperature of 20 liters of a gas is changed from 0°C to 273°C at constant pressure. The NEW volume of the gas will be _____ liters.
    A. 5   B. 10   C. 20   D. 40

30.___

31. An O^{2-} ion has the same electron configuration as
    A. S^{2-} B. Ca^{2+} C. F^- D. K^+

31.___

32. At the end of 3 half-life periods, how much of an 8 gram sample of $^{226}_{88}Ra$ will remain unchanged? _____ grams.
    A. 1   B. 2   C. 3   D. 4

32.___

33. The MAXIMUM number of electrons that can occupy the third principal energy level is
    A. 8   B. 10   C. 18   D. 32

33.___

34. Element X exists in three isotopic forms. The isotopic mixture consists of 10.0% ^{10}X, 20.0% ^{11}X, and 70.0% ^{12}X. What is the AVERAGE atomic mass of this element?
    A. 11.0   B. 11.6   C. 12.0   D. 12.4

34.___

35. Which electron configuration represents an element having the HIGHEST first ionization energy?
    A. $1s^1$ B. $1s^2$ C. $1s^2 2s^1$ D. $1s^2 2s^2$

35.___

KEY (CORRECT ANSWERS)

1. C	11. C	21. A	31. C
2. D	12. B	22. B	32. A
3. C	13. C	23. A	33. C
4. D	14. D	24. B	34. B
5. D	15. D	25. B	35. B
6. A	16. A	26. A	
7. B	17. D	27. B	
8. D	18. A	28. D	
9. C	19. D	29. C	
10. B	20. B	30. D	

TEST 3

DIRECTIONS: Each question or incomplete statement is followed by several suggested answers or completions. Select the one that BEST answers the question or completes the statement. *PRINT THE LETTER OF THE CORRECT ANSWER IN THE SPACE AT THE RIGHT.*

1. The temperature at which a substance in the liquid state freezes is the same as the temperature at which the substance
   A. melts   B. sublimes   C. boils   D. condenses
          1.____

2. A sample of gaseous substance contains 3.01×10^{23} molecules. The number of moles of the substance in this sample is
   A. 1.00   B. 2.00   C. 0.25   D. 0.50
          2.____

3. The temperature of a sample of water increases from 30°C to 40°C as 100 calories of heat is added.
   What is the mass of the sample of water?
   _____ grams.
   A. 1   B. 10   C. 100   D. 1,000
          3.____

4. A(n) _____ may be heterogeneous.
   A. substance   B. element
   C. compound   D. mixture
          4.____

5. The neutral atoms in a given sample of an element could have different
   A. mass numbers   B. atomic numbers
   C. numbers of protons   D. numbers of electrons
          5.____

6. A 1.00 mole sample of a gas is at STP.
   If the temperature remains constant and the pressure is doubled, the new volume will be _____ liters.
   A. 11.2   B. 22.4   C. 33.6   D. 44.8
          6.____

7. How many orbitals are completely filled in an atom of nitrogen in the ground state?
   A. Five   B. Two   C. Three   D. Four
          7.____

8. Which atom in the ground state has only one unpaired electron in its valence shell?
   A. Boron   B. Carbon   C. Nitrogen   D. Oxygen
          8.____

9. Which pair of atoms represents different isotopes of the same element?
   A. $^{39}_{18}Ar$ and $^{39}_{19}K$ B. $^{58}_{27}Co$ and $^{59}_{28}Ni$
   C. $^{12}_{6}C$ and $^{13}_{6}C$ D. $^{35}_{17}Cl$ and $^{35}_{17}Cl$
          9.____

10. The TOTAL number of electrons in the second principal energy   10.___
    level of a calcium atom in the ground state is
    A. six   B. two   C. eight   D. eighteen

11. The electron-dot symbol $:\overset{..}{\underset{..}{X}}\cdot$ 11.___

    represents an element.
    According to the chart at
    the right, this element
    could have an electro-
    negativity of
    A. 1.5
    B. 2.0
    C. 3.5
    D. 4.0

Ionization Energies and Electronegativities							
IA							**0**
313 ◄─── First Ionization Energy (kcal/mole of atoms)							567
H	◄─── Electronegativity						He
	IIA	**IIIA**	**IVA**	**VA**	**VIA**	**VIIA**	
124 Li 1.0	215 Be 1.5	191 B 2.0	260 C 2.5	336 N 3.0	314 O 3.5	402 F 4.0	497 Ne
119 Na 0.9	176 Mg 1.2	138 Al 1.5	188 Si 1.8	254 P 2.1	239 S 2.5	300 Cl 3.0	363 Ar
100 K 0.8	141 Ca 1.0	138 Ga 1.6	187 Ge 1.8	231 As 2.0	225 Se 2.4	273 Br 2.8	323 Kr
96 Rb 0.8	131 Sr 1.0	133 In 1.7	169 Sn 1.8	199 Sb 1.9	208 Te 2.1	241 I 2.5	280 Xe
90 Cs 0.7	120 Ba 0.9	141 Tl 1.8	171 Pb 1.8	185 Bi 1.9	Po 2.0	At 2.2	248 Rn
Fr 0.7	Ra						

12. The number of protons in an atom of ^{36}Cl is   12.___
    A. 17   B. 18   C. 35   D. 36

13. Which is the electron configuration of a noble gas atom in   13.___
    the excited state?
    A. $1s^1$ B. $1s^1 2s^1$ C. $1s^2 2s^2$ D. $1s^2 2s^2 2p^2$

14. When a chlorine atom reacts with a sodium atom to form an   14.___
    ion, the chlorine atom will _____ electron(s).
    A. lose one   B. lose two
    C. gain one   D. gain two

15. The CORRECT formula for iron (III) oxide is   15.___
    A. FeO_3 B. Fe_2O_3 C. Fe_3O D. Fe_3O_2

16. Given the unbalanced equation: 16.___
    $(NH_4)_3PO_4 + Ba(NO_3)_2 \rightarrow Ba_3(PO_4)_2 + NH_4NO_3$.
    What is the coefficient in front of the NH_4NO_3 when the
    equation is completely balanced with the smallest whole-
    number coefficients?
    A. Six   B. Two   C. Three   D. Four

17. At 25°C, hydrogen bonds are STRONGEST between molecules of   17.___
    A. CH_4 B. NH_3 C. H_2O D. HCl

18. Which atom will form the MOST polar bond with hydrogen?   18.___
    A. F   B. Cl   C. Br   D. I

19. A proton (H^+) would be MOST likely to form a coordinate covalent bond with   19.___

(A)
$$H:C:H$$
with H above and H below (CH$_4$)

(C) $H:C::C:H$

(B) $H:O:$ with H below, and dots

(D) $\begin{bmatrix} H \\ H:N:H \\ H \end{bmatrix}^+$

20. Which represents a transition element?   20.___
    A. He   B. Se   C. Be   D. Fe

21. Which Period contains four elements which are gases at STP?   21.___
    A. One   B. Two   C. Three   D. Four

22. An atom in the ground state with eight valence electrons would MOST likely be classified as a(n)   22.___
    A. active metal   B. inactive metal
    C. noble gas   D. halogen

23. The atomic number of a metalloid in Period 4 is   23.___
    A. 19   B. 26   C. 33   D. 36

24. Which electron configuration represents the atom in Period 2 with the LARGEST covalent atomic radius?   24.___
    A. $1s^2 2s^1$ B. $1s^2 2s^2$ C. $1s^2 2s^2 2p^1$ D. $1s^2 2s^2 2p^2$

25. Which element is a liquid at STP?   25.___
    A. K   B. I   C. Ag   D. Hg

26. The volume of 0.25 mole of oxygen at STP is _____ liters.   26.___
    A. 0.25   B. 0.50   C. 5.6   D. 11.2

27. A compound has the empirical formula CH_2 and a molecular mass of 42.
    Its molecular formula is   27.___
    A. CH_2 B. C_2H_4 C. C_3H_6 D. C_4H_8

28. The percent by mass of Li in $LiNO_3$ (formula mass = 69) is CLOSEST to _____ percent.   28.___
    A. 6   B. 10   C. 18   D. 20

29. Which gas is MOST dense at STP?   29.___
    A. $CO(g)$ B. $NO(g)$ C. $N_2(g)$ D. $O_2(g)$

30. Given the reaction: $2C_8H_{18}(g) + 25O_2(g) \rightarrow 16CO_2(g) + 18H_2O(g)$.
    The TOTAL number of liters of O_2 required for the complete combustion of 4.00 liters of C_8H_{18} is   30.___
    A. 25.0   B. 50.0   C. 100.   D. 200.

31. Indicate which of the following saturated solutions is the MOST concentrated at 20°C?   31.____
    A. NaCl   B. KCl   C. $NaNO_3$ D. KNO_3

32. Which reaction has a positive heat of reaction (ΔH) at 1 atmosphere and 298°K?   32.____
    A. $CH_4(g) + 2O_2(g) \rightarrow CO_2(g) + 2H_2O(\ell)$
    B. $CO(g) + \frac{1}{2}O_2(g) \rightarrow CO_2(g)$
    C. $NH_4Cl(s) \rightarrow NH_4^+(aq) + Cl^-(aq)$
    D. $H^+(aq) + OH^-(aq) \rightarrow H_2O(\ell)$

33. Which change represents an increase in the entropy of a system?   33.____

                    H_2O
    A. $C_6H_{12}O_6(s) \xrightarrow{} C_6H_{12}O_6(aq)$
    B. $H_2O(\ell) \rightarrow H_2O(s)$
    C. $CO_2(g) \rightarrow CO_2(s)$
    D. $C_2H_5OH(g) \rightarrow C_2H_5OH(\ell)$

34. Which change may occur in a reaction system when a catalyst is added?   34.____
The
    A. equilibrium point is reached more rapidly
    B. potential energy of the reactants increases
    C. potential energy of the products decreases
    D. heat of reaction becomes smaller

35. According to the table at the right, which compound is LEAST soluble in water?   35.____
    A. AgBr
    B. $BaSO_4$
    C. $PbCrO_4$
    D. ZnS

Constants for Various Equilibria at 1 atm and 298 K

$H_2O = H^+(aq) + OH^-(aq)$		$K_w = 1.0 \times 10^{-14}$
$CH_3COO^-(aq) + H_2O = CH_3COOH(aq) + OH^-(aq)$		$K_b = 5.6 \times 10^{-10}$
$NH_3(aq) + H_2O = NH_4^+(aq) + OH^-(aq)$		$K_b = 1.8 \times 10^{-5}$
$CO_3^{2-}(aq) + H_2O = HCO_3^-(aq) + OH^-(aq)$		$K_b = 2.1 \times 10^{-4}$
$Ag(NH_3)_2^+(aq) = Ag^+(aq) + 2NH_3(aq)$		$K_{eq} = 6.3 \times 10^{-8}$
$N_2(g) + 3H_2(g) = 2NH_3(g)$		$K_{eq} = 6.7 \times 10^{5}$
$H_2(g) + I_2(g) = 2HI(g)$		$K_{eq} = 3.5 \times 10^{1}$

Compound	K_{sp}	Compound	K_{sp}
AgCl	1.6×10^{-10}	$PbCl_2$	1.6×10^{-5}
AgBr	7.7×10^{-13}	$PbCrO_4$	1.8×10^{-14}
AgI	1.5×10^{-16}	PbI_2	1.4×10^{-8}
$BaSO_4$	1.1×10^{-10}	ZnS	1.6×10^{-20}

KEY (CORRECT ANSWERS)

1. A	11. D	21. B	31. C
2. D	12. A	22. C	32. C
3. B	13. B	23. C	33. A
4. D	14. C	24. A	34. A
5. A	15. B	25. D	35. D
6. A	16. A	26. C	
7. B	17. C	27. C	
8. A	18. A	28. B	
9. C	19. B	29. D	
10. C	20. D	30. B	

EXAMINATION SECTION

TEST 1

1. A physical property which determines the method of collection of a gas in a laboratory is its
    A. solubility in water   B. color
    C. state   D. ease of liquefaction

    1.___

2. The antidote for lye that has come into contact with the skin is application of
    A. ammonia water followed by tincture of iodine
    B. petroleum jelly
    C. copious water followed by boric acid
    D. 2% tincture of iodine

    2.___

3. The simplest crystalline symmetry in a solid is
    A. cubic   B. rhombic   C. triclinic   D. tetragonal

    3.___

4. If a given substance can crystallize in two or more forms, it is called
    A. isomorphic   B. isotopic   C. isotropic   D. polymorphic

    4.___

5. The heat of crystallization is numerically equal to the heat of
    A. solution   B. formation   C. vaporization D. fusion

    5.___

6. The gram molecular volume of ozone equals ____ liters.
    A. 22.4   B. 44.8   C. 48.0   D. 67.2

    6.___

7. One mole of hydrogen and one mole of iodine are placed in a 1 liter container of 500°C.
    If the equilibrium constant equals 45.9, the equilibrium concentration of hydrogen, expressed in moles/liter, equals
    A. .228   B. .772   C. 1.54   D. 1.772

    7.___

8. The conjugate base of H_3O^+ is
    A. H^+ B. H_2O C. OH^- D. H_2O_2

    8.___

9. Water at 100°C has a vapor pressure, expressed in mm. of Hg, equal to
    A. 0   B. 100   C. 760   D. 1013

    9.___

10. The inert gas with the LOWEST boiling point is
    A. helium   B. radon   C. argon   D. xenon

    10.___

11. The scientist credited with the earliest investigations on dialysis is
    A. Einstein   B. Graham   C. Tyndall   D. Cottrell

    11.___

12. The formula for hydrazoic acid is 12.___
    A. HN_3 B. H_3N C. H_4N_2 D. HNO_2

13. In the sulfite process for paper making, wood chips are 13.___
heated with
    A. $Ca(HSO_3)_2$ B. $Ca(HSO_4)_2$ C. $Na_2S_4O_6$ D. $Na_2S_2O_8$

14. A substance sometimes used as a base in paints has the 14.___
formula
    A. $Pb(OH)_2 \cdot 2PbCO_3$ B. $PbCrO_4$
    C. PbS D. $Pb(C_2H_3O_2)_2 \cdot 3H_2O$

15. A potentially hazardous mixture frequently employed as a 15.___
propellant in amateur rockets is
    A. $Zn + S$ B. $C_2H_5OH + O_2$
    C. $C_3H_5(OH)_3 + O_3$ D. $C_3H_5(NO_3)_3 + C_7H_5(NO_2)_3$

16. The number of grams of potassium required to react with 16.___
bromine to produce 10 mols. of potassium bromide is
APPROXIMATELY
    A. 78.2   B. 159.8   C. 238.0   D. 391.0

17. When manganese dioxide is heated to a temperature of 17.___
535°C, the substances produced are oxygen and
    A. MnO B. MnO_3 C. Mn_3O_4 D. Mn_2O_7

18. When steam is passed through a solution of $H_2S_2O_8$, the 18.___
substance that is formed and distills over is
    A. SO_2 B. SO_3 C. H_2SO_4 D. H_2O_2

19. Sodium hydride reacts with water to produce a(n) 19.___
    A. gas   B. salt
    C. acid   D. neutral solution

20. The molarity of a solution of sodium chloride containing 20.___
100 gm. of salt per 400 ml. of solution is about
    A. 0.25   B. 1.71   C. 4.27   D. 58.50

21. At 0°C and 1 atmosphere pressure, 49 ml. of oxygen and 21.___
23.5 ml. of nitrogen will dissolve in 1 liter of water.
The volume of air, in milliliters, under standard conditions that will dissolve in 1 liter of water is about
    A. 25.5   B. 28.6   C. 72.5   D. 96.0

22. An element that has a specific heat of 0.113 cal/gm/°C 22.___
has an atomic weight of
    A. 14   B. 28   C. 56   D. 113

23. In the reaction: 23.___
$2KMnO_4 + 16HCl \longrightarrow 5Cl_2 + 2MnCl_2 + 2KCl + 8H_2O$,
the reduction product is
    A. Cl_2 B. $MnCl_2$ C. KCl D. H_2O

24. In the reaction:
    $4P + 3KOH + 3H_2O \longrightarrow 3 KH_2PO_2 + PH_3$, phosphorus is
    A. oxidized *only*
    B. reduced *only*
    C. neither oxidized nor reduced
    D. both oxidized and reduced

    24.____

25. Of the following, the salt that hydrolyzes to the
    GREATEST extent is
    A. $NH_4C_2H_3O_2$ B. NH_4Cl C. $NaCl$ D. $CuSO_4$

    25.____

___

KEY (CORRECT ANSWERS)

1. A	11. B
2. C	12. A
3. A	13. A
4. D	14. A
5. D	15. A
6. A	16. D
7. A	17. C
8. B	18. D
9. C	19. A
10. A	20. C

21. B
22. C
23. B
24. D
25. A

___

TEST 2

DIRECTIONS: Each question or incomplete statement is followed by several suggested answers or completions. Select the one that BEST answers the question or completes the statement. *PRINT THE LETTER OF THE CORRECT ANSWER IN THE SPACE AT THE RIGHT.*

1. Of the following, the substance which has the HIGHEST boiling point is
   A. H_2S B. H_2Se C. H_2Te D. H_2O

   1.____

2. The temperature of 1 liter of gas at constant pressure is changed from 0°C to 273°C.
   The new volume of gas, expressed in liters, is
   A. .5   B. 1   C. 2   D. 2.5

   2.____

3. In electrolysis, oxidation takes place at the
   A. anode   B. cathode
   C. anode and cathode   D. anode or cathode

   3.____

4. LeChatelier's principle applies to.
   A. neither chemical nor physical equilibria
   B. chemical and physical equilibria
   C. chemical equilibria only
   D. physical equilibria only

   4.____

5. The atom with atomic number 20 will MOST likely combine chemically with the atom whose atomic number is
   A. 10   B. 14   C. 16   D. 21

   5.____

6. As the atomic number of the elements in the second period of the periodic table increases, the ionization potential
   A. generally increases
   B. generally decreases
   C. first decreases then increases
   D. first increases then decreases

   6.____

7. The heats of formation of MgO and HI are +145,800 and -6,400 calories, respectively.
   This would indicate that
   A. MgO is insoluble in acids
   B. MgO melts at a low temperature
   C. HI is a weak acid
   D. HI is unstable

   7.____

8. The driving force of a chemical reaction is MOST closely related to the concept of
   A. heat of reaction   B. heat of formation
   C. entropy   D. free energy

   8.____

9. Of the following, the element which is NOT a lanthanide is   9.___
    A. Holmium   B. Hafnium   C. Cerium   D. Lutecium

10. The transition element with the LOWEST atomic number is   10.___
    A. actinium   B. sodium   C. scandium   D. lanthanum

11. Raoult's law is concerned PRIMARILY with the lowering of   11.___
the
    A. freezing point   B. vapor pressure
    C. osmotic pressure   D. boiling point

12. In a chemical reaction, equilibrium has been established   12.___
when the
    A. concentration of reactants and resultants are equal
    B. opposing reactions cease
    C. velocity of opposing reactions are equal
    D. temperatures of the opposing reactions are equal

13. In a solution containing 1 mole of alcohol and 4 moles of   13.___
water, the mole fraction of alcohol is
    A. 1/5   B. 1/4   C. 3/4   D. 4/5

14. Chemically pure water may be obtained by the process of   14.___
    A. ion exchange   B. water softening
    C. filtration   D. sedimentation

15. The atom with the electronic structure 2 - 1s, 2 - 2s,   15.___
6 - 2p, 2 - 3s, 1 - 3p is
    A. Al   B. Na   C. He   D. Cr

16. The BASIC conclusion that may be drawn from the experi-   16.___
mental studies with x-rays carried out by H.G.J. Moseley
is that the
    A. frequency of vibration is inversely proportional to
       the atomic number
    B. frequency of vibration is independent of the atomic
       number
    C. atomic number is equal to the positive charge on the
       nucleus
    D. number of protons and neutrons in the nucleus are
       nearly equal

17. When an electron moves from the K level to the L level,   17.___
there is an accompanying
    A. absorption of energy   B. emission of beta particle
    C. emission of gamma rays   D. emission of x-rays

18. The MAXIMUM number of p electrons in any shell is   18.___
    A. 2   B. 6   C. 8   D. 14

19. In the equation $E = mc^2$, when m is measured in grams and   19.___
c is measured in centimeters per second, E is expressed in
    A. BTU's   B. volts
    C. ergs   D. degrees, centigrade

20. The packing fraction is MOST closely related to   20.___
    A. electron spin
    B. dipole moment
    C. increase in relativistic mass
    D. mass defect

21. Nuclear particles which are presently thought to hold the   21.___
nucleus together are
    A. neutrons   B. protons   C. electrons   D. mesons

22. For hydrogen gas, the ratio $\frac{Cp}{Cv}$ is APPROXIMATELY   22.___
    A. 1.25   B. 1.41   C. 1.67   D. 2

23. The half-life of U-238 is APPROXIMATELY   23.___
    A. 2.5 minutes   B. .3 x 10^{-6} seconds
    C. 5580 years   D. 4.5 x 10^9 years

24. The initial step in the conversion of uranium to   24.___
plutonium involves the process of
    A. neutron capture   B. proton bombardment
    C. alpha emission   D. fission

25. Of the following particles, the one whose discovery was   25.___
announced MOST recently is the
    A. neutron   B. meson   C. anti-proton   D. positron

KEY (CORRECT ANSWERS)

1. D	11. B
2. C	12. C
3. A	13. A
4. B	14. A
5. C	15. A
6. A	16. C
7. D	17. A
8. D	18. B
9. B	19. C
10. C	20. D

21. D
22. B
23. D
24. A
25. C

TEST 3

DIRECTIONS: Each question or incomplete statement is followed by
several suggested answers or completions. Select the
one that BEST answers the question or completes the
statement. *PRINT THE LETTER OF THE CORRECT ANSWER IN
THE SPACE AT THE RIGHT.*

1. When chlorine and carbon tetrachloride are added to a   1.___
    solution of an iodide and shaken, the color produced is
    A. brown   B. orange   C. violet   D. yellow

2. An important use of silicon carbide is   2.___
    A. as an abrasive   B. as a catalyst
    C. as an explosive   D. in water purification

3. If an eudiometer tube was filled with 26 ml. of hydrogen   3.___
    and 24 ml. of oxygen and the mixture exploded, there
    would remain uncombined
    A. 2 ml. hydrogen   B. 14 ml. hydrogen
    C. 23 ml. hydrogen   D. 11 ml. oxygen

4. The gas evolved when hydrochloric acid is added to a   4.___
    mixture of iron filings and sulfur is
    A. H_2S B. SO_2 C. SO_3 D. H_2

5. When a colorless gas is dissolved in water and the   5.___
    resulting solution turns red litmus blue, the gas may
    have been which one of the following?
    A. HCl   B. NH_3 C. H_2S D. SO_2

6. Fluorine is the MOST active member of the halogen family   6.___
    because it
    A. is a gas   B. has the smallest atomic radius
    C. has no isotopes   D. combines with lithium

7. In sulfuric acid, the valence number of sulfur is   7.___
    A. plus 2   B. minus 2   C. minus 4   D. plus 6

8. In the fractional distillation of liquid air, the gas   8.___
    among the following which boils off last is
    A. argon   B. helium   C. nitrogen   D. oxygen

9. The element selenium is MOST closely related to which one   9.___
    of the following elements?
    A. Beryllium   B. Oxygen   C. Silicon   D. Sulfur

10. Baking soda is also called   10.___
    A. washing soda   B. caustic soda
    C. soda ash   D. bicarbonate of soda

11. Solder is an alloy of
    A. aluminum and copper   B. copper and tin
    C. mercury and silver   D. tin and lead
                                              11.____

12. A lake is prepared by making a mixture of a colored dye with
    A. $Al(OH)_3$ B. $CaOCl_2$ C. Na_2CO_3 D. NH_4OH
        12.____

13. A substance which will cause permanent hardness in water is
    A. Na_2SO_4 B. K_2SO_4 C. $MgSO_4$ D. $Ca(HCO_3)_2$
        13.____

14. An apparatus which is used in the commercial preparation of sodium metal is named
    A. Davy   B. Downs   C. Glauber   D. Hoffman
        14.____

15. Bleaching powder has the formula
    A. $CaCl_2$ B. $CaOCl$ C. $CaOCl_2$ D. $Ca(ClO_3)_2$
        15.____

16. Pig iron is essentially the same as
    A. low carbon steel   B. wrought iron
    C. cast iron   D. Bessemer steel
        16.____

17. Of the following, an example of a transition element is
    A. aluminum   B. astatine   C. nickel   D. rubidium
        17.____

18. A gas which is lighter than air is
    A. CH_4 B. C_6H_6 C. HCl D. N_2O
        18.____

19. Of the following gases, the one which is odorless and heavier than air is
    A. CO B. CO_2 C. H_2S D. N_2
        19.____

20. The CHIEF impurity in producer gas is
    A. CH_4 B. CO C. CO_2 D. N_2
        20.____

21. The weight, in grams, of 22.4 liters of nitrogen (atomic weight = 14) is
    A. 3   B. 7   C. 14   D. 28
        21.____

22. One liter of a certain gas, under standard conditions, weighs 1.16 grams.
A possible formula for the gas is
    A. C_2H_2 B. CO C. NH_3 D. O_2
        22.____

23. Of the following acids, the one which is MOST commonly found in the home is
    A. $HC_2H_3O_2$ B. HNO_3 C. H_3PO_4 D. H_2SO_4
        23.____

24. Of the following, the one which is an aromatic compound is
    A. benzene   B. ethyl alcohol
    C. iodoform   D. methane
        24.____

25. The complete combustion of carbon disulfide would yield carbon dioxide and
    A. sulfur   B. sulfur dioxide
    C. sulfuric acid   D. water
        25.____

KEY (CORRECT ANSWERS)

1.	C	11.	D
2.	A	12.	A
3.	D	13.	C
4.	D	14.	B
5.	B	15.	C
6.	B	16.	C
7.	D	17.	C
8.	D	18.	A
9.	D	19.	B
10.	D	20.	D

21. D
22. A
23. A
24. A
25. B

———

TEST 4

DIRECTIONS: Each question or incomplete statement is followed by several suggested answers or completions. Select the one that BEST answers the question or completes the statement. *PRINT THE LETTER OF THE CORRECT ANSWER IN THE SPACE AT THE RIGHT.*

1. Spiegeleisen contains iron, carbon, and   1.___
   A. manganese   B. chromium   C. molybdenum   D. nickel

2. A brown gas which becomes pale yellow when cooled with   2.___
   dry ice MOST likely has the formula
   A. NO   B. N_2O C. NO_2 D. N_2O_5

3. The anhydride of chloric acid is   3.___
   A. Cl_2O B. ClO_2 C. Cl_2O_5 D. Cl_2O_7

4. The formation of MOST subterranean limestone caves is   4.___
   caused by underground water containing
   A. ammonia   B. carbon dioxide
   C. limewater   D. strong acids

5. Magnesium alloys are welded frequently in an atmosphere of   5.___
   A. hydrogen   B. oxygen
   C. helium   D. carbon dioxide

6. In ordinary water, the percentage of hydrogen by weight   6.___
   is APPROXIMATELY
   A. 8%   B. 11%   C. 33 1/3%   D. 66 2/3%

7. The valence of an element is equal to the   7.___
   A. number of equivalent weights which can combine with
      8 grams of oxygen
   B. number of atomic weights which can combine with 16
      grams of oxygen
   C. number of its atoms which can combine with 1 atom of
      hydrogen
   D. atomic weight divided by the equivalent weight

8. Rare earth elements usually   8.___
   A. form colorless ions   B. have multiple valences
   C. are inert   D. are diamagnetic

9. Assume that the sulfide X_2S is 80% X by weight.   9.___
   The atomic weight of X, then, is
   A. 23   B. 39   C. 64   D. 128

10. The Ostwald Process is used frequently to prepare   10.___
    A. sulfuric acid   B. ammonia
    C. nitric acid   D. sodium bicarbonate

11. One of the constituents of pyroligneous acid is   11.___
    A. aniline   B. ethanol   C. phenol   D. acetone

12. Low grade ores of metals usually are concentrated by   12.___
    A. puddling   B. roasting   C. flotation   D. reduction

13. One of the products of the reaction of hot concentrated   13.___
sulfuric acid on copper is
    A. hydrogen   B. sulfur trioxide
    C. sulfur   D. sulfur dioxide

14. The tendency of water molecules to polymerize is   14.___
attributable to the
    A. low Van derWaal's forces
    B. peroxide linkage
    C. hydrogen bond
    D. presence of unsaturated linkage

15. Vat dyes are precipitated within the cloth through   15.___
    A. oxidation by the air   B. addition of a mordant
    C. production of a lake   D. soaking in salt solution

16. The solvent employed in the Hall process is   16.___
    A. KHF_2 B. Na_3AlF_6 C. $KAl(SO_4)_2$ D. H_2F_2

17. In the liquid ammonia system, the ion which corresponds   17.___
to the hydroxyl ion in the water system is
    A. NH_4^{+1} B. NH_2^{-1} C. NO_2^{-1} D. NO_3^{-1}

18. One of the raw materials used in the production of iron   18.___
from its ore in the blast furnace is
    A. spiegeleisen   B. limestone
    C. slag   D. calcium phosphate

19. An element which is used in transistors is   19.___
    A. beryllium   B. germanium   C. cadmium   D. titanium

20. Acidified potassium permanganate solution can be   20.___
decolorized by the addition of
    A. Cl_2 B. H_2O_2 C. HNO_3 D. H_2SO_4

21. The principle that no two electrons have the same four   21.___
quantum numbers was first proposed by
    A. Pauli   B. deBroglie   C. Einstein   D. Heisenberg

22. In the liquefaction of gases, use is made of (the)   22.___
    A. LeChatelier's principle B. Boyle's law
    C. Avogadro's hypothesis   D. Joule-Thomson effect

23. The interionic attraction theory involving strong   23.___
electrolytes was proposed by
    A. Van derWaals   B. Arrhenius
    C. Lewis   D. Debye and Huckel

24. The law of partial pressures was formulated by   24.___
   A. Avogadro   B. Graham   C. Dalton   D. Boyle

25. Wohler experimentally disproved the vital force doctrine   25.___
   by heating
   A. NH_4OCN B. NH_4SCN C. NH_4CN D. $(NH_2)_2CO$

KEY (CORRECT ANSWERS)

1. A		11. D	
2. C		12. C	
3. C		13. D	
4. B		14. C	
5. C		15. A	
6. B		16. B	
7. D		17. B	
8. B		18. B	
9. C		19. B	
10. C		20. B	

21. A
22. D
23. D
24. C
25. A

TEST 5

DIRECTIONS: Each question or incomplete statement is followed by
              several suggested answers or completions. Select the
              one that BEST answers the question or completes the
              statement. *PRINT THE LETTER OF THE CORRECT ANSWER IN
              THE SPACE AT THE RIGHT.*

1. X-ray diffraction is associated with the experimental work   1.___
    of
      A. Roentgen   B. Bragg   C. Mendeleef   D. Dempster

2. The charge on the electron was determined FIRST by   2.___
      A. Schrodinger B. Millikan   C. Crookes   D. Hertz

3. Emulsifying agents are generally   3.___
      A. suspensoids   B. protective colloids
      C. ions with high charge   D. lyophobic

4. In titration, the point at which equivalent amounts of a   4.___
    weak acid and a strong base have been mixed together is
    the point called
      A. isoelectric   B. eutectic
      C. equilibrium   D. stoichiometric

5. Of the following substances, the indicator MOST suitable   5.___
    for use in titrating ammonium hydroxide and sulfuric acid is
      A. methyl orange   B. litmus
      C. phenolphthalein   D. alizarin yellow

6. Assume that 30 ml. of .3M H_2SO_4 are needed to neutralize 6.___
    10 ml. of an unknown base.
    The normality of the base will be
      A. .45   B. .9   C. 1.8   D. 4.5

7. A substance sometimes used as a moderator in nuclear   7.___
    reactors is
      A. cadmium   B. Uranium 235 C. lead   D. heavy water

8. Of the following, the radioactive emanations having the   8.___
    GREATEST penetrating ability are the
      A. alpha rays B. beta rays   C. gamma rays D. neutrons

9. The atomic number of an element is always equal to the   9.___
      A. number of neutrons in the nucleus
      B. atomic weight divided by two
      C. weight of the nucleus
      D. electrical charge on the nucleus

10. Maleic and fumaric acids are examples of the type of   10.___
    isomers called
      A. tautomers   B. optical isomers
      C. cis-trans   D. keto-enol

11. Vinyl chloride, vinyl bromide, and vinyl acetate are   11.___
    MOST similar in structure to
    A. ethane   B. ethylene   C. acetylene   D. benzene

12. The paraffin hydrocarbon that has the LOWEST molecular   12.___
    weight and at the same time exhibits isomerism is
    A. propane   B. ethane   C. methane   D. butane

13. Of the following compounds, the one classified as an   13.___
    amino acid is
    A. CH_2NH_2COOH B. CH_3NH_2
    C. CH_2NO_2COOH D. $C_6H_4OH NH_2$

14. Methyl alcohol is produced synthetically on a commercial   14.___
    scale by combining carbon monoxide catalytically with
    A. acetylene   B. hydrogen   C. ethanol   D. methane

15. Of the following organic compounds, the one MOST likely   15.___
    to have optical isomers is
    A. $CH_3CHOHCOOH$ B. CH_3CH_2COOH
    C. $HOOC-CH_2-COOH$ D. CHCOOH
                                  $||$
                                  CHCOOH

Questions 16-19.

DIRECTIONS: Answer Questions 16 to 19 after studying the following
               statement.

    An aqueous solution contains the ions AG^+, Hg_2^{+2}, Cu^{+2}, Fe^{+3},
    Ga^{+2}, and NH_4^+.

16. The ion which forms an insoluble chloride in water   16.___
    solution is
    A. Ag^+ B. Ca^{+2} C. Fe^{+3} D. Cu^{+2}

17. The ion which forms an insoluble sulfide in a .3N HCl   17.___
    solution is
    A. NH_4^+ B. Ca^{+2} C. Cu^{+2} D. Fe^{+3}

18. The ion which can be identified through the use of KCNS is   18.___
    A. Hg_2^{+2} B. Cu^{+2} C. Fe^{+3} D. NH_4^+

19. The ion MOST difficult to remove as a precipitate is   19.___
    A. NH_4^+ B. Ag^+ C. Fe^{+3} D. Hg_2^{+2}

20. The element that produces a violet-colored bead with   20.___
    microcosmic salt when cooled after heating in a reducing
    flame is
    A. copper   B. manganese   C. tungsten   D. titanium

21. Concentrated sulfuric acid is stored in   21.___
    A. wax bottles   B. glass-stoppered bottles
    C. rubber-stoppered bottles   D. copper containers

3 (#5)

22. For best results when demonstrating the electrolysis of   22.___
    water, the laboratory assistant should make available an
    electric current of APPROXIMATELY
        A. 110 volts AC   B. 20 volts AC
        C. 1.5 volts DC   D. 18 volts DC

23. Hematite is an important ore of the metal   23.___
        A. iron   B. boron
        C. magnesium   D. plutonium

24. For the study of the action of metals on acids, the   24.___
    students may be supplied safely with
        A. sodium   B. zinc   C. lithium   D. potassium

25. Metallic potassium should be stored under   25.___
        A. water   B. dilute hydrochloric acid
        C. fluorspar   D. kerosene

KEY (CORRECT ANSWERS)

1. B		11. B
2. B		12. D
3. B		13. A
4. D		14. B
5. A		15. A
6. C		16. A
7. D		17. C
8. C		18. C
9. D		19. A
10. C		20. D

21. B
22. D
23. A
24. B
25. D

EXAMINATION SECTION

TEST 1

DIRECTIONS: Each question or incomplete statement is followed by several suggested answers or completions. Select the one that *BEST* answers the question or completes the statement. *PRINT THE LETTER OF THE CORRECT ANSWER IN THE SPACE AT THE RIGHT.*

1. Two silver electrodes are immersed in an aqueous solution of silver ions and connected to a battery which sends 0.500 amp of current at 2.00 volts through the cell. How many seconds will the current have to flow to deposit 54.0 milligrams of Ag on one of the electrodes? (Ag = 108)   1.___
   A. 275×10^1 B. 9.65×10^1
   C. 1.11×10^2 D. 1.91×10^2

2. A 0.01 M barium hydroxide solution would have an OH^- ion concentration of *approximately*   2.___
   A. 0.01 M   B. 0.02 M.
   C. 0.03 M   D. 1.0×10^{-6} M.

3. To correct the ideal gas law equation to describe a real gas at high pressure, account MUST be taken of the amount of space occupied by the molecules themselves. If B symbolizes this volume factor, the equation for one mole of gas could be   3.___
   A. $\dfrac{PV}{b} = RT$ B. $V = \dfrac{RT}{P} - b$

   C. $P(V-b) = RT$ D. $P(V + b) = RT$

4. What is the *apparent* degree of ionization of a salt of the type A_2B_3 if 3.0 grams dissolved in 1.0×10^2 grams of water makes a solution with a freezing point of -0.97^oC? The formula weight of the compound is 1.5×10^2. The molal freezing point constant for water is 1.86^oC.   4.___
   A. 24%   B. 52%   C. 13%   D. 40%

5. In which gas sample is the number of atoms equal to the number of atoms in 32 grams of SO_2? (C = 12; S = 32; O = 16; H = 1)   5.___
   A. 1.0 gram hydrogen   B. 1.5 grams hydrogen
   C. 16 grams oxygen   D. 32 grams oxygen

6. What is the pH of a 2.5×10^{-1} M HCN solution? ($K_a = 4 \times 10^{-10}$)   6.___
   A. 2.0×10^{-5} B. 2.0
   C. 4.7   D. 5.0

7. A six gram sample of a solution of a monoprotic acid 7.____
(F.W. = 60) required 40 ml of 0.10 M NaOH solution
for neutralization.
What was the percent purity of the acid solution?
   A. 1%   B. 2%   C. 3%   D. 4%

8. On reaction with hydrochloric acid, 72 mg. of magnesium 8.____
metal produced 91 ml of a gas collected over water at
22°C and 630 mm of Hg pressure.
   ____milligrams of aluminum metal would be needed to pro-
duce the same volume of the same gas under the same
conditions. (Mg = 24; Al = 27) (V.P. H_2O at 22°C = 20 mm of
Hg.)
   A. 36   B. 48   C. 54   D. 71

9. If the use of an ammeter and a timing device indicated 9.____
that four moles of electrons were transferred from anode
to cathode in the electrolysis of water, the *total* volume
of the two gases (dry at STP) produced would be *approximately*
   ____ liters.
   A. 22.4   B. 29.8   C. 44.8   D. 67.2

10. What is the oxidation number of phosphorus in phosphoric 10.____
acid, H_3PO_4?
   A. -3   B. +2   C. +3   D. +5

11. In the reaction represented by the equation: 11.____
   $4Al(s) + 3\ O_2(g) \rightarrow 2Al_2O_3(s)$,
How many moles of aluminum are required to react *completely*
with 9.0 moles of oxygen gas?
   A. 9.0   B. 12   C. 27   D. 4.0

12. Consider the equation: 12.____
   $CH_4(g) + 2\ O_2(g) \rightarrow CO_2(g) + 2\ H_2O(\ell)$
How many moles of reactant are in excess when 2.0 moles
of $CH_4(g)$ are ignited in 2.0 moles of $O_2(g)$?
   A. 1.0 mole CH_4 B. 2.0 moles O_2
   C. 0.5 mole CH_4 C. no excess of either reactant

13. In the electrolysis of water what happens at the cathode 13.____
(negative electrode)?
   A. H_2 gas bubbles off   B. O_2 gas bubbles off
   C. Ions are discharged   D. H_2O_2 liquid is formed

14. Consider the diagram for the reaction 14.____
   $A(g) + B(g) \rightarrow C(g) + D(g)$

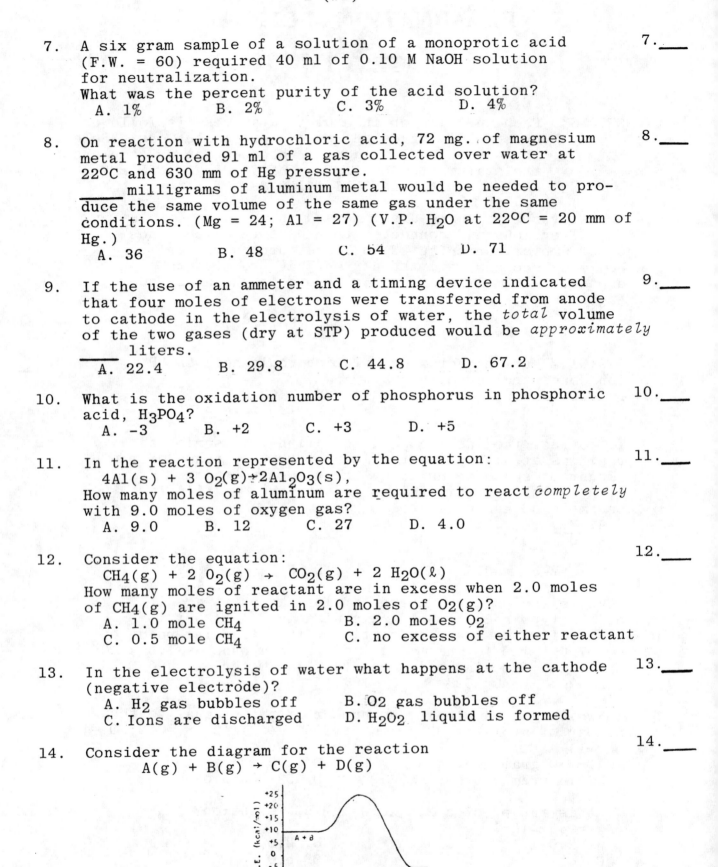

The activation energy for this reaction is ____ Kcal/mol.
A. +5   B. +10   C. +15   D. -15

15. The half-life of radioactive iron, $_{26}^{59}Fe$ is 46 days. What fraction of the original sample of this isotope remains after 184 days?
A. 0.0625   B. 0.125   C. 0.250   D. 0.500   15.____

16. In electroplating, the mass of metal deposited at the cathode is proportional to the   16.____
A. size of the ion
B. activity of the metal
C. temperature of the solution
D. quantity of electric charge passed through the cell

17. A single burst of light is released from an atom. The statement which explains what happens in the atom is that an electron   17.____
A. is changed from a particle to a wave
B. moved from a higher to a lower energy level
C. pulled a proton out of the nucleus
D. pulled a neutron out of the nucleus

18. The electron configuration $1s^2 \ 2s^2 \ 2p^6 \ 3s^1 \ 3p^1$ represents a   18.____
A. sodium ion
B. manganese atom
C. carbon atom in the ground state
D. magnesium atom in an excited state

19. The number of atoms of hydrogen in one molecule of glycerine, $C_3H_5(OH)_3$, is   19.____
A. 14   B. 8   C. 6   D. 5

20. Which compound has the GREATEST ionic character in its bonds?   20.____
A. NaCl   B. $MgCl_2$ C. $AlCl_3$ D. PCl_5

21. What type of bonding is found in a molecule of phosphine, PH_3?   21.____
A. Ionic   B. Covalent
C. Hydrogen bonding   D. Van der Waals

22. In the solid state which type of bonding between particles BEST allows for the conduction of electricity?   22.____
A. Ionic   B. Covalent
C. Metallic   D. Covalent network

23. ____ neutrons are in the isotope $_{15}^{29}P$?   23.____
A. 14   B. 15   C. 16   D. 29

24. Which BEST accounts for the dissolution of solid KNO_3 in H_2O even though the change is endothermic?
    24.___
    A. All nitrates are soluble in H_2O.
    B. The entropy of the system increases.
    C. The free energy of the system increases.
    D. The enthalpy of the system decreases.

25. A 100 ml beaker containing 1.0 M NaCl and a 100 ml beaker containing 2.0 M NaCl are placed in a closed container and maintained at a constant temperature until equilibrium is established.
    What change is apparent?
    25.___
    A. All the liquid disappears from the beaker containing the 2.0 M solution.
    B. The liquid level in the beaker containing the 1.0 M solution falls.
    C. The liquid level in the beaker containing the 2.0 M solution falls.
    D. Both solutions lose water until only solid NaCl is in both beakers.

26. What happens to the velocities of molecules as the temperature of a gas increases?
    26.___
    A. The velocities of all component molecules increase equally.
    B. The velocity range among different molecules will be smaller than at the lower temperature.
    C. The effect on the velocities of the molecules depends on whether the pressure remains constant.
    D. The velocity range among different molecules will be wider than at the lower temperature.

27. A reaction is thermodynamically spontaneous under the stated conditions if it(s)
    27.___
    A. is exothermic
    B. ΔG value is negative
    C. ΔH value is negative
    D. is self-starting at room temperature

Questions 28 - 30

DIRECTIONS: Use the following information in answering questions 28 through 30.
A voltaic cell consists of
$Ni(s)$ | $Ni^{2+}(a=1)$ || $Cu^{2+}(a=1)$ | $Cu(s)$

28. The reaction at the anode of this cell produces
    28.___
    A. Cu^{2+} ions   B. Ni^{2+} ions
    C. SO_4^{2-} ions   D. Cu atoms

29. The internal flow of current in this cell is a movement
    29.___
    A. ONLY of positive ions towards the Ni electrode
    B. ONLY of negative ions towards the Ni electrode
    C. of positive ions towards the Ni electrode and of negative ions towards the Cu electrode
    D. of negative ions towards the Ni electrode and of positive ions towards the Cu electrode

30. The voltage is increased by   30.____
    A. raising the temperature
    B. decreasing the concentration of Cu^{2+}(aq)
    C. decreasing the concentration of Ni^{2+}(aq)
    D. using a $Zn \mid Zn^{2+}$(a=1) half-cell in place of
       the $Cu \mid Cu^{2+}$(a=1) half-cell

31. A 1.00 molal aqueous solution of a crystalline solid   31.____
    begins to freeze at $-1.86^{O}C$. The molecules of the
    solute have a dipole moment.
    These properties suggest the solid is a
    A. compound with identical polar covalent bonds
       arranged symmetrically
    B. compound with a high degree of ionic character
    C. polar compound with a low degree of ionic
       character
    D. compound containing an element which has a low
       ionization energy

32. Which BEST supports the concept of electron transi-   32.____
    tions between quantized energy levels?
    A. In absorption spectra, definite lines are pro-
       duced.
    B. In NMR, the resonance absorption peaks in
       CH_3CH_2OH are in the ratio of 1:2:3.
    C. In electron diffraction patterns of electron
       density, intensity points form regular patterns.
    D. In crystal X-ray diffraction, the refracting
       signals reinforce each other at whole number
       intervals.

33. When a 10.00-milliliter sample of a base is to be   33.____
    titrated with a certain volume of an acid, the volume
    of acid used should be measured from a
    A. graduated cylinder
    B. buret
    C. beaker with graduations on the side
    D. volumetric flask

34. Oxygen gas (O_2) and ozone (O_3) *differ* in the number of   34.____
    A. neutrons in each of the oxygen atoms
    B. protons in each of the oxygen atoms
    C. electrons in each of the oxygen atoms
    D. atoms in each of the molecules

35. When 1.0 mole of a certain compound is formed from its   35.____
    elements, 25 kilojoules of heat energy is released.
    If 2.0 moles of the compound is decomposed into elements,
    what heat energy change takes place?
    ____ kilojoules of heat energy is ____
    A. 25; absorbed   B. 25; released
    C. 50; absorbed   D. 50; released

36. The kinetic energy of a particle is determined from its   36.____
    A. mass *only*   B. volume *only*
    C. speed *only*   D. mass and speed

37. Since a phosphorus atom has 5 electrons in its outer
energy level, a molecule of PH3 would be expected to have
the structures of

   A. H ×̣ P̈ ×̈ H : H   B. H ×̣ P ×̈ H : H

   C. H ×̣ P̈ · H   D. H ·̣ P ×̈·̣ H
             H   H

37.____

38. The periodic table and knowledge about typical elements in
each family of the periodic table would be LEAST useful
in predicting which of the following for an unfamiliar
element?
   A. The formulas for its oxides
   B. Its approximate melting point
   C. The charge on any ion it forms
   D. Its abundance in the Earth's crust

38.____

39. Atoms of which of these elements from the halogen family
have the LARGEST radius?
   A. F (atomic number 9)
   B. Cl (atomic number 17)
   C. Br (atomic number 35)
   D. I (atomic number 53)

39.____

40. A substance is observed to have the following properties:

Odor	None
Solubility in water	Soluble
Solubility in benzene	Almost insoluble
Effect of Bunsen flame	Not melted
Electrical conductivity	
Solid	None
Melted	Good
Water solution	Good

Which statement can be predicted about this substance?
   A. It is a strong oxidizing agent.
   B. There is ionic bonding in the substance.
   C. The substance is *probably* a weak base.
   D. The substance can readily be drawn out into wires.

40.____

KEY (CORRECT ANSWERS)

1. B	11. B	21. B	31. C
2. B	12. A	22. B	32. A
3. C	13. A	23. A	33. B
4. D	14. C	24. B	34. D
5. B	15. A	25. B	35. C
6. D	16. D	26. D	36. D
7. D	17. B	27. B	37. C
8. C	18. D	28. B	38. D
9. D	19. B	29. D	39. D
10. D	20. A	30. C	40. B

TEST 2

DIRECTIONS: Each question or incomplete statement is followed by several suggested answers or completions. Select the one that *BEST* answers the question or completes the statement. *PRINT THE LETTER OF THE CORRECT ANSWER IN THE SPACE AT THE RIGHT.*

1. Upon analysis, the composition by weight of a compound   1.____
   was found to be 22.2% C, 3.7% H, and 74.1% Br.
   What is its empirical formula?
   A. CH_3Br B. C_2H_4Br C. $C_3H_8Br_2$ D. $C_4H_8Br_2$

2. If the electronegativities of H and P are both 2.1, and   2.____
   the covalent single bond energy values for phosphorus and
   hydrogen are:
   P-P   18.9 kcal/mole
   H-H   103.4 kcal/mole
   What is the BEST estimate of the covalent single bond
   energy for a P-H bond, in kcal/mole?
   A. 61.2   B. 70.6   C. 112.9   D. 122.3

3. According to the law of Dulong and Petit, the BEST predic-   3.____
   tion for the specific heat of osmium is ____ g C^o.
   A. 0.012 cal   B. 0.033 cal   C. 0.083 cal   D. 30.1 cal

4. The molal freezing point constant for benzene is 4.9 C^o 4.____
   for a one molal solution and its normal freezing point is
   5.5°C. When 3.4 g of an unknown non-electrolyte is
   dissolved in 50.0 g of benzene, the solution freezes at 0.60 C.
   What is the *apparent* mass of a mole of the compound?
   A. 23 g   B. 26 g   C. 34 g   D. 68 g

5. The combustion of propane is represented by the following   5.____
   equation:
   $C_3H_8(g) + 5O_2(g) \rightleftharpoons 3CO_2(g) + 4H_2O(g)$
   The amount of heat produced by the combustion of one mole
   of propane is ____ Kcal.
   A. 152   B. 488   C. 513   D. 538

6. When 2.40 g of a certain volatile liquid is heated, the   6.____
   volume of the resulting vapor is 821 ml at a temperature
   of 127° C at standard pressure. The molecular weight of
   this substance is about ____ g/mole.
   A. 30.5   B. 65.6   C. 96.0   D. 126

7. What is the *approximate* mole fraction of sugar in a 0.50   7.____
   molar aqueous solution?
   A. 1/112   B. 1/56   C. 1/55.5   D. 18/342

8. Sodium hydroxide solution is used to titrate 2.0 g $(COOH)_2$ to form a sodium oxalate solution. The end point is reached when 26 ml of NaOH solution has been used.
What is the molarity of the NaOH solution?
   A. 0.43   B. 0.85   C. 1.7   D. 3.4

8.___

9. A certain radioactive species undergoing decay by beta minus emission has a half-life of 5.0 years. *Approximately* how many years would it take for 8.75% of a sample of 400 mg of this species to disintegrate?
   A. 4.4   B. 5.8   C. 9.4   D. 15

9.___

10. The ionization constant of a certain weak acid, HA, is 2.0×10^{-6}. What is the pH of a buffer solution prepared by adding 0.10 mole of solid NaA to 1.0 liter of 1.0 M HA? Neglect volume change.
    A. 2.8   B. 4.7   C. 5.7   D. 6.7

10.___

11. Oxygen gas will effuse through a small orifice at a rate of 16.0 liters/hr. What is the rate of effusion of UF_6 under the same conditions?
    A. 2.08×10^{-1} liters/hr
    B. 6.32×10^{-1} liters/hr
    C. 3.40 liters/hr
    D. 4.82 liters/hr

11.___

12. An excess of $S_8(s)$ is heated with a metallic element until the metal is completely reacted and the excess $S_8(s)$ is burned away.
The equivalent weight of the metal from these data is ___ g/equiv.
   Mass of crucible, lid ,and metal   = 55.00 g
   Mass of crucible and lid   = 41.00 g
   Mass of crucible, lid, and residue = 61.88 g
    A. 2.04   B. 6.88   C. 32.6   D. 64.0

12.___

13. When 0.600 mole of $BaCl_2$ is mixed with 0.250 mole of $K_3AsO_4(aq)$, what is the MAXIMUM number of moles of solid $Ba_3(AsO_4)_2$ which could be formed?
    A. 0.125   B. 0.200   C. 0.250   D. 0.375

13.___

14. How many grams of Al will be required to release 30.2 ml of H_2 gas collected over water at $29.0^\circ C$ and 654 Torr (mm Hg)? (The vapor pressure of water at $29.0^\circ C$ is 30.0 Torr.)
    A. 9.0×10^{-3} g   B. 1.8×10^{-2} g
    C. 2.7×10^{-2} g   D. 3.6×10^{-2} g

14.___

15. When sodium melts, the heat of transition is 0.63 kcal/mole and the entropy change is 1.7 cal per mole per $^\circ K$.
The melting point of sodium metal based on these data is ___ $^\circ K$.
    A. 370   B. 470   C. 540   D. 1100

15.___

16. In the equilibrium reaction, $2NO_2(g) \rightleftharpoons N_2O_4(g)$ $(K_e = 8.81)$, what is the molar concentration of nitrogen tetroxide at equilibrium if the nitrogen dioxide concentration is 0.200 moles/liter?

    A. 4.53×10^{-3} B. 2.27×10^{-2}
    C. 1.76×10^{-1} D. 3.52×10^{-1}

16.____

17. For the reaction, $H_2(g) + 1/8\ S_8(s) \rightleftharpoons H_2S(g)$, ΔG^O is -7.90 kcal/mole.
The value of ΔS^O for this reaction is ____ cal/mole K^O.

    A. -124   B. -42.6   C. 0.124   D. 10.4

17.____

18. A solution is prepared by adding 1.00×10^2 ml of 0.100 M NaOH to 2.00×10^2 of 0.100 M HCN.
What is the pH of the mixture?

    A. 5.6   B. 7.0   C. 9.4   D. 10.6

18.____

19. If $E = E^O - \dfrac{0.059}{n} \log \dfrac{[\text{oxidized form}]}{[\text{reduced form}]}$ at $298^O K$, what will happen to the oxidation potential when the Zn^{2+} (aq) ion concentration in a $Zn \mid Zn^{2+}$ half-cell is reduced to 0.10M from the standard 1.0M? It will be

    A. decreased by about 0.59 V
    B. increased by about 0.030 V
    C. increased by about 0.059 V
    D. increased by a factor of 10

19.____

20. What is the approximate molar concentration of the Ag^+ ion in a saturated aqueous solution of Ag_2CrO_4?

    A. 4.8×10^{-13} B. 1.4×10^{-6}
    C. 7.8×10^{-5} D. 1.6×10^{-4}

20.____

21. Which structure represents a nonpolar molecule with one or more polar bonds?

    A.   B. Cl - Cl

    C.   D. Br-Be-Br

21.____

22. The molarity of a solution made by diluting 20 cm^3 of 6.0 M HCl to 600 cm^3 is ____ M.

    A. 0.12   B. 0.20   C. 0.60   D. 1.2

22.____

23. In neutralizing 0.015 mole of H_3PO_3, 0.030 mole of NaOH was consumed.
Which equation describes this reaction?

    A. $H_3PO_3 + NaOH \rightarrow NaPO_3 + H_2O$
    B. $H_3PO_3 + NaOH \rightarrow NaH_2PO_3 + H_2O$
    C. $H_3PO_3 + 3\ NaOH \rightarrow NaPO_3 + 3\ H_2O$
    D. $H_3PO_3 + 2\ NaOH \rightarrow Na_2HPO_3 + 2\ H_2O$

23.____

24. In the equation:
$$BaCl_2(aq) + Na_2SO_4(aq) \rightarrow BaSO_4(s) + 2\ NaCl(aq)$$
What is the net ionic equation for this reaction?
A. $Cl^-(aq) + Na^+(aq) \rightarrow NaCl(aq)$
B. $Cl_2{}^{2-}(aq) + Na_2{}^{2+}(aq) \rightarrow 2\ NaCl(aq)$
C. $Ba^{2+}(aq) + SO_4{}^{2-}(aq) \rightarrow BaSO_4(s)$
D. $BaCl_2(s) + Na_2SO_4(s) \rightarrow$
$Ba^{2+}(aq) + 2\ Cl^-(aq) + 2\ Na^+(aq) + SO_4{}^{2-}(aq)$

24.____

25. Which of these is the STRONGEST organic (carboxylic) acid?

Acid	K_a
A. Formic	1.76×10^{-4}
B. Lactic	1.38×10^{-4}
C. Benzoic	6.30×10^{-5}
D. Acetic	1.75×10^{-5}

25.____

26. What is the hydrogen ion concentration, (H^+), of an acid that has a pH of 3? M
A. 10^{-3} B. 10^{-1} C. 10^3 D. 10^6

26.____

27. Which of these graphs BEST represents the relationship between the volume and the pressure of a sample of gas at constant temperature?

27.____

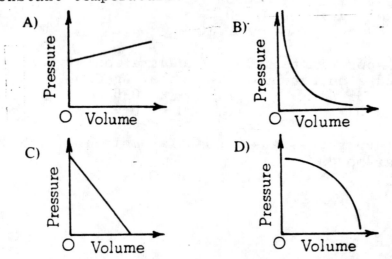

28. It is possible to make water boil at room temperature (about 20°C) by
A. putting it in a pressure cooker
B. sufficiently reducing the pressure on the water
C. increasing the kinetic energy of the molecules
D. dissolving a sufficient amount of salt in the water

28.____

29. Suppose that an atom of thorium (atomic number 30, atomic mass 232) captures a neutron.
What are the properties of the atom that is formed?

29.____

	Atomic Number	Atomic Mass
A.	89	231
B.	90	232
C.	90	233
D.	91	232

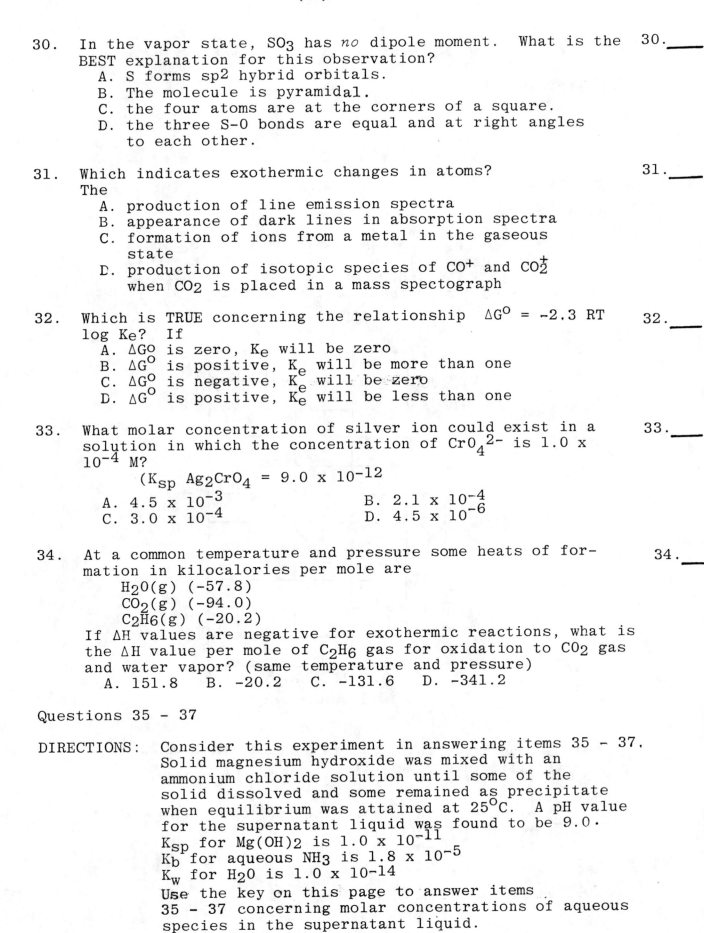

30. In the vapor state, SO_3 has *no* dipole moment. What is the   30.___
    BEST explanation for this observation?
    A. S forms sp^2 hybrid orbitals.
    B. The molecule is pyramidal.
    C. the four atoms are at the corners of a square.
    D. the three S-O bonds are equal and at right angles
       to each other.

31. Which indicates exothermic changes in atoms?   31.___
    The
    A. production of line emission spectra
    B. appearance of dark lines in absorption spectra
    C. formation of ions from a metal in the gaseous
       state
    D. production of isotopic species of CO^+ and $CO_2^{\pm}$
       when CO_2 is placed in a mass spectograph

32. Which is TRUE concerning the relationship $\Delta G^O = -2.3$ RT   32.___
    log K_e?   If
    A. ΔG^O is zero, K_e will be zero
    B. ΔG^O is positive, K_e will be more than one
    C. ΔG^O is negative, K_e will be zero
    D. ΔG^O is positive, K_e will be less than one

33. What molar concentration of silver ion could exist in a   33.___
    solution in which the concentration of CrO_4^{2-} is 1.0×10^{-4} M?
         (K_{sp} $Ag_2CrO_4 = 9.0 \times 10^{-12}$
    A. 4.5×10^{-3} B. 2.1×10^{-4}
    C. 3.0×10^{-4} D. 4.5×10^{-6}

34. At a common temperature and pressure some heats of for-   34.___
    mation in kilocalories per mole are
         $H_2O(g)$ (-57.8)
         $CO_2(g)$ (-94.0)
         $C_2H_6(g)$ (-20.2)
    If ΔH values are negative for exothermic reactions, what is
    the ΔH value per mole of C_2H_6 gas for oxidation to CO_2 gas
    and water vapor? (same temperature and pressure)
         A. 151.8   B. -20.2   C. -131.6   D. -341.2

Questions 35 - 37

DIRECTIONS: Consider this experiment in answering items 35 - 37.
            Solid magnesium hydroxide was mixed with an
            ammonium chloride solution until some of the
            solid dissolved and some remained as precipitate
            when equilibrium was attained at 25^OC. A pH value
            for the supernatant liquid was found to be 9.0.
            K_{sp} for $Mg(OH)_2$ is 1.0×10^{-11}
            K_b for aqueous NH_3 is 1.8×10^{-5}
            K_w for H_2O is 1.0×10^{-14}
            Use the key on this page to answer items
            35 - 37 concerning molar concentrations of aqueous
            species in the supernatant liquid.

A. 5.6 x 10^{-1} B. 3.6 x 10^{-1}
C. 1.0 x 10^{-1} D. 1.0 x 10^{-5}

35.   What is   OH$^-$?   35.___

36.   What is   Mg^{2+} ?   36.___

37.   What is   NH$_4^+$?   37.___

Questions 38 - 39

DIRECTIONS: Answer questions 38 - 39 on the basis of the
              curve below.
              The curve represents the solubility of a
              certain salt in 100 grams of water. Points
              A, B, C, and D represent the concentrations
              and temperatures of four solutions of the same
              salt in four different beakers.

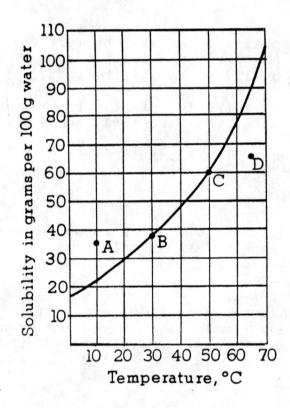

38.   If a crystal of this salt is added to each of the solutions,   38.___
      crystallization occurs in
         A. A   B. B   C. C   D. D

39.   _____ grams of this salt are needed to make a saturated   39.___
      solution in 1,000 grams of water at 50°C.
         A. 50   B. 60   C. 500   D. 600

40. Proteins are giant molecules prepared from small molecules   40. ___
that are amino acids. Which of these is the structural
formula for an amino acid?

A.
```
   H     O
   |    //
  HC - C - OH
   |
  NH2
```

B.
```
   H   H
   |   |
  HC - NH
   |
   H
```

C.
```
   H     O
   |    //
  HC - C - OH
   |
   H
```

D.
```
   H   H   H
   |   |   |
  HC - C - C - H
   |   |   |
   H   H   H
```

KEY (CORRECT ANSWERS)

1. B	11. D	21. C	31. A
2. A	12. C	22. B	32. D
3. B	13. A	23. C	33. C
4. D	14. B	24. D	34. D
5. B	15. A	25. A	35. D
6. C	16. D	26. A	36. C
7. A	17. D	27. B	37. B
8. C	18. C	28. B	38. A
9. D	19. B	29. C	39. D
10. B	20. D	30. A	40. A

TEST 3

DIRECTIONS: Each question or incomplete statement is followed by several suggested answers or completions. Select the one that *BEST* answers the question or completes the statement. *PRIN THE LETTER OF THE CORRECT ANSWER IN THE SPACE AT THE RIGHT.*

1. The crystal lattice binding energy of sodium chloride is 180 kilocalories per mole, but *only* 1.28 kilocalories per mole are required for dissolution of the salt in water.
   An explanation could be that
   A. the lattice energy is NOT involved in the dissolving process for solids
   B. water is a polar compound
   C. the process of hydration liberates 178.72 kilocalories per mole
   D. the heat of solution is 178.72 kilocalories per mole
   E. the solubility of sodium chloride increases only *slightly* with increase in temperature

   1.____

2. The following table indicates the probable electron distribution in the outside two shells of certain elements. Which *one* should have the GREATEST tendency to exist in different oxidation states in compounds?

   A. $s^2 p^6$ $\quad\quad$: s^2

   B. s^2 $\quad\quad$: $s^2 p^6$

   C. $s^2 p^6$ $\quad\quad$: s^1

   D. $s^2 p^6 d^6$ $\quad\quad$: s^2

   E. $s^2 p^6 d^{10}$ $\quad\quad$: s^2

   2.____

3. Bonds with highest degree of ionic character are formed between two elements having respectively ____ ionization potential and ____ electron affinity.
   A. high; high $\quad\quad$ B. high; low $\quad\quad$ C. low; low
   D. low; high $\quad\quad$ E. intermediate; intermediate

   3.____

4. A 0.1 aqueous solution of a pure compound has a pH of *approximately* 7.
   The solution could NOT contain
   A. hydronium ions $\quad\quad\quad$ B. ammonium acetate
   C. sodium chloride $\quad\quad\quad$ D. nitrate ions
   E. copper (II) sulfate

   4.____

5. A one liter vessel contains three moles of a gas at 273° Centigrade. The pressure in the cylinder expressed in atmosphere is
   A. 33.6 $\quad$ B. 67.2 $\quad$ C. 100.8 $\quad$ D. 134.4 $\quad$ E. 145.6

   5.____

6. A solid was sealed in a can of air at 100°C. After
   some time it was observed that the pressure in the can
   increased and the temperature decreased to 70°C.
   One could, therefore, conclude that
      A. pressure and temperature are inversely proportional
      B. a reaction was taking place between the solid and
         the air
      C. some gas was being formed
      D. pressure and volume are inversely proportional
      E. Charles' Law does NOT *always* work.

6.___

7. If calcium hydroxide is completely ionized in a dilute
   solution, which relationship is correct? { } indicates
   molar concentration.
      A. $[Ca(OH)_2] = [OH^-]$ B. $[Ca^{++}] = [OH^-]$
      C. $2[Ca^{++}] = [OH^-]$ D. $[Ca^{++}] = 2[OH^-]$
      E. $[Ca^{++}] = [OH^- 2]$

7.___

8. In the endothermic dissolution of NH_4NO_3, the GREATEST
   energy change is associated with the
      A. decomposition of the salt to NH_3 and HNO_3
      B. separation of the ions from the crystals
      C. hydration of the ions in solution
      D. hydrolysis of the slat to form ammonia water and
         HNO_3
      E. protolysis of the ammonium ion to form NH_3 and
         H_3O^+ ion

8.___

9. Liquid compounds that do NOT conduct an electric current
   unless they are dissolved in water probably have molecules
   with _____ bonding.
      A. a high degree of ionic   B. symmetrical covalent
      C. macromolecular   D. polar covalent
      E. nonpolar

9.___

10. If the use of an ammeter and a timing device indicated
    that three moles of electrons were transferred from anode
    to cathode in the electrolysis of water, the total volume
    of the two gases (dry at STP) produced would have been
    approximately _____ liters.
       A. 22.4   B. 67.2   C. 33.6   D. 50.4   E. 16.8

10.___

11. The solution with the LOWEST freezing point would be
       A. 1 molar HOAc
       B. 1 molar $BaCl_2$
       C. 1 molar sugar ($C_{12}H_{22}O_{11}$)
       D. 1 molar alcohol(C_2H_5OH)
       E. 1 molar NaCl

11.___

12. Which chemical species could be classified as both a
    Brönsted acid and base?
       A. HSO_4^- B. CO_3^{--} C. NH_4^+
       D. S^{--} E. Such a species does NOT exist

12.___

13. Copper metal reacts with dilute nitric acid according   13.____
    to
    $3 \, Cu + 8 \, H^+ + 2 \, NO_3^- = 3 \, Cu^{++} + 2 \, NO\uparrow + 4H_2O$
    How many moles of nitric acid would be needed to
    produce one mole of nitric oxide?
        A. one   B. two   C. three   D. four   E. eight

14. As compared to a one molar aqueous solution of acetic   14.____
    acid, an equal volume of one molar hydrochloric acid
        A. would have a higher pH value
        B. would require a larger volume of 0.1 M sodium
           hydroxide for neutralization
        C. would have a higher hydronium ion molar concentration
        D. would produce a solution with a higher pH value if
           just neutralized with sodium hydroxide
        E. would produce a larger volume of hydrogen (STP) if
           reacted with an active metal such as zinc

15. Two allotropic forms of carbon are diamond and graphite.   15.____
    Diamond is harder than graphite because in diamond
        A. the van der Waal's forces between molecules are
           stronger
        B. the planar covalent bonding between atoms is
           greater
        C. some of the electrons are shared by several atoms
        D. there is tetrahedral covalent bonding
        E. its structure has double bonds which give great
           strength to the crystal

16. Ionization potential data for Group 1 (Alkali) metals   16.____
    indicate that Li holds its electron *most tightly*.
    Oxidation potential data indicate that Li gives off its
    electron *most readily*. Which of these statements, all
    of which are TRUE, would be a plausible explanation of this
    seeming discrepancy?
        A. Less energy is needed for the separation of an electron
           in solution (oxidation potential) than for the
           removal of an electron from an isolated gaseous
           atom (ionization potential).
        B. Ionization potential is an endothermic measurement;
           oxidation potential is an exothermic measurement.
        C. Lithium (solid) is in a polymerized structure, $(Li)_x$
        D. The very small lithium ion has a large heat of hy-
           dration to offset the higher energy required to
           pull off the electron.
        E. Lithium is the BEST reducing agent of the group.

Questions 17 - 23

A section of a common form of the Periodic Table is printed on the next
page with elements indicated by atomic numbers *only*. Use this table
to aid you in answering question 17 through 23.

	IA	IIA	IIIB	IVB	VB	VIB	VIIB	VIIIB			IB	IIB	IIIA	IVA	VA	VIA	VIIA	VIIIA
1																		2
2	3	4											5	6	7	8	9	10
3	11	12											13	14	15	16	17	18
4	19	20	21	22	23	24	25	26	27	28	29	30	31	32	33	34	35	36
5	37	38	39	40	41	42	43	44	45	46	47	48	49	50	51	52	53	54
6	55	56	57-71	72	73	74	75	76	77	78	79	80	81	82	83	84	85	86
7	87	88	89-103															

17. The electronic configuration for element 34 can be indicated by the following "spectroscopic shorthand": (Neon core) $3s^2$, $3p^6$, $3d^{10}$, $4s^2$, $4p^4$.   One could use this information and/or the Periodic Table to predict that

    A. element 34 forms bonds with a high degree of ionic character with element 15
    B. element 34 would form ions in water solution with a charge of -4
    C. element 34 is less "metallic" than element 8
    D. one atom of element 34 would combine chemically with 3 atoms of element 12
    E. element 34 forms compounds in which its "oxidation number" varies from -2 to +6

17.____

18. From periodic table positions <u>alone</u>, one would predict that element

    A. 37 gains electrons more readily than element 3
    B. 9 is a better reducing agent than element 35
    C. 35 is a better oxidizing agent than element 9
    D. 3 loses electrons less readily than element 37
    E. 86 loses electrons most readily of all elements listed

18.____

19. From its position in the periodic table, which of these statements about element 15 would one expect to be TRUE?

    A. Its oxide is a better base (proton acceptor) than the oxide of element 11.
    B. Its MAXIMUM positive oxidation number is less than that of element 11.
    C. Its compounds have lower melting points than the compounds of element 11.
    D. Its compounds have bonds with a high degree of ionic character.
    E. It has a greater tendency to lose electrons than does element 11.

19.____

Questions 20 - 23

DIRECTIONS: Select an answer from the following five atomic
number values for questions 20 - 23. You may
use a value once, more than once, or *not at all.*

A. 88   B. 9   C. 17   D. 4   E. 16

20. This element is naturally radioactive.   20.____

21. This element has two s and four p electrons in its   21.____
outermost energy level.

22. This element has the smallest atomic radius of the   22.____
five elements listed.

23. The ion of this element is a better reducing agent   23.____
than ions of the other four elements listed.

24. The sample of gas which contains the same number of   24.____
molecules as 44 grams of CO_2 gas (C = 12, O = 16, S = 32)
is ____ gram(s) of ____ gas.
   A. 1; hydrogen   B. 16; oxygen   C. 34; H_2S
   D. 44; SO_2 E. 44; SO_3

25. How many milliliters of 6.0 M hydrochloric acid are   25.____
needed to prepare 300 milliliters of 0.30 M solution?
   A. 1.5   B. 15   C. 3.0   D. 30   E. 90

26. A sample of a pure compound was found to contain *only*   26.____
0.250 gram of hydrogen, 1.500 grams of carbon, and
8.875 grams of chlorine.
What is an empirical formula for this compound?
   (H = 1, C = 12, Cl = 35.5)
   A. CH_3Cl B. CH_2Cl C. CH_2Cl_2
   D. $CHCl_3$ E. $C_2H_2Cl_4$

27. Oxygen combined with 6.0 grams of element X to form   27.____
8.0 grams of oxide.
The equivalent weight of element X is
   A. 6.0   B. 2.0   C. 8.0   D. 14   E. 24

28. A current of 0.100 ampere was passed through a copper   28.____
(II) sulfate solution for 2 hours, 40 minutes, and 50
seconds.
The MAXIMUM weight of copper that could have been deposited
is ____ grams.   (Cu = 63.5)
   A. 0.032   B. 0.318   C. 0.635
   D. 31.8   E. 33.6

Questions 29 - 38

Use the reading passage on the following page to aid you in
answering questions 29 - 38 if you think the discussion will
be helpful. To save time, answer the questions directly if you
can.

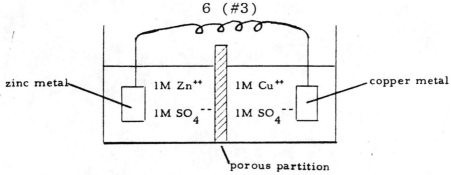

zinc metal · · · · copper metal · · · porous partition

The above galvanic cell operates on the principle that two
separated half-reactions can be made to take place simultaneously
with electron transfer occurring through a wire. In the galvanic
cell above, the following reaction takes place:

$$Zn\ (s) + Cu^{++} \rightleftarrows Zn^{++} + Cu\ (s)$$

A porous partition separates the container into two compartments
but still permits diffusion of ions between them. A voltmeter
connected between two dissimilar elements in a galvanic cell
shows a characteristic voltage which depends in magnitude
upon the nature of the dissimilar elements and upon the concentration of the corresponding metallic ions in the solutions
in which the metal is placed. This characteristic voltage
is an indication of the relative tendencies of elements to
ionize in solution. This voltage also measures the work
required to move electrons around the circuit and is, therefore,
an indication of the tendency for a chemical reaction to take
place.

The voltage observed in all galvanic cells arises from a voltage
at the anode and from a voltage at the cathode. It is impossible
to measure the voltage of a single electrode since any circuit
must contain two electrodes. It is necessary, therefore, to
assign an arbitrary value to one electrode and compare the
voltage at the other electrode to this standard. The standard
hydrogen electrode (H_2 at 1 atmosphere pressure and 1 M H_3O^+
concentration) is arbitrarily chosen as a standard and its value
fixed at zero. As a result, in any cell which contains the
hydrogen electrode, the entire measured voltage is attributed
to the half-reaction at the other electrode. Such assigned
voltages for metals bathed in their respective solutions at
1 molar concentrations are called oxidation potentials.

The abbreviated table shown on the following page lists the
voltages when the half-reaction proceeds from left to right
and the concentrations are standard. As the reaction proceeds,
the voltage will drop.

Half Reaction	Potential Volts	Half Reaction	Potential Volts
Li (s) = Li$^+$ + e$^-$	+3.05	Cu (s) = Cu^{++} + 2e$^-$	-0.34
Na (s) = Na$^+$ + e$^-$	+2.71	2I$^-$ = I$_2$ + 2e$^-$	-0.54
Mg (s) = Mg^{++} + 2e$^-$	+2.37	Ag (s) = Ag$^+$ + e$^-$	-0.80
Al (s) = Al^{+++} + 3e$^-$	+1.66	Hg (l) = Hg^{++} + 2e$^-$	-0.85
Zn (s) = Zn^{++} + 2e-	+0.76	2Br- = Br$_2$ + 2e$^-$	-1.09
Fe (s) = Fe^{++} + 2e$^-$	+0.44	2H$_2$O = O$_2$ (g) + 4H$^+$ + 4e$^-$	-1.23
Pb (s) = Pb^{++} + 2e$^-$	+0.126	2Cl- = Cl$_2$ (g) + 2e$^-$	-1.36
H$_2$ (g) = 2H$^+$ + 2e$^-$	0	4H$_2$O+Mn^{++} =MnO$_4^-$ + 8H$^+$ +5e$^-$	-1.51
		2F$^-$ = F$_2$ (g) + 2e$^-$	-2.87

Use the following key to answer questions 29 - 33 concerning the galvanic cell indicated by the diagram on page 6. You may use an answer once, more than once, or ~~not at all~~.

    A. Copper (II) ions
    B. Zinc ions
    C. Zinc metal
    D. Copper metal
    E. Sulfate ions

29. What is the BEST reducing agent of the chemical species listed? 29.___

30. What is the chemical species that is reduced as the cell operates? 30.___

31. What is the electrode of the cell at which reduction takes place as the cell operates? 31.___

32. What chemical species moves toward the zinc electrode as the cell operates? 32.___

33. What is the source of electrons that flow through the connecting wire? 33.___

Refer to the abbreviated Standard Electrode Potential Table to answer questions 34 - 38.

34. Which is the STRONGEST oxidizing agent in the series listed? 34.___
    A. Li   B. Na$^+$ C. H$^+$ D. Cl$^-$ E. F$_2$

35. Which element or ion will oxidize Zn to Zn^{++}, but
will not oxidize Cu to Cu^{++} ion?
    A. Fe   B. H^+ C. F_2 D. Hg^{++} E. Mg^{++}

35.____

36. Which element will NOT dissolve in dilute hydrochloric acid?
    A. Aluminum   B. Copper   C. Magnesium
    D. Sodium   E. Zinc

36.____

37. Galvanic action is *probably* responsible for the
corrosion of metals.
You would expect the LEAST amount of oxidation of iron
to take place with iron metal
    A. immersed in a slightly acid solution
    B. immersed in a bromide solution
    C. in contact with zinc metal and both immersed in
       water
    D. in contact with copper metal and both immersed in
       a slightly acid solution
    E. in a slightly acid solution of copper ions

37.____

38. When all conditions are *standard*, the voltage value
for the zinc-copper galvanic cell diagrammed on page
10 is
    A. 0.34   B. 0.42   C. 0.76   D. 0.88   E. 1.10

38.____

39. A bell jar is placed over a beaker of water (A) and a
beaker of one molal sugar solution (B). When equilibrium
is reached, there will be
    A. equal numbers of sugar and water molecules in each
       beaker
    B. a decrease in the number of molecules of sugar in
       B
    C. a decrease in the volume of liquid in beaker B
    D. *no* change in either A or B
    E. an increase in the number of molecules of water in
       B

39.____

40. What volume of HCl aqueous solution having a specific
gravity of 1.19 and containing 37.2% HCl by weight would
be needed to prepare 6.00×10^2 milliliters of
6.00×10^{-2} M HCL? (H = 1; Cl = 35.5)
    A. 2.97 liters   B. 2.97 milliliters
    C. 29.7 milliliters   D. 0.297 milliliters
    E. NONE of the above is correct

40.____

41. Which of these statements explains why hydrogen chloride
remains a nonconductor when dissolved in a solvent such
as toluene?
    A. Toluene is nonpolar
    B. Hydrogen chloride is nonpolar
    C. Hydrogen chloride will not release protons in
       toluene
    D. Toluene is a molecular compound
    E. None of the above

41.____

42. At 25°C the solubility product constant for AgCl is approximately 1.0 x 10-10. The solubility of AgCl in water at 25°C in moles per liter is *approximately*
   A. 1.0 x 10-10   B. 1.0 x 10-5
   C. 1.4 x 10-3   D. 1.0 x 10-20
   E. 1.1 x 10-3

42.___

43. To determine the extent of solubility of an unknown salt in water, 25 grams of a solution of the unknown salt was evaporated and gave 5.0 grams of dry salt. From this information <u>alone</u> one would conclude that the solubility of the salt is ____ per 100 grams of water.
   A. 5.0 grams   B. 20 grams
   C. 25 grams   D. more than 25 grams
   E. could not be determined from the information given

43.___

44. At any given temperature and pressure the relative diffusion rates of CH_4 and SO_2 are
   (H = 1, C = 12, O = 16, S = 32)
   A. 1 to 2   B. 2 to 1   C. 2 to 3
   D. 1 to 4   E. 4 to 1

44.___

45. A water solution is 0.50 molar with respect to sodium acetate and is 0.20 molar with respect to acetic acid. What is the pH value for this solution?
   (Ionization constant for acetic acid,
   HAc, is 1.8 x 10-5
   Log_{10} of 7 = approximately 0.85
   Log_{10} of 9 = approximately 0.95
   Log_{10} of 18 = approximately 0.25)
   A. 8.8   B. 4.2   C. 6.1   D. 4.7   E. 5.1

45.___

KEY (CORRECT ANSWERS)

1. C	11. B	21. E	31. D	41. C
2. D	12. A	22. B	32. E	42. B
3. D	13. D	23. E	33. C	43. E
4. E	14. C	24. C	34. E	44. B
5. D	15. D	25. B	35. B	45. E
6. C	16. D	26. C	36. B	
7. C	17. E	27. E	37. C	
8. B	18. D	28. B	38. E	
9. D	19. C	29. C	39. E	
10. D	20. A	30. A	40. B	

EXAMINATION SECTION
TEST 1

DIRECTIONS: Each question or incomplete statement is followed by several suggested answers or completions. Select the one that *BEST* answers the question or completes the statement. *PRINT THE LETTER OF THE CORRECT ANSWER IN THE SPACE AT THE RIGHT.*

1. Boyle's and Charles' Laws are readily explained in terms of the
    A. theory of generalized relativity
    B. kinetic - molecular theory
    C. DeBroglie wave theory
    D. Le Chatelier's principle

    1. ___

2. "The properties of the elements are periodic functions of their atomic numbers" is a statement attributed to
    A. Mendeleef   B. Dobereiner
    C. Meyer   D. Moseley

    2. ___

3. The development of the ultramicroscope makes use of the
    A. Edison effect   B. Tyndall effect
    C. Stark effect   D. Raman effect

    3. ___

4. The irregular zigzag movement of extremely minute particles when suspended in a liquid or gas was *FIRST* observed by
    A. Tyndall   B. Dalton   C. Brown   D. Graham

    4. ___

5. The Nelson, Vorce, and Hooker cells are used in the production of which one of the following?
    A. Oxygen   B. Aluminum   C. Chlorine   D. Manganese

    5. ___

6. Nitrogen may be prepared in the laboratory by heating which one of the following?
    A. Ammonium nitrate   B. Ammonium nitrite
    C. Ammonium nitride   D. Ammonium carbonate

    6. ___

7. When titrating a weak base with a strong acid, the *MOST SUITABLE* of the following indicators to use is
    A. phenolphthalein   B. methyl orange
    C. brom thymol blue   D. litmus

    7. ___

8. A compound possessing no dipole moment is which one of the following?
    A. Water   B. Carbon tetrachloride
    C. Hydrogen chloride   D. Carbon monoxide

    8. ___

9. The direct chemical reaction between dry HCl and SO_3 produces which one of the following?
    A. Monatomic chlorine   B. Sulfuric acid
    C. Sulfuryl chloride   D. Chlorosulfonic acid

    9. ___

10. The strength of a solution containing 49 grams of sulfuric   10. ___
    acid (at. wgts: H-1; S-32; 0-16) dissolved in a liter of
    solution is one
       A. molar   B. normal   C. molal   D. formal

11. A green flame formed over a boiling alcoholic solution may   11. ___
    indicate the presence in the solution of which one of the
    following?
       A. Boron   B. Lithium   C. Strontium   D. Tungsten

12. Realgar and orpiment are important native compounds of   12. ___
       A. bismuth   B. mercury   C. arsenic   D. manganese

13. The Lewis concept of acids and bases postulates the accept-   13. ___
    ance or donation of a/n
       A. proton   B. pair of electrons
       C. hydroxyl ion   D. amphiprotic particle

14. A few drops of chlorine water are added to a mixture of   14. ___
    solutions of sodium iodide and sodium fluoride and the
    whole is shaken with carbon disulfide. The new mixture,
    upon standing, will appear
       A. colored light green   B. colored orange
       C. colored violet   D. colorless

15. Of the following, the gas having a diffusion rate three   15. ___
    times as rapid as that of steam is (at. wgts: C - 12; H - 1;
    0 - 16; He - 4):
       A. helium   B. hydrogen
       C. carbon dioxide   D. methane

16. The parent substance in the family of sulfa drugs used in   16. ___
    chemotherapy is
       A. sulfanilamide   B. sulfapyridine
       C. sulfathiazole   D. sulfadiazine

17. Glucose and fructose differ structurally in that glucose   17. ___
    is a/n
       A. aldehyde and fructose is an ether
       B. ketone and fructose is an aldehyde
       C. aldehyde and fructose is a ketone
       D. ketone and fructose is an ether

18. Calcium hydrogen sulfite is an important reagent used in   18. ___
    the manufacture of which one of the following?
       A. Rayon   B. Paper
       C. Pyroxlin   D. Orlon

19. Al(OH)$_3$ is used commercially in the dyeing industry as a   19. ___
       A. mordant   B. lake   C. water purifier   D. dye

20. Galena is an ore of   20. ___
       A. aluminum   B. lead   C. mercury   D. tin

21. Molecules of nitrogen tetroxide, N_2O_4, are
    A. yellow   B. brown   C. green   D. colorless

21. ___

22. A water solution of H_2S is called
    A. sulfurous acid   B. hydrosulfurous acid
    C. sulfuric acid   D. hydrosulfuric acid

22. ___

23. The iodine number of an organic compound is a measure of its degree of
    A. solubility   B. stability
    C. unsaturation   D. volatility

23. ___

24. In the production of blister copper, the *LAST* traces of copper oxide are removed by stirring the molten copper with
    A. vanadium   B. stainless steel
    C. graphite   D. green wood poles

24. ___

25. Methyl alcohol and air passing through a heated tube containing a mixture of iron powder and molybdenum oxide, forms
    A. carbon monoxide   B. ethanol
    C. carbon dioxide   D. formaldehyde

25. ___

26. Which one of the following statements about transition elements is true?
    A. They have complete shells.
    B. They generally contain incomplete 3rd, 4th, 5th or 6th inner shells.
    C. They all contain incomplete 3rd shells.
    D. They are all non-metals.

26. ___

27. In the pure liquid state, which one of the following will be a good conductor of electrical current?
    A. Glacial acetic acid   B. Sulfuric acid
    C. Hydrogen chloride   D. Potassium nitrate

27. ___

28. When we divide 6.3 by the specific heat of a substance, we get its approximate
    A. atomic weight   B. molecular weight
    C. density   D. specific gravity

28. ___

29. Zinc is used to separate gold and silver from copper and lead in the
    A. Parkes process   B. Goldschmidt process
    C. Mond process   D. Duplex process

29. ___

30. When an excess of CO_2 is passed through limewater, the white precipitate *FIRST* formed goes into solution as
    A. calcium carbonate   B. calcium bicarbonate
    C. sodium carbonate   D. calcium oxalate

30. ___

31. Helium gas will diffuse
    A. four times as rapidly as SO_2 gas

31. ___

B. at one-half the rate of H_2 gas

C. eleven times as rapidly as CO_2 gas

D. at one-seventh the rate of N_2 gas

32. The uncancelled spin of an unpaired electron in the atom of silver explains its
    A. paramagnetism   B. ferromagnetism
    C. diamagnetism   D. electrical conductivity

32. ____

33. Diffusion occurs *MOST RAPIDLY* in which one of the following?
    A. Solids   B. Liquids
    C. Gases   D. Gels

33. ____

34. In the structural formula for C_6H_6, which one of the following is true?
    A. Carbon is considered to be tetravalent.
    B. Carbon is considered to be monovalent.
    C. There are triple bonds.
    D. The compound is shown to be a saturated hydrocarbon.

34. ____

35. The members of the copper sub-group
    A. tend to be very active
    B. increase in ability with an increase in atomic radius
    C. occur chemically uncombined in nature
    D. have low electrical conductivity

35. ____

36. Which one of the following statements about an ion exchanger is true?
    A. It has an unlimited ability to exchange Na^+ ions for Ca^{++} ions.
    B. It is usually a very small molecule.
    C. It is negatively charged.
    D. It is commonly used as a water softener.

36. ____

37. A magnet will cause the *GREATEST* deflection of a beam of
    A. gamma rays   B. neutrons
    C. electrons   D. alpha particles

37. ____

38. When acid is added to milk, a curd is formed because
    A. the hydronium ion coagulates the negatively charged particles
    B. milk is a supersaturated solution
    C. calcium phosphate precipitates
    D. the fat in the milk is homogenized

38. ____

39. At the boiling point of a liquid, its vapor pressure is
    A. greater than the prevailing atmospheric pressure

39. ____

B. equal to the prevailing atmospheric pressure
C. lower than the prevailing atmospheric pressure
D. unrelated to the prevailing atmospheric pressure

40. Two metals whose melting points are below 30° Centigrade are 40. ___
    A. sodium and potassium   B. cesium and gallium
    C. calcium and magnesium   D. indium and thallium

41. In which one of the following groups are there three mem-   41. ___
    bers of the alkaline-earth family of metals?
    A. Aluminum, strontium, titanium
    B. Lithium, sodium, potassium
    C. Magnesium, barium, calcium
    D. Rubidium, cesium, francium

42. The function of ethylene dibromide, $C_2H_4Br_2$, in "ethyl"   42. ___
    gasoline is to
    A. improve the anti-knock qualities
    B. lower the flash point
    C. help remove the lead as $PbBr_2$
    D. increase the volatility

43. Lithopone, a pigment in white paint, is a mixture of   43. ___
    A. barium sulfide and zinc sulfate
    B. lead carbonate and lead hydroxide
    C. barium sulfate and zinc sulfide
    D. lead oxide and lead sulfate

44. Of the following pairs, the one containing examples of   44. ___
    metalloid elements in the Periodic Table is
    A. sodium and potassium   B. fluorine and chlorine
    C. calcium and magnesium   D. boron and silicon

45. A compound that produces a green residue in the cobalt ni-   45. ___
    trate test, and, with $FeSO_4$ and concentrated H_2SO_4, produces
    a brown ring is, *PROBABLY*,
    A. aluminum sulfate   B. zinc nitrate
    C. copper (II) carbonate   D. barium chloride

46. Tin is one of the constituents used in the alloy known as   46. ___
    A. type metal   B. sterling silver
    C. brass   D. stainless steel

47. The weak intermolecular forces of attraction that are caused 47. ___
    by temporary dipoles are called
    A. ionic forces   B. ligancy forces
    C. van der Waals' forces   D. coordination forces

48. Nylon is a copolymer of   48. ___
    A. urea and formaldehyde
    B. phenol and formaldehyde
    C. hexamethylenediamine and adipic acid
    D. vinyl chloride and vinyl alcohol

49. According to the orientation rules in organic chemistry,   49. ___
ortho-para directing groups are generally
   A. positive atoms or groups
   B. unsaturated groups
   C. negative atoms or groups
   D. groups which decrease the electron density around the
     m position

50. Nitrous oxide, commonly known as laughing gas, is generally 50. ___
prepared by the
   A. heating and decomposition of ammonium nitrate
   B. action of dilute nitric acid on copper
   C. heating and decomposition of ammonium nitrite
   D. action of concentrated nitric acid on copper

KEY (CORRECT ANSWERS)

1. B	11. A	21. D	31. A	41. C
2. D	12. C	22. D	32. A	42. C
3. B	13. B	23. C	33. C	43. C
4. C	14. C	24. D	34. A	44. D
5. C	15. B	25. D	35. C	45. B
6. B	16. A	26. B	36. D	46. A
7. B	17. C	27. D	37. C	47. C
8. B	18. B	28. A	38. A	48. C
9. D	19. B	29. A	39. B	49. C
10. B	20. B	30. B	40. B	50. A

TEST 2

DIRECTIONS: Each question or incomplete statement is followed by several suggested answers or completions. Select the one that *BEST* answers the question or completes the statement. *PRINT THE LETTER OF THE CORRECT ANSWER IN THE SPACE AT THE RIGHT.*

1. A temperature of absolute zero Kelvin is, of the following, 1. ____
   CLOSEST to
   A. -459°C   B. -273°C   C. -241°F   D. 0°C

2. Naphthalene, $C_{10}H_8$, is *MOST SOLUBLE* in which of the follow- 2. ____
   ing solvents?
   A. Water   B. Alcohol
   C. Benzene   D. Acetic Acid

3. The number of molecules of water needed to convert one   3. ____
   molecule of P_2O_5 into orthophosphoric acid is
   A. 1   B. 2   C. 3   D. 4

4. The *MOST PROBABLE* valence of an element with an electronic   4. ____
   distribution of $1s^2\ 2s^2\ 2p^6\ 3s^2\ 3p^1$, is
   A. +1   B. +2   C. +3   D. -1

5. $_{20}Ca^{40}$ and $_{18}A^{40}$ are examples of   5. ____

   A. isotopes   B. isomers   C. isobars   D. lanthanides

6. Heavy water made from $_1H^3$ and $_8O^{18}$ has a molecular weight 6. ____
   of
   A. 18   B. 20   C. 22   D. 24

7. Atoms have radii *CLOSEST* in size to which one of the fol-   7. ____
   lowing?
   A. 1×10^{-4} mm   B. 1×10^{-8} cm

   C. 1×10^{-12} cm   D. 1×10^{-8} Angstrom units

8. Considering energy levels, the *MOST PROBABLE* electronic con- 8. ____
   figuration for element No. 28 would be which one of the following?
   A. 2, 8, 18   B. 2, 8, 10, 8
   C. 2, 8, 8, 8, 2   D. 2, 8, 16, 2

9. If 50.0 ml of 0.10 molar NaCl, 20.0 ml. of 0.30 molar
   $CaCl_2$, and 30.0 ml. of 0.20 molar $Ca(NO_3)_2$ are mixed, the
   resulting concentration of Ca^{++} ions is

   A. one-half that of Cl^- ions   B. 0.12 M
   C. 0.25M   D. 1.00M

9. ___

10. A 0.0100 molal solution of the compound AB in water has a
    freezing point of -0.0193°C. The percentage of the AB
    molecules which have been dissociated by the water is
    A. 0.01%   B. 0.4%   C. 1.0%   D. 4.0%

10. ___

11. In order to convert 50.0 ml. of 3.50 molar H_2SO_4 into 2.00
    molar H_2SO_4, the volume of water which must be added is

    A. 1.75 ml.   B. 37.50 ml.   C. 87.50 ml.   D. 1,700 ml.

11. ___

12. The volume of 0.25 molar H_3PO_4 necessary to neutralize
    25 ml. of 0.30 molar $Ca(OH)_2$ is

    A. 8.3 ml.   B. 20 ml.   C. 50 ml.   D. 75 ml.

12. ___

13. If 10 ml. of 0.1 molar NaOH are added to 10 ml. of 0.1
    molar HCl, the pH of the resulting mixture will be

    A. 0   B. 3   C. 7   D. 12

13. ___

14. An element X is found to combine with oxygen to form a com-
    pound with the molecular formula X_4O_6. If 8.40 g. of the
    element X combine with 6.50 g. of oxygen, the atomic weight
    of the element is
    A. 24.0 a.m.u.   B. 33.6 a.m.u.
    C. 50.4 a.m.u.   D. 118.7 a.m.u.

14. ___

15. A solution containing 90 grams of a carbohydrate dissolved
    in 1,000 grams of water has a boiling point of 100.26°
    Centigrade. If the boiling point constant is 0.52°, the
    molecular weight of the carbohydrate is
    A. 90   B. 180   C. 342   D. 360

15. ___

16. A metallic element has a specific heat of 0.097 cal./gm.
    Its atomic weight is *CLOSEST* to which one of the following?
    A. 27   B. 40   C. 56   D. 64

16. ___

17. How many pounds of iron can be extracted from one ton of
    Fe_2O_3 (atomic weights: Fe = 56; O = 16)?

    A. 140   B. 560   C. 700   D. 1,400

17. ___

18. The density of sulfur dioxide, SO_2, in grams per liter, is   18. ___

    A. 0.77   B. 1.25   C. 1.98   D. 2.93

19. The pOH of a solution having a hydrogen ion concentration   19. ___
    of 1×10^{-5} gram ions per liter is

    A. 2   B. 5   C. 7   D. 9

20. It has been experimentally determined that, in a molecule   20. ___
    of water, the bond angle between the two hydrogen atoms
    which are attached to a single oxygen atom, is *CLOSEST* to
    which one of the following?
    A. 45 degrees   B. 90 degrees
    C. 105 degrees   D. 180 degrees

21. Of the following groups of elements, the one which consists   21. ___
    ENTIRELY of transuranium elements is
    A. U, Pa, Pu   B. Am, Cm, Cf
    C. Fm, No, Po   D. Es, Md, Tl

22. If one mole of "X" replaces two moles of "Y", and four moles   22. ___
    of "Y" unite with one mole of oxygen, the equivalent weight
    of element "Y" is
    A. 0.50 gram mole of "X"
    B. 0.75 gram mole of "X"
    C. 1.00 gram mole of "X"
    D. 1.50 gram mole of "X"

23. When 100 grams of ice at 0°C melt, the process requires   23. ___
    which one of the following?
    A. Evolution of 80 calories
    B. Absorption of 800 calories
    C. Evolution of 5,600 calories
    D. Absorption of 8,000 calories

24. The *MAXIMUM* number of cubic structures which crystalline   24. ___
    solids may assume is
    A. 1   B. 2   C. 3   D. 4

25. The mol fraction of methanol in a water solution containing   25. ___
    80% methanol (At. Wgts: C-12; H-1; O-16) is, of the follow-
    ing, *CLOSEST* to
    A. 0.3   B. 0.5   C. 0.7   D. 0.9

26. The pH of a 1×10^{-4}M potassium hydroxide solution is   26. ___

    A. 10^{-4} B. 4   C. 10   D. 4×10^{-4}

27. The number of electron orbitals in an "f" subshell is   27. ___
    A. 1   B. 2   C. 5   D. 7

28. Approximately how many grams of copper will be deposited   28. ___
    from a solution of $CuSO_4$ by 0.5 faraday of electricity
    (At. Wgts: Cu - 64; S - 32; O - 16)?

    A. 16   B. 32   C. 48   D. 64

29. The number of elements in each of the "long" periods in the   29. ___
    Periodic Table is
    A. 2   B. 8   C. 18   D. 32

30. If the solubility product of $BaSO_4$ is 1.5×10^{-9}, its solu-   30. ___

    bility in water is

    A. 1.5×10^{-9} moles per liter

    B. 3.9×10^{-5} moles per liter

    C. 7.5×10^{-5} moles per liter

    D. less than in dilute sulfuric acid

31. If the dissociation constant of NH_4OH is 1.8×10^{-5}, the   31. ___

    concentration of OH^- ions, in moles per liter, of a 0.1

    molar NH_4OH solution, is

    A. 1.80×10^{-6} B. 1.34×10^{-3}

    C. 4.20×10^{-3} D. 5.00×10^{-2}

32. Using a calorimeter containing 3,000 g. of water, a chemist   32. ___
    noted that the temperature changes from 20.123°C to
    20.316°C when 0.1 mole of $BaSO_4$ is formed from Ba^{++} ions

    and $SO_4^=$ ions by precipitation. The amount of heat given
    off when 1 mole of $BaSO_4$ is formed from its ions is

    A. 0.643 kcal   B. 1.00 kcal
    C. 1.93 kcal   D. 5.79 kcal

33. In the dichromate ion, chromium has an oxidation state of   33. ___
    A. -2   B. 0   C. +3   D. +6

34. Chemical analysis of a gas shows that it contains one atom   34. ___
    of carbon for each two atoms of hydrogen. If its density is
    1.25 g. per liter at standard temperature and pressure, its
    formula is
    A. CH_2 B. C_2H_4 C. $C_{10}H_5$ D. C_3H_6

35. The process, $_1H^2 + _1H^3 \rightarrow _2He^4 + _0n^1$, represents the type of   35. ___
    reaction known as
    A. fission   B. chemical   C. autocatalytic   D. fusion

36. A correct expression for the conversion of mass into energy   36. ___
    is which one of the following?
    A. $E = mc$ B. $m = c^2/E$

    C. $c = \sqrt{E/m}$ D. $E = m/c^2$

37. Of the following, the compound possessing optical isomerism   37. ___
    is
    A. $CH_3 \cdot CH_2OH$

    B. $CH_2OH \cdot CHOH \cdot CH_2OH$

    C. CCl_2F_2

    D. $CH_3 \cdot CHOH \cdot C_2H_5$

38. In the properly balanced equation for the reaction,   38. ___

    $$KClO_3 \rightarrow KCl + O_2,$$

    the integer which should be placed before the O_2 is

    A. 1   B. 2   C. 3   D. 4

39. Which one of the following is an illustration of a revers-   39. ___
    ible reaction?
    A. $Pb(NO_3)_2 + 2NaI \rightarrow PbI_2 + 2NaNO_3$

    B. $AgNO_3 + NaCl \rightarrow AgCl + NaNO_3$

    C. $2Na + 2HOH \rightarrow 2NaOH + H_2$

    D. $KNO_3 + NaCl \rightarrow KCl + NaNO_3$

40. Of the following, the gas which is less dense than air and   40. ___
    very soluble in water is:
    A. HCl B. NH_3 C. N_2 D. CO

41. Aqua regia is a mixture of   41. ___
    A. HNO_3 and H_2SO_4
    B. HCl and HNO_3
    C. H_2SO_4 and HCl
    D. $H \cdot COOH$ and $CH_3 \cdot COOH$

42. The heaviest of the following particles is

    A. S^{-2} B. S^0 C. S^{+4} D. S^{+6}

42. ____

43. Iodic acid has the formula,

    A. HIO B. HIO_2 C. HIO_3 D. HIO_4

43. ____

44. Of the following pairs, the one containing two compounds which illustrate the Law of Multiple Proportions, is

    A. $FeCl_2$ and $FeCl_3$

    B. Na_2SO_4 and $NaHSO_4$

    C. O_2 and O_3

    D. KNO_3 and $NaNO_3$

44. ____

45. When lead nitrate is heated, the products formed are indicated in which one of the following choices?

    A. Pb, N_2, O_2 B. Pb, N_2O, O_2

    C. PbO, NO, O_2 D. PbO, NO_2, O_2

45. ____

46. During the charging of a lead storage battery, the reaction occurring at the cathode is represented by

    A. $Pb^{++} + 2e \rightarrow Pb$

    B. $Pb^{++} + SO_4^{--} \rightarrow PbSO_4$

    C. $Pb \rightarrow Pb^{++} + 2e$

    D. $PbSO_4 + 2H_2O \rightarrow PbO_2 + 4H^+ + SO_4^{--} + 2e$

46. ____

47. The correct formula for plaster of Paris is

    A. $Ca_3(PO_4)_2$ B. $CaSO_4 \cdot 2H_2O$

    C. $Ca(OH)_2 \cdot CaSO_4$ D. $(CaSO_4)_2 \cdot H_2O$

47. ____

48. When copper roofing weathers, it becomes coated with a green film of

    A. $Cu_2(OH)_2CO_3$ B. $CuCO_3 \cdot CuO$

    C. $Cu(OH)_2 \cdot CuOH$ D. Cu_2S

48. ____

49. The correct formula for hydroxylamine is

    A. NH_2OH B. NH_4OH

    C. $HONH \cdot NHOH$ D. $HONHNH_2$

49. ____

50. Which one of the following is detected by the addition of   50. ___
    both bromine water and barium chloride in the presence of
    hydrochloric acid?

    A. $S^=$ B. $SO_3^=$ C. $SO_4^=$ D. $S_2O_8^=$

KEY (CORRECT ANSWERS)

1. B	11. B	21. B	31. B	41. B
2. C	12. B	22. A	32. D	42. A
3. C	13. C	23. D	33. D	43. C
4. C	14. D	24. C	34. B	44. A
5. C	15. B	25. C	35. D	45. D
6. D	16. D	26. C	36. C	46. A
7. B	17. D	27. D	37. D	47. D
8. D	18. D	28. A	38. C	48. A
9. B	19. D	29. C	39. D	49. A
10. D	20. C	30. B	40. B	50. B

TEST 3

DIRECTIONS: Each question or incomplete statement is followed by several suggested answers or completions. Select the one that *BEST* answers the question or completes the statement. *PRINT THE LETTER OF THE CORRECT ANSWER IN THE SPACE AT THE RIGHT.*

1. Of the following, the compound that obeys the "octet" rule is
    A. CO_2 B. BCl_3 C. PCl_5 D. OsF_8
    1. ___

2. Of the following, the mixture which is the *POOREST* conductor of an electric current is one containing equal volumes of
    A. 0.1 M $CaCl_2$ and 0.1 M glucose

    B. 0.1 M NH_4OH and 0.1 M sucrose

    C. 0.1 M $HC_2H_3O_2$ and 0.1 M $CuSO_4$

    D. 0.1 M H_2SO_4 and 0.1 M $Ba(OH)_2$
    2. ___

3. In qualitative analysis, the group III precipitates which can be formed are in which one of the following groups?
    A. PbS, CuS, HgS

    B. Hg_2Cl_2, AgCl, $PbCl_2$

    C. CoS, NiS, FeS

    D. $BaCO_3$, $SrCO_3$, $CaCO_3$
    3. ___

4. Fehling's solution and Benedict's solution are reduced by glucose to form
    A. CuO   B. Cu_2O C. $Cu(OH)_2$ D. $Cu(CO)_4$
    4. ___

5. According to the Brönsted-Lowry theory of acids and bases, when H_2O acts as a base, its conjugate acid is
    A. H^+ B. OH^- C. H_3O^+ D. OH^+
    5. ___

6. The chemical formula for borax is
    A. B_2O_3 B. B_4C C. H_3BO_3 D. $Na_2B_4O_7$
    6. ___

7. The general formula for the benzene series of hydrocarbons is
    A. C_nH_n B. C_nH_{2n+2} C. C_nH_{2n-2} D. C_nH_{2n-6}
    7. ___

8. When $CaCN_2$ reacts with steam or hot water, the nitrogen compound formed is   8. ___
   A. N_2O B. NO   C. NO_2 D. NH_3

9. A reagent used to test for the Fe^{++} ion is   9. ___
   A. NH_4CNS B. $K_3Fe(CN)_6$ C. $K_4Fe(CN)_6$ D. H_2SO_4

10. Elemental phosphorus is obtained commercially by heating a   10. ___
    mixture of
    A. P_2O_3 and C

    B. P_2S_3, O_2 and C

    C. $Ca_3(PO_4)_2$ and H_2SO_4

    D. $Ca_3(PO_4)_2$, SiO_2 and C

11. Hydrazine, which is being used as a rocket fuel, has the   11. ___
    chemical formula
    A. $H_2N \cdot NH_2$ B. $H_2N \cdot NOH$

    C. $C_6H_5HN \cdot NH_2$ D. $CH_3 \cdot NH_2$

12. The raw materials used in the Solvay Process are   12. ___
    A. NaCl, NH_3 and H_2O

    B. NH_3, CO_2 and H_2O

    C. NaCl, NH_3 and CO_2

    D. NH_3, CO_2, NaCl and H_2O

13. In the nuclear reaction,   13. ___

$$_{13}Al^{27} + {}_1H^2 \rightarrow {}_{12}Mg^{25} + Z,$$

    the symbol "Z" represents which one of the following?

    A. 4 $_1H^1$ B. 2 $_1H^2$

    C. $_2He^4$ D. $_1H^3 + {}_1H^1$

14. A compound contains 26.6% K, 35.4% Cr, and 38.0% O. Its   14. ___
    SIMPLEST formula is
    A. $KCrO_3$ B. K_2CrO_4 C. $KCrO_7$ D. $K_2Cr_2O_7$

15. An example of a resonance hybrid, among the following, is   15. ____
    A. CO_2 B. SO_2 C. H_2O_2 D. NH_3

16. An example of a polar covalent bond is found in which one   16. ____
    of the following?
    A. H_2O B. CCl_4 C. O_2 D. CO_2

17. The one of the following equations which is representative   17. ____
    of neutralization is

    A. $CaCl_2 \rightarrow Ca^{++} + 2Cl^-$

    B. $H_3O^+ + Cl^- \rightarrow HCl_{(g)} + H_2O_{(1)}$ | (1) = liquid
                                                                  | (g) = gas

    C. $2Ag^+ + 2NO_3^- + Zn^0 \rightarrow 2Ag^0 + Zn^{++} + 2NO_3$

    D. $H_3O^+ + OH^- \rightarrow 2H_2O_{(1)}$

18. Accepting the definition that an acid is a proton donor,   18. ____
    the acid in the following reaction,

    $NH_3 + H_2O \rightarrow NH_4^+ + OH^-$, is

    A. NH_3 B. H_2O C. NH_4^+ D. OH^-

19. A gas used in the synthesis of methyl alcohol is   19. ____
    A. CH_4 B. CO_2 C. H_2 D. O_2

20. The substance, among the following, with the highest vapor   20. ____
    pressure is
    A. solid $Na_2SO_4 \cdot 10H_2O$

    B. liquid CS_2

    C. liquid H_2SO_4

    D. solid I_2

21. Which one of the following statements about $AgNO_3$ is true?   21. ____
    A. $AgNO_3$ has a negative heat of solution.

    B. The precipitation of $AgNO_3$ is endothermic.

    C. The hydration energy of $AgNO_3$ is negative.

    D. The hydration energy of $AgNO_3$ exceeds its lattice energy.

22. In the balanced reaction for
    $Zn + HNO_3 \rightarrow Zn(NO_3)_2 + NH_4NO_3 + H_2O$,

    the coefficient before the symbol for nitric acid is
    A. 3   B. 5   C. 10   D. 15

    22. ___

23. Magnesia mixture is added to an acidic solution of an un-
    known substance, and, thereafter, a white, crystalline pre-
    cipitate forms. The unknown substance *MOST LIKELY* contained

    A. SO_4^{--} B. CO_3^{--} C. PO_4^{---} D. HCO_3^{-}

    23. ___

24. Slaked lime is added to soil *CHIEFLY* to
    A. supply needed nitrogen
    B. adjust the soil's acidity
    C. precipitate carbonate compounds
    D. make the soil porous

    24. ___

25. Taconite is an ore used to obtain
    A. aluminum   B. titanium   C. tantalum   D. iron

    25. ___

26. In the electrolytic extraction of aluminum from its oxide,
    the purified ore is dissolved in
    A. bauxite   B. alcohol
    C. de-ionized water   D. cryolite

    26. ___

27. Of the following pairs of elements, the one containing two
    metals *MOST CLOSELY* related in chemical activity is
    A. aluminum and lead
    B. tin and gold
    C. iron and platinum
    D. calcium and magnesium

    27. ___

28. An atom containing 9 electrons, 10 neutrons, and 9 protons
    has a mass number of
    A. 9   B. 18   C. 19   D. 28

    28. ___

29. The neutrons in an atom
    A. equal the total number of electrons and protons
    B. revolve about the nucleus in elliptical orbits
    C. contribute to the nuclear charge
    D. vary in number with different isotopes

    29. ___

30. In the formula $Al_2(NO_3)_3$, the total number of atoms repre-
    sented is
    A. 5   B. 11   C. 14   D. 18

    30. ___

31. When concentrated sulfuric acid acts on carbohydrates, the
    process is termed
    A. esterification   B. neutralization
    C. hydrolysis   D. dehydration

    31. ___

32. Coke is used in metallurgical processes *CHIEFLY* as a
    32. ___
    - A. flux
    - B. diluent
    - C. reducing agent
    - D. co-precipitant

33. The destructive distillation of bituminous coal is a commercial source of which one of the following?
    33. ___
    - A. Ammonia
    - B. Nitric acid
    - C. Nitric oxide
    - D. Nitrous oxide

34. Oxygen may be prepared by pupils with greatest safety in the high school laboratory by employing which one of the following?
    34. ___
    - A. H_2O_2 (3%) and MnO_2

    - B. $KClO_3$ and MnO_2

    - C. $KClO_3$

    - D. Na_2O_2 and H_2O

35. Of the following first aid measures, the most effective in case one inhales bromine vapor, is to
    35. ___
    - A. swallow sodium thiosulfate solution
    - B. breathe fresh air
    - C. use glycerol
    - D. breathe weak ammonia fumes

36. Of the following hazardous mixtures, the one *NOT* used in high school classroom instruction is
    36. ___
    - A. zinc dust and sulfur
    - B. thermite
    - C. potassium chlorate and charcoal
    - D. hydrogen and air

37. Of the following, the physical property *LEAST* frequently used in chemistry instruction is
    37. ___
    - A. taste
    - B. odor
    - C. solubility
    - D. density

38. Of the following, the reagent frequently used in gas analysis to absorb carbon monoxide is
    38. ___
    - A. cuprous chloride
    - B. calcium chloride
    - C. pyrogallic acid
    - D. sodium peroxide

39. Of the following reagents, the one used to separate cupric ions from cadmium ions is
    39. ___
    - A. ammonium hydroxide
    - B. hydrogen sulfide
    - C. sodium cyanide
    - D. sodium thiocyanate

40. The pH of a 0.3M solution of HCl is *CORRECTLY* expressed by
    40. ___
    - A. log 3.3
    - B. antilog 3.3
    - C. 1/log 3.3
    - D. log 0.3

41. A solution with $_pH = 2$ is more acid than one with a $_pH = 6$ 41. ___

    by a factor of

    A. 4   B. 12   C. 400   D. 10,000

42. The addition of sodium acetate crystals to one liter of 0.1M   42. ___
    acetic acid will produce a(n)
    A. increase in the value of K_{eq}

    B. decrease in the value of K_{eq}

    C. increase in the $_pH$ value

    D. decrease in sodium ion concentration

43. The plastic "nylon" is best described as which one of the   43. ___
    following?
    A. Polymerized hydrocarbon   B. **Polyamide**
    C. Polyester   D. Polyurthane

44. The number of liters of air needed to burn completely   44. ___
    8 liters of acetylene is
    A. 40   B. 60   C. 80   D. 100

45. One would expect to find the term isotactic used in con-   45. ___
    nection with which one of the following?
    A. Plastics   B. Dyes   C. Textiles   D. Metals

46. Of the following, a metallic compound which is increasing   46. ___
    in importance as a lubricant is
    A. graphite   B. iron oxide
    C. molybdenum disulfide   D. tungsten oxide

47. A monopropellant is a rocket fuel that combines within its   47. ___
    molecule both fuel and oxidizing agent. Of the following,
    the substance that *BEST* fits this description is
    A. hydrogen peroxide   B. fuming nitric acid
    C. nitromethane   D. decaborane

48. Carbon dioxide is an illustration of a molecule which is   48. ___
    A. polar with polar bonds
    B. non-polar with polar bonds
    C. non-polar with non-polar bonds
    D. polar with non-polar bonds

49. Cis-trans isomers generally   49. ___
    A. contain an asymmetric carbon atom
    B. rotate the plane of polarized light
    C. are enantiomorphs
    D. contain double-bonded carbon atoms

50. According to the Brönsted-Lowry theory, which one of the following is a substance classified as a base?

    A. Cl^-

    B. H_3O^+

    C. NH_4^+

    D. CH_3COOH

50. ___

_____

KEY (CORRECT ANSWERS)

1. A	11. A	21. A	31. D	41. D
2. D	12. D	22. C	32. C	42. C
3. C	13. C	23. C	33. A	43. B
4. B	14. D	24. B	34. A	44. D
5. C	15. B	25. D	35. D	45. A
6. D	16. A	26. D	36. C	46. C
7. D	17. D	27. D	37. A	47. C
8. D	18. B	28. C	38. A	48. B
9. B	19. C	29. D	39. C	49. D
10. D	20. B	30. C	40. A	50. A

_____

TEST 4

DIRECTIONS: Each question or incomplete statement is followed by several suggested answers or completions. Select the one that *BEST* answers the question or completes the statement. *PRINT THE LETTER OF THE CORRECT ANSWER IN THE SPACE AT THE RIGHT.*

1. Substances which furnish a pair of electrons to form a co-ordinate covalent bond are called   1. ____
   A. acids   B. bases   C. amphiprotic   D. non-polar

2. The tendency of hydrogen fluoride to polymerize is explained   2. ____
   by the fact that it
   A. is a strong acid
   B. reacts vigorously with glass
   C. is electrovalent
   D. has a high dipole moment

3. $K_2Cr_2O_7 + HCl \rightarrow KCl + CrCl_3 + Cl_2 + H_2O$ 3. ____

   In the completely balanced equation for the above reaction, the coefficient for Cl_2 is

   A. 1   B. 2   C. 3   D. 4

4. Which one of the following is the formula for calcium   4. ____
   cyanamide?
   A. $CaCNH_2$ B. $CaCN_2$

   C. $CaCN(NH_2)$ D. $Ca(CN)_2$

5. Which one of the following is an *ALTERNATE* name for methyl   5. ____
   n-propyl methane?
   A. Isohexane   B. Butane   C. N-octane   D. Pentane

6. Fluorine is normally produced by the   6. ____
   A. reduction of the fluoride ion
   B. action of chlorine on potassium fluoride
   C. electrolysis of sodium fluoride solution
   D. electrolysis of potassium hydrogen fluoride

7. Bleaching powder may be made by passing chlorine over which   7. ____
   one of the following?
   A. Calcium carbonate
   B. Hydrated calcium sulfate
   C. Anhydrous calcium sulfate
   D. Calcium hydroxide

8. The formula for phosphorus acid is   8. ____

   A. H_3PO_3 B. H_2PO_3 C. HPO_3 D. H_3PO_2

9. Two elements frequently used for making transistors are
   A. carbon and hydrogen   B. iridium and tungsten
   C. niobium and columbium   D. silicon and germanium

9. ___

10. The percentage of iron in an ore which is 80% hematite
   (at. wgts: $Fe - 56$, $0 = 16$) is, *APPROXIMATELY*,
   A. 28   B. 35   C. 56   D. 70

10. ___

11. If 27 grams of aluminum (at. wgt.= 27) are added to 1 liter
   of 3N cupric sulfate solution (at. wgt. Cu = 64), the number of grams of copper displaced is
   A. 32   B. 64   C. 96   D. 128

11. ___

12. During the laboratory preparation of chlorine, the manganese
   dioxide is
   A. oxidized   B. reduced
   C. precipitated   D. left unchanged

12. ___

13. Which one of the following substances is a tertiary alcohol?
   A. $CH_3CH_2CH_2OH$ B. $CH_3CHOHCH_3$

   C. $(CH_3)_3CCH_2OH$ D. $(CH_3)_3COH$

13. ___

14. Amides may be converted into amines by the reaction named
   after
   A. Perkin   B. Claisen   C. Hofmann   D. Gatterman

14. ___

15. A clathrate may be properly defined as a
   A. hydrate   B. solid solution
   C. zeolite   D. cage compound

15. ___

16. At present, *MOST* phthalic anhydride is produced from
   A. benzene   B. turpentine
   C. anthracene   D. naphthalene

16. ___

17. Which of the following substances contains an asymmetric
   carbon atom?
   A. CHClBrF   B. $CFBrCl_2$

   C. $C(OH)HBr_2$ D. $CH(OH)I_2$

17. ___

18. The name of the compound with the formula $(CH_3CO)_2O$ is
   A. acetone   B. di-acetyl
   B. dimethylglyoxime   D. acetic anhydride

18. ___

19. Of the following solvents, the one *MOST* likely to dissolve
   an ionic solute is
   A. carbon tetrachloride   B. methanol
   C. pentane   D. butyl ether

19. ___

20. Of the following, the molecule whose shape is *NOT* linear is
   A. CO   B. CO_2 C. H_2O D. HCl

20. ___

21. The anhydride of $HClO_4$ is

    A. ClO_3 B. ClO_2 C. Cl_2O_5 D. Cl_2O_7

21. ___

22. In the equation,

$$2Fe^{+++} + S^{--} \rightarrow 2Fe^{++} + S^{\circ},$$

the substance formed as a result of a reduction is

    A. Fe^{+++} B. S° C. Fe^{++} D. S^{--}

22. ___

23. Of the following elements, the one that is *NOT* extracted commercially from sea water or marine plants is

    A. Ba   B. Mg   C. Br_2 D. I_2

23. ___

24. How many chloride ions immediately surround each sodium ion in the sodium chloride crystal?

    A. 2   B. 4   C. 6   D. 8

24. ___

25. Of the following, the one that is *NOT* an amphoteric hydroxide is

    A. zinc hydroxide   B. lead hydroxide
    C. aluminum hydroxide   D. calcium hydroxide

25. ___

26. The formula for plaster of Paris is

    A. $CaSO_4$ B. $CaSO_4 \cdot 2H_2O$

    C. $CaSO_4 \cdot 1/2H_2O$ D. $CaSO_4 \cdot H_2O$

26. ___

27. The formula for potassium manganate is

    A. $KMnO_4$ B. K_2MnO_4 C. K_2MnO_3 D. K_2MnO_2

27. ___

28. The iron triad of elements also contains

    A. cobalt and nickel   B. manganese and chromium
    C. palladium and platinum   D. vanadium and titanium

28. ___

29. The formula for sodium bismuthate is

    A. $Na_2Bi_4O_7$ B. $NaBiO_2$ C. $Na_2Bi_2O_4$ D. $NaBiO_3$

29. ___

30. The phosphonium ion has the formula,

    A. PH_2^- B. $P(OH)_2^+$ C. $H_2PO_4^-$ D. PH_4^+

30. ___

31. Radioactive Pb^{201} has a half-life of 8 hours. Starting with 1 gram of this isotope, how much will remain at the end of 24 hours?

    A. 1/2 gram   B. 1/3 gram   C. 1/8 gram   D. none

31. ___

32. Which one of the following statements is true of aluminum   32. ____
    in the thermite reaction?
    A. It gains electrons and is oxidized.
    B. It gains electrons and is reduced.
    C. It loses electrons and is oxidized.
    D. It loses electrons and is reduced.

33. Through radioactive decay, $_{92}U^{234}$, may be transformed into   33. ____

    $_{82}Pb^{206}$. This process involves the loss of

    A. 7 alpha particles and 4 electrons
    B. 6 alpha particles, 1 neutron and 3 protons
    C. 8 alpha particles and 6 electrons
    D. 6 alpha particles, 3 electrons and 2 deuterons

34. The radioactive disintegration of $_{14}Si^{27}$ yields $_{13}Al^{27}$ and   34. ____
    a(n)
    A. proton   B. neutron   C. positron   D. electron

35. Which one of the following elements is produced by irradi-   35. ____
    ating a bismuth target with high energy helium ions?
    A. Californium   B. Astatine   C. Americium   D. Niobium

36. The barium ion may be separated from strontium ions by em-   36. ____
    ploying
    A. Na_2CO_3 and HCl   B. $K_4Fe(CN)_6$ and NH_4NO_3

    C. $(NH_4)_2CO_3$ and NH_4OH D. K_2CrO_4 and $HC_2H_3O_2$

37. The reagent, dimethylglyoxime, is used in a confirmatory   37. ____
    test for the element,
    A. iron   B. calcium   C. nickel   D. cobalt

38. The group reagent for the silver group in qualitative ana-   38. ____
    lysis is
    A. H_2S B. $H_2S + NH_3$ C. $(NH_4)_2CO_3$ D. HCl

39. If a halide soluble in water gave a white precipitate when   39. ____
    dilute nitric acid and a solution of sodium chloride were
    added, the original salt was silver
    A. chloride   B. bromide   C. fluoride   D. iodide

40. Since lead has an atomic weight of 207.2 and a density of   40. ____
    11.4 g/c.c, its atomic volume is
    A. 1.13 c.c.   B. 9.1 c.c.   C. 18.2 c.c.   D. 36.4 c.c.

41. A Tyndall effect would *MOST LIKELY* be observed in which one   41. ____
    of the following?
    A. Solution   B. Precipitate   C. Sol   D. Solvent

42. Of the following, the metal that does *NOT* give a red flame   42. ____
    test is
    A. lithium   B. barium   C. strontium   D. rubidium

43. Assuming that n = energy level, quantum mechanics postulates   43. ____
    that the electron population of any energy level in an atom
    is limited to
    A. 2n   B. $2n^2$ C. $2n^2 + 2$ D. $2n^2 - 2$

44. Albert Einstein was awarded the Nobel prize for his study   44. ____
    of
    A. generalized relativity
    B. photochemistry
    C. non-Euclidean geometry
    D. special theory of relativity

45. The formula for hydroxylamine hydrochloride is   45. ____
    A. NH_2Cl B. $NH_2OH \cdot HCl$

    C. $(NH_2OH)Cl$ D. $(NH_2Cl)OH$

46. Manganese is dissimilar to most transition elements because   46. ____
    it reacts with
    A. oxygen   B. chlorine   C. sulfur   D. water

47. 45 ml of lithium hydroxide were needed to completely neutral- 47. ____
    ize 30 ml of 2M phosphoric acid. The molarity of the lithium
    hydroxide was
    A. 1.3   B. 2.0   C. 2.7   D. 4.0

48. When 14 grams of phosphoric acid (mol. wgt. = 98) are dis- 48. ____
    solved in 250 grams of water, the resulting solution is
    A. 0.14 molar   B. 0.19 normal
    C. 0.28 normal   D. 0.57 molal

49. An atom containing an odd number of electrons is   49. ____
    A. paramagnetic   B. diamagnetic
    C. ferromagnetic   D. hypermagnetic

50. Of the following isotopes, the one that is *NOT* radioactive   50. ____
    is
    A. Co^{60} B. I^{131} C. Ca^{40} D. Sr^{90}

KEY (CORRECT ANSWERS)

1. B	11. C	21. D	31. C	41. C
2. D	12. B	22. C	32. C	42. B
3. C	13. D	23. A	33. A	43. B
4. B	14. C	24. C	34. C	44. B
5. D	15. D	25. D	35. B	45. B
6. D	16. D	26. C	36. D	46. D
7. D	17. A	27. B	37. C	47. D
8. A	18. D	28. A	38. D	48. D
9. D	19. B	29. D	39. C	49. A
10. C	20. C	30. D	40. C	50. C

TEST 5

DIRECTIONS: Each question or incomplete statement is followed by several suggested answers or completions. Select the one that *BEST* answers the question or completes the statement. *PRINT THE LETTER OF THE CORRECT ANSWER IN THE SPACE AT THE RIGHT.*

1. Of the following groups of elements, the one containing   1. ___
   ONLY artificially produced elements is
       A. polonium, francium, actinium
       B. protactinium, neptunium, radon
       C. berkelium, rhenium, hafnium
       D. curium, californium, americium

2. Van der Waals' forces between molecules increase with in-   2. ___
   creasing
       A. temperature   B. number of electrons
       C. ionic radius   D. ionization potential

3. If, at standard temperature and pressure, 25 liters of a   3. ___
   gas weigh 50 grams, the molecular weight of the gas is
   CLOSEST to which one of the following?
       A. 22   B. 34   C. 45   D. 56

4. The mol fraction of nitrogen in a mixture containing 70   4. ___
   grams of nitrogen, 128 grams of oxygen, and 44 grams of
   carbon dioxide, is
       A. 0.29   B. 0.33   C. 0.36   D. 0.50

5. If the K_{sp} for CaC_2O_4 is 2.6×10^{-9}, the concentration of   5. ___
   oxalate ion needed to form a precipitate in a solution con-
   taining 0.02 moles per liter of calcium ions, is

       A. 1.0×10^{-9} B. 1.3×10^{-7}

       C. 2.2×10^{-5} D. 5.2×10^{-11}

6. If 5.2 grams of non-volatile solute are dissolved in 125   6. ___
   grams of water and the boiling point of the solution was
   100.78°C, the molecular weight of the solute is, *APPROXI-
   MATELY,*
       A. 14   B. 28   C. 42   D. 56

7. If a saturated solution of $La_2(C_2O_4)_3$ contains 1.1×10^{-6} 7. ___
   moles/liter, the solubility product constant for this sub-
   stance is
       A. 1.2×10^{-12} B. 1.6×10^{-30}

       C. 1.6×10^{-34} D. 1.7×10^{-28}

8. A catalyst employed in the Friedel-Crafts synthesis is　　　　　8. ___
   A. sodium　　　　　　　　　　B. cuprous chloride
   C. aluminum chloride　　　　D. magnesium iodide

9. The Goldschmidt process would be represented by which one　　9. ___
   of the following reactions?
   A. $ZnS + O_2 \rightarrow ZnO + SO_2$

   B. $3MnO_2 + 4Al \rightarrow 3Mn + 2Al_2O_3$

   C. $2Al_2O_3 \rightarrow 4Al + 3O_2$

   D. $2Al + 3ZnCl_2 \rightarrow 2AlCl_3 + 3Zn$

10. In the cell, $Cu/Cu^{++} // Zn^{++}/Zn$, the electromotive force　10. ___
    may be increased to the greatest extent by
    A. increasing the copper ion and zinc ion concentrations
    B. decreasing the copper ion and zinc ion concentrations
    C. increasing the copper ion concentration and decreasing
       the zinc ion concentration
    D. decreasing the copper ion concentration and increasing
       the zinc ion concentration

11. If a certain element forms an oxide in which the oxygen is　　11. ___
    20% of the compound by weight, the equivalent weight of
    this element is
    A. 32　　　　　　B. 40　　　　　　C. 64　　　　　　D. 128

12. At standard temperature and pressure, the density of CCl_4　12. ___
    vapor (at. wgts: C = 12; Cl = 35.5) in grams/liter is
    A. 2.56　　　　　B. 3.70　　　　　C. 4.52　　　　D. 6.88

13. The Mond process is one used in the metallurgy of　　　　　　13. ___
    A. titanium　　　B. nickel　　　C. iron　　　　D. copper

14. The formula for the iron ore, siderite, is　　　　　　　　　14. ___
    A. Fe_2O_3　　　　B. $FeSiO_3$　　　C. $FeCO_3$　　　D. $Fe(OH)_2$

15. The term, beneficiation, refers to　　　　　　　　　　　　15. ___
    A. plastics development　　　B. ore enrichment
    C. dye research　　　　　　　D. rocket research

16. Experimental evidence that atomic nuclei could cause large　16. ___
    deflections of alpha particles, was first obtained by
    A. Thomson　　　B. Fermi　　　C. Rutherford　　　D. Dirac

17. If the specific heat of a metallic element is given as　　　17. ___
    0.214 cal/g, the atomic weight of this element is CLOSEST
    to which one of the following?
    A. 6.6　　　　　　B. 12.0　　　　　C. 30.0　　　　D. 66.0

18. Of the following, the ONLY compound that does NOT contain a　18. ___
    double or triple bond is
    A. H_2O　　　　　B. HCN　　　　　C. CO　　　　　D. N_2

19. The maximum number of p-type orbitals possible in any sub-shell is
    A. 2   B. 3   C. 5   D. 7

19. ___

20. Of the following, the elements whose compounds are most often colored are the
    A. alkali metals   B. alkaline earth metals
    C. halogens   D. transition elements

20. ___

21. The new international standard adopted for the determination of atomic weights is
    A. F^{19} B. O^{16} C. Ca^{40} D. C^{12}

21. ___

22. Of the following, a molecule which is a typical example of a resonance hybrid is that of
    A. SO_2 B. HCl   C. H_2O D. CH_4

22. ___

23. Of the following elements, the one possessing the largest atomic radius is
    A. cesium   B. magnesium   C. lead   D. uranium

23. ___

24. The label on a bottle of sulfuric acid indicates: 80% H_2SO_4 by weight; sp. gravity 1.727; molecular weight 98. The molarity of this acid is *CLOSEST* to which one of the following?
    A. 9.8   B. 10.2   C. 14.1   D. 16.6

24. ___

25. If a compound contains 21.6% Na, 33.3% Cl, and 45.1% O, (atomic weights: Na = 23; Cl = 35.5; O = 16), the empirical formula for the compound is
    A. NaClO   B. $NaClO_2$ C. $NaClO_3$ D. $NaClO_4$

25. ___

26. The percent of nitrogen in the compound NH_4NO_3 (atomic weights: N=14; O=16; H=1) is *CLOSEST* to which one of the following?
    A. 17.5%   B. 35.5%   C. 52.5%   D. 70.5%

26. ___

27. Acetylene belongs to the hydrocarbon series having the general formula,
    A. C_nH_{2n+2} B. C_nH_{2n} C. C_nH_{2n-2} D. C_nH_n

27. ___

28. The electron configuration for neon is
    A. $1s^2\ 2s^2\ 2p^3$ B. $1s^2\ 2s^2\ 2p^4$
    C. $1s^2\ 2s^2\ 2p^5$ D. $1s^2\ 2s^2\ 2p^6$

28. ___

29. In the following reaction,

$$2 SO_{2(g)} + O_{2(g)} \rightleftharpoons 2 SO_{3(g)} + heat,$$

the yield of SO_3 is favored by
   A. increasing the pressure and the temperature
   B. increasing the pressure and decreasing the temperature
   C. decreasing the pressure and increasing the temperature
   D. decreasing the pressure and the temperature

29. ___

30. Millikan's oil-drop experiment determined the
   A. value of the ratio e/m
   B. number of electrons in the K orbit
   C. value of the charge on the electron
   D. magnitude of Planck's constant

30. ___

31. The maximum number of electrons held in an "f" subshell is
   A. 6   B. 10   C. 14   D. 18

31. ___

32. The theory postulating complete ionization of strong electrolytes was advanced by
   A. Arrhenius   B. Ostwald
   C. Bronsted   D. Debye and Huckel

32. ___

33. In determining electrode potentials, the standard reference electrode is the
   A. calomel electrode   B. Weston cell
   C. hydrogen electrode   D. cadmium electrode

33. ___

34. Of the following, the element possessing the *HIGHEST* electro negativity is
   A. lithium   B. cesium   C. fluorine   D. astatine

34. ___

35. The Heisenberg principle postulates that
   A. the momentum and position of an electron cannot be known simultaneously
   B. two electrons may not occupy the same orbital
   C. for every proton there must exist an anti-proton
   D. every radioactive decay results in the production of isotopic lead

35. ___

36. If a current deposits 9 grams of aluminum (atomic weight equals 27) in 10 minutes, how many grams of magnesium will it deposit in 20 minutes?
   A. 12   B. 16   C. 18   D. 24

36. ___

37. The *MOST PROBABLE* structural formula for the compound whose empirical formula is C_3H_6O, and which can reduce Benedict's reagent, is
   A. $CH_3.CH_2.CHO$ B. $CH_2 = CH.CH_2OH$

   B. 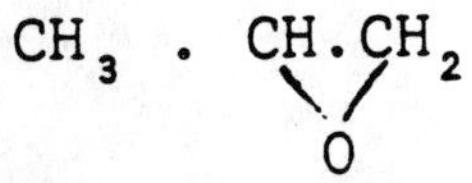 $CH_3 . CH.CH_2$ D. $CH_3.O.CH = CH_2$
          $\diagdown \diagup$
             O

37. ___

38. The relative difference in boiling points of hydrogen oxide   38. ____
    and hydrogen sulfide may be correctly attributed to
       A. chelation   B. hydrogen bonding
       C. van der Waals' forces   D. coordinate covalence

39. The electron sub-shell constructed of three orbitals per-   39. ____
    pendicular to each other is designated by the letter
       A. s   B. p   C. d   D. f

40. The Marsh test may be used to detect small quantities of   40. ____
       A. mercury   B. arsenic   C. tin   D. methane

41. The statement, If 0.003 moles of gas are dissolved in 900   41. ____
    grams of water under 1 atmosphere pressure, 0.006 moles will
    be dissolved if the pressure is 2 atmospheres, illustrates
       A. Dalton's Law of Partition   B. Graham's Law
       C. Henry's Law   D. Boyle's Law

42. If under similar conditions, 1 liter of helium requires   42. ____
    40 minutes to flow through an orifice and 1 liter of an un-
    known gas requires 4 hours, the molecular weight of the
    unknown gas is *CLOSEST* to which one of the following?
       A. 6   B. 12   C. 24   D. 144

43. The scientist who devised the mass spectrograph for the   43. ____
    detection of isotopes was
       A. Moseley   B. Lawrence   C. Aston   D. Fermi

44. Which one of the following substances can be used effect-   44. ____
    ively as a water softener?
       A. Sodium tetraborate   B. Calcium bicarbonate
       C. Ferric chloride   D. Calcium silicate

45. $CH_3CO \cdot OC_2H_5$ is an example of which one of the following?   45. ____

       A. Alcohol   B. Soap   C. Acid   D. Ester

46. Of the following, the formula which represents an unsatu-   46. ____
    rated organic compound is
       A. C_6H_{14} B. C_4H_8 C. C_CH_7OH D. $C_2H_4Cl_2$

47. A device used to measure the number of nuclear disintegra-   47. ____
    tions per minute is called a
       A. Geiger counter .   B. cyclotron
       C. cloud chamber   D. electrometer

48. Because of dangers inherent in the process, special pre-   48. ____
    cautions should be taken in diluting concentrated
       A. HNO_3 B. HCl C. H_2SO_4 D. $H_2C_2O_4$

49. As the atomic number of the halogens increases, the halogens 49. ___
    A. lose their outermost electrons less easily
    B. become less dense
    C. become lighter in color
    D. gain electrons less easily

50. A water solution of which one of the following will have a   50. ___
    pH of less than 7?
    A. $CuSO_4$ B. Na_3PO_4 C. KCl   D. Na_2CO_3

———

KEY (CORRECT ANSWERS)

1. D	11. A	21. D	31. C	41. C
2. B	12. D	22. A	32. D	42. D
3. C	13. B	23. A	33. C	43. C
4. B	14. C	24. C	34. C	44. A
5. B	15. B	25. C	35. A	45. D
6. B	16. C	26. B	36. D	46. B
7. D	17. C	27. C	37. A	47. A
8. C	18. A	28. D	38. B	48. C
9. B	19. B	29. B	39. B	49. D
10. C	20. D	30. C	40. B	50. A

———

SCIENCE READING COMPREHENSION
EXAMINATION SECTION

DIRECTIONS FOR THIS SECTION:
Each question or incomplete statement is followed by several suggested answers or completions. Select the one that BEST answers the question or completes the statement. *PRINT THE LETTER OF THE CORRECT ANSWER IN THE SPACE AT THE RIGHT.*

TEST 1

PASSAGE

Photosynthesis is a complex process with many intermediate steps. Ideas differ greatly as to the details of these steps, but the general nature of the process and its outcome are well established. Water, usually from the soil, is conducted through the xylem of root, stem and leaf to the chlorophyl-containing cells of a leaf. In consequence of the abundance of water within the latter cells, their walls are saturated with water. Carbon dioxide, diffusing from the air through the stomata and into the intercellular spaces of the leaf, comes into contact with the water in the walls of the cells which adjoin the intercellular spaces. The carbon dioxide becomes dissolved in the water of these walls, and in solution diffuses through the walls and the plasma membranes into the cells. By the agency of chlorophyl in the chloroplasts of the cells, the energy of light is transformed into chemical energy. This chemical energy is used to decompose the carbon dioxide and water, and the products of their decomposition are recombined into a new compound. The compound first formed is successively built up into more and more complex substances until finally a sugar is produced.

Questions 1-8.

1. The union of carbon dioxide and water to form starch results in an excess of   1. ...
    A. hydrogen   B. carbon   C. oxygen
    D. carbon monoxide E. hydrogen peroxide
2. Synthesis of carbohydrates takes place   2. ...
    A. in the stomata
    B. in the intercellular spaces of leaves
    C. in the walls of plant cells
    D. within the plasma membranes of plant cells
    E. within plant cells that contain chloroplasts
3. In the process of photosynthesis, chlorophyl acts as a   3. ...
    A. carbohydrate   B. source of carbon dioxide
    C. catalyst   D. source of chemical energy
    E. plasma membrane
4. In which of the following places are there the GREATEST   4. ...
   number of hours in which photosynthesis can take place
   during the month of December?
    A. Buenos Aires, Argentina B. Caracas, Venezuela
    C. Fairbanks, Alaska   D. Quito, Ecuador
    E. Calcutta, India
5. During photosynthesis, molecules of carbon dioxide enter   5. ...
   the stomata of leaves because
    A. the molecules are already in motion
    B. they are forced through the stomata by the son's rays
    C. chlorophyl attracts them
    D. a chemical change takes place in the stomata
    E. oxygen passes out through the stomata

1

6. Besides food manufacture, another USEFUL result of photo- 6. ...
   synthesis is that it
   A. aids in removing poisonous gases from the air
   B. helps to maintain the existing proportion of gases in
      the air
   C. changes complex compounds into simpler compounds
   D. changes certain waste products into hydrocarbons
   E. changes chlorophyl into useful substances
7. A process that is almost the exact reverse of photosynthesis 7. ...
   is the
   A. rusting of iron   B. burning of wood
   C. digestion of starch   D. ripening of fruit
   E. storage of food in seeds
8. The leaf of the tomato plant will be unable to carry on 8. ...
   photosynthesis if the
   A. upper surface of the leaf is coated with vaseline
   B. upper surface of the leaf is coated with lampblack
   C. lower surface of the leaf is coated with lard
   D. leaf is placed in an atmosphere of pure carbon dioxide
   E. entire leaf is coated with lime

TEST 2

PASSAGE

The only carbohydrate which the human body can absorb and oxidize
is the simple sugar glucose. Therefore, all carbohydrates which are
consumed must be changed to glucose by the body before they can be
used. There are specific enzymes in the mouth, the stomach, and the
small intestine which break down complex carbohydrates. All the
monosaccharides are changed to glucose by enzymes secreted by the
intestinal glands, and the glucose is absorbed by the capillaries
of the villi.

The following simple test is used to determine the presence of a
reducing sugar. If Benedict's solution is added to a solution containing glucose or one of the other reducing sugars and the resulting mixture is heated, a brick-red precipitate will be formed. This
test was carried out on several substances and the information in the
following table was obtained. "P" indicates that the precipitate was
formed and "N" indicates that no reaction was observed.

Material Tested	Observation
Crushed grapes in water	P
Cane sugar in water	N
Fructose	P
Molasses	N

Questions 1-2.
1. From the results of the test made upon crushed grapes in 1. ...
   water, one may say that grapes contain
   A. glucose   B. sucrose   C. a reducing sugar
   D. no sucrose   E. no glucose
2. Which one of the following foods probably undergoes the 2. ...
   LEAST change during the process of carbohydrate digestion
   in the human body?
   A. Cane sugar   B. Fructose   C. Molasses
   D. Bread   E. Potato

TEST 3

PASSAGE

The British pressure suit was made in two pieces and joined around the middle in contrast to the other suits, which were one-piece suits with a removable helmet. Oxygen was supplied through a tube, and a container of soda lime absorbed carbon dioxide and water vapor. The pressure was adjusted to a maximum of 2 1/2 pounds per square inch (130 millimeters) higher than the surrounding air. Since pure oxygen was used, this produced a partial pressure of 130 millimeters, which is sufficient to sustain the flier at any altitude.

Using this pressure suit, the British established a world's altitude record of 49,944 feet in 1936 and succeeded in raising it to 53,937 feet the following year. The pressure suit is a compromise solution to the altitude problem. Full sea-level pressure can not be maintained, as the suit would be so rigid that the flier could not move arms or legs. Hence a pressure one third to one fifth that of sea level has been used. Because of these lower pressures, oxygen has been used to raise the partial pressure of alveolar oxygen to normal.

Questions 1-9.

1. The MAIN constituent of air not admitted to the pressure   1. ...
   suit described was
      A. oxygen   B. nitrogen   C. water vapor
      D. carbon dioxide   E. hydrogen
2. The pressure within the suit exceeded that of the surround- 2. ...
   ing air by an amount equal to 130 millimeters of
      A. mercury   B. water   C. air
      D. oxygen   E. carbon dioxide
3. The normal atmospheric pressure at sea level is   3. ...
      A. 130 mm   B. 250 mm   C. 760 mm
      D. 1000 mm   E. 1300 mm
4. The water vapor that was absorbed by the soda lime came   4. ...
   from
      A. condensation
      B. the union of oxygen with carbon dioxide
      C. body metabolism
      D. the air within the pressure suit
      E. water particles in the upper air
5. The HIGHEST altitude that has been reached with the British 5. ...
   pressure suit is about
      A. 130 miles   B. 2 1/2 miles   C. 6 miles
      D. 10 miles   E. 5 miles
6. If the pressure suit should develop a leak, the   6. ...
      A. oxygen supply would be cut off
      B. suit would fill up with air instead of oxygen
      C. pressure within the suit would drop to zero
      D. pressure within the suit would drop to that of the
         surrounding air
      E. suit would become so rigid that the flier would be
         unable to move arms or legs
7. The reason why oxygen helmets are unsatisfactory for use   7. ...
   in efforts to set higher altitude records is that
      A. it is impossible to maintain a tight enough fit at
         the neck

3

  B. oxygen helmets are too heavy
  C. they do not conserve the heat of the body as pressure suits do
  D. if a parachute jump becomes necessary, it can not be made while such a helmet is being worn
  E. oxygen helmets are too rigid
8. The pressure suit is termed a compromise solution because   8. ...
  A. it is not adequate for stratosphere flying
  B. aviators can not stand sea-level pressure at high altitudes
  C. some suits are made in two pieces, others in one
  D. other factors than maintenance of pressure have to be accommodated
  E. full atmospheric pressure can not be maintained at high altitudes
9. The passage implies that   9. ...
  A. the air pressure at 49,944 feet is approximately the same as it is at 53,937 feet
  B. pressure cabin planes are not practical at extremely high altitudes
  C. a flier's oxygen requirement is approximately the same at high altitudes as it is at sea level
  D. one-piece pressure suits with removable helmets are unsafe
  E. a normal alveolar oxygen supply is maintained if the air pressure is between one third and one fifth that of sea level

—

TEST 4

PASSAGE

Chemical investigations show that during muscle contraction the store of organic phosphates in the muscle fibers is altered as energy is released. In doing so, the organic phosphates (chiefly adenoisine triphosphate and phospho-creatine) are transformed an-aerobically to organic compounds plus phosphates. As soon as the organic phosphates begin to break down in muscle contraction, the glycogen in the muscle fibers also transforms into lactic acid plus free energy; this energy the muscle fiber uses to return the organic compounds plus phosphates into high-energy organic phosphates ready for another contraction. In the presence of oxygen, the lactic acid from the glycogen decomposition is changed also. About one-fifth of it is oxidized to form water and carbon dioxide and to yield another supply of energy. This time the energy is used to transform the re-maining four-fifths of the lactic acid into glycogen again.
Questions 1-5.
1. The energy for muscle contraction comes directly from the   1. ...
  A. breakdown of lactic acid into glycogen
  B. resynthesis of adenosine triphosphate
  C. breakdown of glycogen into lactic acid
  D. oxidation of lactic acid
  E. breakdown of the organic phosphates

4

2. Lactic acid does NOT accumulate in a muscle that   2. ...
    A. is in a state of lacking oxygen
    B. has an ample supply of oxygen
    C. is in a state of fatigue
    D. is repeatedly being stimulated
    E. has an ample supply of glycogen
3. The energy for the resynthesis of adenosine triphosphate   3. ...
    and phospho-creatine comes from the
    A. oxidation of lactic acid
    B. synthesis of organic phosphates
    C. change from glycogen to lactic acid
    D. resynthesis of glycogen
    E. change from lactic acid to glycogen
4. The energy for the resynthesis of glycogen comes from the   4. ...
    A. breakdown of organic phosphates
    B. resynthesis of organic phosphates
    C. change occurring in one-fifth of the lactic acid
    D. change occurring in four-fifths of the lactic acid
    E. change occurring in four-fifths of glycogen
5. The breakdown of the organic phosphates into organic com-   5. ...
    pounds plus phosphates is an
    A. anobolic reaction   B. aerobic reaction
    C. endothermic reaction   D. exothermic reaction
    E. anaerobic reaction

TEST 5

PASSAGE

And with respect to that theory of the origin of the forms of
life peopling our globe, with which Darwin's name is bound up as
closely as that of Newton with the theory of gravitation, nothing
seems to be further from the mind of the present generation than
any attempt to smother it with ridicule or to crush it by vehemence
of denunciation. "The struggle for existence," and "natural selection," have become household words and every-day conceptions. The
reality and the importance of the natural processes on which Darwin
founds his deductions are no more doubted than those of growth and
multiplication; and, whether the full potency attributed to them is
admitted or not, no one is unmindful of or at all doubts their vast
and far-reaching significance. Wherever the biological sciences are
studied, the "Origin of Species" lights the path of the investigator;
wherever they are taught it permeates the course of instruction. Nor
has the influence of Darwinian ideas been less profound beyond the
realms of biology. The oldest of all philosophies, that of evolution, was bound hand and foot and cast into utter darkness during the
millennium of theological scholasticism. But Darwin poured new life-
blood into the ancient frame; the bonds burst, and the revivified
thought of ancient Greece has proved itself to be a more adequate
expression of the universal order of things than any of the schemes
which have been accepted by the credulity and welcomed by the super-
stition of seventy later generations of men.

Questions 1-7.
1. Darwin's theory of the origin of the species is based on   1. ...
    A. theological deductions   B. the theory of gravitation
    C. Greek mythology
    D. natural processes evident in the universe
    E. extensive reading in the biological sciences
2. The passage implies that   2. ...
    A. thought in ancient Greece was dead
    B. the theory of evolution is now universally accepted
    C. the "Origin of Species" was seized by the Church
    D. Darwin was influenced by Newton
    E. the theories of "the struggle for existence" and
       "natural selection" are too evident to be scientific
3. The idea of evolution   3. ...
    A. was suppressed for 1,000 years
    B. is falsely claimed by Darwin
    C. has swept aside all superstition
    D. was outworn even in ancient Greece
    E. has revolutionized the universe
4. The processes of growth and multiplication   4. ...
    A. have been replaced by others discovered by Darwin
    B. were the basis for the theory of gravitation
    C. are "the struggle for existence" and "natural selection"
    D. are scientific theories not yet proved
    E. are accepted as fundamental processes of nature
5. Darwin's treatise on evolution   5. ...
    A. traces life on the planets from the beginning of time
       to the present day
    B. was translated from the Greek
    C. contains an ancient philosophy in modern, scientific
       guise
    D. has had a profound effect on evolution
    E. has had little notice outside scientific circles
6. The theory of evolution   6. ...
    A. was first advanced in the "Origin of Species"
    B. was suppressed by the ancient Greeks
    C. did not get beyond the monasteries during the millennium
    D. is philosophical, not scientific
    E. was elaborated and revived by Darwin
7. Darwin has contributed GREATLY toward   7. ...
    A. a universal acceptance of the processes of nature
    B. reviving the Greek intellect
    C. ending the millennium of theological scholasticism
    D. a satisfactory explanation of scientific theory
    E. easing the struggle for existence

TEST 6

PASSAGE

The higher forms of plants and animals, such as seed plants and vertebrates, are similar or alike in many respects but decidedly different in others. For example, both of these groups of organisms carry on digestion, respiration, reproduction, conduction, growth, and exhibit sensitivity to various stimuli. On the other hand, a number of basic differences are evident. Plants have no excretory systems comparable to those of animals. Plants have no heart or similar pumping organ. Plants are very limited in their movements. Plants have nothing similar to the animal nervous system. In addition, animals can not synthesize carbohydrates from inorganic substances. Animals do not have special regions of growth, comparable to terminal and lateral meristems in plants, which persist throughout the life span of the organism. And, finally, the animal cell "wall" is only a membrane, while plant cell walls are more rigid, usually thicker, and may be composed of such substances as cellulose, lignin, pectin, cutin, and suberin. These characteristics are important to an understanding of living organisms and their functions and should, consequently, be carefully considered in plant and animal studies. Questions 1-7.

1. Which of the following do animals lack?   1. ...
   A. Ability to react to stimuli
   B. Ability to conduct substances from one place to another
   C. Reproduction by gametes
   D. A cell membrane
   E. A terminal growth region

2. Which of the following statements is false?   2. ...
   A. Animal cell "walls" are composed of cellulose.
   B. Plants grow as long as they live.
   C. Plants produce sperms and eggs.
   D. All vertebrates have hearts.
   E. Wood is dead at maturity.

3. Respiration in plants takes place   3. ...
   A. only during the day
   B. only in the presence of carbon dioxide
   C. both day and night
   D. only at night
   E. only in the presence of certain stimuli

4. An example of a vertebrate is the   4. ...
   A. earthworm   B. starfish   C. amoeba
   D. cow   E. insect

5. Which of the following statements is true?   5. ...
   A. All animals eat plants as a source of food.
   B. Respiration, in many ways, is the reverse of photosynthesis.
   C. Man is an invertebrate animal.
   D. Since plants have no hearts, they can not develop high pressures in their cells.
   E. Plants can not move.

6. Which of the following do plants lack?   6. ...
   A. A means of movement   B. Pumping structures
   C. Special regions of growth
   D. Reproduction by gametes
   E. A digestive process

7. A substance that can be synthesized by green plants but NOT 7. ...
  by animals is
   A. protein   B. cellulose   C. carbon dioxide
   D. uric acid   E. water

7

TEST 7

PASSAGE

Sodium chloride, being by far the largest constituent of the mineral matter of the blood, assumes special significance in the regulation of water exchanges in the organism. And, as Cannon has emphasized repeatedly, these latter are more extensive and more important than may at first thought appear. He points out "there are a number of circulations of the fluid out of the body and back again, without loss." Thus, by example, it is estimated that from a quart and one-half of water daily "leaves the body" when it enters the mouth as saliva; another one or two quarts are passed out as gastric juice; and perhaps the same amount is contained in the bile and the secretions of the pancreas and the intestinal wall. This large volume of water enters the digestive processes; and practically all of it is reabsorbed through the intestinal wall, where it performs the equally important function of carrying in the digested foodstuffs. These and other instances of what Cannon calls "the conservative use of water in our bodies" involve essentially osmotic pressure relationships in which the concentration of sodium chloride plays an important part.

Questions 1-11.

1. This passage implies that   1. ...
   A. the contents of the alimentary canal are not to be
      considered within the body
   B. sodium chloride does not actually enter the body
   C. every particle of water ingested is used over and
      over again
   D. water can not be absorbed by the body unless it con-
      tains sodium chloride
   E. substances can pass through the intestinal wall in
      only one direction
2. According to this passage, which of the following processes 2. ...
   requires MOST water? The
   A. absorption of digested foods
   B. secretion of gastric juice
   C. secretion of saliva
   D. production of bile
   E. concentration of sodium chloride solution
3. A body fluid that is NOT saline is   3. ...
   A. blood   B. urine   C. bile
   D. gastric juice E. saliva
4. An organ that functions as a storage reservoir from which   4. ...
   large quantities of water are reabsorbed into the body is
   the
   A. kidney   B. liver   C. large intestine
   D. mouth   E. pancreas
5. Water is reabsorbed into the body by the process of   5. ...
   A. secretion   B. excretion   C. digestion
   D. osmosis   E. oxidation
6. Digested food enters the body PRINCIPALLY through the   6. ...
   A. mouth   B. liver   C. villi
   D. pancreas   E. stomach

8

7. The metallic element found in the blood in compound form   7. ...
   and present there in larger quantities than any other
   metallic element is
   A. iron   B. calcium   C. magnesium
   D. chlorine   E. sodium

8. An organ that removes water from the body and prevents   8. ...
   its reabsorption for use in the body processes is the
   A. pancreas   B. liver   C. small intestine
   D. lungs   E. large intestine

9. In which of the following processes is sodium chloride   9. ...
   removed MOST rapidly from the body?
   A. Digestion   B. Breathing   C. Oxidation
   D. Respiration   E. Perspiration

10. Which of the following liquids would pass from the ali-   10. ...
    mentary canal into the blood MOST rapidly?
    A. A dilute solution of sodium chloride in water
    B. Gastric juice
    C. A concentrated solution of sodium chloride in water
    D. Digested food
    E. Distilled water

11. The reason why it is unsafe to drink ocean water even   11. ...
    under conditions of extreme thirst is that it
    A. would reduce the salinity of the blood to a dangerous
       level
    B. contains dangerous disease germs
    C. contains poisonous salts
    D. would greatly increase the salinity of the blood
    E. would cause salt crystals to form in the blood stream

—

TEST 8

PASSAGE

The discovery of antitoxin and its specific antagonistic effect
upon toxin furnished an opportunity for the accurate investigation
of the relationship of a bacterial antigen and its antibody. Toxin-
antitoxin reactions were the first immunological processes to which
experimental precision could be applied, and the discovery of principles of great importance resulted from such studies. A great deal
of the work was done with diphtheria toxin and antitoxin and the
facts elucidated with these materials are in principle applicable
to similar substances.

The simplest assumption to account for the manner in which an
antitoxin renders a toxin innocuous would be that the antitoxin
destroys the toxin. Roux and Buchner, however, advanced the opinion
that the antitoxin did not act directly upon the toxin, but affected
it indirectly through the mediation of tissue cells. Ehrlich, on
the other hand, conceived the reaction of toxin and antitoxin as a
direct union, analogous to the chemical neutralization of an acid by
a base.

The conception of toxin destruction was conclusively refuted by
the experiments of Calmette. This observer, working with snake
poison, found that the poison itself (unlike most other toxins)
possessed the property of resisting heat to 100 degrees C, while its
specific antitoxin, like other antitoxins, was destroyed at or about

9

70 degrees C. Nontoxic mixtures of the two substanues, when subjected to heat, regained their toxic properties. The natural inference from these observations was that the toxin in the original mixture had not been destroyed, but had been merely inactiviated by the presence of the antitoxin and again set free after destruction of the antitoxin by heat.

Questions 1-10.

1. Both toxins and antitoxins ORDINARILY   1. ...
   A. are completely destroyed at body temperatures
   B. are extremely resistant to heat
   C. can exist only in combination
   D. are destroyed at 180°F
   E. are products of nonliving processes

2. MOST toxins can be destroyed by   2. ...
   A. bacterial action   B. salt solutions
   C. boiling   D. diphtheria antitoxin
   E. other toxins

3. Very few disease organisms release a true toxin into the   3. ...
   blood stream. It would follow, then, that
   A. studies of snake venom reactions have no value
   B. studies of toxin-antitoxin reactions are of little
      importance
   C. the treatment of most diseases must depend upon in-
      formation obtained from study of a few
   D. antitoxin plays an important part in the body defense
      against the great majority of germs
   E. only toxin producers are dangerous

4. A person becomes susceptible to infection again immediate-   4. ...
   ly after recovering from
   A. mumps   B. tetanus   C. diphtheria
   D. smallpox   E. tuberculosis

5. City people are more frequently immune to communicable   5. ...
   diseases than country people are because
   A. country people eat better food
   B. city doctors are better than country doctors
   C. the air is more healthful in the country
   D. country people have fewer contacts with disease car-
      riers
   E. there are more doctors in the city than in the country

6. The substances that provide us with immunity to disease   6. ...
   are found in the body in the
   A. blood serum   B. gastric juice   C. urine
   D. white blood cells   E. red blood cells

7. A person ill with diphtheria would MOST likely be treated   7. ...
   with
   A. diphtheria toxin   B. diphtheria toxoid
   C. dead diphtheria germs   D. diphtheria antitoxin
   E. live diphtheria germs

8. To determine susceptibility to diphtheria, an individual   8. ...
   may be given the
   A. Wassermann test   B. Schick test
   C. Widal test   D. Dick test
   E. Kahn test

9. Since few babies under six months of age contract diph-   9. ...
   theria, young babies PROBABLY
   A. are never exposed to diphtheria germs

10

B. have high body temperatures that destroy the toxin
   if acquired
C. acquire immunity from their mothers
D. acquire immunity from their fathers
E. are too young to become infected

10. Calmette's findings   10. ...
   A. contradicted both Roux and Buchner's opinion and
      Ehrlich's conception
   B. contradicted Roux and Buchner, but supported Ehrlich
   C. contradicted Ehrlich, but supported Roux and Buchner
   D. were consistent with both theories
   E. had no bearing on the point at issue

TEST 9

PASSAGE

In the days of sailing ships, when voyages were long and uncertain, provisions for many months were stored without refrigeration
in the holds of the ships. Naturally no fresh or perishable foods
could be included. Toward the end of particularly long voyages the
crews of such ships became ill and often many died from scurvy. Many
men, both scientific and otherwise, tried to devise a cure for scurvy.
Among the latter was John Hall, a son-in-law of William Shakespeare,
who cured some cases of scurvy by administering a sour brew made from
scurvy grass and water cress.

The next step was the suggestion of William Harvey that scurvy
could be prevented by giving the men lemon juice. He thought that
the beneficial substance was the acid contained in the fruit.

The third step was taken by Dr. James Lind, an English naval surgeon, who performed the following experiment with 12 sailors, all of
whom were sick with scurvy: Each was given the same diet, except
that four of the men received small amounts of dilute sulfuric acid,
four others were given vinegar and the remaining four were given
lemons. Only those who received the fruit recovered.

Questions 1-7.

1. Credit for solving the problem described above belongs to   1. ...
   A. Hall, because he first devised a cure for scurvy
   B. Harvey, because he first proposed a solution of the
      problem
   C. Lind, because he proved the solution by means of an
      experiment
   D. both Harvey and Lind, because they found that lemons
      are more effective than scurvy grass or water cress
   E. all three men, because each made some contribution

2. A good substitute for lemons in the treatment of scurvy is   2. ...
   A. fresh eggs   B. tomato juice   C. cod-liver oil
   D. liver   E. whole-wheat bread

3. The number of control groups that Dr. Lind used in his ex-   3. ...
   periment was
   A. one   B. two   C. three   D. four   E. none

4. A substance that will turn blue litmus red is   4. ...
   A. aniline   B. lye   C. ice
   D. vinegar   E. table salt

5. The hypothesis tested by Lind was: 5. ....
   A. Lemons contain some substance not present in vinegar.
   B. Citric acid is the most effective treatment for scurvy.
   C. Lemons contain some unknown acid that will cure scurvy.
   D. Some specific substance, rather than acids in general,
      is needed to cure scurvy.
   E. The substance needed to cure scurvy is found only in
      lemons.

6. A problem that Lind's experiment did NOT solve was: 6. ....
   A. Will citric acid alone cure scurvy?
   B. Will lemons cure scurvy?
   C. Will either sulfuric acid or vinegar cure scurvy?
   D. Are all substances that contain acids equally effective
      as a treatment for scurvy?
   E. Are lemons more effective than either vinegar or sul-
      furic acid in the treatment of scurvy?

7. The PRIMARY purpose of a controlled scientific experiment   7. ...
   is to
   A. get rid of superstitions
   B. prove a hypothesis is correct
   C. disprove a theory that is false
   D. determine whether a hypothesis is true or false
   E. discover new facts

TEST 10

PASSAGE

The formed elements of the blood are the red corpuscles or erythrocytes, the white corpuscles or leucocytes, the blood platelets, and
the so-called blood dust or hemoconiae. Together, these constitute
30-40 per cent by volume of the whole blood, the remainder being
taken up by the plasma. In man, there are normally 5,000,000 red
cells per cubic millimeter of blood; the count is somewhat lower in
women. Variations occur frequently, especially after exercise or a
heavy meal, or at high altitudes. Except in camels, which have elliptical corpuscles, the shape of the mammalian corpuscle is that of
a circular, nonnucleated, bi-concave disk. The average diameter
usually given is 7.7 microns, a value obtained by examining dried
preparations of blood and considered by Ponder to be too low. Ponder's own observations, made on red cells in the fresh state, show
the human corpuscle to have an average diameter of 8.8 microns.
When circulating in the blood vessels, the red cell does not maintain a fixed shape but changes its form constantly, especially in
the small capillaries. The red blood corpuscles are continually
undergoing destruction, new corpuscles being formed to replace them.
The average life of red corpuscles has been estimated by various in-
vestigators to be between three and six weeks. Preceding destruction, changes in the composition of the cells are believed to occur
which render them less resistant. In the process of destruction, the
lipids of the membrane are dissolved and the hemoglobin which is
liberated is the most important, though probably not the only, source
of bilirubin. The belief that the liver is the only site of red cell
destruction is no longer generally held. The leucocytes, of which

there are several forms, usually number between 7000 and 9000 per cubic millimeter of blood. These increase in number in disease, particularly when there is bacterial infection.

Questions 1-10.

1. Leukemia is a disease involving the   1. ...
   A. red cells   B. white cells   C. plasma
   D. blood platelets E. blood dust

2. Are the erythrocytes in the blood increased in number after 2. ...
   a heavy meal? The paragraph implies that this
   A. is true   B. holds only for camels
   C. is not true   D. may be true
   E. depends on the number of white cells

3. When blood is dried, the red cells   3. ...
   A. contract   B. remain the same size
   C. disintegrate   D. expand
   E. become elliptical

4. Ponder is probably classified as a professional   4. ...
   A. pharmacist   B. physicist   C. psychologist
   D. physiologist   E. psychiatrist

5. The term "erythema" when applied to skin conditions sig-   5. ...
   nifies
   A. redness   B. swelling   C. irritation
   D. pain   E. roughness

6. Lipids are insoluble in water and soluble in such solvents 6. ...
   as ether, chloroform and benzene. It may be inferred that
   the membranes of red cells MOST closely resemble
   A. egg white   B. sugar   C. bone
   D. butter   E. cotton fiber

7. Analysis of a sample of blood yields cell counts of   7. ...
   4,800,000 erythrocytes and 16,000 leucocytes per cubic
   millimeter. These data suggest that the patient from whom
   the blood was taken
   A. is anemic
   B. has been injuriously invaded by germs
   C. has been exposed to high-pressure air
   D. has a normal cell count
   E. has lost a great deal of blood

8. Bilirubin, a bile pigment, is   8. ...
   A. an end product of several different reactions
   B. formed only in the liver
   C. formed from the remnants of the cell membranes of
      erythrocytes
   D. derived from hemoglobin exclusively
   E. a precursor of hemoglobin

9. Bancroft found that the blood count of the natives in the   9. ...
   Peruvian Andes differed from that usually accepted as nor-
   mal. The blood PROBABLY differed in respect to
   A. leucocytes   B. blood platelets C. cell shapes
   D. erythrocytes   E. hemoconiae

10. Hemoglobin is probably NEVER found   10. ...
    A. free in the blood stream
    B. in the red cells
    C. in women's blood
    D. in the blood after exercise
    E. in the leucocytes

_____

13

TEST 11

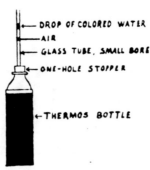

DROP OF COLORED WATER
AIR
GLASS TUBE, SMALL BORE
ONE-HOLE STOPPER

THERMOS BOTTLE

Questions 1-7.
1. The device shown in the diagram above indicates changes   1. ...
   that are measured more accurately by a(n)
      A. thermometer   B. hygrometer   C. anemometer
      D. hydrometer   E. barometer
2. If the device is placed in a cold refrigerator for 72   2. ...
   hours, which of the following is MOST likely to happen?
      A. The stopper will be forced out of the bottle.
      B. The drop of water will evaporate.
      C. The drop will move downward.
      D. The drop will move upward.
      E. No change will take place.
3. When the device was carried in an elevator from the first   3. ...
   floor to the sixth floor of a building, the drop of colored
   water moved about 1/4 inch in the tube. Which of the following is MOST probably true? The drop moved
      A. *downward* because there was a decrease in the air pressure
      B. *upward* because there was a decrease in the air pressure
      C. *downward* because there was an increase in the air tem-
         perature
      D. *upward* because there was an increase in the air temper-
         ature
      E. *downward* because there was an increase in the tempera-
         ture and a decrease in the pressure
4. The part of a thermos bottle into which liquids are poured   4. ...
   consists of
      A. a single-walled, metal flask coated with silver
      B. two flasks, one of glass and one of silvered metal
      C. two silvered-glass flasks separated by a vacuum
      D. two silver flasks separated by a vacuum
      E. a single-walled, glass flask with a silver-colored
         coating
5. The thermos bottle is MOST similar in principle to   5. ...
      A. the freezing unit in an electric refrigerator
      B. radiant heaters
      C. solar heating systems
      D. storm windows
      E. a thermostatically controlled heating system
6. In a plane flying at an altitude where the air pressure is   6. ...
   only half the normal pressure at sea level, the plane's
   altimeter should read, *approximately,*
      A. 3000 feet   B. 9000 feet   C. 18000 feet
      D. 27000 feet   E. 60000 feet

14

7. Which of the following is the POOREST conductor of heat?   7. ...
   A. Air under a pressure of 1.5 pounds per square inch
   B. Air under a pressure of 15 pounds per square inch
   C. Unsilvered glass
   D. Silvered glass
   E. Silver

TEST 12

PASSAGE

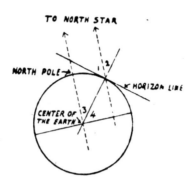

The latitude of any point on the earth's surface is the angle between a plumb line dropped to the center of the earth from that point and the plane of the earth's equator. Since it is impossible to go to the center of the earth to measure latitude, the latitude of any point may be determined indirectly as shown in the accompanying diagram.

It will be recalled that the axis of the earth, if extended outward, passes very near the North Star. Since the North Star is, for all practical purposes, infinitely distant, the line of sight to the North Star of an observer on the surface of the earth is virtually parallel with the earth's axis. Angle 1, then, in the diagram represents the angular distance of the North Star above the horizon. Angle 2 is equal to angle 3, because when two parallel lines are intersected by a straight line, the corresponding angles are equal. Angle 1 plus angle 2 is a right angle and so is angle 3 plus angle 4. Therefore, angle 1 equals angle 4 because when equals are subtracted from equals the results are equal.

Questions 1-10.

1. If an observer finds that the angular distance of the North   1. ...
   Star above the horizon is 30°, his latitude is
   A. 15°N   B. 30°N   C. 60°N   D. 90°N   E. 120°N

2. To an observer on the equator, the North Star would be   2. ...
   A. 30° above the horizon   B. 60° above the horizon
   C. 90° above the horizon   D. on the horizon
   E. below the horizon

3. To an observer on the Arctic Circle, the North Star would   3. ...
   be
   A. directly overhead   B. 23 1/2° above the horizon
   C. 66 1/2° above the horizon
   D. on the horizon
   E. below the horizon

4. The distance around the earth along a certain parallel of   4. ...
   latitude is 3600 miles. At that latitude, how many miles
   are there in one degree of longitude?
      A. 1 mile   B. 10 miles   C. 30 miles
      D. 69 miles   E. 100 miles
5. At which of the following latitudes would the sun be   5. ...
   DIRECTLY overhead at noon on June 21?
      A. 0°   B. 23 1/2°S   C. 23 1/2°N
      D. 66 1/2°N   E. 66 1/2°S
6. On March 21 the number of hours of daylight at places on   6. ...
   the Arctic Circle is
      A. none   B. 8   C. 12   D. 16   E. 24
7. The distance from the equator to the 45th parallel, meas-   7. ...
   ured along a meridian, is, *approximately,*
      A. 450 miles   B. 900 miles   C. 1250 miles
      D. 3125 miles   E. 6250 miles
8. The difference in time between the meridians that pass   8. ...
   through longitude 45°E and longitude 105°W is
      A. 6 hours   B. 2 hours   C. 8 hours
      D. 4 hours   E. 10 hours
9. Which of the following is NOT a great circle or part of a   9. ...
   great circle?
      A. Arctic Circle   B. 100th meridian   C. Equator
      D. Shortest distance between New York and London
      E. Greenwich meridian
10. At which of the following places does the sun set EARLIEST 10. ...
    on June 21?
      A. Montreal, Canada   B. Santiago, Chile
      C. Mexico City, Mexico   D. Lima, Peru
      E. Manila, P.I.

KEY (CORRECT ANSWERS)

TEST 1	TEST 4	TEST 7	TEST 9	TEST 11
1. C	1. A	1. A	1. E	1. A
2. E	2. B	2. A	2. B	2. C
3. C	3. C	3. D	3. B	3. B
4. A	4. C	4. C	4. D	4. C
5. A	5. D	5. D	5. D	5. D
6. B		6. C	6. A	6. C
7. B	TEST 5	7. E	7. D	7. A
8. C	1. D	8. D		
	2. B	9. E	TEST 10	TEST 12
TEST 2	3. A	10. E	1. B	1. B
1. C	4. E		2. D	2. D
2. B	5. D	TEST 8	3. A	3. C
	6. E	1. D	4. D	4. B
TEST 3	7. A	2. C	5. A	5. C
1. B		3. C	6. D	6. C
2. A	TEST 6	4. E	7. B	7. D
3. C	1. E	5. D	8. A	8. E
4. C	2. A	6. A	9. D	9. A
5. D	3. C	7. D	10. E	10. B
6. D	4. D	8. B		
7. D	5. B	9. C		
8. E	6. B	10. D		
9. C	7. B			

SCIENCE READING COMPREHENSION
EXAMINATION SECTION

DIRECTIONS: This section consists of a long reading passage, followed by questions based on the text. Each question consists of a statement followed by several suggested answers, only one of which is correct. After reading the passage, choose the letter of the BEST answer among the suggested answers, basing your answer upon what is stated or implied in the passage, and on your own understanding of science. *PRINT THE LETTER OF THE CORRECT ANSWER IN THE SPACE AT THE RIGHT.*

PASSAGE

SALIVA

Composition of Saliva

Before summarizing present knowledge of the composition of saliva, it is important to emphasize the difficulties of investigating this problem. First, saliva is produced by three pairs of large glands and the smaller glands of the oral mucosa (labial, lingual, buccal, and palatial), whose secretions differ in composition and whose relative contribution to the mixed saliva present in the mouth varies with conditions. Saliva may also contain fluid from the gingival pocket (gingival, or crevicular fluid). Since little is known about the factors which decide the relative secretion rates of each source, this variable is difficult to control. The composition of the saliva produced from any one gland varies with the rate of flow which itself varies with the type, intensity, and duration of stimulus used for obtaining the sample. Consequently, the composition of saliva may vary with changes in the stimulus. Although much more reproducible results are obtained by analyzing the secretion of separate glands, rather than mixed saliva, even then variations are found such as changes at different times of the day or differences related to meals. Secondly, the presence of suspended matter (mostly bacteria, epithelial cells, and mucin) raises the question whether or not saliva should be centrifuged before analysis. Centrifuged saliva gives lower figures for some constituents than does uncentrifuged; if, on the other hand, the suspended matter is not removed, it frequently interferes with the analytical techniques. Thirdly, the processes of living bacteria in saliva and the spontaneous loss of CO_2 after collection causes changes in the composition on standing, hence the accuracy of some analyses depends on the length of time elapsing between collection and analysis. Fourthly, some analytical methods which have been worked out for other biological fluids have sometimes been used on saliva, although later work has shown that for accurate results with saliva, the methods need modification. Fifthly, it is difficult to collect saliva under conditions which are physiological; saliva stimulated by chewing wax or rubber bands which is so frequently used may differ from that produced in response to food.

Saliva varies greatly in different individuals and in the same individual under different circumstances, and few average figures for its composition can be obtained which have any meaning or significance unless large groups of, say several hundred people, are studied under standardized conditions.

Properties of Saliva

In samples of parotid saliva from 384 subjects, the mean specific gravity varied between 1·0024 and 1·0061 at rates of flow of 0·32 and 0·94 ml min^{-1}, respectively. The osmotic pressure is between half and three-quarters that of blood, but sublingual saliva has approximately the same osmotic pressure as blood.

Viscosity and Spinnbarkeit

Saliva is a viscous fluid and also shows the property of *spinnbarkeit*, i.e., the ability to be drawn out into long elastic threads.

The cause of the viscosity of so dilute a solution as saliva is not understood. Gottschalk (1961) suggested that the mutual repulsion of the highly-ionized sialate groups at the end of the side-chains of glycoproteins would tend to keep the polypeptide core stretched and the molecule elongated. Molecules of this shape make their solution viscous by the considerable friction incurred in the movement relative to one another. There is considerable doubt, however, about the validity of this explanation of viscosity because the sialate contents of human parotid and submandibular saliva are similar, whereas their viscosities are very different and the viscosity of saliva can change without the release of the sialate from the side-chains. Schrager & Oates (1971) showed that the side-chains end in sulphate groups which might perform the role originally suggested for sialate. Large numbers of water molecules become attached to the glycoproteins, and the great bulk of these hydrated molecules may contribute to the viscosity of saliva, an effort not dependent on highly-changed side-chains. The viscosity and spinnbarkeit of wax-stimulated saliva are much lower than those of resting saliva collected by draining from the mouth. It may be speculated that the high viscosity of resting saliva may be due to an effect of rate of flow or to the fact that a higher proportion of the saliva collected in this way comes from the submandibular and sublingual glands. This does not appear to have been adequately studied, perhaps because difficulties arise in measuring the saliva from submandibular and sublingual ducts, owing to its consisting of an aqueous and semigelatinous phase and also the rapidity with which its viscosity changes.

The relative viscosities of the three main secretions after acetic acid stimulation were found by Schneyer (1955) to be: parotid 1.5, submaxillary 3.4, and sublingual 13.4.

The Buffering Power of Saliva

The buffering power (the power to resist changes of pH when acid or alkali are added) of a complex solution like saliva will vary at different parts of the pH range. Salivary buffers consist of bicarbonates, phosphates, and proteins. This has been shown by Lilenthal

(1955), who measured the buffering power of saliva before and after the removal of bicarbonate by a current of CO_2 free air at pH_5, and before and after dialysis, which removed both phosphates and bicarbonate but which does not remove the larger proteins.

Removal of the bicarbonate greatly reduced the buffering power and dialysis removed the whole of it. He concluded that bicarbonate is the most important buffer, that phosphate plays some part, but that, contrary to previous views, the proteins can be disregarded as buffers in saliva over the physiological pH range, but are the chief buffers of plaque. Buffers work by converting any highly-ionized acid or alkali which is tending to alter the pH of a solution, into a more weakly-ionized substance (that is, one which released fewer H^+ or OH^- ions). Bicarbonates release the weak carbonic acid when an acid is added, and since this acid is rapidly decomposed into water and CO_2, which leaves the solution, the result is not the accumulation of a weaker acid (as with most buffers) but the complete removal of acid. Bicarbonates are, therefore, very effective buffers against acid and are important in reducing pH changes in plaque after meals. Unstimulated saliva, which has a much lower bicarbonate content, is a less powerful buffer near neutrality.

Ericsson (1959) studied the diurnal variation in buffering power of saliva in five subjects. He found that (1) it was high immediately on rising in the morning. but rapidly fell; (2) it increased about a quarter of an hour after meals but usually fell within half to one hour after meals; and (3) there was an upward trend in the buffering power throughout the day until evening when it usually tended to fall.

The Reducing Power of Saliva

In any complex, biological system like saliva with its teeming flora, some chemical reactions in progress will be oxidations and others reductions. The algebraic sum of these reactions is such that mixed saliva normally has reducing properties.

In addition to bacterial reductions, saliva contains a complex mixture of substances with reducing properties which have been mistakenly assumed in the past to be glucose. These reducing substances are present in saliva collected from the duct, as well as in *mouth* saliva. They include carbohydrate split-off from glycoproteins, nitrites, and some unidentified substances of low molecular weight.

Functions of Saliva

Saliva has many functions and, although not essential for the maintenance of life, it makes important and varied contributions to the efficient working and protection of the body.

Digestive Functions

The only important digestive enzyme present in saliva is ptyalin or salivary amylase. This enzyme digests starch provided it has been previously cooked; heat breaks up the outer envelope of starch granules, after which their contents form a colloidal suspension which the enzyme can attack. The envelope does not consist of cellulose, as frequently stated, but of a specially insoluble type of starch which is made soluble by heat.

The amylase activity of saliva from different individuals shows great variation. Low amylase activity will no more than delay the digestion of starch since pancreatic juice contains powerful amylase activity. Activity has been found to be low before breakfast and to rise during the morning with a less consistent tendency to fall during the rest of the day. Parotid saliva has a concentration at least four times that of submandibular saliva and extracts of human sublingual glands (post-mortem material) contain no activity at all. The effect of flow rate on amylase concentration is uncertain: some workers have found that it is not affected but more recent results suggest a rise in concentration as the flow rate increases. With mixed saliva, however, the activity rises with increased rates of flow; this occurs because the proportion of the more active parotid saliva increases with increased stimuli. Sucrose and salt produce a higher amylase activity than other taste stimuli in the parotid. Crystaline salivary amylase has been prepared, and it is similar to pancreatic amylase but electrophoretic studies show that the two enzymes are not identical. Amylase is stated to be absent from the salivas of the cat and dog, and this is probably true of other carnivorous animals, though few have been tested.

It is clear that food remains in the mouth for too short a time to allow much digestion of starch to occur. However, after a large meal, the pH of the food which enters the stomach last remains nearly neutral for up to 30 minutes or more, the gastric hydrochloric acid soaks into the food and lowers the pH, amylase is inactivated and is eventually digested by pepsin, like any other protein.

It is possible that the main action of salivary amylase is to digest starch from food residues which remain in the mouth after meals, rather than to contribute to digestion as a whole.

The Antibacterial Function of Saliva

Although bacteria are always present, wounds in the mouth rarely become infected. This fact suggests that saliva contains some means of keeping in check harmful bacteria and that the organisms normally present in the mouth are those which have become resistant to salivary inhibition.

Many antibacterial actions of saliva have been observed, but opinions differ as to their relative importance. Dog saliva inhibits many bacteria more powerfully than does human, and this is believed to account at least partly for the freedom of the dog from dental caries.

Saliva has some mechanical action in removing bacteria from the mouth and conveying them to the stomach where most of them are killed and digested by the gastric juice. Although bacterial growth on some surfaces of the mouth is greatly restricted by this means, it probably has little effect on the bacteria in sheltered places such as the crevices between the teeth.

Microscopical examination of smears of saliva shows the presence of phagocytic leucocytes, and although the majority are disintegrating, ingested bacteria can be demonstrated within those cells which remain alive.

Leucotaxin and Opsonins

Two properties of saliva have been described which may be related to its antibacterial power: (1) saliva increases capillary permeability, and (2) mixed saliva possesses leucotactic activity, i.e., the power of attracting polymorphonuclear leucocytes, but this is absent from saliva collected from the ducts and is greatly reduced after thorough brushing of the teeth and the dorsum of the tongue. The activity returns within 1-3 hours in different individuals. Evidently, the *leucotaxin* (a polypeptide with the above properties) is produced by proteolytic enzymes of bacteria acting on the proteins of saliva. Whether the leucotaxin in saliva plays any part in the normal supply of leucocytes in the mouth is not known, but if the tissues are injured, it would gain access to the damaged area and by its dual action may promote the accumulation of leucocytes. Plaque also contains a leucotaxin which can be demonstrated in extracts and is much more active than in saliva. Its presence may account for the increased number of leucocytes passing through the gingival tissue when inflamed and with much plaque present.

Leucocytes thoroughly washed free of plasma and suspended in saline do not phagocytose bacteria, but if a trace of plasma is added, phagocytosis readily occurs. The substances in plasma which make bacteria more *palatable* to leucocytes are called *ipsonins*, now thought to be IgM and certain constituents of complement. Saliva contains opsonins, but being immunoglobulins, they are much less active than in plasma. Saliva from caries-free individuals has been stated to show more opsonic activity than caries-active saliva.

In addition to the above mechanisms, saliva contains chemical substances which exert a direct bacteriocidal action. Even bacteria normally found in saliva are weakly inhibited in vitro but it is obvious that these organisms have at least some degree of resistance to the oral antibacterial factors, otherwise they would not survive in the mouth. There is an erratic variation in the antibacterial potency of saliva from different individuals and from the same individuals at different times.

The Nature of the Antibacterial Substances in Saliva

In 1922, Fleming discovered in tears, nasal secretion, saliva, egg white, and in most tissues and body fluids a substance which dramatically kills and dissolves the organism Micrococcus iysodeikticus and, more slowly, many other species of bacteria. This substance is called *lysozyme* or *muramidase*, an enzyme which splits the 1:4 links between N-acetylmuramic acid and N-acetylglucosamine, these links being present in the walls of certain bacteria, the splitting of which causes their death and disintegration. If these polysaccharides are absent from a species of bacteria, then it is not destroyed by lysozyme.

Saliva and gingival fluid have higher concentrations than plasma, but its concentration decreases with stimulation. The effectiveness of lysozyme in saliva is probably reduced by the presence of mucin which inhibits its action. There is contradictory evidence on the effectiveness of lysozyme against the indigenous flora of the mouth; one group of workers were unable to detect any effect on over 100 strains of oral bacteria, but another group stated that the viability of most cariogenic and noncariogenic streptococci was reduced by lysozyme, although the bacteria were not fully lysed.

In addition to lysozyme, at least one other antibacterial factor exists as a normal constituent of parotid and submandibular saliva in concentrations varying sixteen-fold in different subjects. Most of the experiments have been carried out on lactobacilli, but it is active on many organisms. Its activity was shown by dialysis to consist of two fractions, a small ion which dialysed and a large molecule which remained inside the dialysing membrane. The small ion was identified as thiocyanate and the non-dialysable constituent as the enzyme perixidase. With hydrogen **peroxide** (present in saliva as a product of bacterial metabolism), these substances react to form an unstable antibacterial factor, possibly cyanosulphurous acid (HO_2SCN), cyanosulphuric acid (HO_3SCN) or sulphur dicyanoxide.

If this were the only reaction, the addition of catalase (which decomposes hydrogen **peroxide**) would be expected to abolish the effect whereas it only reduced it, thus showing the existence of a second factor not dependent on hydrogen peroxide but also inactive without thiocyanate. Experiments with ^{14}C thiocyanate show that the product in the presence of hydrogen peroxide is volatile, whereas that formed without hydrogen is not.

The activity of this factor does not seem to have been compared in saliva from caries-active and caries-free subjects.

The concentration of immunoglobulins (mainly IgA) in saliva is about 1.35 that of plasma, and it does not contain complement. Gingival fluid contains IgG, IgA, IgM, and complement in a ratio similar to that of plasma but only one-third the concentration; they may have an action localized to the gingivae but owing to dilution by the saliva are unlikely to have much effect in the mouth generally. The concentration of IgA in both parotid and submandibular saliva falls with increased rate of flow from an average of 33 mg 100 ml^{-1} (resting flow to 6.7 mg 100 ml^{-1} with vigorous stimulation with acid.

Another factor is a globulin which Green (1959) isolated from caries-free saliva (but was occasionally found in low concentration in caries-active saliva) which attaches itself to lactobacilli and is stated to inhibit their growth and bring about their lysis. It also has some effect on streptococci. This work contained some discrepancies and Geddes (1972) was unable to confirm it.

Bacterial Antagonisms

Some organisms are unable to survive in the mouth because they are killed in the presence of other salivary organisms. This topic has been reviewed and new results published by Donohue & Tyler (1975). The effect has been demonstrated by pouring a suspension of one species or organism over previously grown colonies of other organisms killed by UV light. On further incubations, the organisms may fail to grow in the vicinity of the dead colonies.

As well as unidentified factors, hydrogen peroxide and lactic acid (which is said to have antibacterial properties greater than can be accounted for by its pH) are products of salivary bacteria which antagonize other species in the oral flora. There is uncertainty about the extent of this antagonism in vivo, particularly by hydrogen peroxide which might be broken down by catalase in the plaque. However, it seems likely that, at least in some parts of the plaque, bacterial activity is kept in check by these antagonisms.

Certain oral streptococci synthesize bacteriocins-bactericidal substances which are active against some strains of the same or closely-related species as those that produce them, but not against unrelated species. Bacteriocins produced in the mouth could influence the particular strains which flourish in this environment.

In germ-free rats, a mixture of three species of organisms produced less caries than any of these species alone because one of the organisms removed lactic acid which, as the main metabolic product dissolving enamel, thereby reduced the intensity of the acid attack.

There is evidence that saliva acts as a barrier to the penetration of substances into the oral mucosa. Various dyes were placed on the oral mucosa of rats and their penetration was measured in histological sections from animals killed at intervals. The penetration was much greater if saliva flow had been previously inhibited by the injection of hyoscine. This work followed a previous finding that carcinogens diffused through the skin much more readily than through the oral mucosa; skin transplanted into the mouth also became more resistant to diffusion. The oral mucosa allows between ten and one hundred times as much water to pass through as the skin.

Saliva and Blood Coagulation

When freshly-shed blood is diluted with saliva, its clotting time is reduced, an activity destroyed by trypsin but enhanced by chymotrypsin.

This property of saliva has been studied quantitatively by Diku (1960) whose main findings were as follows: (1) if blood is diluted with saline, the clotting time is reduced to about 40% of normal but when diluted with saliva, it is reduced to 10% of normal, the effect being similar whether the blood:saliva ratio was 4:1 or 1:1; (2) saliva from all three glands as well as both sediment and supernatant from whole saliva all contained the coagulation factors normally present in serum; (3) whole saliva contains factors which act like tissue thromboplastins; (4) whole saliva could replace the platelet factor in experimental clotting but parotid or submandibular saliva could only do so partially; (5) saliva as secreted from the ducts

7

does not contain factor V but whole saliva and its sediment did contain some of the factor.

Saliva as a Lubricant

The glycoproteins, which are the main proteins of saliva, have the important property of giving saliva its slimy character. The moistening of the food is important for bolus formation and its lubrication facilitates swallowing. Claude Bernard found that a horse with a parotid fistula has great difficulty in swallowing dry food. In man, the lubrication of the mouth is necessary for clear speech. The accurate positioning of the tongue in relation to the teeth becomes difficult when the mouth is dry. The lubricating function of saliva is perhaps best appreciated when salivary flow is inhibited during nervousness or embarrassment. Under these circumstances, the swallowing of dry food or clear speaking in public becomes very difficult.

Saliva and Water Balance

Cannon (1937) first observed that the drying of the mouth due to excessive evaporation of saliva, as during prolonged talking, acted as a stimulus to salivary flow, the *dry mouth reflex*, and its existence has been thoroughly confirmed. One of the theories of the nature of thirst is that it results from drying of the mucous membrane in the pharynx. If the mouth becomes dry, and the dry mouth reflex operates, salivary flow is stimulated which prevents drying of the pharynx and, according to this theory, thirst is avoided. If the body tissues are short of water, the reflex does not occur, and in these circumstances, thirst follows and drying of the mouth thus encouraging the individual to put the situation right by taking a drink. This suppression of the dry mouth reflex does not require an actual loss of fluid by the body, but occurs after meals, when several liters of fluid are transferred from the blood and tissues into the gut as digestive juices. This could explain the thirst which frequently follows a meal. It is now thought that thirst follows from some stimulus, probably a rise in osmotic pressure of the blood, acting on the thirst center in the hypothalamus, but as thirst is quenched immediately after drinking - long before blood osmotic pressure could be changed - there is probably some additional effect in the mouth or pharynx which could be influenced by the dry mouth reflex.

Saliva and Taste

The sensation of taste is produced only by substances in solution. Some foods, such as fruits, contain such a high proportion of water that probably all the substances which have a taste are already in solution and their taste may be perceived as soon as they are released by mastication. Other foods, biscuits for example, contain relatively little water and before their taste becomes apparent, saliva must dissolve out the flavored constituents. By this means, saliva not only makes eating more pleasurable but may assist in the detection of unwholesome contaminants of food.

Desalivated rats show increased water intake and impaired taste discrimination; for example, when presented with either water or sodium chloride solution on different days, between 53 and 65% of the fluid drank by the control rats was saline, whereas the desalivated drank up to 93% saline. When solutions of acid or bitter substances were given, control rats drank very little of the sapid solution (i.e., with a taste), whereas, with certain concentrations, the desalivated rats preferred them.

Saliva and Dental Caries

The Composition of Saliva and Dental Caries

Many attempts have been made to relate the composition of saliva to the presence or absence of caries. There are several fundamental difficulties in the approach to the caries problem. In addition to the difficulties already mentioned in establishing normal standards for the composition of saliva, it is equally difficult to assess quantitatively the degree of dental carie. A common method of assessing caries is to enumerate the number of decayed, missing, or filled teeth (DMFT, or simply DMF) either present on a particular examination or developing over a period. The DMF figure assumes that all missing teeth were extracted because they were carious (which is approximately true for young subjects) but makes no distinction between a small and a large filling. A more refined method of scoring caries is to record the numbers of decayed, missing, or filled surfaces (DMFS). This takes into account the severity of the attack on each tooth. The age of the subject is important in considering the annual change in DMF because the incidence of new cavities falls off with advancing age; it is undecided whether this is caused by a change in the resistance of the tooth or whether it is merely because the most vulnerable parts of the teeth become carious in youth. When comparing the salivas of caries-active and caries-free individuals, it is difficult to get two equally large groups because caries-free individuals of a mature age are rare and difficult to find in westernized countries. This inequality in the size of the groups tends to lower the statistical significance of the results.

It has been suggested that saliva from caries-free individuals has higher values than the average for the following (but none of them are fully confirmed or apply to all caries-free subjects): rate of flow (and therefore higher pH and buffering power), calcium and phosphorus concentrations, ammonia concentration or ammonia production during incubation, the concentrations of adenosine triphosphate and fructose diphosphate, the aldolase activity, and the oxygen uptake of the bacteria (suggesting a more rapid destruction of sugar and the oxidation of the end-products by caries-free saliva), opsonin activity, general antibacterial activity and an antibacterial substance specific to lactobacilli and streptococci, the number of leucocytes in intact condition and differences in the proportion of epithelial cells to leucocytes. Some workers have found a higher, others a lower, amylase activity in caries-free people. Some of these claims are unconfirmed;

others are either disputed. The two differences which have gained the widest acceptance, but even these are not unanimously agreed, are in the smaller number of acid-producing organisms, especially Lactobacillus acidophilus or Streptococcus mutans in the saliva of caries-free individuals, and a higher rate of flow and, therefore, a buffering power. It seems likely that there is no single factor common to all caries-free subjects.

Changes Occurring During the Incubation of Saliva

If saliva is incubated for 24 hours, its pH rises to over 8.0 owing to ammonia production. A powerful putrid odor develops. These changes are presumably similar to those occurring some hours after a meal, or during sleep, which lead to halitosis.

A very different series of changes takes place if saliva is incubated with carbohydrate, and these have been studied extensively in the hope that they may throw some light on this role of carbohydrate in caries. The pH begins to fall after about an hour and reaches 5.0 within three hours in most salivas, but these changes are usually much slower in saliva from caries-free subjects. The acid arises from bacterial breakdown of the carbohydrate to lactic and other acids. Ammonia production and putrefactive changes are suppressed. These changes resemble those occurring in the plaque after a carbohydrate meal except that in saliva they are much slower because the bacteria are less concentrated. After six to eight hours incubation, the pH reaches about 4.0 after which acid production ceases; unlike plaque, saliva incubated with carbohydrates shows no tendency for a final rise in pH unless the carbohydrate concentration is very low (less than 0.5).

These changes are of interest in showing that saliva contains both acid-producing and alkali-producing bacteria and that the group which becomes dominant depends on whether carbohydrate is present or not.

During the first hour or so of the incubation of saliva without added carbohydrate, the pH may fall slightly before it begins to rise. This occurs because the carbohydrate fraction of the salivary glyco-proteins may be metabolized and converted into acids but their amounts are too small to produce a marked fall in pH. This effect is not always detected because the pH of fresh saliva is unstable owing to loss of CO_2 and the slight fall in pH may, therefore, be obscured. Oxygen uptake also occurs without added carbohydrates, and the amino acids released from salivary protein by bacterial enzymes are the main substrates.

When saliva is centrifuged, a slimy, semi-solid mixture of bacteria and protein separates out which is often referred to as *salivary sediment*. This material is sometimes used in experiments as a substitute for plaque (the salivary sediment system or SSS), although many chemical and bacteriological differences have been shown between plaque and sediment. The bacteria resemble those from the tongue rather than those of plaque and the water content is higher, 90% compared with 80-85% for plaque, and it does not concentrate calcium or phosphate to the same degree as plaque. In spite of these differences, it resembles plaque more than saliva in that acid production during incubation with sugar begins immediately after the sugar is added and reaches its lowest pH value within about half an hour or less (saliva takes over four hours).

If salivary sediment is washed with water or saline, its capacity for producing acid from carbohydrate falls greatly but can be restored if the sediment is suspended in the supernatant fraction of centrifuged saliva. Evidently, saliva contains co-factors necessary for bacterial metabolism. They have not been fully identified but one factor appears to be a polypeptide or small protein which probably stimulates growth and this energy-requiring process in turn stimulates glycolysis. Another factor is of low molecular weight and is possibly urea.

A fraction of saliva called the *pH rise factor* or *sialin* which stimulates glucose uptake by bacteria has also been detected. If the glucose concentration is above 0.5%, this factor increases acid production, but if the concentration is very low (0.05%), the increased uptake of glucose caused by the factor leads to its more rapid exhaustion so that the system reaches sooner the conditions of absence of carbohydrates which, as mentioned above, favor base production. It is likely that the salivary factor which stimulates glycolysis is similar or identical to the pH rise factor.

Halitosis

Halitosis (foetor oris, bad breath) is a condition which is almost universal if the odor of breath on waking is included. It increases in the intervals between meals and is reduced by eating. Halitosis tends to increase with advancing age.

Halitosis has been measured by trapping the odoriferous substances of breath by expiring into a column surrounded by liquid nitrogen which froze them. They were then warmed up and their odor measured in an osmoscope in which air containing the odor is quantitatively diluted until the odor disappears. The strength of the odor is estimated by the amount of dilution needed.

Unpleasant odors in the mouth could arise from the alimentary canal, from the lungs, or from bacterial activity in the mouth itself. Most of the evidence suggests that if subjects with gross disease are excluded, breath odors arise almost entirely from the mouth. For example, when measurements were made (on 200 normal subjects) of the odor of the breath collected from expired air, the value was almost identical to that obtained by circulating atmospheric air through the mouth so that it picked up odors from the mouth only. The main factors producing mouth odor are: (1) stagnation of food debris or epithelial cells which may arise from reduced saliva flow or reduced friction in the mouth. The accumulated material is then broken down by the oral bacteria. (2) Tissue destruction as in periodontal disease or caries also leads to substrates which can give rise to odors. (3) The smell of certain foods such as garlic cling to the mouth, presumably the odoriferous constituents tend to become absorbed on to the oral mucosa. Saliva itself readily gives rise to bad odors, especially during mouth breathing, prolonged talking, or hunger. Eating reduces halitosis partly because it increases saliva flow and friction in the mouth, with the effect of removing the sources of odor, and possibly because if the food contains carbohydrate, the growth of acid-producing bacteria is encouraged and bacteria which metabolize proteins and protein derivatives are suppressed because they cannot compete for the limited growth factors in saliva.

Analysis of mouth air by gas chromatography showed that H_2S and methyl mercaptan were the constituents responsible for approximately 90% of the odor, a third minor constituent being dimethyl sulphide. Surprisingly, the usual products of putrefaction - the tryptophane derivatives (skolole, indole, other amines and ammonia) were found to be unimportant - although present in saliva, they were insufficiently volatile at the pH of saliva to be detected as smells. The unpleasant odor seems to depend on the presence of -SH groups and was, therefore, favored by H transfer (reduction, which converts -S-S groups into -SH) and inhibited if H transfer was prevented, i.e., if oxidation is favored.

Saliva incubated for 60-90 minutes produced similar odoriferous substances. Plaque suspended in saliva supernatant required much longer periods of incubation to produce a comparable amount of odoriferous material. Addition of the sulphur containing amino acids showed that they were the substrates from which the odor was produced, the mercaptan being the dominating product from methionine and H_2S from cysteine and cystine. The epithelial cells are the main source of these amino acids in the mouth.

Methods of preventing halitosis are still inadequate, but temporary improvement follows mouth rinsing, tooth brushing, and especially rubbing epithelial cells from the tongue. In one experiment, rinsing the mouth with water reduced the concentration of volatile sulphur compounds in the mouth air immediately on waking, but they returned to about 80% of their initial value within one hour. If the teeth are thoroughly brushed with various dentifrices, however, their concentrations returned one hour later to only between 15 and 30% of the initial value. This is further evidence that the odor originated in the mouth. Other methods of dealing with halitosis are: (1) antiseptic mouthwashes which inhibit the bacterial activity, (2) in view of the above biochemical findings, oxidizing agents (by preventing H transfer) would be expected to reduce halitosis, and (3) frequent drinks and means of stimulating saliva flow would also be expected to be beneficial but do not appear to have been tested in controlled experiments.

DIRECTIONS: Each question or incomplete statement is followed by
            several suggested answers or completions. Select the
            one that BEST answers the question or completes the
            statement. *PRINT THE LETTER OF THE CORRECT ANSWER
            IN THE SPACE AT THE RIGHT.*

1. Bacteriocins   1.___
   A. are produced by streptococci and are effective against
      bacterial species unrelated to streptococci
   B. include hydrogen peroxide and lactic acid
   C. could influence the natural selection of the oral
      bacterial strains
   D. have their activity destroyed by catalase

2. Spinnbarkeit is   2.___
   A. known to be due to glycoprotein side-chains
   B. dependent on the bicarbonate concentration
   C. not a property of saliva from the minor salivary
      glands
   D. lower for wax-stimulated saliva than resting saliva

3. Lysozyme   3.___
   A. concentration in saliva decreases with stimulated flow
   B. is effective against all types of bacteria
   C. action is enhanced by mucin
   D. is generally felt to be completely ineffective against
      cariogenic bacteria

4. Halitosis is adequately prevented by   4.___
   A. breath mints   B. mouthwashes
   C. toothbrushing   D. none of the above

5. The substance(s) in plasma which make(s) bacteria easier   5.___
   to phagocytize is(are)
   A. IgA   B. IgG
   C. IgM   D. opsonins

6. The composition of saliva changes on standing because   6.___
   A. composition of saliva varies with rate flow
   B. composition varies with the intensity and duration
      of the stimulus
   C. analytical techniques were not properly modified
   D. of the presence of live bacteria

7. As the number of species of bacteria in the oral cavity   7.___
   increases, the caries rate
   A. is likely to *decrease*
   B. will *increase* because each species can produce caries
      at its own individual rate
   C. will *increase* unless fluoride is used
   D. will *increase* unless the body steps up its production
      of salivary antibacterials

8. Incubation of saliva WITHOUT added carbohydrate   8.___
   A. results in a gradual and sustained fall in pH
   B. leads to a pH change due to ammonia production
   C. results in a sharp and immediate rise in pH due to
      bicarbonate
   D. results in an unchanged pH due to buffering

9. The incidence of new caries
   A. *decreases* with increasing amylase activity
   B. *decreases* with advancing age
   C. correlates well with the composition of saliva
   D. *increases* with decreased number of acid-producing organisms

9. ___

10. Antibacterials in saliva are
    A. secreted by the salivary glands and made by activity
    B. formed by the reaction of hydrogen peroxide and lactic acid
    C. active due to the pH decrease they cause
    D. neutralized by gastric juices

10. ___

11. Oxidizing agents
    A. cause halitosis
    B. lead to stagnation of debris
    C. may prevent hydrogen transfer
    D. lead to the formation of -SH groups from -S-S

11. ___

12. Saliva incubated with carbohydrate
    A. reaches pH5
    B. shows no change in pH for saliva from caries-free subjects
    C. reaches pH8 owing to ammonia production
    D. forms salivary glycoproteins

12. ___

13. The pH is approximately 5.5 after the addition of
    A. 0.3 ml of 0.02N HCL to saliva
    B. 0.5 ml of 0.02N HCL to saliva
    C. 1.5 ml of 0.02N HCL to saliva
    D. none of the above

13. ___

14. The outer envelope of starch granules
    A. is easily digested by salivary enzymes
    B. is made soluble by heat
    C. consists of cellulose
    D. occurs as a colloidal suspension in its natural state

14. ___

15. Organisms normally present in saliva
    A. are easily killed and digested by direct bactericidal action of saliva
    B. are identical to those in tears, nasal secretions, and body fluids
    C. are killed and digested by gastric juice
    D. show opsonic activity

15. ___

16. The MAIN proteins of saliva
    A. are digestive enzymes
    B. are pH rise factors
    C. display bactericidal activity
    D. function as lubricants

16. ___

17. Saliva contains
    A. the coagulation factors   B. complement
    C. pepsin   D. all of the above

17. ___

14

18. To collect saliva under physiological conditions, one may   18.___
    A. chew on wax
    B. chew on rubber bands
    C. collect it from the ducts
    D. none of the above

19. Skin transplanted into the mouth becomes more resistant   19.___
    to diffusion due to
    A. the bacteriocins
    B. injections of hyoscine
    C. saliva acting as a barrier
    D. the absence of carcinogens

20. Analysis of centrifuged saliva differs from uncentrifuged   20.___
    because
    A. it is collected from the ducts
    B. composition varies with rate flow
    C. saliva contains suspended matter
    D. mixed saliva was analyzed

21. The LAST significant salivary buffer at physiological pH   21.___
    is
    A. bicarbonate   B. proteins
    C. phosphates   D. carbonates

22. Indole and skatole are   22.___
    A. unimportant in the production of halitosis
    B. volatile constituents of saliva
    C. putrefaction products of histidine
    D. not found in saliva

23. Blood has about the same osmotic pressure as   23.___
    A. parotid saliva   B. sublingual saliva
    C. crevicular fluid   D. all of the above

24. Which of the following is the source of *highest* amylase   24.___
    activity?
    A. Crevicular fluid   B. Submandibular gland
    C. Sublingual gland   D. Parotid gland

25. Contribution to the reducing properties of saliva is   25.___
    from
    A. overall reactions of mixed saliva
    B. bacterial actions
    C. saliva collected from the ducts
    D. all of the above

26. The clotting time of blood is FASTEST when mixed with   26.___
    A. saline   B. parotid saliva
    C. submandibular saliva   D. whole saliva

27. Leucotactic activity of saliva is   27.___
    A. greatest in the saliva collected from the ducts
    B. greatest after thorough brushing of the teeth and
       tongue
    C. greater than that of plaque
    D. due to a polypeptide

15

28. Salivary amylase
   A. is essential for the digestion of cooked starches
   B. is digested by pepsin
   C. has its greatest activity in the intestine when the pH is higher than in the stomach
   D. spreads sugar digestion

28. ___

29. Salivary flow is inhibited by
   A. bacteria
   B. pH changes
   C. skin resistant to diffusion being transplanted into the mouth
   D. none of the above

29. ___

30. Most of the odor of halitosis is due to
   A. odoriferous gases formed in the lungs
   B. hydrogen sulfide and methyl mercaptan
   C. gases formed in the stomach
   D. dental caries

30. ___

31. Analytical methods which have been worked out for studying the composition of the biological fluids
   A. may be applied directly to study saliva
   B. can easily be used to determine whether saliva was collected by chewing wax or in response to food
   C. must be modified when applied to saliva
   D. are ideal for determining the individual differences in saliva

31. ___

32. Saliva is different from plaque in that plaque
   A. does not contain buffers
   B. shows no pH change after a carbohydrate meal
   C. shows a pH rise after a carbohydrate meal
   D. contains more highly concentrated bacteria

32. ___

33. An osmoscope is used to measure
   A. the osmotic pressure of saliva
   B. the number of live bacteria in saliva
   C. the strength of odors
   D. all of the above

33. ___

34. Salivary amylase activity terminates
   A. approximately three minutes after starting
   B. when the carbohydrates are completely digested
   C. when stomach acid comes in contact with it
   D. all of the above

34. ___

35. Localized loss of moisture from the mouth
   A. causes a change of osmotic pressure in the blood
   B. stimulates the dry mouth reflex
   C. stimulates the entry of fluids into the gut
   D. improves bolus formation

35. ___

36. The clotting time of blood is SHORTEST when mixed with
   A. saliva from the ducts   B. saline
   C. whole saliva   D. parotid saliva

36. ___

16

37. It is well established that caries incidence correlates   37.___
    with
    A. ammonia production during incubation
    B. opsonin activity
    C. antibacterial activity
    D. none of the above

38. The thirst center is located in the   38.___
    A. hypothalamus   B. parotid
    C. sublingual   D. oropharynx

39. Salivary sediment   39.___
    A. forms when saliva is incubated with carbohydrates
    B. is a mixture of protein and bacteria
    C. is essentially the same as plaque
    D. remains in the duct after collection of saliva

40. An enzyme which splits a chemical bond between N-acetyl-   40.___
    muramic acid and N-acetylglucosamine is
    A. lysozyme   B. amylase
    C. catalase   D. peroxidase

41. Average figures for the composition of saliva are BEST   41.___
    obtained
    A. by analysis of resting saliva
    B. by studying saliva collected from the ducts
    C. when several hundred people are studied
    D. by incubating saliva in the absence of carbohydrates

42. Saliva from the submandibular gland as compared to that   42.___
    from the parotid
    A. has greater amylase activity
    B. has constant composition from individual to individual
    C. does not contain glycoproteins
    D. has higher viscosity

43. Carbonic acid in saliva   43.___
    A. is a major contributor to caries formation
    B. decomposes rapidly
    C. helps accumulate weaker acids
    D. all of the above

44. The hydrogen peroxide found in saliva   44.___
    A. is formed by muramidase
    B. plays a major role in the buffering capacity
    C. is a bacterial product
    D. is not formed in caries-free subjects

45. Dog saliva does NOT contain   45.___
    A. amylase   B. antibacterials
    C. buffers   D. bacteria

46. Incubation of saliva with or without carbohydrate   46.___
    results in
    A. ammonia formation
    B. a pH change
    C. changes which resemble those following a carbohydrate
       meal
    D. increased lactic acid formation

47. The composition of saliva varies with the   47.___
   A. rate of flow
   B. intensity of the stimulus
   C. identity of the stimulus
   D. all of the above

48. Leucocytes washed free of plasma and suspended in saline   48.___
   A. will rapidly disintegrate
   B. do not phagocytose bacteria
   C. exert a direct bactericidal activity
   D. will display erratic antibacterial potency

49. The dominant bacteria of saliva, acid-producing or alkali-   49.___
    producing, depends on
   A. whether it was collected from minor or major salivary
      glands
   B. what percentage is crevicular fluid
   C. the presence or absence of carbohydrate
   D. the intensity of halitosis

50. The MAIN bacterial product dissolving enamel is   50.___
   A. hydrogen peroxide   B. lactic acid
   C. acetic acid   D. ammonia

KEY (CORRECT ANSWERS)

1. C	11. C	21. B	31. C	41. C
2. D	12. A	22. A	32. D	42. D
3. A	13. D	23. B	33. C	43. B
4. D	14. B	24. D	34. C	44. C
5. D	15. C	25. D	35. B	45. A
6. D	16. D	26. D	36. C	46. B
7. A	17. A	27. D	37. D	47. D
8. B	18. D	28. B	38. A	48. B
9. B	19. C	29. D	39. B	49. C
10. A	20. C	30. B	40. A	50. B

SCIENCE READING COMPREHENSION

EXAMINATION SECTION

DIRECTIONS: This section consists of a long reading passage, followed by questions based on the text. Each question consists of a statement followed by several suggested answers, only one of which is correct. After reading the passage, choose the letter of the BEST answer among the suggested answers, basing your answer upon what is stated or implied in the passage, and on your own understanding of science. *PRINT THE LETTER OF THE CORRECT ANSWER IN THE SPACE AT THE RIGHT.*

PASSAGE

PHARMACOLOGICAL STUDIES OF STIMULANTS AND DEPRESSANTS

ABSTRACT

A group of experiments is described in which chimpanzees and orangutans are utilized as subjects in research projects designed to evaluate the effects of stimulant and depressant drugs on learning and performance. Efficiency of performance on a task which measures spaced responding was impaired when subjects smoked cigarettes containing Δ^5-tetrahydrocannabinol prior to testing. In a sequential learning task, these subjects also demonstrated reduced performance when stimulant drugs were orally administered before testing. Depressant drugs did not produce comparable decrements in sequential learning performance. Physical and behavioral tolerance and dependence on ethanol were investigated in rhesus monkey subjects using a variety of experimental procedures, including forced oral acceptance, intragastic intubation, intravenous infusion, and conditioned voluntary oral acceptance.

Chimpanzees, orangutans, and gorillas are the largest of all nonhuman primate species and constitute the great ape family. In our studies, we have generally utilized chimpanzees (Pan troglodytes) from the great ape colony of the Yerkes Regional Primate Research Center of Emory University. Chimpanzees tend to be inquisitive subjects that perform well on a wide variety of behavioral tasks. Although none of the research projects undertaken are terminal experiments, there are obviously greater risks in some procedures than others. For that reason, in studies involving surgical preparation, indwelling catheters, and the like, the rhesus monkey (Macaca mulatta) has been our primary subject.

LEARNING AND PERFORMANCE

With the chimpanzee, we have focused our attention on evaluating the effects of potentially psychoactive compounds on learning and performance. One of the earliest experiments of this type was designed to examine the effects of smoking cigarettes containing Δ^9-tetrahydrocannabinol (Δ^9-THC) on spaced responding. The behavioral task used involved lever pulling performance for M & M candy rewards on a DRL schedule (differential reinforcement low), in which the subject was required to pause for a minimum of either 10 sec. or 20 sec. before pulling a lever that would deliver an M & M candy reward. For example, on a DRL 10-sec. schedule, the subject was required to wait at least 10 sec. before responding to obtain the reward. If a response was made prior to the end of the 10 sec. interval, the timer was reset and the subject was again required to pause 10 sec. or more to obtain a reinforcement.

Prior to initiation of drug testing, pretraining on both the smoking and DRL task was completed. To facilitate absorption of the Δ^9-THC, two chimpanzees and one orangutan (Pongo pygmaeus) were trained to make long draws on a pipe that was inserted through the wall of the testing cage. One end of the pipe contained a lighted cigarette, and the subject was required to maintain constant negative pressure on the pipe for approximately 5 sec. or longer before an M & M candy reinforcer was delivered. On drug days, the cigarettes smoked by the subjects were injected with Δ^9-THC such that the total putative dose of the drug was varied from 1.8 mg/kg to 6.2 mg/kg. Following the smoking session, behavioral testing on the DRL task was initiated. As can be seen in Fig. 1, the results of this experiment indicated that the efficiency of responding (rewards obtained/total response) decreased below control levels when the cigarette contained Δ^9-THC. This reduction in performance was observed in all three subjects.

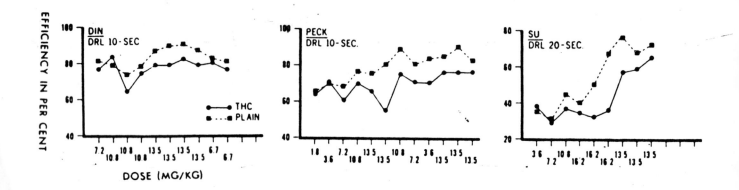

Figure 1. Efficiency of responding (reinforcements/responses) per 30-min. DRL test session for three great apes. Doses of Δ^9-THC as indicated on the abscissa were administered every 3-4 days and performance on those days compared to intervening control days.

Although this approach demonstrated the feasibility of using large adult ape subjects (40-70 kg) for psychopharmacological research, two major problems remained. (a) Rigorous control over the dose of drug via inhalation proved very difficult, since variable amounts of inhalation by the animal were still possible. Further, routine monitoring of the blood concentrations of inhaled compounds was not practical because of the size of the subjects and the lack of practical analytical procedures for measuring substances such as Δ^9-THC in biological fluids. (b) Performance on the DRL task could not be directly related to the effects of drugs on the process of learning, since the subjects were all given extensive training on the task prior to drug testing. For these reasons, we shifted to oral administration of all drugs and adopted a sequential response task to assess the effects of drugs on learning.

This sequential response task was first described by Boren and Devine and is uniquely suited to the problem in at least three respects. First, the subject is required to learn a relatively complex sequential response chain rather than a simple visual discrimination or light tracking task. Second, a stimulus fading procedure is used so that learning is guided in a standardized manner. Initially, brightness cues are used to shape the animal's response. These cues are then gradually diminished so that the animal has to rely more and more on memory rather than brightness discrimination. This procedure has proved to be more efficient in sequential learning than nonfading techniques. Third, and most important, while the basic nature of the task is the same over sessions, the subject is required to learn a new sequence on each day. Thus, the learning deficit or enhancement associated with various orally administered drugs can be assessed using a nonhuman primate species closely related to man.

We have used a modified version of this task consisting of a manipulandum panel with six horizontally mounted Lindsley response levers. A transilluminated circular disk was mounted 10 cm above each of the six levers. These lights served as visual cues signaling the correct lever to pull at a given time. The saliency of these brightness cues was varied across eight levels of illumination, ranging from high contrast (the correct lever fully lighted with the other five off) to no contrast (all levers, including the correct one, at full brightness). Below the manipulandum panel was a food receptacle into which M & M candy reinforcers were delivered from a dispenser. These reinforcers were delivered each time the animal pulled the final lever in a correct sequence of levers. When an error was made, a 7-sec. timeout went into effect during which a buzzer was sounded and the house lights and all lever lights were extinguished. Each day testing began with maximum light cues followed by a gradual fading out of the discriminable brightness feature, thereby forcing the subject to learn the position of the correct levers. The length of the lever pulling sequence was also systematically increased from one lever to six levers. The fading procedure was first used with the shortest sequence length of one. Each correct lever response was followed by a reduction in the brightness cue by one level while each error resulted in the light cue "backing up" to the level used on the previous trial. At the eighth level, all stimulus lights were identically illuminated and consequently, no longer functioned as a cue. Therefore, a correct response at the eighth level indicated that the animal had learned the correct position of the lever(s). Thus, the brightness cue was systematically faded out through eight

3

equal intensity changes, so that the stimulus lights provided no cue to the correct sequence of levers when acquisition of the behavioral chain was completed. When the subject correctly completed sequence one, the sequence was increased to a two-lever chain. The subject was now required to pull two levers in the correct sequence to obtain reinforcement. Again, maximal brightness cues were used on the initial trials but were progressively faded out with each correct response. When the subject successfully completed the sequence to two levers at the eighth level of illumination, demonstrating that he had learned to discriminate the correct two-lever sequence by position, the sequence was lengthened to three levers and the process repeated.

Daily test sessions were terminated either when 50 minutes had elapsed or when the subject has successfully completed a sequence of six levers, whichever occurred first. Since a new lever sequence was presented each day, a new sequence was learned each day. Thus, this task provided learning data for each day of testing. Therefore, learning (acquisition) on those days when a particular drug was administered could be compared with intervening control days when only placebo was given.

The primary dependent measure obtained from this task is the maximum sequence length completed during the 50-min. test sessions. In general, drugs that have a depressant or tranquilizing action (butabarbital, secobarbital, glutethimide, and diazepam) have little effect on learning as measured by the sequential task when the doses are kept below the level where obvious general physical impairment occurs. However, stimulants (benzphetamine, d-amphetamine, diethylpropion, phendimetrazine, and phentermine) do produce decreases in learning, depending on the potency of the drug and the size of dose, even though no overt symptoms of general impairment are present (see Fig. 2).

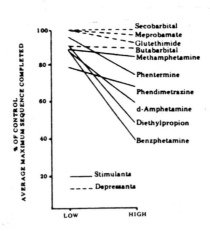

Figure 2. The effect of a series of drugs on learning as measured by the maximum sequence length achieved during a test session. Performance on drug testing days is indicated as a percent of that on the control days that immediately preceded the drug administration days.

4

ETHANOL TOLERANCE AND DEPENDENCE

In our laboratory, physical dependence on ethanol has been produced in young chimpanzees by including alcohol in their liquid diet in gradually increasing doses. With rhesus monkeys, ethanol physical dependence has been produced using this same procedure and also by using nasogastric intubation of ethanol in liquid diet two to three times per day, and by constant infusion of ethanol solutions through surgically implanted intrajugular catheters. All procedures have resulted in the production of physical dependence as evidenced by the emergence of withdrawal symptoms when blood ethanol concentrations decreased from previously elevated values achieved during the chronic administration period. In general, these studies demonstrated that chronic administration of ethanol in sufficient amounts and at appropriate intervals to maintain blood ethanol concentrations above zero for a period of 4 or more days was necessary to produce observable signs of physical dependence. Further, blood methanol was observed to accumulate during these periods of chronic ethanol administration, probably due to competitive inhibition of the enzyme system that catalyzes the metabolism of both alcohols. This buildup of methanol, which is toxic in primates, may have some significance in the development of physical dependence.

In addition to physical dependence, the addictive process is characterized by the development of tolerance to ethanol. Both metabolic and behavioral tolerance have been investigated in these animals. The rate of disappearance of ethanol from the blood was determined at frequent intervals during periods of chronic ethanol administration. In both chimpanzees and rhesus monkeys, disappearance rates increased with chronic administration and the magnitude of the increase was significantly and positively correlated with the quantity of ethanol administered. This effect was reversible as demonstrated by a return of disappearance rates to baseline values following termination of chronic ethanol administration.

Behavioral or functional tolerance associated with ethanol intake has also been investigated in our laboratory using rhesus monkeys that had been extensively trained on a two-choice discrimination reversal task. Performance of this task under baseline conditions or following administration of a placebo that was isocaloric to the ethanol dose was compared to performance 90-min. following the nasogastric administration of 3 q/kg of ethanol. Upon initiation of ethanol administration, performance decrements were significant. However, over a 36-day period during which this same dose of ethanol was given each day prior to testing, performance gradually returned to control levels, indicating the development of functional tolerance (see Fig. 3). Blood ethanol concentration measured at the end of each test session averaged 235 mg/dl and did not vary significantly, suggesting that the changes in performance were not due simply to increased disappearance rates and, consequently, lower blood ethanol concentration at time of testing. Subsequent testing demonstrated that this tolerance was retained at both a 24-day and a 1-year interval following the original alcohol test period.

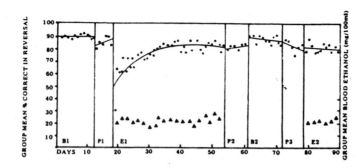

Figure 3. Group mean percentage of correct responses during trials 2-10 following cue reversal or a two choice discrimination-reversal task. Scores for individual animals were obtained by calculating the mean percentage of correct responses during reversal for each daily test session; equations for the lines were calculated using the method of least squares. Ethanol (3 g/kg) was administered nasogastrically 90 min. prior to the test session on days 19 through 54 and days 70 through 90 (El and E2). Group mean blood ethanol concentrations (▲) are shown for these days. Placebo solutions of isocaloric lactose were similarly administered during the 6-day placebo periods (P1, P2, and P3). During baseline testing (B1 and B2), no solutions were administered prior to testing.

In this series of studies, we have demonstrated the development of both physical dependence and tolerance to alcohol in nonhuman primates. These are two primary aspects of the addictive process and their development in nonhuman primates is a demonstration that these animals are suitable models for the systematic experimental investigation of alcoholism.

More recently, our efforts have been directed toward the investigation of behavioral dependence on alcohol in rhesus monkeys and on the development of procedures for quantitatively evaluating the severity of the withdrawal syndrome in dependent monkeys.

To study the development of behavioral dependence, we have designed an experiment that examines the effects of a conditioning procedure in which oral consumption of ethanol is accompanied by simultaneous intravenous (i.v.) ethanol infusion on voluntary oral intake. The taste of the drug is temporally paired with the apparently reinforcing pharmacological effects. Animals with intrajugular catheters were trained to make contact with a drinking tube to initiate the delivery of fluid both orally and i.v. During conditioning, 0.1 g/kg of ethanol was administered per response. Initially, the delivery was entirely by i.v. infusion, but gradually the dose was partitioned between the oral and i.v. components with the i.v. concentration decreasing as the oral concentration was increased, until the entire dose was delivered orally. A free choice between water and an 18% ethanol solution was then made available to the animal.

Of five monkeys for which data are available for the post-conditioning choice period, increased voluntary oral intake of ethanol was demonstrated in three animals. In one animal, intake exceeded 10.5 g/kg per day for 10 of the first 11 days following conditioning and withdrawal symptoms were observed on the day when intake decreased to 6.6 g/kg per day. Unfortunately, this animal died on the 14th day following conditioning. In a second animal, intake averaged 5-8 g/kg per day for 9 weeks following conditioning and in the third, the range was 3-5 g/kg per day for 2 weeks. In both these latter animals, ethanol intake declined following these periods of elevation, but was again increased following a 2-week period of forced ethanol intake. In the remaining two animals, intake was slightly elevated following conditioning, but returned to preconditioning levels within 2 weeks. Preconditioning mean ethanol intake in the entire group of monkeys did not exceed 1.5 g/kg per day at ethanol concentrations ranging from 1 to 12%. At concentrations of 12-18%, mean intake ranges from 1.5 to 2.5 g/kg per day. Thus, the quantity of ethanol consumed after conditioning by the three animals described above represents a considerable increase above control levels.

The development of methods for reproducibly and quantitatively assessing physical dependence during ethanol withdrawal has also been investigated using rhesus monkeys. Physiological tremor was chosen as the parameter to measure, since increased tremor is one of the earliest and most universal symptoms of ethanol withdrawal and since it could be recorded frequently during withdrawal with minimal disturbance to the animal. A transducer was strapped to the leg of a chair-restrained monkey and tremor was recorded on a paper chart for visual examination and on magnetic tape for further analysis by computer. Recordings were made each hour for a 33-hour withdrawal period that followed a 4-day period of ethanol administration. These tremor measurements were compared to control measurements from a 33-hour period following 4 days of chair restraint during which no ethanol was administered. After a 1-week recovery period, each animal began another cycle. Physical dependence was induced by constant infusion of ethanol solutions through intrajugular catheters to maintain blood ethanol concentration at one of four levels: 50, 100, 200, or 300 mg/dl. Each of these blood ethanol concentrations was examined in each animal in a counterbalanced order. During withdrawal, an observational score was also obtained each hour based on a rating scale of withdrawal symptoms.

These procedures have been followed with four rhesus monkeys, and the data from these studies are currently being evaluated. Analyses of variance have shown that baseline tremor measurements repeated in a single animal are statistically distinguishable, indicating that these measurements must be repeated before each ethanol administration period and used as a basis of comparison for the accompanying withdrawal period. During withdrawal, we generally observe an increase in tremor frequency and data analysis is in progress to statistically evaluate the observed differences and to determine the reproducibility of the procedure.

In the studies described above, we have attempted to develop procedures for using nonhuman primate subjects for systematically investigating the effect of stimulant and depressant drug on learning and the behavioral and physical aspects of ethanol usage. Although major research projects with chimpanzees and rhesus monkeys are necessarily restricted to relatively specialized institutional settings, these animals can prove extremely useful animal models of psychopharmacological processes that have major implications for serious public health problems in this country and throughout the world.

DIRECTIONS: Each question or incomplete statement is followed by several suggested answers or completions. Select the one that BEST answers the question or completes the statement. *PRINT THE LETTER OF THE CORRECT ANSWER IN THE SPACE AT THE RIGHT.*

1. The experiments in which ethanol was given both *orally* and 1.___
   intravenously were designed to study the development of
   A. metabolic tolerance   B. behavioral tolerance
   C. behavioral dependence   D. functional tolerance

2. In the experiments in which Δ^9-THC was smoked, the amounts 2.___
   of drug inhaled
   A. were controlled by forcing the subjects to maintain
      a constant pressure on the pipe for 5 seconds before
      getting a reward
   B. were controlled by using a 10 second differential
      reinforcement schedule
   C. were maintained constant by injecting measured amounts
      of the drug into the cigarettes
   D. proved to be impossible to control rigorously

3. In experiments in which physical dependence was studied, 3.___
   hourly comparisons of tremor were made between a subject
   A. after 4 days of chair restraint and the same subject
      after another 4 days of chair restraint and alcohol
      administration
   B. after four days of chair restraint and another subject
      similarly treated
   C. after four days of chair restraint and another subject
      after four days of chair restraint and alcohol adminis-
      tration
   D. with a blood ethanol level of 50 mg/dl and another
      subject with blood ethanol level of 300 mg/dl

4. According to this article, the BEST kind of task to be 4.___
   used in assessing the effects of drugs on learning would
   be one that is
   A. learned prior to drug administration
   B. basically a new procedure each time
   C. learned for the first time under the influence of the
      drug
   D. independent of any rewards

8

5. Given the design of these experiments, behavioral   5.___
   dependence could be said to have been established if,
   after a period of conditioning, the animals
       A. chose to drink a great deal of alcohol
       B. appeared to have an aversion to alcohol
       C. manifested withdrawal symptoms if alcohol were not
          available
       D. showed a rapid rate of ethanol metabolism

6. Metabolic studies of the blood of chimpanzees during   6.___
   chronic ethanol administration indicate
       A. ethanol accumulates in the blood
       B. the rate of methanol disappearance is increased
       C. the rate of ethanol disappearance is increased
       D. the magnitude of the increase in the rate of ethanol
          disappearance is inversely related to the quantity
          of ethanol given

7. In the two weeks following conditioning, ethanol ingestion 7.___
       A. was substantially greater in three animals than in the
          preconditioning period
       B. was approximately the same as in the preconditioning
          period
       C. could not be followed in more than one animal because
          the others died
       D. was very low, in the range of 1.5 g/kg/day

8. In these experiments, when the subjects that had been   8.___
   treated with a drug for several weeks demonstrated an
   accelerated rate of disappearance of that drug from the
   blood, it was considered evidence for
       A. functional tolerance   B. behavioral tolerance
       C. metabolic tolerance   D. addiction

9. The test that was used in the investigation of behavioral   9.___
   tolerance associated with chronic ethanol administration
   was
       A. not described in detail in the article
       B. the same as the task used in the tests involving Δ^9-THC
       C. a sequential response task
       D. a task on a differential reinforcement schedule

10. A _____ test was used in the investigation of behavioral 10.___
    tolerance associated with chronic ethanol administration.
       A. behavioral task on a differential reinforcement schedule
       B. sequential response task
       C. visual discrimination task
       D. two-choice discrimination-reversal task

11. The functional tolerance to ethanol that was developed   11.___
       A. persisted for as long as a year after the original
          testing (36-day) period
       B. could not be demonstrated 24 days after the 36-day test
       C. could not be clearly demonstrated during the 36-day
          period
       D. could only be demonstrated if alcohol continued to be
          given on a daily basis

9

12. Signs of physical dependence on ethanol were produced   12.___
    A. by nasogastric administration of 3 g/kg of ethanol
    B. by nasogastric administration of three doses of
       ethanol in one day
    C. by nasogastric administration of one dose of ethanol/
       day for three days
    D. when blood ethanol concentrations were maintained
       above zero for four or more days

13. When an error was made during an SRT training session,   13.___
    A. a buzzer delivered a shock to the animal
    B. an M & M candy reinforcer was retracted
    C. a 2-second timeout went into effect
    D. all the house lights and lever lights were extinguished

14. In testing for the development of behavioral tolerance in   14.___
    response to chronic ethanol administration, evidence was
    sought that
    A. performance continues to deteriorate throughout the
       course of the experiment
    B. after initial impairment, performance tends to improve
       even though blood levels of ethanol are held constant
    C. removal of alcohol leads to withdrawal symptoms
    D. blood levels of ethanol decrease even though equal
       doses of ethanol are given

15. One of the MAJOR objectives of the studies using ethanol   15.___
    was to
    A. demonstrate some of the characteristics of the
       addiction process
    B. determine what are lethal amounts of ethanol for non-
       human primates
    C. study behavior in intoxicated monkeys
    D. determine the rate of blood ethanol disappearance in
       addicted subjects

16. A MAJOR drawback to the use of chimpanzees and other   16.___
    large apes in psychopharmacologic investigation is
    A. their size
    B. their inquisitive nature
    C. that they are poor models for experiments on the
       effects of drugs on behavior
    D. that their use is restricted to specialized institu-
       tional settings

17. The sequential response task (SRT) proved to be a better   17.___
    measure of learning than the DRL spaced response test
    because SRT
    A. proved to be more appropriate to monkeys
    B. made it possible to compare learning acquisition on
       drug days with learning on placebo days
    C. was less distracting than the DRL spaced response test
    D. does not depend on visual cues, whereas the DRL spaced
       response test does

18. Following the period of ethanol administration, recordings 18.___
    of leg tremor were made during the succeeding
    A. four days   B. thirty-three hours
    C. one week   D. eleven days

19. Which of the following would be evidence of the development 19.___
    of behavioral dependence on alcohol?
    A. A rapid rate of ethanol metabolism
    B. Appearance of withdrawal symptoms when alcohol is not
       available
    C. An aversion to alcohol on the part of the animals
    D. A tendency to drink a great deal of alcohol

20. An integral procedure in training for sequential response 20.___
    task testing is the
    A. use of a stimulus fading device
    B. surgical preparation of the brain for placement of
       indwelling catheters
    C. use of a candy reinforcer before and after each lever
       pull
    D. use of a board having many levers, each a different
       color

21. Which of the following drugs was labeled a stimulant? 21.___
    A. Ethanol   B. Diethylpropion
    C. Δ⁹-THC   D. Meprobamate

22. Which of the following statements CORRECTLY describes some 22.___
    aspect of sequential response task testing?
    A. The subject is required to repeat the same task every
       day.
    B. The test session is 50 minutes, or less if the subject
       has successfully learned the sequence of levers.
    C. M & M candy reinforcers are delivered at 10 and 20
       second intervals.
    D. The six levers are uniformly illuminated.

23. In the ethanol ingestion experiments in which animals were 23.___
    conditioned, how many animals were available for post-
    conditioning testing?
    A. One   B. Five   C. Six   D. Eleven

24. In the experiments in which withdrawal was quantitatively 24.___
    assessed, physical dependence was produced in monkeys by
    A. allowing them free access to ethanol in their
       drinking water
    B. restraining them in a chair and forcing them to drink
       18% ethanol
    C. inducing a fine tremor of the leg
    D. maintaining blood ethanol concentration at four levels,
       ranging between 50 and 300 mg/dl

25. According to this study, the BEST way to evaluate the 25.___
    effect of a drug on learning is to test the ability of
    the animal, while under the effect of the drug, to
    A. learn a new task each test day
    B. repeat the same task each test day

11

C. repeat the same task over a long period, with no
intervening training
D. do the same task each test day, but at a different
rate of speed

26. The reason for giving ethanol both orally and by intra-   26.___
venous infusion is to
A. make the animals more intoxicated than they would
have been with oral ingestion alone
B. demonstrate that orally administered ethanol disappears more rapidly from the blood than intravenously
administered ethanol
C. provide a reward for animals undergoing task training
D. temporally pair the taste of ethanol with the pharmacological effects produced by intravenous administration

27. The MAJOR point made in this report is that   27.___
A. learning ability is adversely affected by drugs
B. inhalation of a drug via smoking is not as reliable
a way of delivering a drug as oral administration
C. nonhuman primates made good models for the study of
effects of drugs on learning and behavior
D. monkeys become addicted to Δ^9-THC

28. Which of the following observations, made during or after   28.___
chronic administration of ethanol, makes it possible to
say that ethanol causes physical dependence?
A. Withdrawal symptoms occurred when blood levels of
ethanol fell.
B. Methanol was observed to accumulate in the blood.
C. Rate of disappearance of ethanol from the blood
increased.
D. Performance of discrimination-reversal tasks was
adversely affected.

29. Which of the following terms is a synonym for *behavioral*   29.___
tolerance?
A. Metabolic tolerance   B. Physical dependence
C. Functional tolerance   D. Discrimination tolerance

30. Nonhuman primates are good models for experiments on   30.___
human alcohol use because
A. they develop a great fondness for alcohol
B. they can be given large quantities of alcohol over
long periods of time without deleterious effects
C. it is possible and convenient to monitor blood
ethanol levels from minute to minute
D. it was possible to demonstrate two primary aspects
of the human addictive process in the nonhuman
primates

31. The MAJOR disadvantage of the spaced task for studying   31.___
the effects of drugs on learning is that it is
A. too simple
B. learned entirely before the administration of drugs
and cannot be varied thereafter

12

C. too dependent on extraneous clues, like lights
D. too distracting for use in nonhuman primates

32. For experiments in which procedures were involved, the   32.___
    animal of choice was the
    A. chimpanzee   B. orangutan
    C. gorilla   D. rhesus monkey

33. The use of large apes for research on the effects of drugs 33.___
    on behavior
    A. was first demonstrated in chimpanzees trained to do
       a sequential response task
    B. was shown to be feasible in a limited number of
       experiments on Δ^9-THC treated chimpanzees
    C. is severely limited by the natural inquisitiveness
       of large apes
    D. is limited by the inability of large apes to learn
       sequential tasks

34. Nasogastric administration of 3 g/kg of ethanol every day   34.___
    for over a month led to
    A. a progressive and continuing decrease in performance
       levels
    B. relatively constant blood ethanol levels at the end
       of each session
    C. a decreased rate of disappearance of ethanol from the
       blood
    D. a significant increase in body weight

35. To which of the following nonhuman primates does the   35.___
    name Pan Troglodyte apply?
    A. Chimpanzees   B. Orangutans
    C. Gorillas   D. Rhesus monkeys

36. Metabolic tolerance to alcohol was established by the   36.___
    fact that during chronic administration of ethanol
    A. its rate of disappearance from the blood increased
    B. methanol accumulated in the blood
    C. ethanol was converted into methanol
    D. the rate of ethanol disappearance from the blood
       increased and remained elevated long after termination
       of ethanol administration

37. A MAJOR advantage of the sequential response task in   37.___
    studies of the effects of drugs on learning is that
    A. while the basic nature of the task remains the same,
       the animal must learn a new procedure each day
    B. the nature of the task forces the animal to rely more
       on brightness cues than on memory
    C. it provides a good test of color discrimination
    D. the six-lever sequence appears ideally suited to
       nonhuman primates

13

38. Figure 1 indicates that
    A. the great ape named *Din* has the lowest tolerance to THC
    B. in general, the efficiency in the response of all three apes was reduced when THC was taken
    C. the 20 second DRL was experimentally most effective
    D. the great ape named *Peck* initially had the most efficient responses

38.___

39. The experiments using ethanol demonstrate that
    A. ethanol severely impairs the learning of a sequential response task
    B. many aspects of human drug addiction can be reproduced and studied in nonhuman primates
    C. it is impossible to demonstrate true withdrawal in monkeys
    D. depressant drugs are antagonists of stimulant drugs

39.___

40. What was the MAJOR point made in this article?
    A. Learning ability is adversely affected by drugs.
    B. Smoking and drug usage is hazardous to the health of nonhuman primates and, therefore, of humans.
    C. Nonhuman primates make good models for the study of the effects of drugs on learning and behavior.
    D. Rhesus monkeys are more effective subjects for drug-effect studies than other primates.

40.___

41. Which of the following drugs produced a *decrease* in learning at dosage levels NOT associated with general physical impairment?
    A. Secobarbital   B. Glutethimide
    C. Phentermine   D. Butabarbital

41.___

42. Which of the following statements CORRECTLY describes a procedure in sequential response task testing?
    A. The subject is required to learn a new task sequence every day.
    B. The testing period is the length of time required to complete a sequence of six levers, no matter how long this takes.
    C. M & M candy reinforcers are delivered at 10 and 20 second intervals.
    D. The six levers are illuminated at an unvarying intensity of light.

42.___

43. At the end of the conditioning period in the ethanol ingestion experiments,
    A. all the ethanol was delivered orally
    B. all the ethanol was delivered intravenously
    C. 18% of the ethanol was delivered intravenously
    D. no ethanol was delivered

43.___

44. One of the MAJOR problems encountered in the experiments on the effect of smoking on spaced responding was the fact that
    A. large apes tend to be too inquisitive for this kind of study

44.___

14

B. the subjects were all given extensive training on the task prior to drug testing so that performance could not be directly related to the effects of drugs
C. the subjects refused to smoke cigarettes containing Δ^9-THC
D. the 10-second DRL schedule proved to be too short

45. An IMPORTANT part of the procedure for training for sequential task testing involves the
   A. use of light cues of varying intensity
   B. routine monitoring of blood concentrations of inhaled compounds
   C. use of a candy reinforcer before and after each lever pull
   D. use of transilluminated discs of various colors

45.___

46. Learning, as measured by sequential response task testing, is considered to have taken place when the animal
   A. correctly pulls a number of levers in sequence with all stimulus lights identically illuminated
   B. pulls the same number of levers in the same sequence one day after learning the sequence
   C. no longer required the M & M candy reward to pull the levers in the correct sequence
   D. correctly pulls a number of levers, each with a different brightness cue, in sequence

46.___

47. Alterations in blood methanol levels during chronic ethanol administration
   A. led to a decrease in physical tolerance to ethanol
   B. causes a change in the disappearance rate of ethanol in the blood
   C. may be caused by competitive inhibition of the enzyme system that metabolizes both alcohols
   D. were interpreted as evidence for physical dependence on methanol

47.___

48. Physical dependence on ethanol has been produced in chimpanzees by
   A. administering ethanol by means of a nasogastric tube
   B. infusing ethanol through surgically implanted catheters
   C. substituting ethanol for the drinking water
   D. including alcohol in their liquid diet in increasing doses

48.___

49. In the study of the development of behavioral tolerance, performance of a task by an ethanol-treated subject was compared with performance of that task by
   A. other subjects given a placebo isocaloric with ethanol
   B. the same subject given a placebo isocaloric with ethanol
   C. other untreated subjects
   D. untreated subjects 36 days later

49.___

15

50. The effects of administration of diazepam at doses that   50.___
    did not cause general physical impairment were similar
    to those produced by
    A. metamphetamine
    B. drugs having a tranquilizing effect
    C. doses that did cause general physical impairment
    D. drugs classified as stimulants

———

KEY (CORRECT ANSWERS)

1. C	11. A	21. B	31. B	41. C
2. D	12. D	22. B	32. D	42. A
3. A	13. D	23. B	33. B	43. A
4. B	14. B	24. D	34. B	44. B
5. A	15. A	25. A	35. A	45. A
6. C	16. D	26. D	36. A	46. A
7. A	17. B	27. C	37. A	47. C
8. C	18. B	28. A	38. B	48. D
9. A	19. D	29. C	39. B	49. B
10. D	20. A	30. D	40. C	50. B

———

SCIENCE READING COMPREHENSION
EXAMINATION SECTION

DIRECTIONS: This section consists of a long reading passage, followed by questions based on the text. Each question consists of a statement followed by several suggested answers, only one of which is correct. After reading the passage, choose the letter of the BEST answer among the suggested answers, basing your answer upon what is stated or implied in the passage, and on your own understanding of science. *PRINT THE LETTER OF THE CORRECT ANSWER IN THE SPACE AT THE RIGHT.*

PASSAGE

IONIZING RADIATION: RISK AND BENEFIT

X radiation is a form of energy which was discovered by the German physicist, Wilhelm Conrad Roentgen in 1895. Like visible light, radiowaves, and microwaves, x-rays belong to a group of radiations known as the electromagnetic spectrum. Electromagnetic radiations are comprised of units of pure energy called photons or quanta. Unlike corpuscular, or particular, radiations which are composed of subatomic particles, electromagnetic radiations have no mass or weight. Subatomic particles that can be involved in corpuscular radiations include the alpha particle or helium radical, the beta particle or electron, neutrons and protons. Corpuscular radiations can cause ionization; however, for the purposes of the present discussion only electromagnetic radiations capable of causing ionization will be considered.

All photons of electromagnetic radiation travel in direct lines in a wave motion at the speed of 300,000 kilometers per second. Many of our conceptual ideas about wave motion are the result of our sensory experience with the transverse waves which occur in water and in the stretched string of a musical instrument. It is a pity in some way that the same term, wave, is given to both this transverse wave form and the oscillatory movement which is propagated along the direction of travel by electromagnetic radiations. This oscillatory movement, or longitudinal wave propagation, can be seen when a coiled spring is tapped sharply at one end, and as such this is a good paradigm for electromagnetic wave motion. Whereas for transverse waves the wavelength is between successive crests, the wavelength for electromagnetic radiations is the distance between successive areas of compression. This distance can vary enormously and electromagnetic radiations of different wavelengths have different properties. At one end of the spectrum there are very long wavelengths. Electromagnetic radiation of long wavelength is used in the transmission of radio messages. At the other end of the spectrum are the short wavelength radiations such as gamma radiations, which arise from naturally occurring unstable elements, and x-rays which are similar in property to gamma radiations, but are man-made by bombarding a target material with electrons in an x-ray tube. For gamma and x radiations, the wavelengths are so small that they are measured in Angstrom units, where an Angstrom unit is 1/100,000,000 centimeter. The shorter the wavelength, the higher the energy and penetrating power of the photon, and (as all electromagnetic radiations travel at the speed of light) the higher the frequency of waves. X-ray wavelengths used in diagnostic radiology range from approximately 0.1 to 0.5 Angstroms. At such wavelengths, the radiation has sufficient energy to cause ionization of atoms and molecules. If such atoms or molecules are within living systems, there is the potential for biological harm. This is the reason for the paradox that x-rays can cause cancer, can be used to help in diagnosis of disease, and in high doses can be used to destroy cancer cells.

Consideration of the potential benefits of an activity is involved in the decision of risk acceptability. In diagnostic radiology, the risk-benefit equation is difficult to estimate. Risk is generally given in units of equivalent radiation dose, while the benefit is expressed in such terms as lives saved or disease cured. Gibbs and his fellow workers have noted that estimates or risk from low-level radiation usually consider whole-body exposure, which is not generally the case for the diagnostic use of x radiation. Moreover, they indicated that it has not yet been possible to define the value of a life saved in units of dose equivalence. Because of these uncertainties, diagnostic radiation is to be regarded as a potentially noxious agent. Hence, radiological examination should be carried out only if it is likely that the information obtained will be useful for the clinical management of the patient.

Undoubtedly, ionizing radiation in high doses can be harmful. The first report of patient injury from a diagnostic radiological procedure, namely skin burns, was made within a few months of Roentgen's discovery of the x-ray. In that case, the exposure time was one hour, but it is impossible to estimate the dose received. As early as 1902, the first case of cancer attributed to radiation injury was reported in the literature. Nonetheless, the magnitude of the risk (or even if there is a risk) from the small doses of x radiation presently employed for diagnostic purposes is still undetermined.

Various accidents, such as the recent reactor incident at Chernobyl in the Soviet Union, knowledge gained from follow-up studies on survivors from the atom bomb explosions in Hiroshima and Nagasaki at the end of World War II, and experiments subjecting various plant and animal species to ionizing radiation indicate that radiation bioeffects can be divided into two basic types where relatively high doses of radiation are concerned. One category of effects requires a threshold dose be met before detectable change occurs. Such effects are termed non-stochastic, and are primarily a result of cell death. Examples are the acute radiation syndrome and the development of cataracts. On the other hand, stochastic effects show statistical probability of occurrence as a function of dose, but no threshold cutoff for the effect. Examples of stochastic effects are carcinogenesis and genetic mutations.

The problem in evaluating the risk of cancer or mutation in human populations due to the diagnostic use of x radiation is that there is no known method to distinguish between disease resulting from the radiation and that which is spontaneous or due to other factors in the environment. The only way to assess the magnitude of the risk would be to determine the excess incidence of cancer or mutations in an irradiated population. Where the excess incidence is expected to be small, extremely large populations and long periods of observation are required. Land, for example, suggested that the risk of breast cancer from mammography is numerically so small when compared to the spontaneous incidence of one in 13 for breast cancer in U.S. women, that the epidemiologic methods of evaluation would require a population of at least 60 million women followed from age 35 until death. Half of them would receive mammograms and the other half, the control group, would not. It goes without saying that such a study would take at least 40 years to conduct and would be so prohibitively expensive that it is not likely to be carried out. Similar considerations apply to the evaluation of risks from small doses of ionizing radiation of all human cancers and mutations. Hence, it has been common practice to use quantitative estimates and interpolations from observations of human and animal populations exposed to large radiation doses, when attempting to make numeric estimates of the risks to humans from low doses of ionizing radiation.

In view of the uncertainty surrounding possible risks from the diagnostic use of x-rays, the International Commission on Radiological Protection has originated the concept of keeping exposure levels *as low as reasonably achievable*. This concept has been summarized in cryptic acronym form as the ALARA Principle. The three key ways of minimizing exposure to radiation are minimizing the duration of exposure, maximizing the distance from the source, and using barriers such as leaded clothing or screens. Diagnostic x-ray production occurs only when the x-ray tube is energized, and this is only necessary when radiographs are being exposed. The time that the x-ray tube is energized can be reduced by using fast image receptors, and by reducing the number of radiographs taken by high-yield selection criteria of the exposures to be performed. As the intensity of the x-ray beam is inversely proportional to the square of the distance from the source (e.g., when the distance is doubled, the intensity of the beam is reduced by a factor of four, when tripled it is reduced by a factor of nine...) the operator should be as far as possible from the x-ray machine if it is not possible to stand behind a barrier impregnable to the x-rays being used. By conscientious use of the ALARA Principle, the practitioners reduce risks for themselves, their staff, and their patients.

1. Which of the following was the EARLIEST description of   1.____
   ill effects attributed to x radiation?
   A. Cancer in atom bomb survivors
   B. Genetic mutations following mammography
   C. Radiation burns due to prolonged exposure

3

D. Acute radiation syndrome after the Chernobyl incident
E. Cataracts

2. Of the following, which is the electromagnetic radiation   2.___
   having the LONGEST wavelength?
   _____ radiation.
   A. Gamma   B. Alpha   C. Beta
   D. X   E. Radiowave

3. From statements in the passage, it can be inferred that   3.___
   the author PROBABLY is a(n)
   A. sentimentalist whose judgments are influenced primari-
      ly by his emotions
   B. skeptic who refuses to believe anything without
      absolute proof
   C. realist who adheres to practical considerations and
      rejects the impractical
   D. idealist who places his own standards of perfection
      before practical matters
   E. conformist who follows the ideas of authority without
      question

4. Wave motion for x radiation MOST closely resembles the   4.___
   oscillating movement of a
   A. fast-moving helium radical
   B. coiled spring that has been sharply tapped at one end
   C. plucked stretched string of a musical instrument
   D. wave in water caused by disturbance from a fast moving
      motor boat
   E. transverse wave form

5. The paradox of x radiation is stated to be that it   5.___
   A. is used for diagnostic purposes when the risks involved
      have not been fully determined
   B. was discovered, but not invented, as gamma radiation
      is naturally occuring counterpart
   C. can be controlled by mankind
   D. can both cause and cure cancer
   E. none of the above

6. Which of the following electromagnetic radiations carries   6.___
   the MOST energy and is, therefore, MOST penetrating?
   A. Microwaves
   B. Radiowaves
   C. Visible light
   D. Gamma rays
   E. They all have the same energy

7. With which of the following statements would the author   7.___
   of the passage AGREE?
   A. Rigorous experimentation must be carried out to more
      accurately assess damage caused by the diagnostic use
      of x-rays.
   B. Epidemiologic data from individuals receiving high
      doses of radiation can accurately be interpolated to
      assess the effects of low levels of radiation.

4

8. The beta particle is the same as a(n)
   - A. neutron
   - B. photon of pure energy
   - C. proton
   - D. helium radical
   - E. electron

8.___

9. According to the inverse square law, the intensity of radiation received is reduced by a factor of _____ times when a practitioner stands 4 meters away from a source of radiation rather than 1 meter.
   - A. 4
   - B. 0.25
   - C. 16
   - D. 0.06
   - E. 2

9.___

10. The probability of genetic mutation being caused by low levels of x or gamma radiation is believed to be
    - A. stochastic in nature
    - B. greater than the risk of cancer
    - C. threshold dose related
    - D. unrelated to dose
    - E. a result of cell death

10.___

11. The principal difficulty encountered when evaluating the risk of cancer developing due to the use of diagnostic radiology is
    - A. inability to distinguish between disease caused by radiation and that due to other factors
    - B. the relatively long life span of humans
    - C. the size of the population one needs to follow
    - D. the difficulty in obtaining a good control group
    - E. the financial outlay necessary for the study

11.___

12. Of the following, which according to the text are definite-ly capable of causing ionization?
    - I. Visible light
    - II. Gamma radiation
    - III. Microwaves
    - IV. Radiowave radiation

    The CORRECT answer is:
    - A. All of the above
    - B. II, III, and IV
    - C. II *only*
    - D. III *only*
    - E. IV *only*

12.___

13. For diagnostic radiology, which of the following statements is FALSE?
    - A. Potentially noxious radiations are employed.
    - B. This use of x-rays was first developed very shortly after Roentgen's discovery.
    - C. Particulate radiations are not employed.
    - D. Attempts have been made to develop high yield selection criteria.
    - E. Such use of x-rays is excluded from the ALARA Principle as doses are negligible.

13.___

14. Gibbs and his co-workers considered the risk-benefit ratio for the diagnostic use of ionizing radiation
    - A. should be estimated as being equivalent to that for whole body exposure to the same radiation level

14.___

B. is complicated by uncertainties in the definition of the value of a life saved in units of dose equivalence
C. can readily be determined by examining the excess incidence of cancer and mutations in an irradiated population
D. always shows a linear relationship between risk and the radiation dose
E. more than one of the above

15. Which of the following electromagnetic radiations travels 15.___
    at the GREATEST velocity?
    A. X-rays   B. Visible light
    C. Radiowaves   D. Microwaves
    E. None of the above

KEY (CORRECT ANSWERS)

1. C	6. D	11. A
2. E	7. D	12. C
3. C	8. E	13. E
4. B	9. C	14. B
5. D	10. A	15. E

ARITHMETICAL REASONING
EXAMINATION SECTION

DIRECTIONS FOR THIS SECTION:
   Each question or incomplete statement is followed by several suggested answers or completions. Select the one that BEST answers the question or completes the statement. *PRINT THE LETTER OF THE CORRECT ANSWER IN THE SPACE AT THE RIGHT.*

TEST 1

1. The population of a city is, approximately, 7.85 millions. 1. ...
   The area is approximately 200 square miles. The number of
   thousand persons per square mile is
      A. 3.925   B. 39.25   C. 392.5   D. 39250
2. The longest straight line that can be drawn to connect two 2. ...
   points on the circumference of a circle whose radius is 9
   inches is
      A. 9 inches B. 18 inches C. 28,2753 inches D. 4.5 inches
3. It is believed that every even number is the sum of two   3. ...
   prime numbers. Two prime numbers whose sum is 32 are
      A. 7, 25   B. 11, 21   C. 13, 19   D. 17, 15
4. To divide a number by 3000, we should *move the decimal*   4. ...
   point 3 places to the
      A. right and divide by 3   B. left and divide by 3
      C. right and multiply by 3   D. left and multiply by 3
5. The difference between the area of a rectangle 6 ft. by   5. ...
   4 ft. and the area of a square having the *same* perimeter is
      A. 1 sq. ft. B. 2 sq. ft. C. 4 sq. ft. D. none of these
6. The ratio of 1/4 to 3/8 is the *same* as the ratio of   6. ...
      A. 1 to 3   B. 2 to 3   C. 3 to 2   D. 3 to 4
7. If 7 1/2 is divided by 1 1/5, the quotient is   7. ...
      A. 6 1/4   B. 9   C. 7 1/10   D. 6 3/5
8. A farmer has a cylindrical metal tank for watering his   8. ...
   stock. It is 10 ft. in diameter and 3 ft. deep. If one
   cubic foot contains about 7.5 gallons, the *approximate*
   capacity of the tank in gallons is
      A. 12   B. 225   C. 4   D. 1707
9. The fraction which fits in the following series, 1/2, 1/10, 9. ...
   ____, 1/250, is
      A. 1/20   B. 1/100   C. 1/10   D. 1/50
10. In two years, $200 with interest compounded semi-annually   10. ...
    at 4% will amount to
      A. $216.48   B. $233.92   C. $208   D. $216

———

TEST 2

1. With a *tax rate* of .0200, a tax bill of $1050 corresponds   1. ...
   to an *assessed valuation* of
      A. $21,000   B. $52,500   C. $21   D. $1029
2. A sales agent after deducting his commission of 6%, remits   2. ...
   $2491 to his principal. The SALE amounted to
      A. $2809   B. $2640   C. $2650   D. $2341.54
3. The percent equivalent of .0295 is   3. ...
      A. 2.95%   B. 29.5%   C. .295%   D. 295%
4. An angle of 105 degrees is a   4. ...
      A. straight angle   B. acute angle
      C. obtuse angle   D. reflex angle

1

5. A quart is approximately sixty cubic inches. A cu. ft. of   5. ...
water weighs approximately sixty pounds. Therefore, a quart
of water weighs, *approximately,*
   A. 2 lbs.   B. 3 lbs.   C. 4 lbs.   D. 5 lbs.

6. If the *same* number is added to both the numerator and the   6. ...
denominator of a proper fraction, the
   A. value of the fraction is decreased
   B. value of the fraction is increased
   C. value of the fraction is unchanged
   D. effect of the operation depends on the original fraction

7. The *least common multiple* of 3, 8, 9, 12 is   7. ...
   A. 36   B. 72   C. 108   D. 144

8. On a bill of $100, the *difference* between a discount of   8. ...
30% and 20% and a discount of 40% and 10% is
   A. nothing   B. $2   C. $20   D. 20%

9. 1/3 percent of a number is 24. The NUMBER is   9. ...
   A. 8   B. 72   C. 800   D. 7200

10. The cost of importing five dozen china dinner sets, billed   10. ...
at $32 per set, and paying a duty of 40%, is
   A. $224   B. $2688   C. $768   D. $1344

TEST 3

1. A motorist travels 120 miles to his destination at the   1. ...
average speed of 60 miles per hour and returns to the
starting point at the average speed of 40 miles per hour.
His *average speed* for the ENTIRE trip is
   A. 53 miles per hour   B. 50 miles per hour
   C. 48 miles per hour   D. 45 miles per hour

2. A snapshot measures 2 1/2 inches by 1 7/8 inches. It is   2. ...
to be enlarged so that the longer dimension will be 4
inches. The length of the enlarged *shorter* dimension will
be
   A. 2 1/2 inches   B. 3 3/8 inches
   C. 3 inches   D. none of these

3. The approximate distance, s , in feet that an object falls   3. ...
in t seconds when dropped from a height is obtained by use
of the formula $s = 16_t{}^2$. In 8 seconds, the object will fall
   A. 15,384 feet   B. 1,024 feet
   C. 256 feet   D. none of these

4. The PRODUCT of 75^3 and 75^7 is   4. ...
   A. $(75)^{10}$ B. $(75)^{21}$ C. $(5,625)^{10}$ D. $(150)^{10}$

5. The scale of a map is: 3/4 of an inch = 10 miles. If the   5. ...
distance on the map between two towns is 6 inches, the
actual distance is
   A. 45 miles   B. 60 miles   C. 80 miles   D. none of these

6. If $d = m - \dfrac{50}{m}$, and m is a positive number which increases   6. ...
in value, d
   A. increases in value   B. decreases in value
   C. remains unchanged   D. fluctuates up and down in value

7. From a piece of tin in the shape of a square 6 inches on a   7. ...
side, the largest possible circle is cut out.
Of the following, the ratio of the area of the circle to the
area of the original square is *closest* in value to
   A. 4/5   B. 3/5   C. 2/3   D. 1/2

8. A pound of water is evaporated from 6 pounds of sea water   8. ...
   containing 4% salt. The percentage of salt in the *remain-*
   ing solution is
       A. 3 1/3   B. 4   C. 4 4/5   D. none of these
9. If a cubic inch of a metal weighs 2 pounds, a cubic foot   9. ...
   of the *same* metal weighs
       A. 8 pounds   B. 24 pounds   C. 288 pounds   D. none of these
10. Assume that, according to the Federal income tax law, if   10. ...
    the taxable income in the case of a separate return is over
    $4,000, but not over $6,000, the tax is $840 + 26% of the
    excess over $4,000.
    If a taxpayer files a separate tax return and his taxable
    income is $5,500, the tax is
        A. $690   B. $1,230   C. $1,370   D. none of these

TEST 4

1. If the number of square inches in the area of a circle is   1. ...
   equal to the number of inches in its circumference, the
   DIAMETER of the circle is
       A. 4 inches   B. 3 inches   C. 1 inch   D. none of these
2. The *least common multiple* of 20, 24, 32 is   2. ...
       A. 900   B. 1,920   C. 15,360   D. none of these
3. Six quarts of a 20% solution of alcohol in water are mixed   3. ...
   with 4 quarts of a 60% solution of alcohol in water. The
   alcoholic strength of the mixture is
       A. 80%   B. 50%   C. 36%   D. none of these
4. To find the radius of a circle whose circumference is   4. ...
   60 inches,
       A. multiply 60 by π B. divide 60 by 2π
       C. divide 30 by 2π
       D. divide 60 by π and extract the square root of the result
5. A micromillimeter is defined as one millionth of a milli-   5. ...
   meter. A length of 17 micromillimeters may be represented
   as
       A. .00017 mm.   B. 0000017 mm.
       C. .000017 mm.   D. .00000017 mm.
6. If 9x + 5 = 23, the numerical value of 18x + 5 is   6. ...
       A. 46   B. 41   C. 32   D. 23 + 9x
7. When the fractions 2/3, 5/7, 8/11 and 9/13 are arranged in   7. ...
   ascending order of size, the result is
       A. 8/11, 5/7, 9/13, 2/3   B. 5/7, 8/11, 2/3, 9/13
       C. 2/3, 8/11, 5/7, 9/13   D. 2/3, 9/13, 5/7, 8/11
8. If the outer diameter of a metal pipe is 2.84 inches and   8. ...
   the inner diameter is 1.94 inches, the *thickness* of the
   metal is
       A. .45 of an inch   B. .90 of an inch
       C. 1.94 inches   D. 2.39 inches
9. An office manager employs 3 typists at $45 per week, 2   9. ...
   general clerks at $40 per week, and a messenger at $32 per
   week. The *average* weekly wage of these part-time employees is
       A. $37.25   B. $39.00   C. $41.17   D. none of these

10. A rectangular bin 4 feet long, 3 feet wide, and 2 feet high is solidly packed with bricks whose dimensions are 8 inches, 4 inches, and 2 inches. The *number* of bricks in the bin is
    A. 54   B. 648   C. 1,298   D. none of these

10. ...

TEST 5

1. If x is less than 10, and y is less than 5, it follows that
    A. x is greater than y   B. x = 2y
    C. x − y = 5   D. x + y is less than 15

1. ...

2. A dealer sells an article at a loss of 50% of the cost. Based on the selling price, the *loss* is
    A. 25%   B. 50%   C. 100%   D. none of these

2. ...

3. If 8 men get together at a reunion and each man shakes hands once with each of the others, the *total number* of handshakes is
    A. 49   B. 56   C. 64   D. 28

3. ...

4. The world record for cycling a stretch of 20 kilometers is 26 minutes. This corresponds to an average speed of, *approximately*,
    A. 29 miles per hour   B. 46 miles per hour
    C. 32 miles per hour   D. none of these

4. ...

5. The sum, s, of n consecutive integers beginning with 1 can be found by use of the formula $s = \dfrac{n(n+1)}{2}$. The sum of the *first 100 consecutive integers* is
    A. 5,001   B. 5,050   C. 10,000   D. 10,100

5. ...

6. Of the following, the value of $\dfrac{3\sqrt{64.32}}{\sqrt{.041}}$ is closest to
    A. 400   B. 200   C. 20   D. 16

6. ...

7. If each edge of a cube is increased by 2 inches, the
    A. volume is increased by 8 cubic inches
    B. area of each face is increased by 4 square inches
    C. diagonal of each face is increased by 2 inches
    D. sum of the edges is increased by 24 inches

7. ...

8. In a school in which 40% of the enrolled students are boys, 80% of the boys are present on a certain day. If 1,152 boys are present, the *total* school enrollment is
    A. 1,440   B. 2,880   C. 3,600   D. none of these

8. ...

9. An agent received a commission of d% of the selling price of a house. If the commission amounted to $600, the selling price, in dollars, was
    A. $\dfrac{60,000}{d}$ B. $\dfrac{600}{d}$ C. 6 d   D. 600 d

9. ...

10. A ship sails due north from a position 5° 28' South Latitude to a position 6° 43' North Latitude. Given that one minute of latitude is equivalent to 1 nautical mile, the ship has sailed a distance of
    A. 75 nautical miles   B. 371 nautical miles
    C. 731 nautical miles   D. 1,211 nautical miles

10. ...

SOLUTIONS TO ARITHMETICAL REASONING

TEST 1

1. Answer: (B) 39.25

$$\begin{array}{r} 40,000 \\ 200\overline{)\ 8,000,000} \end{array}$$ (number of persons per square mile)
(approximate population)

Answer: 39.25 or (approximately) 40 (thousand persons per sq. mi.)

2. Answer: (B) 18 inches

9" + 9" = 18 inches

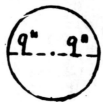

3. Answer: (C) 13, 19
A prime number is an integer which cannot be divided except by itself and one integer; a whole number as opposed to a fraction or a decimal.

4. Answer: (B) 3 places to the left and divide by 3

5. Answer: (A) 1 sq. ft.

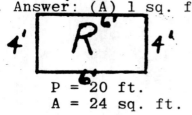 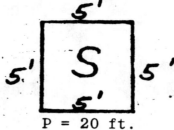

P = 20 ft.   P = 20 ft.   25
A = 24 sq. ft.   A = 25 sq. ft.   -24
                                        ───
                                         1

6. Answer: (B) 2 to 3

$$\frac{1/4}{3/8} = 1/4 \div 3/8 = 1/4 \times 8/3 = 2/3$$

7. Answer: (A) 6 1/4

$$\frac{7\ 1/2}{1\ 1/5} = \frac{15}{2} \div \frac{6}{5} = \frac{15}{2} \times \frac{5}{6} = \frac{25}{4} = 6\frac{1}{4}$$ OR $$\begin{array}{r} 6\frac{3}{12}\ \frac{1}{4} \\ 1.2\overline{)\ 7.5} \end{array}$$

8. Answer: (B) 225

$A = \pi R^2$
$= 3(5)^2$
$= 75$ sq. ft.

$\pi = \dfrac{22}{7} = 3$ (approx.)

Volume of tank = 75 X 3 = 225 cu. ft. (approximate capacity of tank in gallons)

$$\begin{array}{r} 225 \\ \times 7.5 \\ \hline 1125 \\ 1575 \\ \hline 1687.5 \text{ gal.} \end{array}$$

9. Answer: (D) 1/50
A geometric series: each number is multiplied by the same number to get the succeeding number. (Multiply each number by 1/5.)
1, 2, 1/10, 1/50, 1/250   The missing number is 1/50.

10. Answer: (A) $216.48
Compound Interest
4% a year compounded semi-annually is the same as 2% for a half-year.

A. $200
      X .02
      $4.00 Interest for 1st half yr.

$200
+   4
$204 Principal for 1st half yr.

B. $204
      X .02
      $4.08 Interest for 2nd half yr.

$204.00
    4.08
$208.08 Principal for 1st half
         of 2nd year

C. $208.08
      X   .02
      $4.1616 Interest for 1st half
               of 2nd year

$208.08
+ 4.16
$212.24 Principal for 2nd half
         of 2nd year

D. $212.24
      X   .02
      $4.2448 Interest for 2nd half
               of 2nd year

$212.24
+ 4.24
$216.48 Principal at end of 2nd
         half of 2nd year

———

TEST 2

1. Answer: (B) $52,500
   $.0200x = \$1050$ $2x = \$105,000$
   $200x = \$10,500,000$ $x = \$52,500$ (assessed valuation)

2. Answer: (C) $2650
   $\$2491 + .06x = x$
   $x = 2491 + .06x$ Proof
   $1.00x - .06x = 2491$ $\$2650$ $\$2491$
   $.94x = 2491$ X   .06   + 159
   $.94x = 249,100$ $\$159.00$ $\$2650$
         $\$2,650$
   $94\overline{)\,249,100}$

3. Answer: (A) 2.95% $.0295 = 2.95\%$

4. Answer: (C) obtuse angle
   An obtuse angle is an angle greater than $90°$.

5. Answer: (A) 2 lbs.
   A quart   =   60 cu. in.
   60 lbs.   =   1 cu. ft. (or 1728 cu. in.) (12 x 12 x 12)
                  (Keep like units of measure together)
   60 lbs.   =   1728 cu. in.
   1 lb.   = $\frac{1728}{60}$ = approximately .29 cu. in.

   If 29 cu. in. weigh 1 lb., then 60 cu. in. weigh 2 lbs. (approximately). Therefore, a quart weighs 2 lbs. (approximately).

6. Answer: (B) the value of the fraction is increased
   (1) Start with the fraction 2/3   (3) $\frac{3}{2} = \frac{10}{15}$
   (2) $\frac{2 + 2}{3 + 2} = \frac{4}{5}$ (Adding 2 to the numerator
       and the denominator)   (4) $\frac{4}{5} = \frac{12}{15}$

7. Answer: (B) 72
   Common multiple: can be evenly divided by all the numbers.
   Least common multiple: the lowest of these numbers.

8. Answer: (B) $2
   Formula: Step 1. Express percentages as decimals
             Step 2. Subtract each discount from *one*
             Step 3. Multiply all the results
             Step 4. Subtract the product from *one*

Step 1.   .3, .2 and .4, .1
Step 2.   .7, .8 and .6, .9
Step 3.   .7X.8 = .56 (represents percent remaining after the
          .6X.9 = .54 discounts are taken)
Step 4.   1.00   1.00
        - .56   - .54
          .44   .46   The difference is 2%.
Then $100 X .02 = $2.00

9. Answer: (D) 7200

$$\frac{1}{300} x = 24 \quad ; \quad x = 24 \times 300 \quad ; \quad x = 7200$$

10. Answer: (B) $2688

     $32 $1920
    X 60   X   .40
    $1920 Cost of dinner sets before paying duty $768.00 Duty

    $1920
  + 768
    $2688 Cost of dinner sets *after* paying duty

TEST 3

1. Answer: (C) 48 miles per hour
   120 miles = 2 hours (60 mph)
   120 miles = 3 hours (40 mph)
   240 miles = 5 hours = average of 48 mph
2. Answer: (C) 3 inches
   Change 2 1/2 to $\frac{20}{8}$ Change 1 7/8 to $\frac{15}{8}$

   Ratio is 20 to 15 or 4 to 3.
   If the longer dimension is 4 inches, then the shorter is 3 inches.
3. Answer: (B) 1,024 feet
   $s = 16 \times 8^2$ or 16 X 64 or 1024 feet
4. Answer: (A) $(75)^{10}$
   Because the 75 is constant, one needs only to add the exponents
   (7 and 3). Therefore, the product is 75^{10}.
5. Answer: (C) 80 miles
   6 ÷ 3/4 = 6 X 4/3 = 24/3 or 8   8 X 10 miles = 80 miles
6. Answer: (A) increases in value
   By increasing the value of m (by substituting numbers for letters),
   it is obvious that d increases in value.
7. Answer: (A) 4/5
   Area of square = 36 square inches
   Area of circle = πr^2
                  = π 9 (3 X 3)
                  = 3 1/7 X 9
                  = 28 2/7

$$\frac{28 \ 2/7}{36} = \frac{198}{7} \times \frac{1}{36} = \frac{198}{252}$$

```
          .78 + = 78 + %
   ) 198.00
     176 4
      21 60
      20 16
       1 44
```

78 + % is closest to 4/5 (80%)

7

8. Answer: (C) 4 4/5
    .04 X 6 = .24 lbs. of salt in 6 lbs. of salt water.
    When a pound of water is evaporated, the salt content remains
    the same.

$$\frac{.24}{5)\,.24} $$

    .04 4/5 = 4 4/5%

9. Answer: (D) none of these
    1728 cubic inches = 1 cubic foot
       1 cubic inch   = 2 pounds
    1728 cubic inches = 3,456 pounds

10. Answer: (B) $1,230

     $5,500 $1500 X 25% = $390.00
    -4,000   + 840.00
    ───────   ──────────
    $1,500 (excess over 4000) $1230.00 (tax)

───

TEST 4

1. Answer: (A) 4 inches
   Assume there are 100 square inches in the area of a circle and
   100 inches in its circumference.
      A = 1/2 Cr
   100 = 1/2 X 100 X r
   50r = 100
     r = 2
     d = 4

2. Answer: (D) none of these

   $$\begin{array}{l} 2\,)\overline{20 - 24 - 32} \\ \;\;2\,)\overline{10 - 12 - 16} \\ \;\;\;\;2\,)\overline{5 - 6 - 8} \\ \;\;\;\;\;\;\;\;\overline{5 - 3 - 4} \end{array}$$

   2 X 2 X 2 X 5 X 3 X 4 = 480

3. Answer: (C) 36%
      6 quarts X 20% = 120%
      4 quarts X 60% = 240%
   ───────────────────────
     10 quarts   = 360%
      1 quart   = 36%

4. Answer: (B) divide 60 by 2
      C = 2 r
   $2\pi r = 60$ $r = \dfrac{60}{\pi} \times \dfrac{1}{2}$

   $2r = \dfrac{60}{\pi}$ $r = \dfrac{60}{2\pi}$

5. Answer: (C) .000017 mm.
      1 micromillimeter = .000001 mm.
     17 micromillimeters = .000017 mm.

6. Answer: (B) 41
      9x + 5 = 23
      9x = 23 - 5 or 9x = 18
       x = 2
     18x + 5 = 36 + 5 or 41

7. Answer: (D) 2/3, 9/13, 5/7, 8/11
   Find the least common denominator = 3003

   $$\frac{2}{3} = \frac{2002}{3003} \qquad \frac{9}{13} = \frac{2079}{3003} \qquad \frac{5}{7} = \frac{2145}{3003} \qquad \frac{8}{11} = \frac{2184}{3003}$$

   Correct order is 2/3, 9/13, 5/7, 8/11

8. Answer: (A) .45 of an inch
    2.84 inches = outer diameter
    1.94 inches = inner diameter
     .90 inches = thickness (both sides)
     .45 inches = thickness (one side)
9. Answer: (C) $41.17
    3 X 45 = $135
    2 X 40 =   80
    1 X 32 =   32
    ─   ─────
    6          $247 $247 ÷ 6 = $41 1/6 or $41.17
10. Answer: (B) 648
    There are 1728 cu. inches in 1 cu. ft. (12 X 12 X 12)
    4 X 3 X 2 = 24 cu. ft. X 1728 = 41472 cu. in.
    41472 cu. in. ÷ 64 (8 X 4 X 2) = 648 bricks

TEST 5

1. Answer: (D) x + y is less than 15
   If x is less than 10 and y is less than 5, then x + y *MUST* be
   less than 15. None of the others is possible.
2. Answer: (C) 100%
   Based on selling price, the formula is written:
      Cost - Loss = Selling Price
      100% - 50% = 50%
      Loss = 100% of the Selling Price (loss equal to Selling Price)
3. Answer: (D) 28
   A shakes hands with the other 7
   B shakes hands with the other 6 (has already shaken A's)
   and so on ...... Thus 7, 6, 5, 4, 3, 2, 1 = 28 handshakes
4. Answer: (A) 29 miles per hour
   1 kilometer = 5/8 of a mile
   20 kilometers = 20 X 5/8 = 12 1/2 miles
   12 1/2 miles : 26 minutes = x:60 minutes
   $$26x = 750$$
   $$x = 28^{+} \text{ or } 29 \text{ miles per hour}$$
5. Answer: (B) 5,050
   $$s = \frac{n(n+1)}{2} \qquad s = \frac{100(100+1)}{2} \qquad s = \frac{10,100}{2} \qquad s = 5,050$$
6. Answer: (C) 20
   $$3\overline{)64.32} = 4.01 \qquad \frac{4}{.2} = 4 \times \frac{10}{2} = 20$$
   $$2\overline{).041} = .202$$
7. Answer: (D) the sum of the edges is increased by 24 inches
   Since there are 12 edges to a cube and each edge is increased by
   2 inches, the total increase is 24 inches.
8. Answer: (C) 3,600
   $$1152 \div \frac{8}{10} = 1440 \text{ boys enrolled } (1152 \times \frac{10}{8})$$
   $$1440 \div \frac{4}{10} = 1440 \times \frac{10}{4} = 3600 \text{ (total school enrollment)}$$
9. Answer: (A) $\frac{60,000}{d}$
   $$600 \div d = 600 \times \frac{100}{d} = \frac{60,000}{d}$$
10. Answer: (C) 731 nautical miles
    $$
    \begin{array}{ll}
    5°\ 28' & 1° = 60' \\
    6°\ 43' & 11° = 660' \\
    \overline{11°\ 71'} & \quad + 71' \\
    & \overline{731'}
    \end{array}
    $$
        1' = 1 nautical mile
     731' = 731 nautical miles

MATHEMATICS PROBLEM SOLVING
EXAMINATION SECTION

DIRECTIONS FOR THIS SECTION:
Each question or incomplete statement is followed by several suggested answers or completions. Select the one that BEST answers the question or completes the statement. *PRINT THE LETTER OF THE CORRECT ANSWER IN THE SPACE AT THE RIGHT.*

TEST 1

1. If a man travels r miles an hour for h hours and s miles   1. ...
   an hour for t hours, what is his *average* rate in miles per
   hour for the ENTIRE distance traveled?
   A. rh + st   B. $\frac{r}{h} + \frac{s}{t}$ C. $\frac{rh + st}{2}$ D. $\frac{rh + st}{h + t}$
   E. *None of these answers*

2. A certain square 18 feet on a side has the same area as   2. ...
   a rectangle. If *one* side of the rectangle is 9 feet, what
   is the number of feet in the *other* dimension?
   A. 9   B. 2   C. 27   D. 36   E. *None of these answers*

3. A dealer paid 72 cents for a fountain pen listed at 90   3. ...
   cents. What was the *rate* of discount allowed him?
   A. 5%   B. 2%   C. 8%   D. 20%   E. *None of these answers*

4. The tax rate in a certain district is 8 1/2 mills on the   4. ...
   dollar. What would this be if expressed as *dollars per*
   thousand?
   A. $.085   B. $8.50   C. $85   D. $8500
   E. *None of these answers*

5. The wheel of the average bicycle is 28 inches in diameter.   5. ...
   How many feet will be covered in 9 turns of the wheel?
   (Use π = $\frac{22}{7}$)
   A. 21 ft   B. 66 ft   C. 462 ft.   D. 792 ft
   E. *None of these answers*

6. If light travels approximately 186,000 miles a second and   6. ...
   the sun is 93 million miles away, how long does it take a
   ray of light to travel from the sun to the earth? (Find
   answer to the nearest minute.)
   A. 5 min.   B. 2 min.   C. 8 min.   D. 500 min.
   E. *None of these answers*

7. The Acme Company offers a gas range for $63 cash or for $5   7. ...
   down and 10 monthly payments of $6.50 each. The install-
   ment price is what percent GREATER than the cash price?
   (Find answer to the nearest whole percent.)
   A. 7%   B. 9%   C. 10%   D. 11%   E. *None of these answers*

8. The earth revolves through 360 degrees of longitude in   8. ...
   24 hours. How many minutes does it take to revolve through
   1 degree?
   A. .25   B. 6   C. 15   D. 25   E. *None of these answers*

9. A small factory with 3 machines has a job of stamping out   9. ...
   a number of pan covers. The newest machine can do the job
   in 3 days, another machine can do it in 4 days, and the
   third machine can do it in 6 days.
   How many days will it take the factory to do the job, using
   all three machines?
   A. 1 1/3   B. 4 1/3   C. 6   D. 13
   E. *None of these answers*

1

10. If 1 gallon of water is added to 6 quarts of a mixture of   10. ...
    alcohol and water that is 50% alcohol, what percent alcohol
    is the resulting mixture?
       A. 25%   B. 30%   C. 33 1/3%   D. 50%
       E. *None of these answers* _____

TEST 2

1. On a $9840 bill for equipment, what is the *difference* be-   1. ...
   tween a discount of 30% and a discount series of 20% and
   10%?
      A. No difference   B. $196.80   C. $787.20
      D. $2755.20   E. *None of these answers*
2. If the fuel consumption of a 110-horsepower engine is   2. ...
   0.75 lb. per hp per hour, how many pounds of fuel will be
   used in 40 minutes?
      A. 0.50   B. 30   C. 50   D. 55   E. *None of these answers*
3. A clock that loses 4 minutes every 24 hours was set right   3. ...
   at 6 a.m. on January 1. What was the time indicated by
   this clock when the right time was 12 o'clock noon on
   January 6?
      A. 11:36   B. 11:38   C. 11:39   D. 11:40
      E. *None of these answers*
4. The sides of a church spire are four congruent triangles,   4. ...
   each with an altitude of 40 feet and a base of 10 feet.
   Find the area of the spire.
      A. 200 sq. ft.   B. 400 sq. ft.   C. 600 sq. ft.
      D. 1600 sq. ft.   E. *None of these answers*
5. If a man's salary is $b per month and if during a certain   5. ...
   month he spends $c, what *fractional part* of his salary
   does he save?
      A. b-c   B. $\frac{c}{b}$ C. $\frac{b-c}{b}$ D. $\frac{b}{c}$ E. *None of these answers*
6. A bowler has an average of 150 points a game for 12 games.   6. ...
   If he bowls 6 more games, how high an average must he make
   in these games to raise his average for the 18 games to 160?
      A. 170   B. 180   C. 210   D. 225   E. *None of these answers*
7. A store offers for sale five packages of cereal, all of   7. ...
   the same kind and quality but manufactured by different
   firms and containing different amounts. Determine which
   of the following is MOST economical?
      A. 6 oz. for 5¢   B. 1 lb. for 12½¢   C. 11 oz. for 9¢
      D. 14 oz. for 11¢   E. 1 lb. 3 oz. for 16¢
8. From the formula K = 1/2h(b + b₁), find the value of b_1 8. ...
   in terms of K, h and b.
      A. $\frac{2K-b}{h}$ B. $\frac{K}{2h} - b$ C. $\frac{2K-hb}{h}$ D. $\frac{Kh}{2} - b$
      E. *None of these answers*
9. In measuring a distance of 1 mile, an error of 11 feet was   9. ...
   made. Which of the following CORRECTLY represents the size
   of the error?
      A. 1 inch in 40 ft   B. 1 ft. in 150 yd   C. 0.2%
      D. 1:500   E. *None of these answers*
10. A coffee shop blends two kinds of coffee, putting in 2   10. ...
    parts of the 33¢ a pound grade to 1 of the 24¢ grade. If
    the mixture is changed to 1 part of the 33¢ kind and 2

parts of the 24¢ kind, how much will the shop save in blend-
ing 100 lb.?
A. $1 B. $0.90 C. $3 D. $9 E. *None of these answers*

TEST 3

1. What is the largest integer that is a factor of *all three*   1. ...
of the following numbers: 2160, 1344, 1440?
A. 6 B. 8 C. 12 D. 16 E. *None of these answers*
2. Divide 49 by .035.   2. ...
A. 1.4   B. 14   C. 140   D. 1400
E. *None of these answers*
3. Find the value of (4 5/8 - 2 3/4) ÷ 5/4.   3. ...
A. 1   B. 2   C. 1 7/10   D. 2 3/10
E. *None of these answers*
4. Express .3% as a common fraction.   4. ...
A. 1/3   B. 3/10   C. $\frac{3}{100}$ D. $\frac{3}{1000}$
E. *None of these answers*
5. The annual income of a family is budgeted as follows: 5. ...
1/10 for clothing, 1/3 for food, and 1/5 for rent. This
leaves $1320 for other expenses and savings.
Find the annual income.
A. $2156   B. $3600   C. $23,760   D. $39,600
E. *None of these answers*
6. Mr. Smith's tax on his house for a certain year was   6. ...
$283.79. If the tax rate for that year was $3.835 per
$100 of assessed valuation, for what amount was Mr. Smith's
house assessed?
A. $10.88   B. $74   C. $1038.33 D. $7400
E. *None of these answers*
7. A furniture dealer has put a chair on sale with discounts   7. ...
of 25% and 10% from $60, the marked price. How much will
it cost to buy the chair?
A. $13.50   B. $21   C. $39   D. $40.50
E. *None of these answers*
8. The distance between Chicago and Cleveland is 354 miles.   8. ...
If a person leaves Chicago at 9:50 a.m. Central Time and
arrives in Cleveland at 5:30 p.m. the same day Eastern Time,
at what *average* speed does he travel, correct to the nearest
mile?
A. 46 mph   B. 50 mph   C. 53 mph   D. 55 mph
E. *None of these answers*
9. The oil burner in a certain house is used to heat the house 9. ...
and to heat the hot water. During the seven cold months
when the house is heated, an average of 200 gallons of oil
a month is used. In the remaining five months, when the
house is not heated, a total of 200 gallons of oil is used.
What percentage of the year's oil supply is required to
heat water during these five months?
A. 1/8%   B. 7%   C. 12 1/2%   D. 14%
E. *None of these answers*
10. The distance s in feet that a body falls in t seconds is   10. ...
given by the formula $s = 16t^2$. If a body has been falling

3

for 5 seconds, how far will it fall during the 6th second?
    A. 16 ft   B. 80 ft   C. 176 ft   D. 576 ft
    E. *None of these answers*

TEST 4

1. A can do a piece of work in r days and B, who works   1. ...
faster, can do the same work in s days. Which of the
following expressions, if any, represents the number of
days it would take the *two of them* to do the work if they
worked together?
    A. $\dfrac{r + s}{2}$ B. r - s   C. $\dfrac{1}{r} + \dfrac{1}{s}$ D. $\dfrac{rs}{r + s}$
    E. *None of these answers*

2. If y represents the tens digit and x the units digit of a   2. ...
two-digit number, then the number is represented by
    A. y + x   B. yx   C. 10x + y   D. 10y + x
    E. *None of these answers*

3. A certain radio costs a merchant $72, which includes over-   3. ...
head and selling expenses. At what price must he sell it
if he is to make a *profit* of 20% on the selling price?
    A. $86.40   B. $90   C. $92   D. $144
    E. *None of these answers*

4. A formula for infant feeding requires 13 oz. of evaporated   4. ...
milk and 18 oz. of water. If only 10 oz. of milk are
available, how much water, to the nearest ounce, should be
used?
    A. 7 oz.   B. 14 oz.   C. 15 oz.   D. 21 oz.
    E. *None of these answers*

5. A 5-quart solution of sulfuric acid and water is 60% acid.   5. ...
If a gallon of water is added, what percent of the resulting solution is *acid*?
    A. 33 1/3%   B. 40%   C. 48%   D. 50%
    E. *None of these answers*

6. A wooden cone such as that shown in the figure   6. ...
at the right has its entire surface painted. Now
suppose that it is cut into two parts with a saw,
exposing a plane (flat) unpainted surface. All
of the following figures could represent the cut
(unpainted) surface EXCEPT

    1   2   3   4   5

7. In a certain triangle ABC, the three angles are represented 7. ...
by 2x, 3x - 10° and 3x + 30°. What kind of triangle is ABC?
    A. Acute   B. Isosceles C. Obtuse   D. Right
    E. *None of these answers*

8. Two triangles are each equilateral. Which of the follow-   8. ...
ing characteristics *always* belongs to these two triangles?

A. Congruence   B. Equal areas   C. Equal perimeters
D. Similarity   E. *None of these answers*

9. The base of an isosceles triangle is 16 and each of the   9. ...
   equal sides is 10. Find the area of the triangle.
   A. 160   B. 80   C. 36   D. 24   E. *None of these answers*

10. Given a circle A whose diameter is 2 ft and a rectangular   10. ...
    piece of tin B, 10 ft by 4 ft. Find, correct to the near-
    est square foot, the tin that will be left after the great-
    est possible number of circles of the size of A have been
    cut from B.

A. 0 sq. ft.   B. 2 sq. ft.   C. 9 sq. ft.   D. 20 sq. ft.
E. *None of these answers*

TEST 5

1. The number of diagonals, d, in a polygon of n sides is   1. ...
   given by the formula $d = \dfrac{n^2 - 3n}{2}$. If a polygon has 90
   diagonals, how many sides has it?
   A. 8   B. 10   C. 12   D. 15   E. 20

2. A train left Albany for Buffalo, a distance of 290 miles,   2. ...
   at 10:10 a.m. The train was scheduled to reach Buffalo at
   3:45 p.m. If the average rate of the train on this trip
   was 50 miles per hour, it arrived in Buffalo
   A. about 5 minutes ahead of schedule   B. on time
   C. about 5 minutes late   D. about 13 minutes late
   E. more than a quarter of an hour late

3. The expression a^x means that a is to be used as a factor   3. ...
   x times. Therefore, if a^x is squared, the result is
   A. $a^{(x^2)}$ B. a^{2x} C. $2a^{2x}$ D. $2a^x$
   E. *None of these answers*

4. The number of telephones in Adelaide, Australia, is   4. ...
   48,000. If this represents 12.8 telephones per 100 of
   population, the population of Adelaide, to the nearest
   thousand, is
   A. 128,000   B. 375,000   C. 378,000   D. 556,000
   E. *None of these answers*

5. One end of a ladder 32 feet long is placed 10 feet from   5. ...
   the outer wall of a building that stands on level ground.
   How far up the building, to the nearest foot, will the
   ladder reach?
   A. 28 feet   B. 29 feet   C. 30 feet   D. 31 feet
   E. *None of these answers*

6. The length of a rectangle is 3 inches greater than its   6. ...
   width and its area is 88 square inches. An equation that
   may be used to find the width w of the rectangle is:
   A. $3w^2 = 88$ B. $\dfrac{w^2}{3} = 88$ C. $w^2 + 3w - 88 = 0$
   D. $w^2 - 3w = 88$ E. *None of these answers*

7. On a certain map the scale is given as 1" = 1 mile. A boy   7. ...
   copies the map, making each dimension three times as large
   as the given dimensions. On his map how many miles will 6
   inches represent?
      A. 2 miles   B. 3 miles   C. 6 miles   D. 18 miles
      E. *None of these answers*

8. A boy travels on his bicycle at the rate of 6 miles per   8. ...
   hour and his sister on hers at the rate of 5 miles per
   hour. They start at the same time and place and travel
   over the same road in the same direction. After traveling
   for 3 hours the boy turns back.
   How far from the starting point has his sister traveled
   when they meet?
      A. 16 miles   B. About 16.4 miles C. About 16.9 miles
      D. 17 miles   E. *None of these answers*

9. The equation $2x - y - 4 = 0$ is represented graphically be-   9. ...
   low. Which, if any, of the following statements is *false?*
     I. As x increases, y increases.
    II. When $x = 0$, $y = -4$; when $y = 0$, $x = 2$.
   III. The angle marked θ is greater than 45°.
    IV. The graph, if continued, would pass through the point
        $x = 15$, $y = 26$.
      A. I   B. II   C. III   D. IV
      E. *None of these*

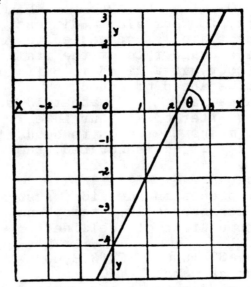

10. If an event can succeed in p ways (all equally probable)   10. ...
    and fail in q ways, the probability that the event will
    succeed is $\dfrac{p}{p + q}$. Which, if any, of the following state-
    ments is TRUE?
      I. The probability of drawing a glass marble in a single
        draw from a bag containing 8 glass marbles and 12 clay
        marbles is 2/3.
     II. The letters x, y and z can be arranged in 6 different
        orders: xyz, zyx, yxz, etc. If one of these arrange-
        ments is chosen at random, the probability that z will
        be the middle letter is 1/6.

III. If one of the integers from 8 to 15 inclusive is chosen at random, the probability that the integer is even is equal to the probability that it is odd.

IV. The probability that a man, aged 40, will live to reach the age of 70 is 4/7.

A. I   B. II   C. III   D. IV   E. *None of these*

SOLUTIONS TO PROBLEMS
TEST 1

1. Answer (D) $\dfrac{rh + st}{h + t}$ Formula: Distance = rate x time

   First distance traveled: rh = r x h
   Second distance traveled: st = s x t
   Total distance traveled: rh + st
   Total time traveled: h + t

   Formula: Distance ÷ time = rate or $\dfrac{rh + st}{h + t}$ = average rate in miles per hour

2. Answer (D) 36

   18^2 = 324 sq. ft., area of square (area of square = $(side)^2$), which is also the area of the rectangle (given).
   Formula: Area of rectangle = length x width
   Let x = the number of feet in other dimension
   ∴ 9x = 324, x = 36 feet.

3. Answer (D) 20%

   Formula: Rate of discount = $\dfrac{\text{amount of discount}}{\text{list price}}$

   by substitution = $\dfrac{90 - 72}{90} = \dfrac{18}{90} = \dfrac{1}{5}$ = 20%

4. Answer (B) $8.50

   10 mills = 1 cent; 100 mills = 10 cents; 1000 mills = 1 dollar
   ∴ $8\frac{1}{2}$ mills per $1 = $8\frac{1}{2}$ x 1000 mills = 8500 mills per $1000 or $8.50 per $1000 (8500 mills ÷ $1000).

5. Answer (B) 66 ft.

   Formula: Circumference = πx diameter
   $= \dfrac{22}{7}$ x 28 in.
   = 88 in.

   Formula: Distance covered = circumference x no. of turns
   = 88 x 9 (given)
   = 792 in.
   = 66 ft. (792 ÷ 12).

6. Answer (C) 8 min. $\dfrac{93,000,000}{186,000}$ = 500 sec.

   ∴ 500 ÷ 60 (60 sec. = 1 min.) = $8\frac{1}{3}$ min. (to the nearest min.)

7. Answer (D) 11%

   Formula: Percent of increase = $\dfrac{\text{amount of increase}}{\text{cash price}}$ x 100%

   Since the installment price = $70 ($5 + 10 x $6.50) and
   the cash price   = $63 (given),
   the installment price is $7 greater.
   ∴ by substitution, percent increase of installment price =
   $\dfrac{\$70 - \$63}{\$63}$ x 100 = $\dfrac{7}{63}$ x 100 = $11\frac{1}{9}$ or 11% (to the nearest whole percent)

7

8. Answer (E) None of these answers
   Change 24 hours to minutes = 1440 min. (24 x 60).
   $\therefore \dfrac{1440}{360}$ = 4 minutes (time it takes the earth to revolve through 1°).

9. Answer (A) $1\frac{1}{3}$
   Formula: $\dfrac{\text{time worked}}{\text{time required}}$ = part of job completed
   Let x = time for all three machines
   Let $\dfrac{x}{3}$ = part of job done by newest machine
   Let $\dfrac{x}{4}$ = part of job done by second machine
   Let $\dfrac{x}{6}$ = part of job done by third machine
   $\therefore \dfrac{x}{3} + \dfrac{x}{4} + \dfrac{x}{6} = 1$ (complete job) or 9x = 12, x = $1\frac{1}{3}$ days.

10. Answer (B) 30%
    Formula: $\dfrac{\text{quantity of alcohol}}{\text{quantity of solution}}$ x 100 = percent alcohol
    6 quarts x 50% alcohol = 3 quarts alcohol
    Second solution contains 6 quarts + 4 quarts (1 gal.) = 10 quarts
    $\therefore \dfrac{3 \text{ quarts}}{10 \text{ quarts}}$ x 100 = 30%.

TEST 2

1. Answer (B) $196.80
   30% of $9840 = $2952; $9840 - $2952 = $6888
   20% of $9840 = $1968; $9840 - $1968 = $7872
   10% of $7872 = $787.20; $7872 - $787.20 = $7084.80
   $\therefore$ $7084.80 - $6888 = $196.80

2. Answer (D) 55   Since 0.75 lb. produces one hp per hr.,
   .75 x 110 = 82.5 lbs. (no. lbs. of fuel used to produce 110 hp in 1 hr.)
   $\dfrac{40}{60}$ = 82.5 or $\dfrac{2}{3}$ x 82.5 = 55 lbs.

3. Answer (C) 11:39
   Total time between the two given dates = 5 days + 6 hrs. or
   5 x 24 + 6 = 126 hrs.
   The object is to find the total number of minutes lost by the clock during the 126 hrs. Let us call this loss x.
   $\therefore \dfrac{4}{24} = \dfrac{x}{126}$ or 24x = 504, x = 21 min. lost
   $\therefore$ the time indicated by the clock at 12 o'clock noon on January 6 was 11:39 (12 o'clock - 21 min.).

4. Answer (E) None of these answers
   Formula: area of triangle = $\frac{1}{2}$ base x altitude
           area of spire   = 4 x $\frac{1}{2}$ base x altitude
           by substitution = 4 x $\frac{1}{2}$ x 10 x 40 = 800 sq. ft.

5. Answer (C) $\dfrac{b - c}{b}$
   If the man earns b and spends c, he saves b - c.
   Formula: $\dfrac{\text{amount saved}}{\text{amount earned}}$ = fractional part of salary saved
   by substitution, $\dfrac{b - c}{b}$ = fractional part of salary saved.

6. Answer (B)   180
The bowler has achieved a total of 1800 points (150 x 12).
His aim is to achieve 2880 points (160 x 18) in 6 more games;
which means 1080 points more (2880 - 1800).
∴ 1080 ÷ 6 = 180 points (the new average he must achieve).

7. Answer (B)   1 lb. for 12½¢
Method: find the cost per oz. in each of the five statements and
        compare.
A. .05 ÷ 6 = $.0083   B. $\frac{.12\frac{1}{2}}{16}$ = $.00781 (most economical)
C. .09 ÷ 11 = $.0081   D. .11 ÷ 14 = $.00785
E. .16 ÷ 19 = $.0084

8. Answer (C) $\frac{2K - hb}{h}$
K = 1/2h(b + b₁) or 2K = h(b + b₁) or 2K = hb + hb₁ or
   2K - hb = hb₁; finally, $\frac{2K - hb}{h}$ = b₁.

9. Answer (C)   0.2%
$\frac{11 \text{ ft.}}{5280 \text{ ft. (1 mile)}}$ = $\frac{1}{480}$ = .002 or .2%.

10. Answer (C) $3
Blend 1: 2 lbs. x .33 + 1 lb. x .24 = .90 per 3 lbs. = .30 per 1 lb.
Blend 2: 1 lb. x .33 + 2 lbs. x .24 = .81 per 3 lbs. = .27 per 1 lb.
Saving per 1 lb., using blend 2 = .03 per 1 lb. (.30 - .27).
Saving per 100 lbs., using blend 2 = $3 (100 x .03).

TEST 3

1. Answer (E)   None of these answers
2160: the factors are 2, 2, 2, 2, 3, 3, 3, 5
1344: the factors are 2, 2, 2, 2, 2, 2, 3, 7
1440: the factors are 2, 2, 2, 2, 2, 2, 3, 3, 5
By inspection, we see that the factors are 2 x 2 x 2 x 2 x 3 = 48

2. Answer (D)   1400
49 ÷ .035 = 49000 ÷ 35 (moving decimals 3 places to the right).
Then solve by using the algorism 35) 49000

3. Answer (E)   None of these answers
The problem may be solved as follows:
$(4\frac{5}{8} - 2\frac{3}{4}) ÷ \frac{5}{4} = (\frac{37}{8} - \frac{11}{4}) ÷ \frac{5}{4} = (\frac{37}{8} - \frac{22}{8}) ÷ \frac{5}{4} = \frac{15}{8} ÷ \frac{5}{4}$
$= \frac{15}{8} × \frac{4}{5} = \frac{3}{2} = 1\frac{1}{2}$

4. Answer (D) $\frac{3}{1000}$ .3% = $\frac{.3}{100}$ = $\frac{3}{1000}$

5. Answer (B) $3600
If x represents the annual income, then $\frac{x}{10}$ = amount spent for
clothing, $\frac{x}{3}$ = amount spent for food, and $\frac{x}{5}$ = amount spent for rent.
∴ $\frac{x}{10} + \frac{x}{3} + \frac{x}{5}$ + $1320 = x. We find x = $3600.

6. Answer (D) $7400
Let x = assessment of Mr. Smith's house.
Since the tax rate was $3.835 per $100., this was = .03835.
Formula: assessment x tax rate = tax paid.
By substitution, .03835x = $283.79. Solving, we find that x=$7400.

9

7. Answer (D) $40.50
   Formula: marked price minus discounts = cost.
   $60 minus $15 (25% x $60) = $45 (price after first discount)
   $45 minus $4.50 (10% x $45, the second discount) = $40.50 (cost).

8. Answer (C) 53 mph
   Time interval = 6 hours 40 min. or $6\frac{2}{3}$ hrs. (Note: In converting
   Central Time to Eastern Time, add 1 hour.)
   Formula: Rate = $\dfrac{\text{Distance}}{\text{Time}} = \dfrac{354}{6\frac{2}{3}} = 354 \times \dfrac{3}{20} = \dfrac{1062}{20} = 53.1$ mph or
   53 mph (to the nearest mile).

9. Answer (C) $12\frac{1}{2}$%
   Year's oil supply = 1600 gallons (200 x 7 = 1400 gallons + 200
   for the remaining 5 months)
   $\therefore \dfrac{200}{1600} = \dfrac{1}{8} = \dfrac{1}{2}$% (percentage of the year's oil supply required
   to heat water during the 5 months when the house is not heated)

10. Answer (C) 176 ft. Formula: $s = 16t^2$
    By substitution, $s = 16 \times 5^2 = 16 \times 25 = 400$ ft. (distance covered
    in 5 seconds). By substitution: $s = 16 \times 6^2 = 16 \times 36 = 576$ ft.
    (distance covered in 6 seconds).
    $\therefore 576 - 400 = 176$ ft. (distance body will fall during 6th sec.)

TEST 4

1. Answer (D) $\dfrac{rs}{r + s}$ Formula: $\dfrac{\text{Time worked}}{\text{Time required}}$ = Part of job done
   Let x = number of days needed when A and B work together.
   Then $\dfrac{x}{r}$ (part of job completed by A when working with B) + $\dfrac{x}{s}$ (part
   of job completed by B when working with A) = 1 (the complete job).
   Then $sx + rx = rs$; $x(s + r) = rs$; $x = \dfrac{rs}{r + s}$.

2. Answer (D) $10y + x$
   Let us assume that the number is 53. Then 5 is the tens digit (y)
   and 3 is the units digit (x). 53 = 10 (5) + (3) = 53.
   Statement (D) is CORRECT.

3. Answer (B) $90 Formula: Selling price = Cost + Profit
   Let x = selling price; therefore, .20x = profit.
   By substitution, x = $72 + .20x or x - .20x = $72 or 80x = $7200
   or x = $90.

4. Answer (B) 14 oz. Let x = amount of water to be added.
   Then 13:18 = 10:x or 13x = 180 or x = 13.8 oz. or 14 oz. (to the
   nearest ounce).

5. Answer (A) $33\frac{1}{3}$%. Explanatory note: The quantity of solution x
   the percentage of solution yields the quantity in solution.
   Therefore, 5 qts. x 60% = 3 qts of acid. Since 1 gallon of water or
   4 qts. is added, the total quantity of solution is now 9 qts.,
   with 3 qts of acid included. Using the formula,
   $\dfrac{\text{quantity of acid}}{\text{quantity of solution}}$ x 100 = percent of acid, $\dfrac{3}{9}$ x 100 = 33 1/3%.

6. Answer (C) By inspection

7. Answer (D) Right
   $2x + (3x - 10°) + (3x + 30°) = 180°$ or $8x + 20° = 180°$ or $x = 20°$.
   Angle $2x = 40°$; angle $3x - 10° = 50°$; and angle $3x + 30° = 90°$.
   Since the triangle contains a right angle, it must be a right
   triangle.

8. Answer (D) Similarity
The triangles are similar since each angle of each triangle is
equal to 60° (a.a.a. = a.a.a.).

9. Answer (E) None of these answers
In isosceles triangle ABC, draw altitude BD; now AD = DC = 8 (since
the altitude of an isosceles triangle is also the median).
Let x = BD; then $(AB)^2 = (AD)^2 + (BD)^2$ (right triangle).
By substitution, $10^2 = 8^2 + x^2$ or $x^2 = 36$, x = 6.
Since the area of a triangle = 1/2 base x altitude, we have
1/2 x 16 x 6 = 48, which is the area of the triangle.

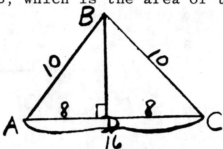

10. Answer (C) 9 sq. ft.   The largest number of circles that can
be cut along the length of the rectangular piece of tin is 5, and
the largest number of circles that can be cut along the width is 2,
since the diameter of the given circle is 2 ft. Therefore, the
maximum number of circles that can be cut is 10 (5 x 2).
To find the area of the tin that will be left, we must find the
area of the rectangle and the area of the 10 circles. Then sub-
tract the area of the ten circles from the area of the rectangle.
Or, briefly stated, area of tin = area of rectangle - area of 10
circles.   Formula: Area of circle = πr^2.
By substitution, area of each circle = $\frac{22}{7}$ x 1 x 1 = 3.14 sq. ft.
The area of all 10 circles = 31.4 sq. ft.
Formula: Area of rectangle - base x altitude. By substitution,
10 x 4 = 40 sq. ft. (area of rectangle).
∴ 40 sq. ft. - 31.4 sq. ft. = 8.6 sq. ft. or 9 sq. ft. (area
of tin left to the nearest sq. ft.).

TEST 5

1. Answer (D) 15   Given d = 90 and the formula d = $\frac{n^2 - 3n}{2}$
∴ 90 = $\frac{n^2 - 3n}{2}$

180 = $n^2 - 3n$ or $n^2 - 3n - 180 = 0$ or (n + 12)(n - 15) = 0
n = -12 (invalid), n = 15

2. Answer (D) About 13 minutes late.
Given distance = 290 miles and average rate = 50 miles per hour
Time = $\frac{Distance}{Rate} = \frac{290}{50} = 5\frac{4}{5}$ hours or 5 hours, 48 minutes
10:10 a.m. + 5 hours, 48 min. = 3:58 p.m. Scheduled time of ar-
rival given as 3:45 p.m.   ∴ 13 minutes late.

3. Answer (B) a^{2x} $(a^x)^2 = a^{2x}$ (by inspection)

4. Answer (B) 375,000   Ratio = $\frac{Number}{Population}$
Given: Number = 48,000 and Ratio = $\frac{12.8}{100}$
∴ $\frac{12.8}{100} = \frac{48,000}{x}$ or 12.8x = 48,000 x 100   x = 375,000

11

5. Answer (C)   30 feet
   The area of a right triangle is formed.
   $x^2 + 10^2 = 32^2$ or $x^2 + 100 = 1024$ or $x^2 = 924$
   x = 30.3 or 30 ft. (to the nearest foot)

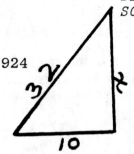

6. Answer (C) $w^2 + 3w - 88 = 0$
   w = width of rectangle   w + 3 = length of rectangle
   Area = length x width or (w + 3) (w)
   .·. $w^2 + 3w = 88$ or $w^2 + 3w - 88 = 0$
7. Answer (A)   2 miles   3:1 = 6:x or 3x = 6 or x = 2 miles
8. Answer (B) About 16.4 miles   Distance covered after 3 hours
   Time = $\dfrac{\text{Distance}}{\text{Rate}}$ Boy - 6 x 3 = 18 miles
                                      Girl - 5 x 3 = 15 miles
      x = distance traveled by   Distance between them - 3 miles
         the girl after first
         3 hours
   3 - x = distance traveled by the boy during this time
   .·. $\dfrac{x}{5} = \dfrac{3 - x}{6}$ (the element of Time is eliminated here since it
                 is the same for both the girl and the boy)
         6x = 15 - 5x or 11x = 15   x = 1.4 miles
   .·. the girl (sister) traveled 15 + 1.4 or 16.4 miles
9. Answer (E)   None of these   The following coordinates of x and y
   may be obtained from the graph: x   0   1   2   3
                                     y -4 -2   0   2
      a. As x increases, y increases.   TRUE (by inspection)
      b. When x = 0, y = -4; when y = 0, x = 2. TRUE (by inspection)
      c. The angle marked θ is greater than 45°. TRUE
         A right angle is formed by the straight line 2x - y - 4 = 0, the
         X axis, and the line x = 3. The leg opposite angle θ consists
         of 2 units and the adjacent leg of 1 unit. θ would be 45° if
         the legs were equal (the acute angles of an isosceles right tri-
         angle are each 45°). The angle must be more than 45° since the
         leg opposite the angle θ is the greater.
      d. The graph, if continued, would pass through the point
         x = 15, y = 26.   TRUE
         The coordinates of a point which lies on a graph will satisfy
         the equation of the graph
         2x - y - 4 = 0 or 2(15) - (26) - 4 = 0 or 30 - 30 = 0   0 = 0
10. Answer (C)   III
    P_{even} = 4 = 8, 10, 12, 14; q_{even} = 4 = 9, 11, 13, 15
         $\dfrac{p}{p + q} = \dfrac{4}{4 + 4} = \dfrac{1}{2}$
    P_{odd} = 4 = 9, 11, 13, 15; q_{odd} = 4 = 8, 10, 12, 14
         $\dfrac{p}{p + q} = \dfrac{4}{4 + 4} = \dfrac{1}{2}$
    .·. c is true inasmuch as $\dfrac{1}{2} = \dfrac{1}{2}$

12

EXAMINATION SECTION
TEST 1

DIRECTIONS: Each question or incomplete statement is followed by several suggested answers or completions. Select the one that BEST answers the question or completes the statement. *PRINT THE LETTER OF THE CORRECT ANSWER IN THE SPACE AT THE RIGHT.*

1. Which of the following proportions is equivalent to $ab = cd$?
   A. $ac = bd$ B. $a/c = d/b$
   C. $ab + cd = 1$ D. $ab - cd = 1$
   E. $a/b = c/d$

   1.___

2. If $x = 3 + 5h$ and $y = 3h - 5$, for what value of h will $x = 2y$?
   A. 68   B. 34   C. 13   D. -4   E. -11

   2.___

3. $\dfrac{\dfrac{1}{x} + \dfrac{1}{x^2}}{\dfrac{1}{x^3}} =$

   A. $2x + 1$ B. $2x$ C. $x(x+1)$

   D. $x + 1$ E. $\dfrac{x + 1}{x^5}$

   3.___

4. If $x = -3/15$, $y = 12$, and $z = 1/10$, then $1/x + y - 1/z =$
   A. 16.9   B. 11 7/10   C. 27/15   D. 14/15   E. -3

   4.___

5. If $2(22/7) = 1/3$ of x, then $x/3 =$
   A. 44/21   B. 22/7   C. 66/7   D. 44/7   E. 132/7

   5.___

6. If $x < y$ and $c = d$, then
   A. $c - y > d - x$ B. $c - x > d$
   C. $y + d > c$ D. $y + c > d$
   E. $c - x > d - y$

   6.___

7. If 85% of $3/x = 8$, then $x =$
   A. .375   B. .032   C. 2.17   D. .300   E. .319

   7.___

8. In the fraction x/y, when 1 is added to the numerator, the fraction equals 1/3. When 3 is added to the denominator of x/y, the fraction equals 1/6. What is x/y?
   A. 2/12   B. 2/9   C. 2/6   D. 6/17   E. 2/3

   8.___

9. If $(.24/.4)(100/48)x = 1$, then $x =$
   A. 8/100   B. 12/150   C. 8/10   D. 10/8   E. 150/12

   9.___

10. If $D_1 = T/R_1$, $D_2 = T/R_2$, D_1 is 75% of D_2, and $R_1 = 1$,   10.____
then $R_2 =$
    A. 3/4   B. $1\frac{1}{2}$ C. $\frac{1}{4}$ D. 4   E. $1\frac{1}{4}$

11. $\dfrac{32/6 + 6/8}{32/6 \times 6/8} =$ 11.____

    A. $\frac{1}{4}$ B. 1   C. 73/48   D. 4   E. 64/9

12. Arrange the following fractions from LEAST to GREATEST: 12.____
3/7, 4/9, 2/5.
    A. 2/5, 4/9, 3/7   B. 3/7, 2/5, 4/9
    C. 4/9, 2/5, 3/7   D. 2/5, 3/7, 4/9
    E. 3/7, 4/9, 2/5

13. If $4/5 + 7/3 - 3/4 + x =$ a whole number, then $x =$ 13.____
    A. 35/60   B. 37/60   C. 3/5   D. 12/5   E. 5

14. What part of a week is 3 hours?   14.____
    A. 1/8   B. 3/28   C. 3/56   D. 1/28   E. 1/56

15. $1 + \dfrac{1}{1 - \dfrac{1}{1+3}} =$ 15.____

    A. 1/5   B. 1 3/4   C. 1 4/5   D. 2 1/3   E. $2\frac{1}{2}$

16. If the diameter of a tube is 2 3/8 inches, then what is   16.____
the APPROXIMATE radius of the tube in feet?
    A. 0.10   B. 0.20   C. 1.19   D. 2.38   E. 14.25

17. If 1 cubic centimeter = .61 cubic inches, APPROXIMATELY   17.____
how many cubic centimeters are there in 1 cubic foot?
    A. 2833   B. 2361   C. 197   D. 105   E. 9

18. If $4/37 = x\%$ of $1/8$, then $x =$ 18.____
    A. 74   B. 8.65   C. 116   D. 12.5   E. 86

19. 166 2/3% of 45 =   19.____
    A. 60   B. 72   C. 75   D. 75 2/3   E. 7500

20. $2\sqrt{20} + \sqrt{45} =$ 20.____

    A. $3\sqrt{65}$ B. $5\sqrt{7}$ C. $7\sqrt{5}$ D. $15\sqrt{5}$ E. $7\sqrt{10}$

21. What is the APPROXIMATE value of $\dfrac{(\sqrt{.3572})(5.473)}{2.18}$?   21.____

    A. .0015   B. .015   C. .15   D. 1.5   E. 15

22. If $\sqrt{16+x} = 4 + 2$, then $x =$ 22.____
    A. -10 B. 2   C. 4   D. 20   E. 36

23. An integer from 1 to 9, inclusive, is selected at random. What is the probability that the integer is a multiple of 3?

    A. 1/9   B. 2/9   C. 3/9   D. 6/9   E. 9/9

23.___

24. If a positive constant is added to each of 5 numbers, then what effect will this have on the mean and standard deviation of these numbers?
The mean
    A. and standard deviation are unchanged
    B. *increases* and standard deviation *increases*
    C. *increases* and standard deviation *decreases*
    D. is unchanged and standard deviation *increases*
    E. *increases* and standard deviation remains the same

24.___

25. If the diagonal of the rectangle shown at the right is 12 cm in length, and the length of one of the sides is 6 cm, then what is the area of the rectangle in square centimeters?

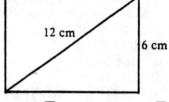

    A. 72   B. $18\sqrt{3}$ C. $18\sqrt{5}$ D. $36\sqrt{3}$ E. $36\sqrt{5}$

25.___

KEY (CORRECT ANSWERS)

1. B		11. C	
2. C		12. D	
3. C		13. B	
4. E		14. E	
5. D		15. D	
6. E		16. A	
7. E		17. A	
8. B		18. E	
9. C		19. C	
10. A		20. C	

21. D
22. D
23. C
24. E
25. D

TEST 2

DIRECTIONS: Each question or incomplete statement is followed by several suggested answers or completions. Select the one that BEST answers the question or completes the statement. *PRINT THE LETTER OF THE CORRECT ANSWER IN THE SPACE AT THE RIGHT.*

1. In the figure shown at the right, the sides of rectangle ABCD are x and y, respectively. A semi-circle is constructed on each side of the rectangle, the diameter of each semi-circle is equal to the length of the corresponding side of the rectangle.
    What is the perimeter of the resulting figure?

    A. $\pi/2(x+y)$
    B. $\pi(x+y)$
    C. $2\pi(x+y)$
    D. $\pi/2(x^2+y^2)$
    E. $\pi(x^2+y^2)$

1.___

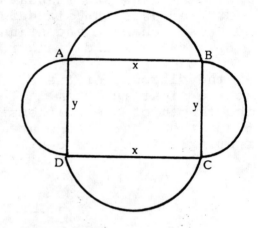

2. What is the measure, in degrees, of ∠BCD in the figure at the right?

    A. 35°
    B. 55°
    C. 90°
    D. 125°
    E. 145°

2.___

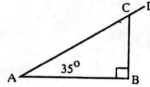

3. In the figure at the right, angle A is drawn in standard position. If the coordinates of the point P on the terminal side of the angle are (-3,4), then what is the sine of the angle A?

    A. -5/4
    B. -3/4
    C. -3/5
    D. 3/5
    E. 4/5

3.___

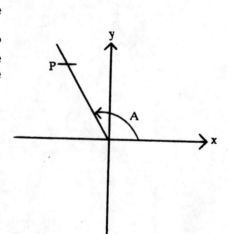

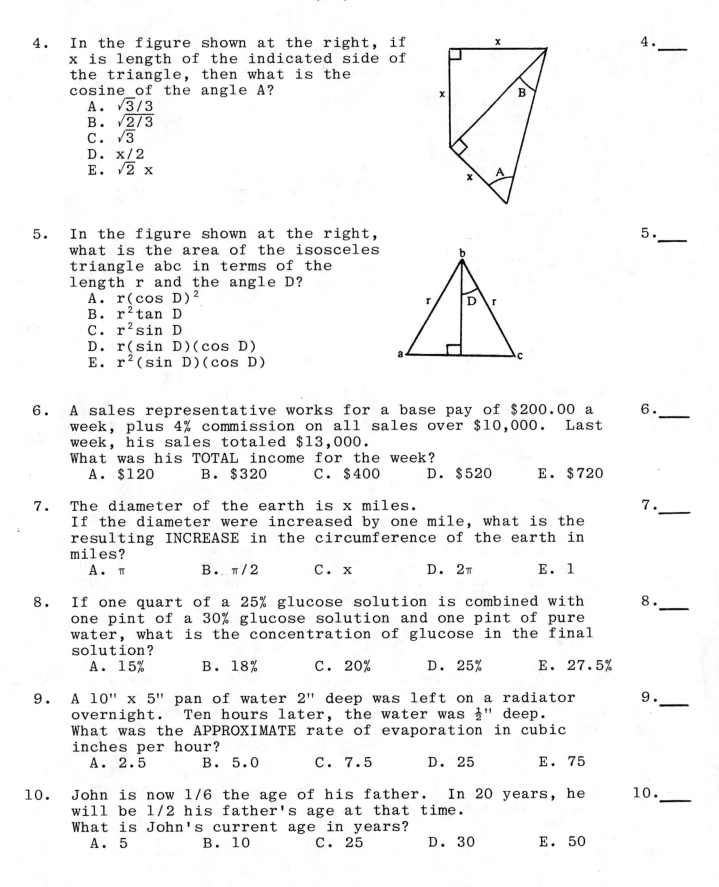

4. In the figure shown at the right, if
   x is length of the indicated side of
   the triangle, then what is the
   cosine of the angle A?
   A. $\sqrt{3}/3$
   B. $\sqrt{2/3}$
   C. $\sqrt{3}$
   D. x/2
   E. $\sqrt{2}$ x

4.___

5. In the figure shown at the right,
   what is the area of the isosceles
   triangle abc in terms of the
   length r and the angle D?
   A. $r(\cos D)^2$
   B. $r^2\tan D$
   C. $r^2\sin D$
   D. $r(\sin D)(\cos D)$
   E. $r^2(\sin D)(\cos D)$

5.___

6. A sales representative works for a base pay of $200.00 a
   week, plus 4% commission on all sales over $10,000. Last
   week, his sales totaled $13,000.
   What was his TOTAL income for the week?
   A. $120   B. $320   C. $400   D. $520   E. $720

6.___

7. The diameter of the earth is x miles.
   If the diameter were increased by one mile, what is the
   resulting INCREASE in the circumference of the earth in
   miles?
   A. π B. $\pi/2$ C. x   D. 2π E. 1

7.___

8. If one quart of a 25% glucose solution is combined with
   one pint of a 30% glucose solution and one pint of pure
   water, what is the concentration of glucose in the final
   solution?
   A. 15%   B. 18%   C. 20%   D. 25%   E. 27.5%

8.___

9. A 10" x 5" pan of water 2" deep was left on a radiator
   overnight. Ten hours later, the water was $\frac{1}{2}$" deep.
   What was the APPROXIMATE rate of evaporation in cubic
   inches per hour?
   A. 2.5   B. 5.0   C. 7.5   D. 25   E. 75

9.___

10. John is now 1/6 the age of his father. In 20 years, he
    will be 1/2 his father's age at that time.
    What is John's current age in years?
    A. 5   B. 10   C. 25   D. 30   E. 50

10.___

11. What is the rate of discount of dental equipment listing   11.___
    at $3,050 and selling for $2,745?
    A. 0.1%   B. 9.0%   C. 10.0%   D. 10.3%   E. 11.1%

12. Shown at the right is a rectangle   12.___
    bounded by streets running north-
    south and east-west.
    If Y is the length of one side
    running north-south and Z is the
    area of the lot, what is the sum
    of the length of the streets
    running east-west?
        A. Z/Y
        B. Z/2
        C. Z - 2Y
        D. Z/2Y
        E. 2Z/Y

13. A 55 minute test consists of four parts with 25 questions   13.___
    each. A student completes the first part in 15 minutes,
    the second in 10 minutes, and the third in 20 minutes.
    How much time does the student have left to spend on each
    of the questions in the remaining fourth part?
        A. 1.8 minutes   B. 1.10 minutes   C. 33 seconds
        D. 27 seconds   E. 24 seconds

14. Brand A of candy sells for $2.00/pound and Brand B for   14.___
    $2.50/pound.
    How many pounds of Brand B should be mixed with $\frac{1}{2}$ pound
    of Brand A to produce candy valued at $2.25/pound?
        A. 0.5   B. 0.6   C. 0.7   D. 0.75   E. 0.8

15. The distributor charges his dealer $100 for 50 units of   15.___
    antiseptic. The dealer in turn sells the units for $2.50
    each, except for 10 units, which were sold at 20% discount.
    What profit is realized by the dealer for the 50 units
    purchased?
        A. No profit   B. $5   C. $10
        D. $20   E. $25

16. In a 500 mile race, Car A averaged 100 miles per hour,   16.___
    and Car B averaged 90 miles per hour.
    Approximately how many miles from the finish line will
    the slower car be when the faster car completes the race?
        A. 5   B. 10   C. 15   D. 45   E. 50

17. A gear with 72 teeth is meshed with one having 24 teeth.   17.___
    If the larger makes 21 revolutions, how many revolutions
    does the SMALLER one make?
        A. 66   B. 63   C. 48   D. 7   E. 3

18. The floor plan layout of a rectangular office calls for   18.___
    locating the center of an examination chair 3 feet and
    4 feet from adjacent walls.
    How many feet from the corner of the room will the center
    of the chair be?
        A. 3   B. 3$\frac{1}{2}$ C. 4   D. 4$\frac{1}{2}$ E. 5

19. At a convention, 1,000 delegates are from the east coast. One hundred delegates are women; 60 of the women are NOT from the east coast.
How many MALE delegates are from the east coast?
    A. 900   B. 850   C. 800   D. 960   E. 940

19.___

20. A crew of 6 men can complete the construction of an office in 60 days. In order to speed up the job, the contractor increases the size of the crew by 1/3.
How many days will he save by the addition of these men?
    A. 10   B. 15   C. 20   D. 40   E. 45

20.___

21. Two teenagers ride a ferris wheel turning at a rate of 10 seconds per revolution. The wheel has a diameter of 50 feet.
What is their APPROXIMATE speed in feet/second?
    A. 5   B. 16   C. 32   D. 50   E. 500

21.___

22. An airplane travels at 500 mph for the first hour of a flight. The plane then encounters headwinds and travels at 450 mph for the remaining hour and one-half of the flight.
What is the AVERAGE speed of the plane, in mph, for the entire flight?
    A. 470   B. 475   C. 480   D. 460   E. 465

22.___

23. A river flows at 3 mph. A man can row at 5 mph in still water.
If he rows one mile upstream and then floats back to the starting place, what is the number of minutes required for the roundtrip?
    A. 30   B. 42   C. 50   D. 60   E. 65

23.___

24. There are two types of animals - chickens and pigs - in a farmer's yard.
If there are 80 heads and 258 feet in the yard, how many chickens are in the yard?
    A. 18   B. 31   C. 46   D. 49   E. 62

24.___

25. Regular gasoline at the local service station sells for $1.16 per gallon. This price includes 15 cents state tax and 8.2 cents Federal tax.
What percent of this sales price goes for tax?
    A. 25   B. 23   C. 20   D. 21   E. 26

25.___

KEY (CORRECT ANSWERS)

1.	B	11.	C
2.	D	12.	E
3.	E	13.	E
4.	A	14.	A
5.	E	15.	D
6.	B	16.	E
7.	A	17.	B
8.	C	18.	E
9.	C	19.	D
10.	A	20.	B

21.	B
22.	A
23.	C
24.	B
25.	C

———

EXAMINATION SECTION

DIRECTIONS: Each question or incomplete statement is followed by several suggested answers or completions. Select the one that BEST answers the question or completes the statement. *PRINT THE LETTER OF THE CORRECT ANSWER IN THE SPACE AT THE RIGHT.*

1. At 7:00 A.M., a student leaves his home in his automobile to drive to school 28 miles away. He averages 50 mph until 7:30 A.M., when his car breaks down. The student has to walk and run the rest of the way.
If he wants to arrive at school at 8:00 A.M., how fast, in mph, must he travel on foot?
   A. 3   B. 4   C. 5   D. 6   E. 7

   1.___

2. Express $1 + \cfrac{1}{2 + \cfrac{1}{3 + \frac{1}{4}}}$ in simplest terms.

   A. 27/28   B. 30/43   C. 1 1/9   D. 1 1/27   E. 1 13/30

   2.___

3. A theater charges $5.00 admission for adults and $2.50 for children. At one showing, 240 admissions brought in a total of $800.
How many adults attended the showing?
   A. 40   B. 80   C. 120   D. 160   E. 266

   3.___

4. $\sqrt{25 + ?} = 5 + 8$
   A. 8   B. 12   C. 64   D. 144   E. 169

   4.___

5. The perimeter of a square is 20.
Which of the following represents the area?
   A. 5   B. 10   C. 20   D. 25   E. 100

   5.___

6. Evaluate the expression $\frac{1}{4} + \frac{3}{8} - \frac{6}{16} - \frac{8}{32}$

   A. 7/16   B. 1/32   C. 1/8   D. 1/4   E. 0

   6.___

7. Bill spent 20% of the money he initially had in his wallet on groceries and 25% on gas. He had $66.00 left.
How much money did he have before he shopped?
   A. $85   B. $100   C. $110   D. $111   E. $120

   7.___

8. Express the product $(2x + 5y)^2$ in simple form.
   A. $4x^2 + 25y^2$ B. $4x^2 + 20xy + 25y^2$
   C. $4x^2 + 10y + 25y^2$ D. $4x^2 - 20xy + 25y^2$
   E. $4x + 25y$

   8.___

9. A student received test grades of 83, 90, and 88. 　　9.___
   What was her grade on a fourth test if the average for
   the four tests is 84?
   　A. 85　　　B. 80　　　C. 75　　　D. 70　　　E. 65

10. A rectangular room is 3 meters wide, 4 meters long, and 　10.___
    2 meters high.
    How far is it from the northeast corner at the floor to
    the southwest corner at the ceiling?
    ____ meters.
    　A. $\sqrt{29}$　　B. $\sqrt{11}$　　C. $\sqrt{9}$　　D. 9　　　E. 5

11. If an electron has a mass of 9.109×10^{-31} kg. and a 　11.___
    proton has a mass of 1.672×10^{-27} kg., approximately
    how many electrons are required to have the same mass
    as one proton?
    　A. 150,000　　　B. 1,800　　　　　C. 5.4×10^{4}
    　D. 5.4×10^{-4}　　E. 15×10^{-58}

12. The introduction of a new manufacturing process will 　12.___
    affect a saving of $1,450 per week over the initial
    8-week production period. New equipment, however, will
    cost $\frac{1}{4}$ of the total savings.
    How much did the equipment cost?
    　A. $11,600.00　　　B. $2,900.00　　　C. $725.00
    　D. $362.50　　　　E. $181.25

13. If P dollars is invested at r percent compounded annually, 　13.___
    at the end of n years it will have grown to $A = P(1 + r)^{n}$.
    An investment made at 16% compounded annually. It grows
    to $1,740 at the end of one year.
    How much was originally invested?
    　A. $150　　　　　B. $278.40　　　　C. $1,461.60
    　D. $1,500　　　　E. $1,700

14. What is $\frac{1}{4}$% of 200?　　　　　　　　　　　　　14.___
    　A. 0.05　　B. 0.5　　　C. 5　　　D. 12.5　　　E. 50

15. Which of the following is .5% of .95?　　　　　　　15.___
    　A. .000475　B. .00475　　C. .0475　　D. .475　　E. 4.75

16. What is the value of (5 lbs. 1 oz)/(3 lbs. 6 oz.) in 　16.___
    ounces?
    　A. 22　　　B. 1.66　　　C. 1.5　　　D. 0.66　　　E. 0.28

17. If 1 inch = 2.54 centimeters, 3/8 centimeter equals 　17.___
    which of the following in inches?
    　A. 6.77　　B. .95　　　C. .39　　　D. .38　　　E. .15

18. If 2x + y = 7 and x - 4y = 4, then x equals which of the 　18.___
    following?
    　A. -15/9　　B. - 1/9　　C. 7/16　　D. 11/9　　E. 32/9

19. What part of an hour is 6 seconds?
    A. 1/600   B. 1/10   C. 1/360   D. 1/60   E. 1/5

20. If 1/3 + 5(x-1) = 8, then which of the following is the value of x?
    A. 8/13   B. 8/5   C. 38/25   D. 38/15   E. 38

21. Which line is perpendicular to the x-axis?
    A. x = 3   B. y = 3   C. x = y
    D. x = y/3   E. y = x/3

22. If a dental hygienist at a certain office is paid H dollars a week, the dental assistant works 36 hours a week at A dollars per hour, and the receptionist works 40 hours a week and receives R dollars every other week, which of the following represents the weekly payroll for these three employees?
    A. H/3 + 36A + 40R/3   B. H + 36A + R/2
    C. H/3 + 12A + R/6   D. 5H + 36 + 20R
    E. H/3 + 12A + 40R

23. Company A ordered five units of anesthetic at $12.00 per unit. Company B ordered 10 units at $13.00 per unit, and Company C ordered 4 at $10.00 per unit. Since all these companies were at one address, the three orders were put on one bill.
    Approximately what percent of the total bill did Company A have to pay?
    A. 5   B. 18   C. 26   D. 36   E. 55

24. Which of the following is the value of A, if 50(A/100) = 2A^2?
    A. 25   B. 1   C. 5/2   D. 1/4   E. 1/2

25. Five-eighths of the employees in a certain company are male. One-fifth of these males are single.
    What percentage of the employees in the company are single males?
    A. 12.5   B. 20.0   C. 25.0   D. 32.0   E. 62.5

26. If x = 20% of y, and z = 35% of x, then z = _____% of y.
    A. 70   B. 57   C. 7   D. 1.75   E. .07

27. Which of the following is the value of the expression
    $\frac{|14-3| - |7-16|}{3|(-2) + 1|}$?

    A. -20/3   B. -2/3   C. 0   D. 2/3   E. 20/3

28. A tank can be filled by a pipe in 30 minutes and emptied by another pipe in 50 minutes.
    How many minutes will it take to fill the tank if both pipes are open?
    A. 45   B. 60   C. 75   D. 80   E. 100

29. If $(4/5)x = (2/5)y$, then which of the following is equal   29.___
    to y/x?
    A. 1/2   B. 2/5   C. 25/8   D. 2   E. 3

30. Which of the following would NOT result in a straight   30.___
    line?
    x =
    A. $1/y$ B. $2y + 5$ C. $(y+6)/(2)$
    D. $5 - y$ E. $4(x+3y)$

31. $\frac{5}{4} + \frac{4}{5} + \frac{3}{2} -$ _____ = a positive integer.   31.___

    A. 10/20   B. 11/20   C. 71/20   D. 3/20   E. 4/20

32. If $\frac{2}{x} + \frac{3}{5} = \frac{4}{3}$, then which of the following is the value of   32.___

    x?
    A. 30/11   B. 30/29   C. 11/30   D. -11/6   E. -5/2

33. Optometry school applicants decreased by 25% during a   33.___
    4-year period. During the same time, the number of
    first-year openings in optometry school increased by 12%.
    If the ratio of applicants to first-year student openings
    had been 3 to 1, then which of the following would be the
    APPROXIMATE ratio at the end of the 4-year period?
    A. 1.5 to 1   B. 2 to 1   C. 3 to 2
    D. 4 to 3   E. 6 to 5

34. If $\sqrt{x-25} = 7 - 5$, then which of the following is the   34.___
    value of x?
    A. 4   B. 27   C. 29   D. 49   E. 729

35. Two cars start at the same point and travel north and   35.___
    west at the rate of 24 and 32 mph, respectively.
    How far apart are they at the end of 2 hours?
    A. 64   B. 80   C. 112   D. 116   E. 100

36. Right triangle ABC with right angle C and AB = 6, BC = 3,   36.___
    find AC.
    A. 3   B. 6   C. 27   D. 33   E. $3\sqrt{3}$

37. When each of the sides of a square is increased by 1 yard,   37.___
    the area of the new square is 53 square yards more than
    that of the original square.
    What is the length of the sides of the original square?
    A. 25   B. 26   C. 27   D. 52   E. 54

38. Evaluate: $3(2)^2 + \sqrt{25} - (-2)^3$.   38.___
    A. 9   B. 24   C. 25   D. 33   E. 76

39. Which of the following is the
    length of the line segment BC
    if AB = 14, AD = 5, and angle
    BAD = 30°?
    A. $\sqrt{221}$
    B. $\sqrt{171}$
    C. $7\sqrt{3}$
    D. 7
    E. 9

39.___

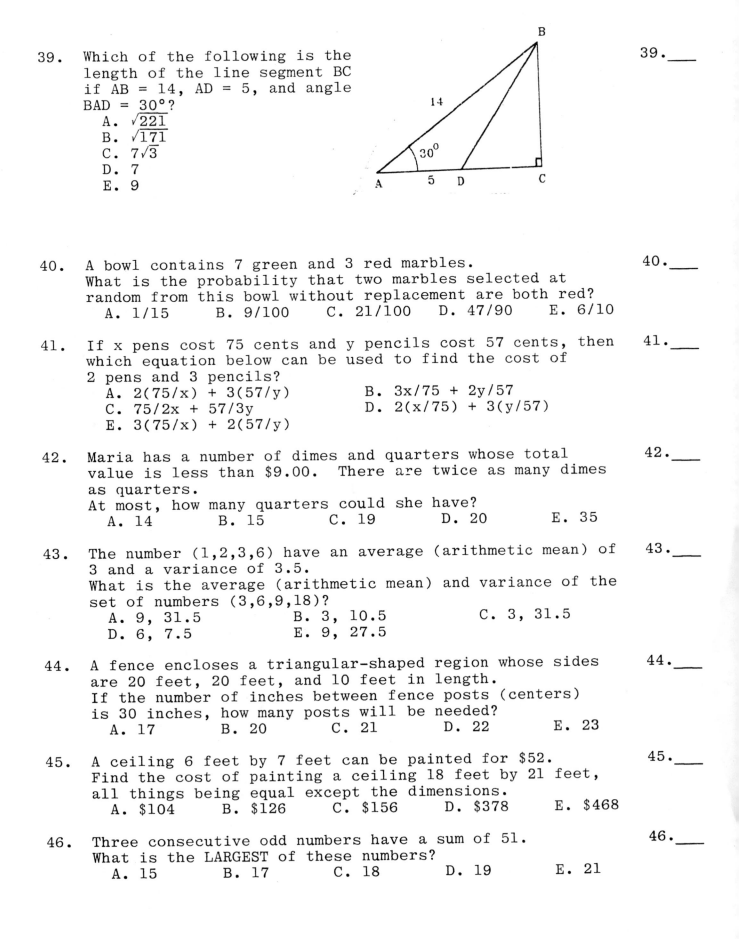

40. A bowl contains 7 green and 3 red marbles.
    What is the probability that two marbles selected at
    random from this bowl without replacement are both red?
    A. 1/15   B. 9/100   C. 21/100   D. 47/90   E. 6/10

40.___

41. If x pens cost 75 cents and y pencils cost 57 cents, then
    which equation below can be used to find the cost of
    2 pens and 3 pencils?
    A. 2(75/x) + 3(57/y)   B. 3x/75 + 2y/57
    C. 75/2x + 57/3y   D. 2(x/75) + 3(y/57)
    E. 3(75/x) + 2(57/y)

41.___

42. Maria has a number of dimes and quarters whose total
    value is less than $9.00. There are twice as many dimes
    as quarters.
    At most, how many quarters could she have?
    A. 14   B. 15   C. 19   D. 20   E. 35

42.___

43. The number (1,2,3,6) have an average (arithmetic mean) of
    3 and a variance of 3.5.
    What is the average (arithmetic mean) and variance of the
    set of numbers (3,6,9,18)?
    A. 9, 31.5   B. 3, 10.5   C. 3, 31.5
    D. 6, 7.5   E. 9, 27.5

43.___

44. A fence encloses a triangular-shaped region whose sides
    are 20 feet, 20 feet, and 10 feet in length.
    If the number of inches between fence posts (centers)
    is 30 inches, how many posts will be needed?
    A. 17   B. 20   C. 21   D. 22   E. 23

44.___

45. A ceiling 6 feet by 7 feet can be painted for $52.
    Find the cost of painting a ceiling 18 feet by 21 feet,
    all things being equal except the dimensions.
    A. $104   B. $126   C. $156   D. $378   E. $468

45.___

46. Three consecutive odd numbers have a sum of 51.
    What is the LARGEST of these numbers?
    A. 15   B. 17   C. 18   D. 19   E. 21

46.___

47. It takes 5 hours for a qualified typist to complete a   47.___
    report. Coffee break begins at 10:15 A.M. It is now
    9:55 A.M.
    How much of the task can the typist be expected to
    complete by coffee break?
    A. 1/8   B. 1/25   C. 1/3   D. 1/5   E. 1/15

48. A container in the form of a rectangular solid is 10   48.___
    feet long, 9 feet wide, and 2 feet deep. The container
    is filled with a liquid weighing 100 pounds per cubic
    foot.
    What is the weight of the liquid in the container in
    pounds?
    A. 90   B. 180   C. 1,800   D. 9,000   E. 18,000

49. The value of cos(π/3) equals the value of   49.___
    A. - cos(2π/3)   B. cos(2π/3)   C. cos(6π/3)
    D. - cos(5π/3)   E. cos(4π/3)

50. If 5 ≤ x ≤ 12 and -2 ≤ y ≤ 9, then $\frac{3x-4}{4+5y^2}$ is as large as   50.___

    possible when x = _____ and y = _____.
    A. 12; 9   B. 12; 0   C. 12; -2   D. 0; 9   E. 0; 0

KEY (CORRECT ANSWERS)

1. D	11. B	21. A	31. B	41. A
2. E	12. B	22. B	32. A	42. C
3. B	13. D	23. C	33. B	43. A
4. D	14. B	24. D	34. C	44. B
5. D	15. B	25. A	35. B	45. E
6. E	16. C	26. C	36. E	46. D
7. E	17. E	27. D	37. B	47. E
8. B	18. E	28. C	38. C	48. E
9. C	19. A	29. D	39. D	49. A
10. A	20. D	30. A	40. A	50. B

EXAMINATION SECTION

DIRECTIONS: Each question or incomplete statement is followed by
several suggested answers or completions. Select the
one that BEST answers the question or completes the
statement. *PRINT THE LETTER OF THE CORRECT ANSWER IN
THE SPACE AT THE RIGHT.*

1. Which ordered pair of numbers (x,y) is the solution of the   1.___
   following system of equations?
   $$3x - 2y = 5$$
   $$2x + 2y = 10$$

   A. (1,1)   B. (1,2)   C. (2,1)   D. (2,3)   E. (3,2)

2. A certain microcomputer's memory contains 16K (K=1,024)   2.___
   storage locations.
   If a program being run uses 12,517 storage locations, how
   many storage locations are still available?
   A. 3,767   B. 3,867   C. 4,867   D. 11,493   E. 16,384

3. (3.5 + 0.3) - 4(0.82 + 1.08) =   3.___

   A. -3.800   B. -0.380   C. 0.304   D. 1.700   E. 4.840

4. Which of the triangles shown below are congruent?   4.___

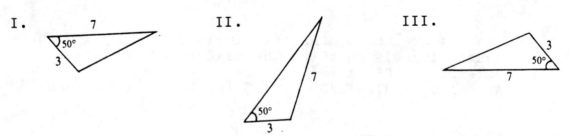

The CORRECT answer is:
   A. I and II
   B. I and III
   C. II and III
   D. All of the above
   E. No triangle is congruent to any other triangle

5. A survey asked a sample of people to choose the better candidate in an upcoming election. Of the people surveyed, 20% said they would vote for Candidate A, 30% for Candidate B, and 50% said they were undecided.
If 1,000 people said they would vote for Candidate A, how many people said they would vote for Candidate B?
   A. 300   B. 1,100   C. 1,500   D. 2,500   E. 5,000

5.___

6. Sheila's salary is $110 per day. Due to financial problems in her company, her employer has asked Sheila to take a 10% cut in pay.
How much will Sheila be earning per day if she takes the cut in pay?
   A. $11   B. $99   C. $100   D. $109   E. $121

6.___

7. The 6 A.M. temperature one day last winter was -13°F. From 6 A.M. until 1 P.M., the temperature rose an average of 3°F per hour.
Which of the following expressions represents the temperature in °F at 1 P.M.?
   A. 7(-13+3)   B. -13-7(3)   C. 7+3(-13)
   D. -13+5(3)   E. -13+7(3)

7.___

8.

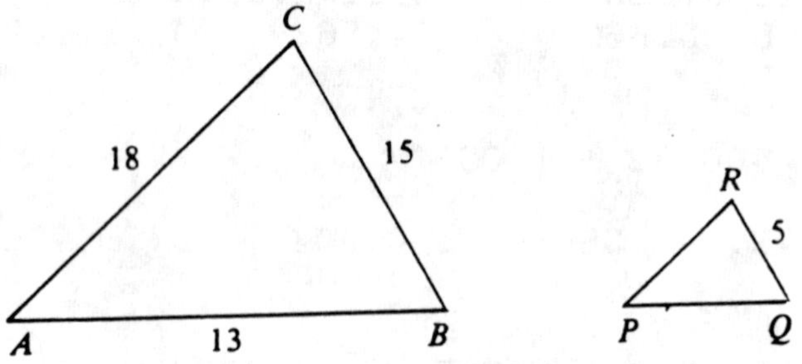

In the figure above, ΔABC is similar to ΔPQR, and the measure of ∠A is equal to the measure of ∠P.
The length of PR is
   A. 4 1/6   B. 4 1/3   C. 5 10/13   D. 6   E. 8

8.___

9. |-5|+|6|+(-5)+6 =
   A. -22   B. -10   C. 2   D. 10   E. 12

9.___

10. A bread recipe calls for ½ cup of butter and 3½ cups of flour. Using this recipe to make enough bread for a party, John will need 1½ cups of butter.
How many cups of flour will he need?
   A. 4½   B. 5½   C. 7½   D. 9½   E. 10½

10.___

11.

Midland Stereo Supply House			
Item	Price each	Quantity ordered	Total for item(s)
Cassette tapes	$ 4.50	6	
Stereo headphones	$36.00	1	
Record protectors	$ 0.10	25	
		Subtotal	$
		Add 4% sales tax	+
		Shipping	+ 1.50
		Total	$

11.___

What would be the TOTAL cost of the order shown above?
A. $42.10   B. $65.50   C. $67.00   D. $69.62   E. $69.68

12. The distance, in miles, from an observer to the horizon is 1.35 times the square root of the observer's elevation, in feet.
If an observer's elevation is 16 feet, how many miles away is the horizon?
A. 5.4   B. 7.0   C. 10.8   D. 11.9   E. 48.6

12.___

13. If 3x - 2y = 6, then y equals which of these expressions?

A. $-\frac{3}{2}x - 3$ B.   B. $\frac{3}{2}x + 6$ C. $\frac{3}{2}x - 3$

D. $\frac{2}{3}x + 3$ E. 3x - 3

13.___

14.

Age	Number of Students
14	50
15	180
16	180
17	340
18	210
19	40
Total	1,000

14.___

The ages of the students attending City High School this year are listed in the table above.
If a student is picked at random from this school, what is the probability that he or she will be 18 or older?
A. 1/25   B. 1/4   C. 1/3   D. 1/2   E. 3/4

15.   15.____

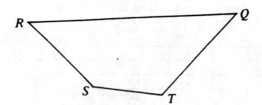

In quadrilateral QRST above, the measures of ∠Q, ∠R, and
∠S are 45°, 45°, and 140°, respectively.
The measure of ∠T is _____ degrees.
    A. 120   B. 130   C. 135   D. 140   E. 220

16.   If x = -3 and y = -2, then the GREATEST value is   16.____

        A. |x-y| B. |x|-|y| C. |x|-y

        D. x-|y| E. x-y

17.   17.____

Name	Height in Inches
Adam	65
Barbara	64
Chris	69
Daniel	64
Ella	65

What is the average (arithmetic mean) height, in inches,
of the 5 people whose heights are listed in the table above?
    A. 65.0   B. 65.2   C. 65.4   D. 66.0   E. 66.5

18.   The Jones family wants to buy a refrigerator that costs   18.____
      $750. They agree to pay 15% of the cost initially and
      the balance in 5 equal monthly payments without interest.
      How much will each monthly payment be?
        A. $112.50 B. 127.50   C. $129.50 D. $147.00 E. $150.00

19.   What is the SMALLEST positive integer that gives a   19.____
      remainder of 1 when divided by any of the integers 12,
      18, and 27?
        A. 121   B. 109   C. 61   D. 55   E. 37

20.   A serving of a certain cereal, with milk, provides 35%   20.____
      of the potassium required daily by the average adult.
      A serving of this cereal with milk contains 112 milligrams
      of potassium.
      How many milligrams of potassium does the average adult
      require each day?
        A. 35   B. 39   C. 147   D. 320   E. 392

21. Three people share $198 in the ratio 1:3:7.
    To the nearest dollar, how much is the LARGEST share?
    A. $18   B. $28   C. $54   D. $126   E. $134

21.___

22. Which of the following is a factorization of the poly-
    nomial $2x^2 + x - 10$?
    A. $2(x^2+x-5)$ B. $(2x+2)(x-5)$ C. $(2x+5)(x-2)$
    D. $(2x-5)(x+2)$ E. $(2x+10)(x-1)$

22.___

23. In the figure at the right,
    B, E, and C are collinear;
    A, D, and C are collinear;
    E is halfway between B and C;
    and $\overline{DE}$ and $\overline{AB}$ are each per-
    pendicular to $\overline{BC}$.
    If $\overline{BE}$ is 40 units long and
    $\overline{AB}$ is 60 units long, how
    many units long is the
    perimeter of quadrilateral
    ABED?
    A. 100
    B. 140
    C. 180
    D. 200
    E. 220

23.___

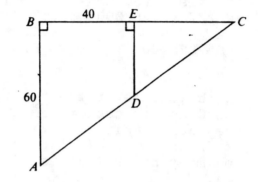

24. The circle graph at the right
    represents the relative sizes
    of the sources of a tax dollar.
    The degree measure of the central
    angle of the sector labeled
    Income is _____ degrees.
    A. 40
    B. 72
    C. 100
    D. 120
    E. 144

24.___

25. $\sqrt{8} + \sqrt{16} + 3\sqrt{2} - \sqrt{3} =$

    A. $4 + 5\sqrt{2} - \sqrt{3}$ B. $11\sqrt{2} - \sqrt{3}$ C. $3\sqrt{26} - \sqrt{3}$
    D. $15 - \sqrt{3}$ E. $3\sqrt{23}$

25.___

26. Two lines have the equations $2x+y = 4$ and $x-2y = 7$,
    respectively.
    At what (x,y) point do they intersect?
    A. (3,-2)   B. (6,-5)   C. (5,-6)   D. (-3,-2)   E. (-2,3)

26.___

27.

x	0	2	4	6	8	10
y	4	7	10	13	16	19

Which of these equations expresses the relationship shown in the above table?
   A. y = 2x   B. y = x+4   y = x+9
   D. 2y = 3x+4   E. 2y = 3x+8

27.____

28. A life insurance policy costs $0.75 per month for each $1,000 worth of insurance.
At this rate, how much would someone have to pay in a year for $25,000 worth of this insurance?
   A. $225.00   B. $187.50   C. $156.25
   D. $75.00   E. $18.75

28.____

29. In the circle at the <u>right</u>, <u>which</u> has O as its center, $\overline{OA}$ and $\overline{AB}$ are each 4 units long.
If $\overline{OE}$ is perpendicular to $\overline{AB}$, how many units long is $\overline{OE}$?
   A. $\sqrt{3}$
   B. 2
   C. 3
   D. $2\sqrt{3}$
   E. 4

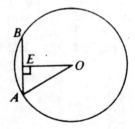

29.____

30. If the solutions of the equation $2x^2 - kx + 6 = 0$ are x = 1 and x = 3, then k =
   A. -4   B. 4   C. 7   D. 8   E. 10

30.____

31. If f(x) = x + 3 and g(x) = 3 - x, what is the value of f[g(3)]?
   A. 6   B. 3   C. 0   D. -3   E. -6

31.____

32. Let x equal the numerator of a certain fraction. The denominator of that fraction is 2 more than the numerator. When 5 is added to both the numerator and the denominator, the resulting fraction equals 5/6.
Which of these equations determines the correct value of x, the numerator of the original fraction?

   A. $\frac{x+5}{x+3} = \frac{5}{6}$ B. $\frac{x+3}{x+5} = \frac{5}{6}$ C. $\frac{x+5}{x+7} = \frac{5}{6}$

   D. $\frac{x+5}{2x+5} = \frac{5}{6}$ E. $\frac{2x+5}{x+5} = \frac{5}{6}$

32.____

33. A man throwing darts at a dart board hit the board on 95% of the throws he made. He hit the board 114 times. Which equation determines the CORRECT value of x, the number of throws he made?

    A. $(0.95)114 = x$ B. $0.95x = 114$ C. $114x = 95$

    D. $\frac{x}{95} = 114$ E. $x = \frac{0.95}{114}$

33.____

34. Which equation determines the line that is parallel to the line with the equation $y = 3x+1$ and intersects the line with the equation $y = 6x-1$ at the y-axis?
y =
    A. $3x-1$ B. $2x-1$ C. $\frac{1}{3}x - 1$ D. $\frac{1}{3}x + 1$ E. $\frac{1}{2}x - 1$

34.____

35.

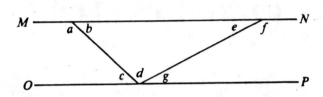

    In the figure above, 2 line segments intersect $\overline{MN}$ and $\overline{OP}$, $\overline{MN}$ is parallel to $\overline{OP}$, and a, b, c, d, e, f, and g are the measures, in degrees, of the indicated angles. Which of these statements is NOT necessarily true?
    A. $b = 180° - d - c$ B. $e = 180° - d - c$
    C. $a = 180° - c$ D. $f = 180° - g$
    E. $g = 180° - f$

35.____

36. If $x = -2$, $y = 3$, and $z = -5$, then the product xyz is how much GREATER than the sum $x + y + z$?
    A. -34 B. -26 C. 20   D. 26   E. 34

36.____

37. If $n! = (n)(n-1)(n-2)...(2)(1)$, then $5! =$
    A. 12   B. 15   C. 30   D. 120   E. 54,321

37.____

38. For all x, $(2x+3)^2 + 2(2x+4) - 2$ equals which of these expressions?
    A. $4x^2 + 4x + 11$ B. $(4x+15)(x+1)$
    C. $(2x+5)(2x+3)$ D. $(2x+5)(2x+2)$
    E. $(2x+5)(2x-3)$

38.____

39. What is TRUE about the solutions of the equation $x^2 - 3x = -2$?
    They are
    A. real and unequal   B. real and equal
    C. real and negative   D. irrational and negative
    E. imaginary

39.____

40. If the retail price of a dinette set is $1\frac{1}{3}$ times the   40. ___
     wholesale price, and the retail price of a dinette set
     is \$200.00, what is its wholesale price?
       A. \$133.33   B. \$150.00   C. \$166.67
       D. \$266.67   E. \$300.00

KEY (CORRECT ANSWERS)

1. E	11. D	21. D	31. B
2. B	12. A	22. C	32. C
3. A	13. C	23. C	33. B
4. B	14. B	24. E	34. A
5. C	15. B	25. A	35. A
6. B	16. C	26. A	36. E
7. E	17. C	27. E	37. D
8. D	18. B	28. A	38. C
9. E	19. B	29. D	39. A
10. E	20. D	30. D	40. B

ABSTRACT REASONING
SPATIAL RELATIONS/TWO DIMENSIONS

COMMENTARY

Since intelligence exists in many forms or phases and the theory of differential aptitudes is now firmly established in testing, other manifestations and measurements of intelligence than verbal or purely arithmetical must be identified and measured.

The spatial relations test, including that phase designated as spatial perception, involves and measures the ability to solve problems, drawn up in the form of outlines or pictures, which are concerned with the shapes of objects or the interrelationship of their parts. While, concededly, little is known about the nature and scope of this aptitude, it appears that this ability is required in science, mathematics, engineering, and drawing courses and curricula. Accordingly, tests of spatial perception involving the reconstruction of two-dimensional patterns, are presented in this section.

It is to be noted that the relationships expressed in spatial tests are geometric, definitive, and exact. Keeping these basic characteristics in mind, the applicant is to proceed to solve the spatial perception problems in his own way. There is no set method of solving these problems. The examinee may find that there are different methods for different types of spatial problems. Therefore, the BEST way to prepare for this type of test is to *TAKE* and study the work-practice problems in two-dimensional patterns provided in this section.

ABSTRACT REASONING
SPATIAL RELATIONS/TWO DIMENSIONS

The tests of spatial relations that follow consist of items which involve the visualization of two dimensions.

Each of the items of these tests consists of a line of figures -- a complete figure on the left and four lettered alternatives of component parts on the right, only one of which can be fitted together exactly to form the complete figure on the left.

The candidate is then required to select that choice of component parts which could be fitted together to form the complete figure given at the left.

———

SAMPLE QUESTIONS AND EXPLANATIONS

DIRECTIONS: The items in this part constitute a test of spatial relations involving two dimensions. Each item consists of a line of figures. The first figure is the complete figure. This is followed by four lettered choices of component parts, only one of which can be fitted together exactly to form the first (complete) figure.
Rules to be followed:
1. The lettered choice of component parts selected as the answer must have the same number of parts as the first (complete) figure.
2. The parts must fit exactly.
3. The parts may be turned around but may not be turned over.

1.

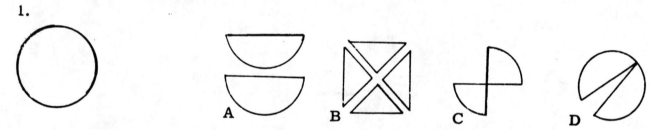

The correct answer is D. When the two parts of D are completely closed, they form the complete figure on the left.

2.

The correct answer is B. When the two parts of B are reversed in position, they form the complete figure on the left.

2

TEST 1

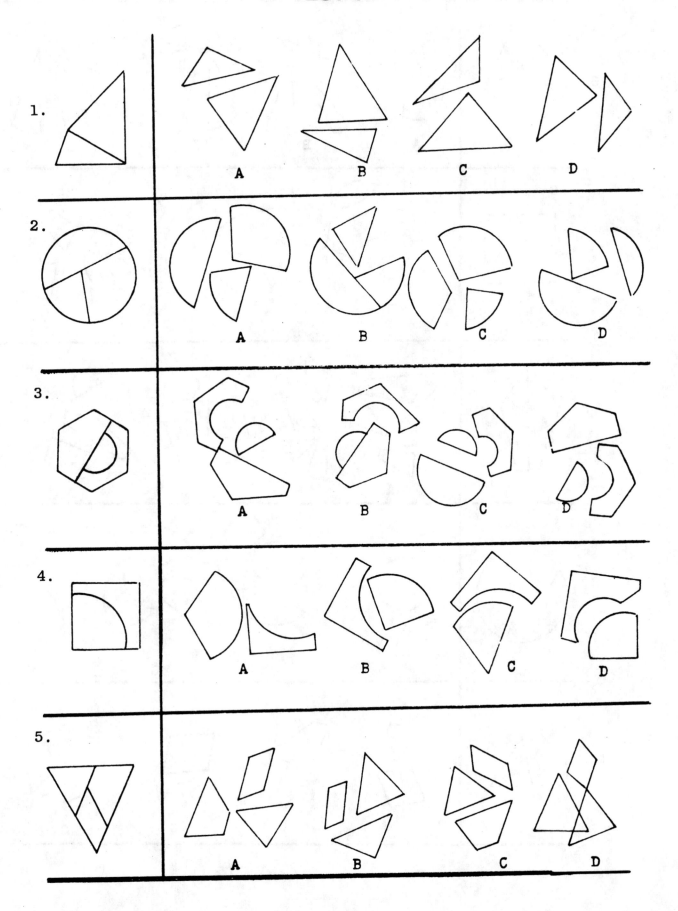

1. A   B   C   D

2. A   B   C   D

3. A   B   C   D

4. A   B   C   D

5. A   B   C   D

TEST 2

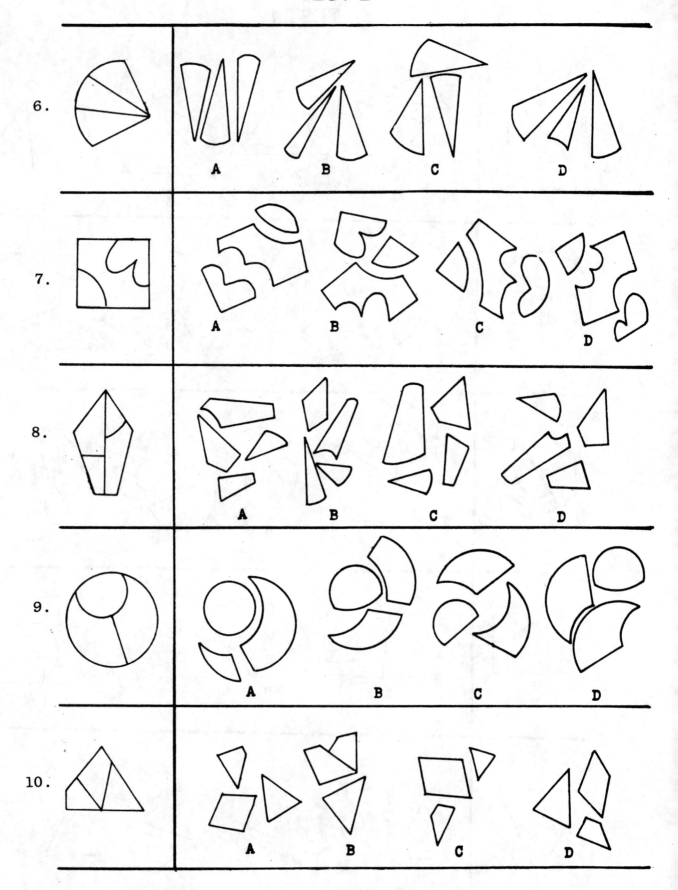

6.

A   B   C   D

7.

A   B   C   D

8.

A   B   C   D

9.

A   B   C   D

10.

A   B   C   D

4

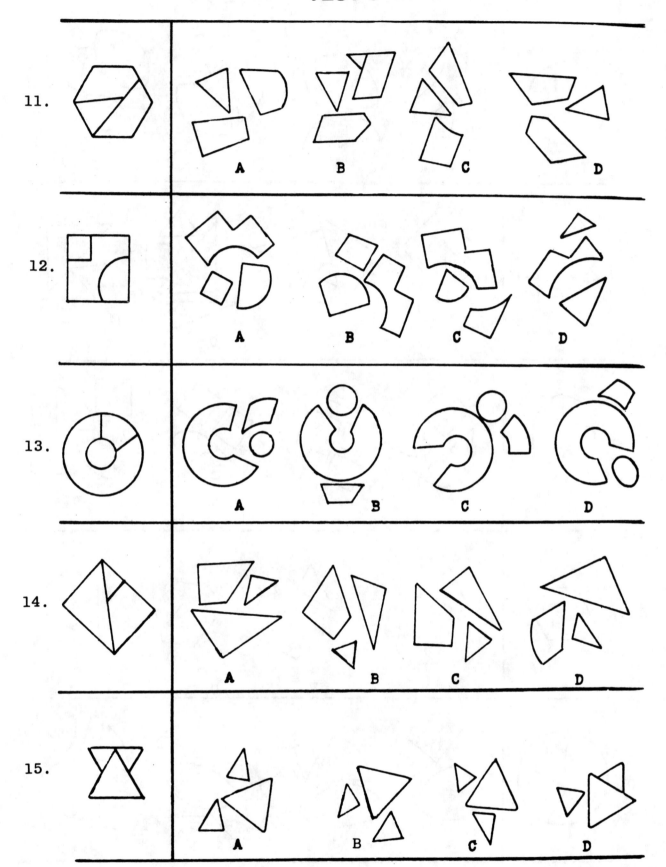

11.

    A   B   C   D

12.

    A   B   C   D

13.

    A   B   C   D

14.

    A   B   C   D

15.

    A   B   C   D

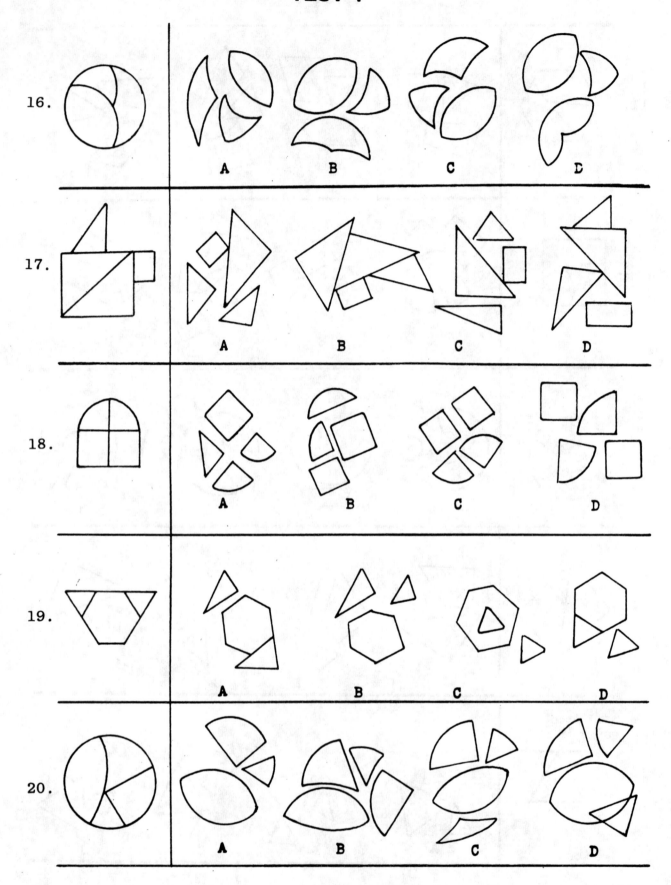

16.

A   B   C   D

17.

A   B   C   D

18.

A   B   C   D

19.

A   B   C   D

20.

A   B   C   D

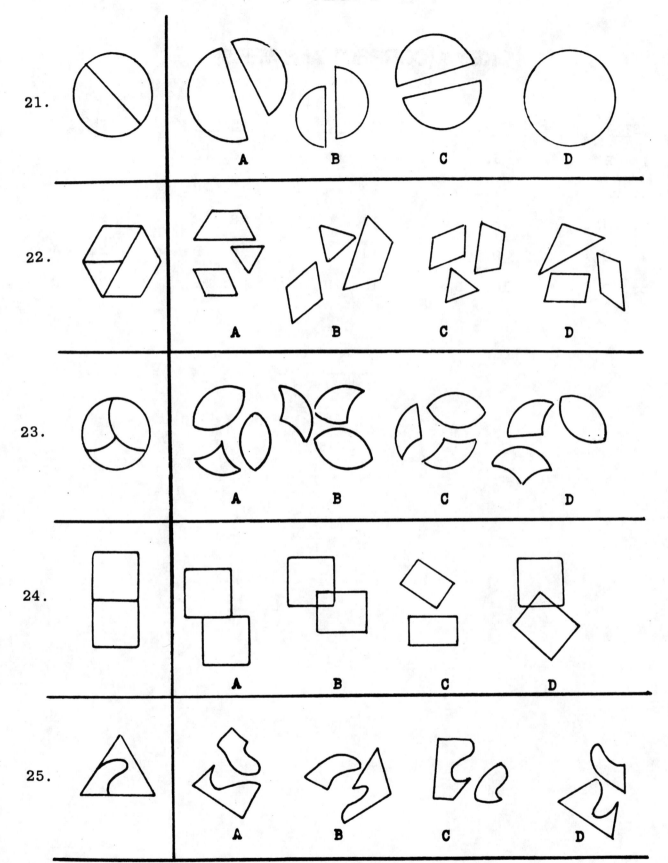

21.   A   B   C   D

22.   A   B   C   D

23.   A   B   C   D

24.   A   B   C   D

25.   A   B   C   D

KEYS (CORRECT ANSWERS)

TEST 1	TEST 2	TEST 3	TEST 4	TEST 5
1. B	6. C	11. D	16. B	21. C
2. A	7. B	12. A	17. B	22. B
3. D	8. A	13. C	18. C	23. B
4. B	9. D	14. A	19. D	24. A
5. C	10. B	15. D	20. B	25. D

ABSTRACT REASONING

SPATIAL RELATIONS/TWO DIMENSIONS

COMMENTARY

Since intelligence exists in many forms or phases and the theory of differential aptitudes is now firmly established in testing, other manifestations and measurements of intelligence than verbal or purely arithmetical must be identified and measured.

The spatial relations test, including that phase designated as spatial perception, involves and measures the ability to solve problems, drawn up in the form of outlines or pictures, which are concerned with the shapes of objects or the interrelationship of their parts. While, concededly, little is known about the nature and scope of this aptitude, it appears that this abiluty is required in science, mathematics, engineering, and drawing courses and curricula. Accordingly, tests of spatial perception involving the reconstruction of two-dimensional patterns, are presented in this section.

It is to be noted that the relationships expressed in spatial tests are geometric, definitive, and exact. Keeping these basic characteristics in mind, the applicant is to proceed to solve the spatial perception problems in his own way. There is no set method of solving these problems. The examinee may find that there are different methods for different types of sptial problems. Therefore, the BEST way to prepare for this type of test is to *TAKE* and study the work-practice problems in two-dimensional patterns provided in this section.

———

ABSTRACT REASONING
SPATIAL RELATIONS/TWO DIMENSIONS

DIRECTIONS FOR THIS SECTION:
Each of the items in these Tests numbered 1 to 52 is followed by a group of five (5) figures lettered A,B,C,D, and E. Two of these lettered figures, when put together, make the drawing that appears unlettered in the upper left corner. Write on the answer sheet the letters of the two figures which, when put together, are *MOST NEARLY* the same as the unlettered figure.

TEST 1

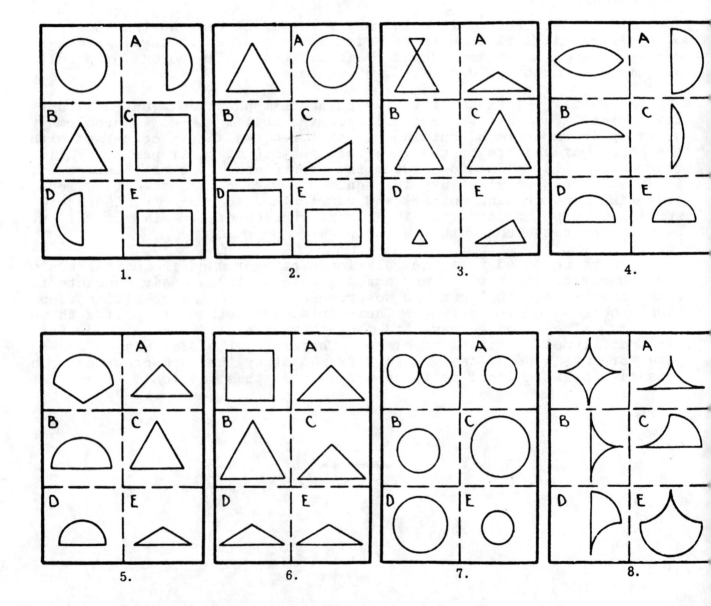

TEST 2

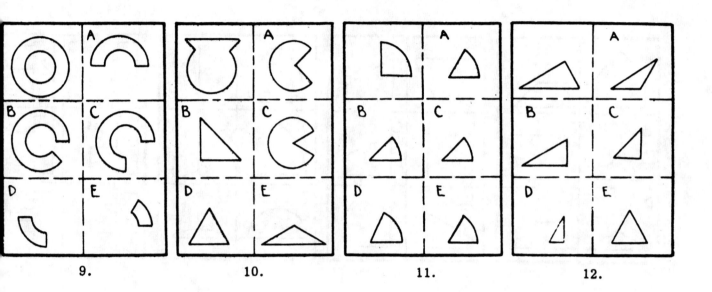

9.   10.   11.   12.

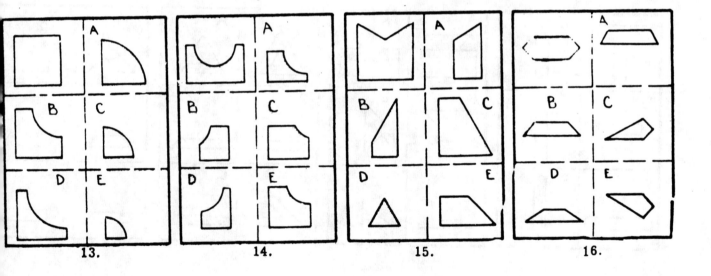

13.   14.   15.   16.

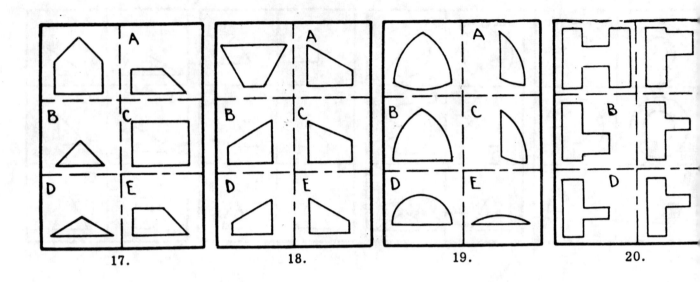

17. 18. 19. 20.

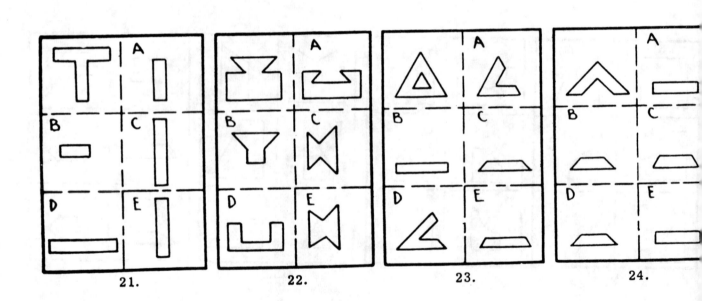

21. 22. 23. 24.

TEST 4

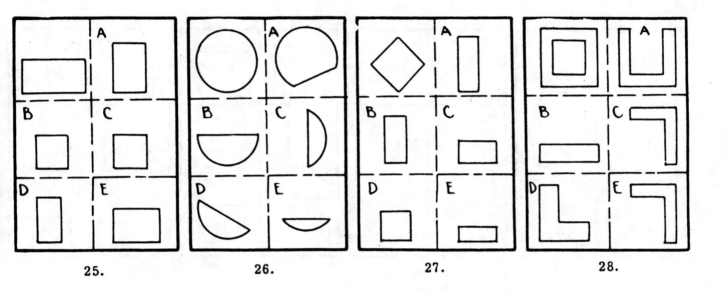

25.   26.   27.   28.

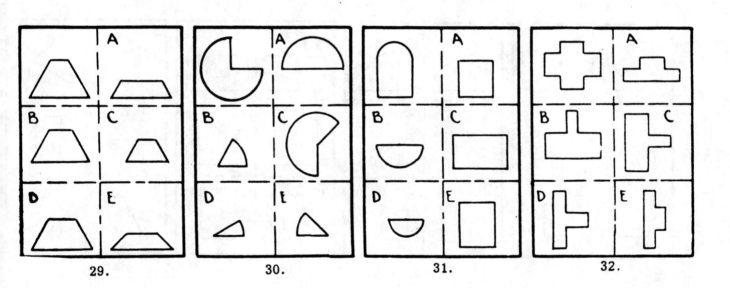

29.   30.   31.   32.

5

TEST 5

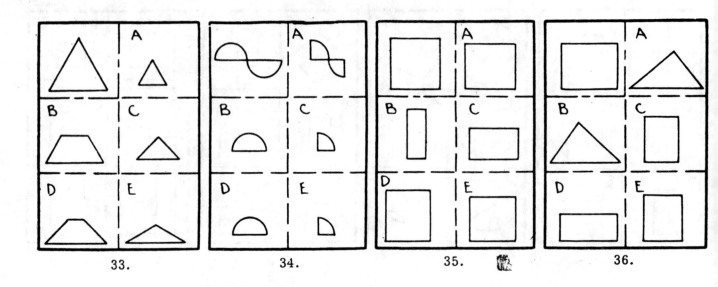

33.   34.   35.   36.

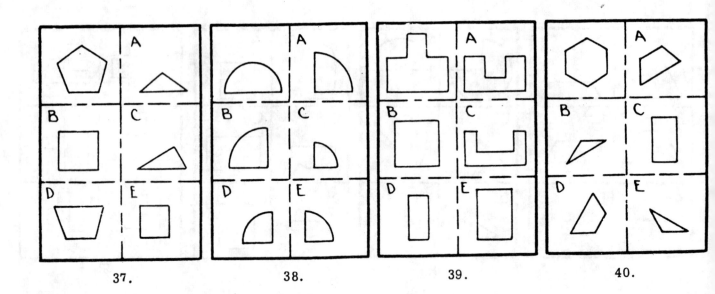

37.   38.   39.   40.

TEST 6

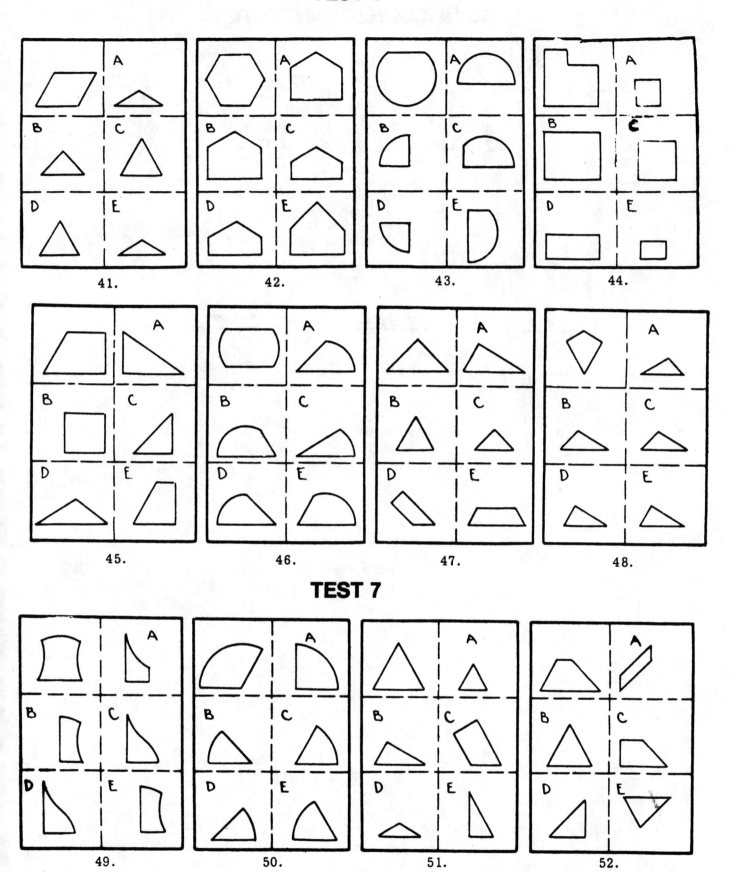

41. 42. 43. 44.

45. 46. 47. 48.

TEST 7

49. 50. 51. 52.

KEYS (CORRECT ANSWERS)

TEST 1	TEST 2	TEST 3	TEST 4
1. AD	9. CD	17. AE	25. BC
2. BC	10. AB	18. DE	26. AE
3. BD	11. BC	19. BE	27. CE
4. BC	12. BD	20. CD *or*	28. CE
5. BE	13. BC	DE *or*	29. AC
6. AC	14. AD	CE	30. CE
7. AE	15. CD	21. AE	31. AD
8. AB	16. CE	22. AC	32. AE
		23. AE	
		24. BD	

TEST 5	TEST 6	TEST 7
33. AB	41. CD	49. BE
34. BD	42. CD	50. CE
35. BC	43. CE	51. BE
36. AB	44. CD	52. AE
37. AD	45. AD	
38. DE	46. AD	
39. AD	47. CD	
40. AD	48. DE	

8

ABSTRACT REASONING

SPATIAL RELATIONS/THREE DIMENSIONS

COMMENTARY

Since intelligence exists in many forms or phases and the theory of differential aptitudes is now firmly established in testing, other manifestations and measurements of intelligence than verbal or purely arithmetical must be identified and measured.

The spatial relations test, including that phase designated as spatial perception, involves and measures the ability to solve problems, drawn up in the form of outlines or pictures, which are concerned with the shapes of objects or the interrelationship of their parts. While, concededly, little is known about the nature and scope of this aptitude, it appears that this ability is required in science, mathematics, engineering, and drawing courses and curricula. Accordingly, tests of spatial perception involving the reconstruction of three-dimensional patterns, are presented in this section.

It is to be noted that the relationships expressed in spatial tests are geometric, definitive, and exact. Keeping these basic characteristics in mind, the applicant is to proceed to solve the spatial perception problems in his own way. There is no set method of solving these problems. The examinee may find that there are different methods for different types of spatial problems. Therefore, the BEST way to prepare for this type of test is to *TAKE* and study the work-practice problems in three-dimensional patterns provided in this section.

———

SPATIAL RELATIONS/THREE DIMENSIONS

The tests of spatial relations that follow consist of items which involve the visualization of three dimensions.

Each of the items of these tests consists of a line of figures -- a question figure in stretchout or open form on the left and five lettered figures on the right, one of which will most closely represent the stretchout or open figure when the latter is folded together.

The candidate is then required to select the figure which will most closely represent the stretchout or open figure when the latter is folded together.

___

SAMPLE QUESTIONS AND EXPLANATIONS

DIRECTIONS: The items in this part constitute a test of spatial relations involving three dimensions. Each item consists of a line of figures. The first figure is the question figure which appears in stretchout or open form. This is followed by five lettered figures which appear in three-dimensional form. When the stretchout or open figure is folded together, which of the five figures will it most closely represent?

Rules to be followed:
1. The stretchout figure may be folded along the lines or rolled where necessary.
2. The edges of the stretchout figure must meet exactly, with no overlapping or empty spaces between them.

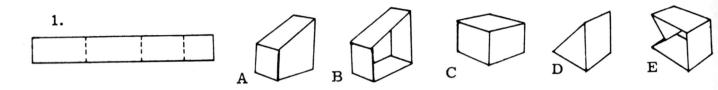

The correct answer is B. This is a simple fold of a four-sided figure.

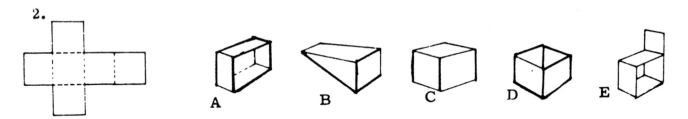

The correct answer is C. This represents the product of a continuous fold from any point to form a cube (six-sided solid).

2

TEST 1

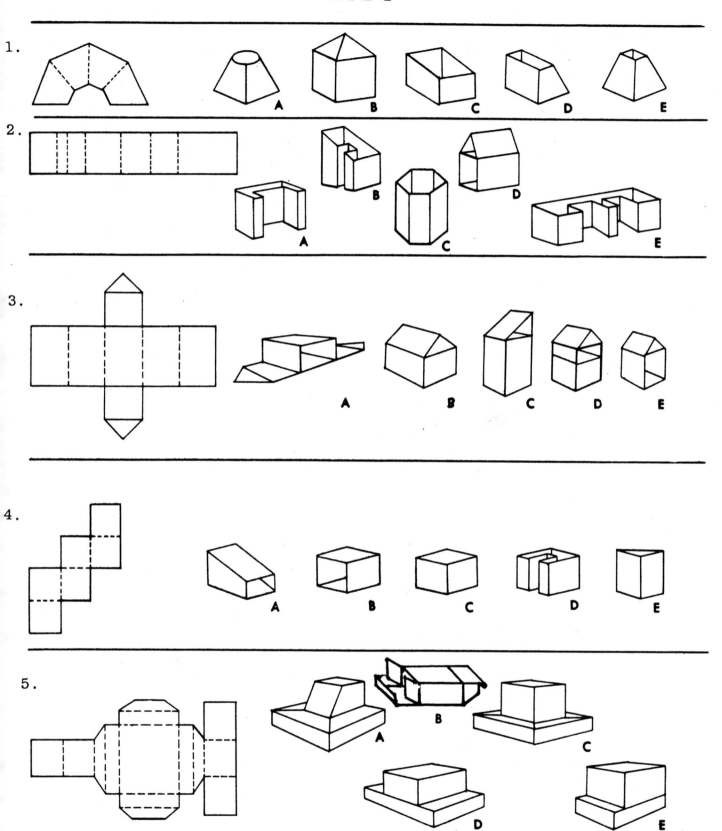

TEST 2

1. F   G   H   K   M

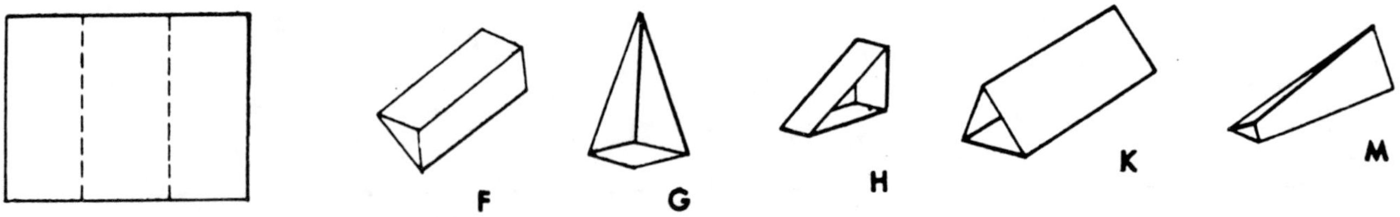

2. F   G   H   K   M

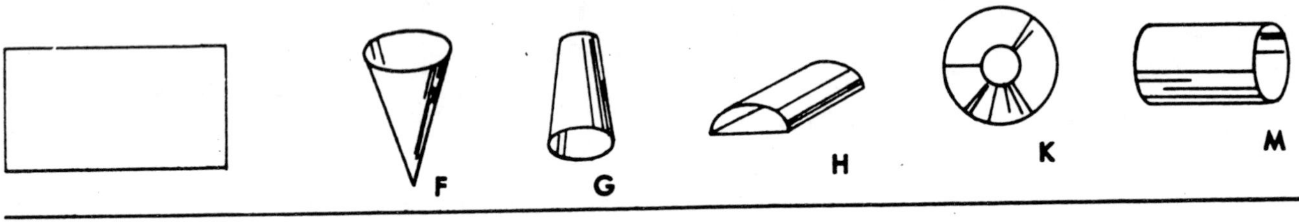

3. F   G   H   K   M

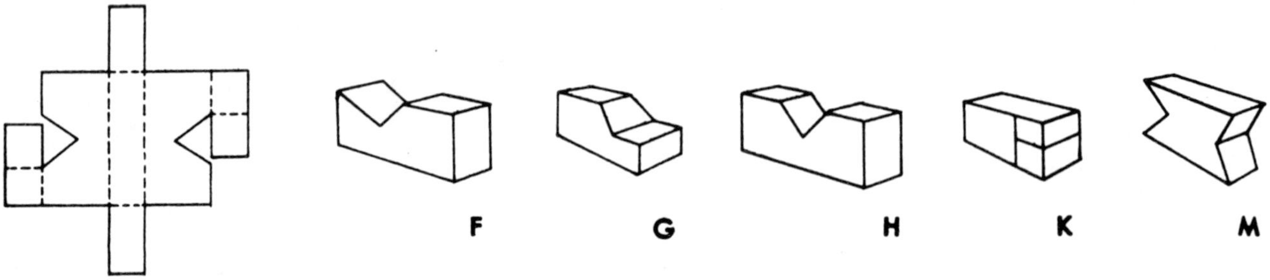

4. F   G   H   K   M

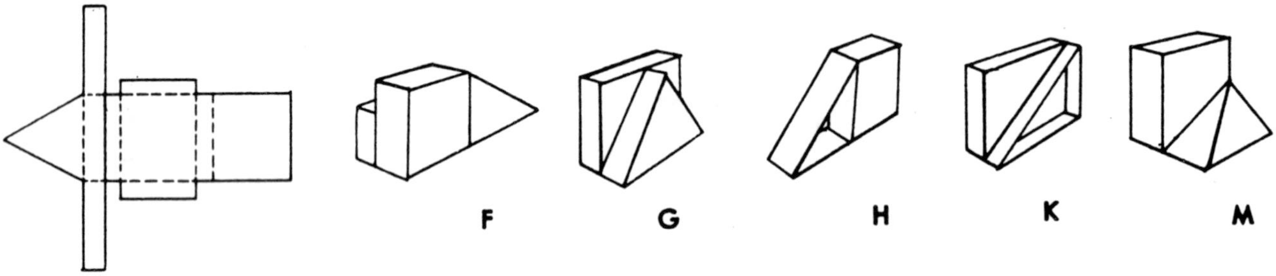

5. F   G   H   K   M

4

TEST 3

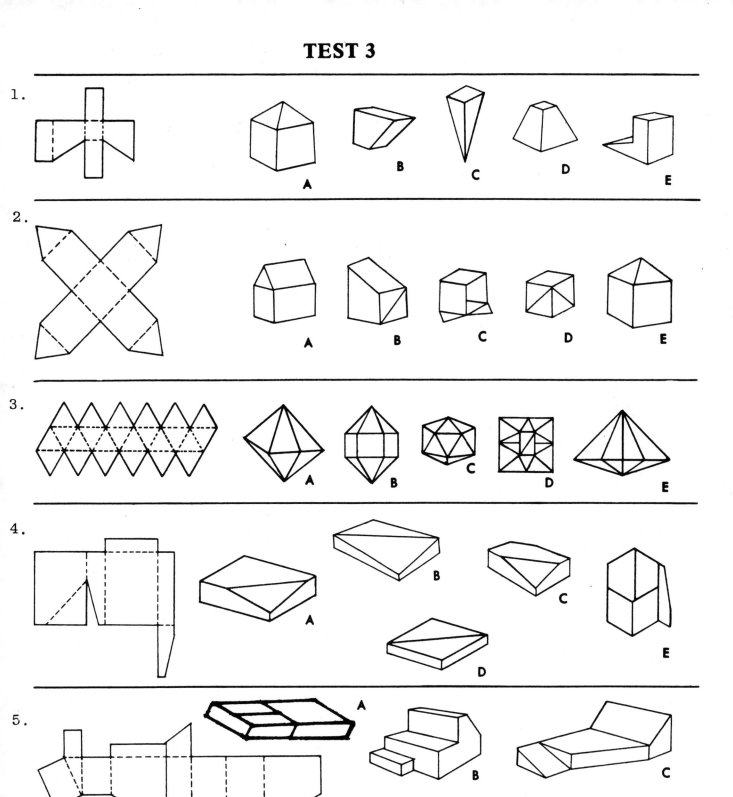

TEST 4

1.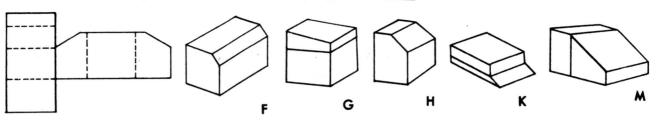

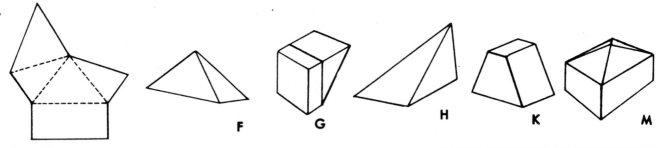

2.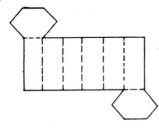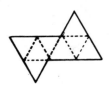

3.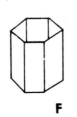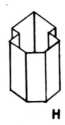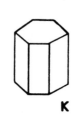

4.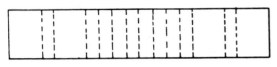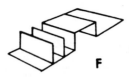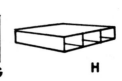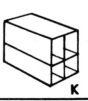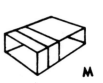

5.

KEY (CORRECT ANSWERS)
EXPLANATION OF ANSWERS

TEST 1   EXPLANATION

1. E   Straight edges form square-top hollow pyramid
2. A   Count panels for key
3. B   Solid "house" shape
4. C   Solid cube shape
5. C   Fold all sides toward center

TEST 2

1. K   Simple three-panel fold
2. M   Roll left to right
3. H   Fold all sides toward the center
4. G   Fold all sides toward the center
5. G   A continuous fold from any point to form a
                dodecahedron (based on a single pentagon form)

TEST 3

1. B   Fold toward the center
2. E   Cube with pyramid on top
3. C   Continuous fold to form an icositetrahedron
                (24 planes); based on equilateral triangles
4. A   Size of triangular fold is the key
5. C   Fold all sides toward the center

TEST 4

1. H   Fold from left to right
2. F   Pyramid with base
3. M   Continuous fold to form an octahedron, based
                on two pyramids, bottom to bottom
4. K   Hexagon (solid)
5. G   Count panels and start fold from the center,
                working both sides together

ANSWER SHEET

TEST NO. _____ PART _____ TITLE OF POSITION _____

PLACE OF EXAMINATION _____ DATE _____

(CITY OR TOWN)   (STATE)

RATING

USE THE SPECIAL PENCIL.   MAKE GLOSSY BLACK MARKS.

	A B C D E		A B C D E		A B C D E		A B C D E		A B C D E
1		26		51		76		101	
2		27		52		77		102	
3		28		53		78		103	
4		29		54		79		104	
5		30		55		80		105	
6		31		56		81		106	
7		32		57		82		107	
8		33		58		83		108	
9		34		59		84		109	
10		35		60		85		110	

Make only ONE mark for each answer.   Additional and stray marks may be counted as mistakes.   In making corrections, erase errors COMPLETELY.

	A B C D E		A B C D E		A B C D E		A B C D E		A B C D E
11		36		61		86		111	
12		37		62		87		112	
13		38		63		88		113	
14		39		64		89		114	
15		40		65		90		115	
16		41		66		91		116	
17		42		67		92		117	
18		43		68		93		118	
19		44		69		94		119	
20		45		70		95		120	
21		46		71		96		121	
22		47		72		97		122	
23		48		73		98		123	
24		49		74		99		124	
25		50		75		100		125	

ABSTRACT REASONING

SPATIAL RELATIONS/THREE DIMENSIONS

COMMENTARY

Since intelligence exists in many forms or phases and the theory of differential aptitudes is now firmly established in testing, other manifestations and measurements of intelligence than verbal or purely arithmetical must be identified and measured.

The spatial relations test, including that phase designated as spatial perception, involves and measures the ability to solve problems, drawn up in the form of outlines or pictures, which are concerned with the shapes of objects or the interrelationship of their parts. While, concededly, little is known about the nature and scope of this aptitude, it appears that this ability is required in science, mathematics, engineering, and drawing courses and curricula. Accordingly, tests of spatial perception involving the reconstruction of three-dimensional patterns, are presented in this section.

It is to be noted that the relationships expressed in spatial tests are geometric, definitive, and exact. Keeping these basic characteristics in mind, the applicant is to proceed to solve the spatial perception problems in his own way. There is no set method of solving these problems. The examinee may find that there are different methods for different types of spatial problems. Therefore, the BEST way to prepare for this type of test is to *TAKE* and study the work-practice problems in three-dimensional patterns provided in this section.

SAMPLE QUESTION

In question 1 through 30 a flat pattern will be presented. This pattern is to be folded into a three dimensional figure. The correct figure is one of the four given at the right of the pattern. There is only one correct figure in each set. The outside of the pattern is what is seen at the left.

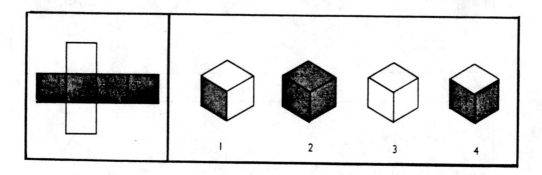

One of the above figures (1,2,3,4,) can be formed from the flat pattern given at the left. The only figure that corresponds in the pattern is 4. If the shaded surfaces are looked at as the sides of the box, then all four sides must be shaded, while the top and bottom are white.

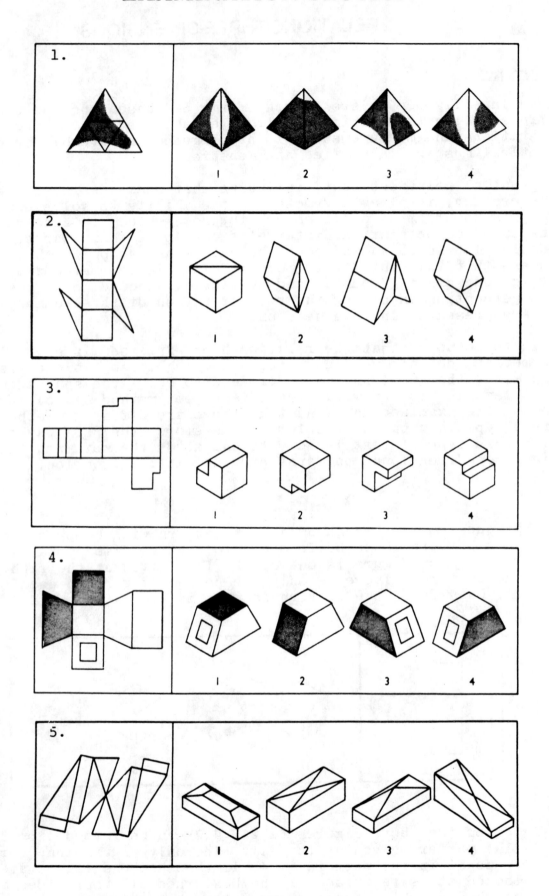

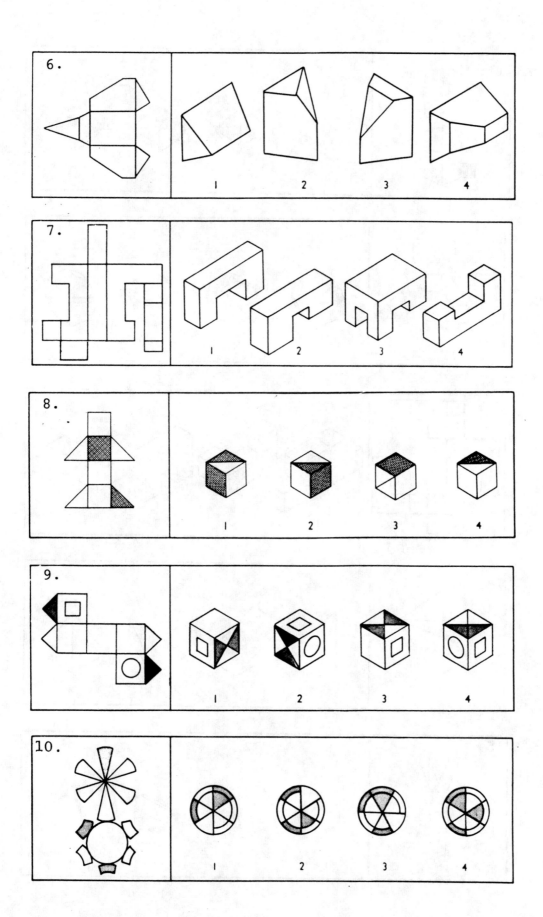

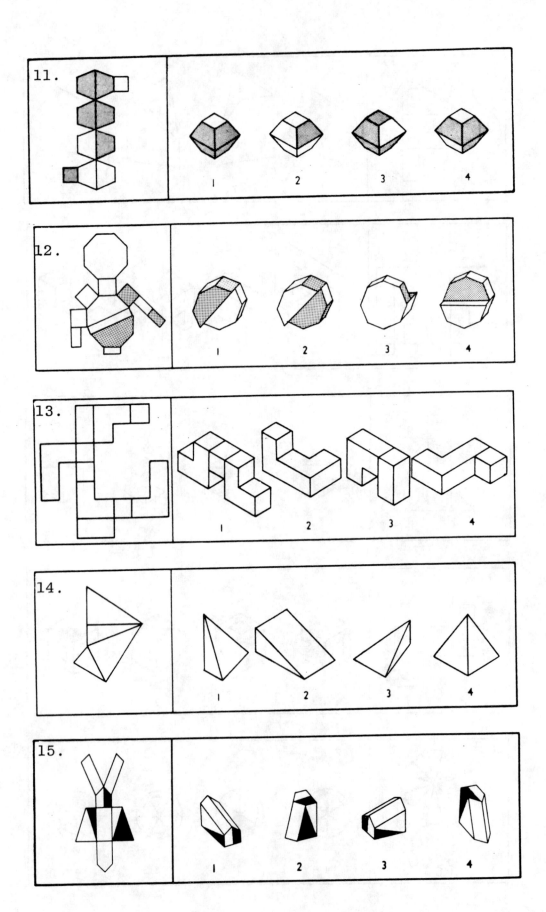

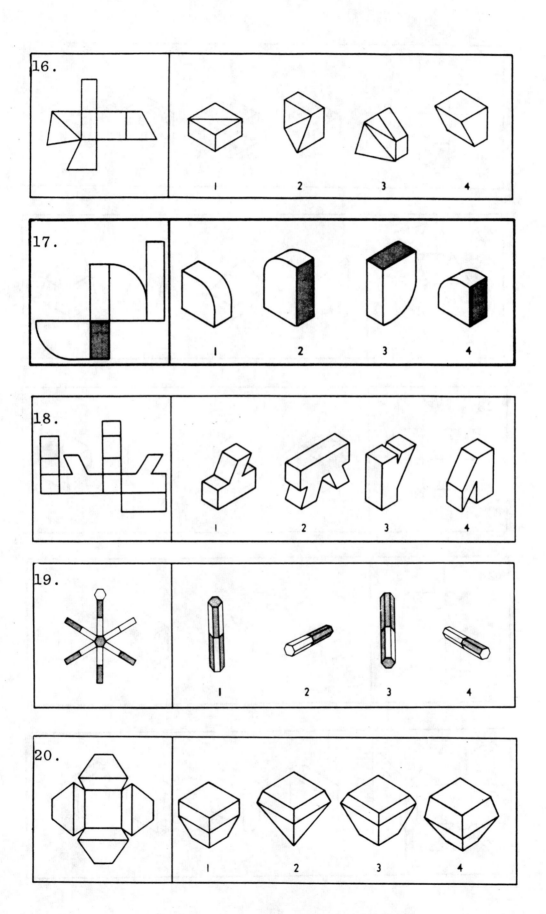

21.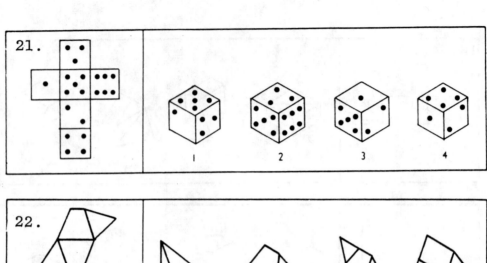

22.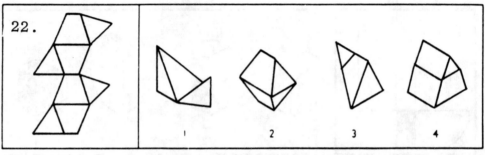

23.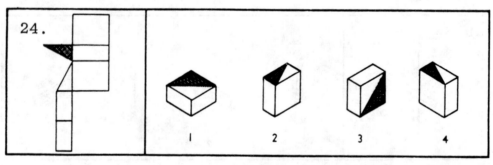

24.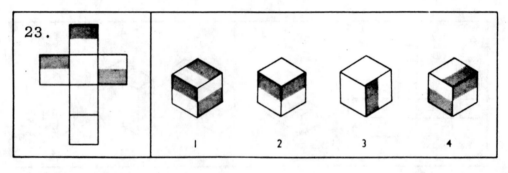

25.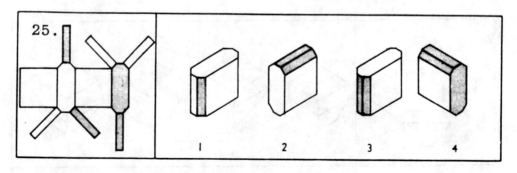

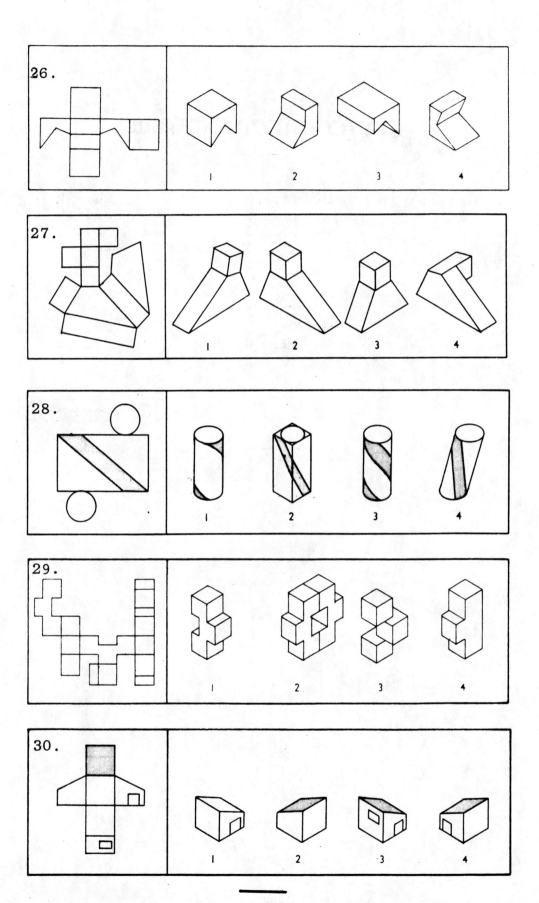

KEY (CORRECT ANSWERS)

1.	4	11.	1	21.	2
2.	2	12.	2	22.	2
3.	2	13..	2	23.	3
4.	3	14.	1	24.	4
5.	3	15.	1	25.	3
6.	3	16.	2	26.	4
7.	4	17.	3	27.	1
8.	1	18.	1	28.	1
9.	1	19.	4	29.	1
10.	1	20.	3	30.	2

———

ABSTRACT REASONING

SPATIAL RELATIONS

COMMENTARY

Since intelligence exists in many forms or phases and the theory
of differential aptitudes is now firmly established in testing, other
manifestations and measurements of intelligence than verbal or purely
arithmetical must be identified and measured.

The spatial relations test, including that phase designated as spatial perception, involves and measures the ability to solve problems,
drawn up in the form of outlines or pictures, which are concerned with
the shapes of objects or the interrelationship of their parts. While,
concededly, little is known about the nature and scope of this aptitude,
it appears that this ability is required in science, mathematics, engineering, and drawing courses and curricula. Accordingly, tests of
spatial perception involving the reconstruction of three-dimensional pat
terns, are presented in this section.

It is to be noted that the relationships expressed in spatial tests
are geometric, definitive, and exact. Keeping these basic characteristics in mind, the applicant is to proceed to solve the spatial perception problems in his own way. There is no set method of solving these
problems. The examinee may find that there are different methods for
different types of spatial problems. Therefore, the BEST way to prepare for this type of test is to *TAKE* and study the work-practice problems in three-dimensional patterns provided in this section.

————————

EXAMINATION SECTION

TEST 1

For questions 1 through 15

The pictures that follow are top, front, and end views of various solid objects. The views are without perspective. That is, the points in the viewed surface are viewed along parallel lines of vision. The projection of the object looking DOWN on it is shown in the upper left-hand corner (TOP VIEW). The projection looking at the object from the FRONT is shown in the lower left-hand corner (FRONT VIEW). The projection looking at the object from the END is shown in the lower right-hand corner (END VIEW). These views are ALWAYS in the same positions and are labeled accordingly.

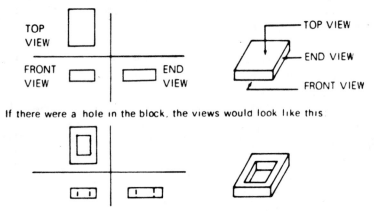

If there were a hole in the block, the views would look like this.

Note that lines that cannot be seen on the surface in some particular view are DOTTED in that view.

In the problems that follow, two views will be shown, with four alternatives to complete the set. You are to select the correct one and mark its number on the answer sheet.

EXAMPLE: Choose the correct END VIEW.

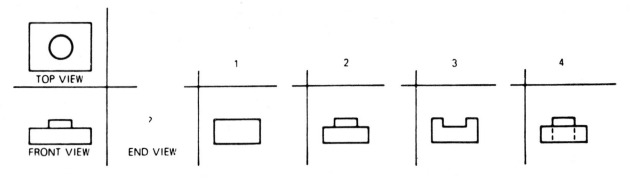

The front view shows that there is a smaller block on the base and that there is no hole. The top view shows that the block is round and in the center of the base. The answer, therefore, must be number 2.

In the problems that follow, it is not always the end view that must be selected; sometimes it is the top view or front view that is missing. Now, proceed to the questions marking the number of the correct view on your answer sheet.

2

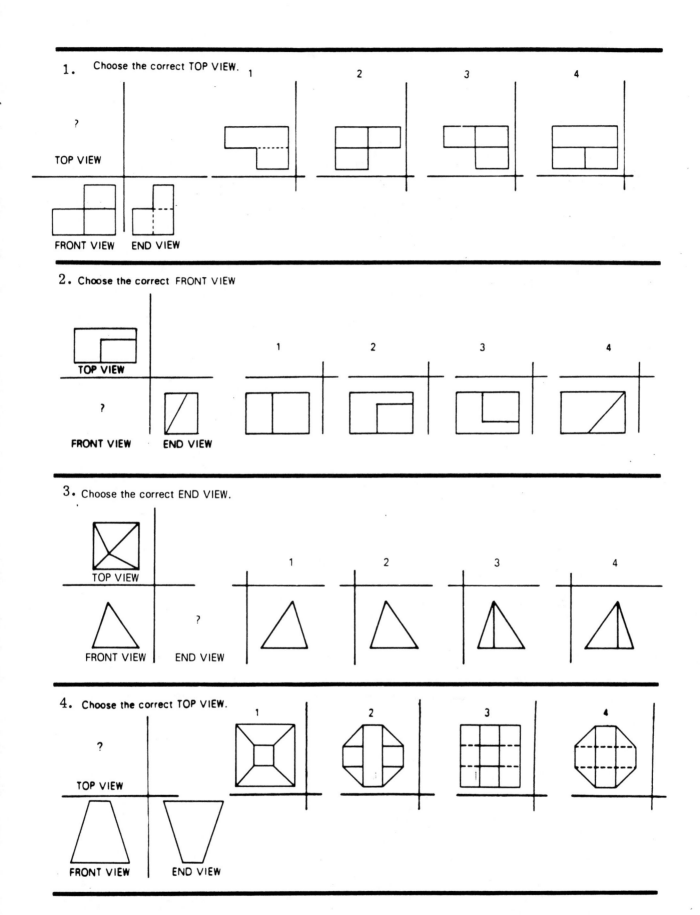

1. Choose the correct TOP VIEW.

2. Choose the correct FRONT VIEW

3. Choose the correct END VIEW.

4. Choose the correct TOP VIEW.

3

5. Choose the correct END VIEW.

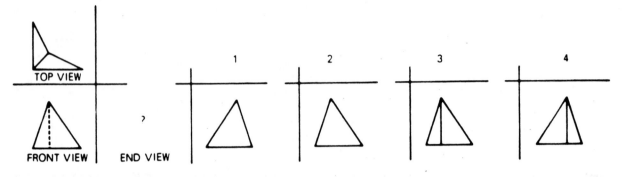

TOP VIEW

FRONT VIEW | END VIEW

?

1   2   3   4

6. Choose the correct TOP VIEW.

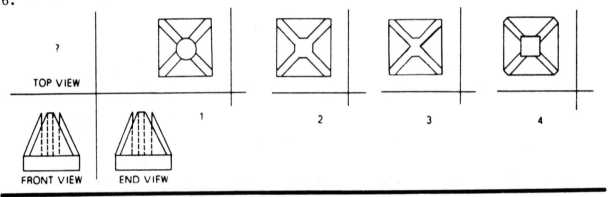

?

TOP VIEW

FRONT VIEW | END VIFW

1   2   3   4

7. Choose the correct END VIEW.

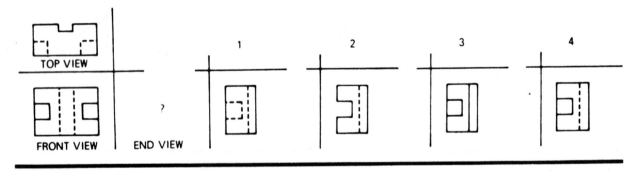

TOP VIEW

FRONT VIEW | END VIEW

?

1   2   3   4

8. Choose the correct END VIEW.

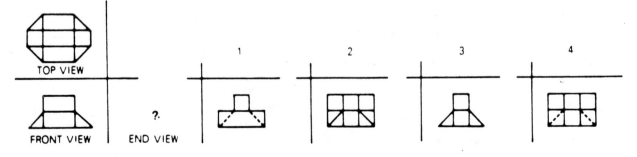

TOP VIEW

FRONT VIEW | END VIEW

?.

1   2   3   4

9. Choose the correct FRONT VIEW

TOP VIEW

1   2   3   4

?

FRONT VIEW   END VIEW

10. Choose the correct TOP VIEW.

1   2   3   4

?

TOP VIEW

FRONT VIEW   END VIEW

11. Choose the correct TOP VIEW.

1   2   3   4

?

TOP VIEW

FRONT VIEW   END VIEW

12. Choose the correct TOP VIEW.

1   2   3   4

?

TOP VIEW

FRONT VIEW   END VIEW

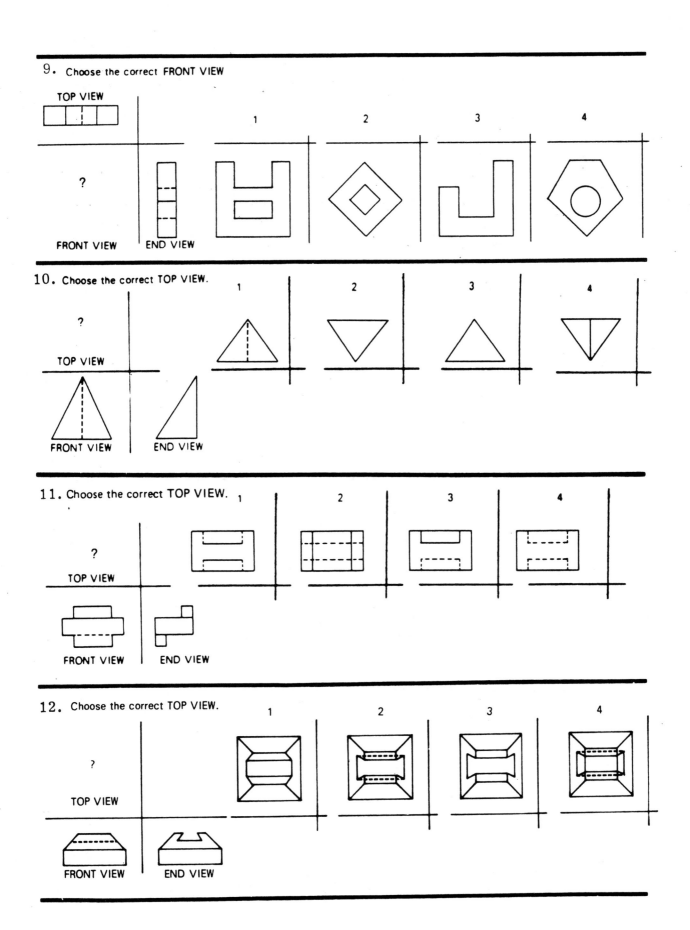

13. Choose the correct END VIEW.

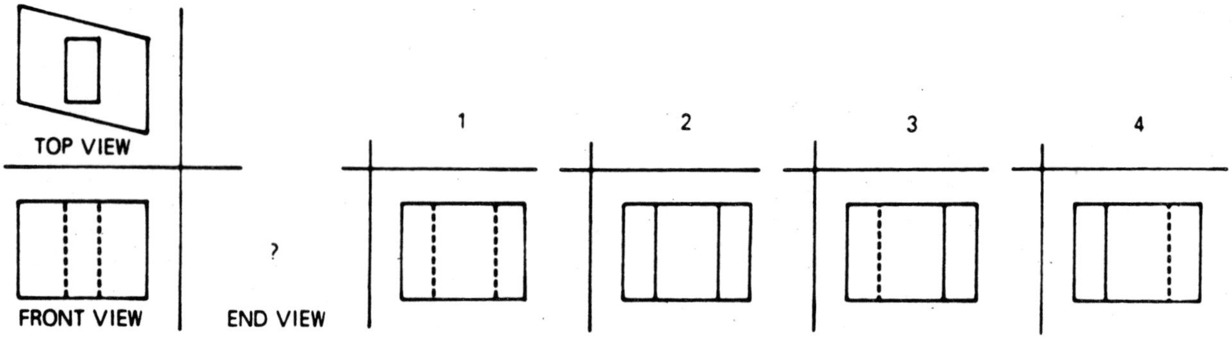

TOP VIEW

FRONT VIEW   END VIEW

?

1   2   3   4

14. Choose the correct FRONT VIEW

TOP VIEW

?

FRONT VIEW   END VIEW

1   2   3   4

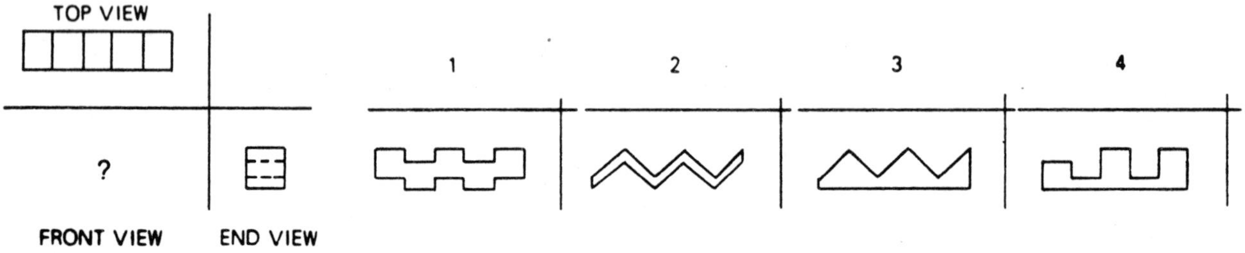

15. Choose the correct FRONT VIEW

TOP VIEW

?

FRONT VIEW   END VIEW

1   2   3   4

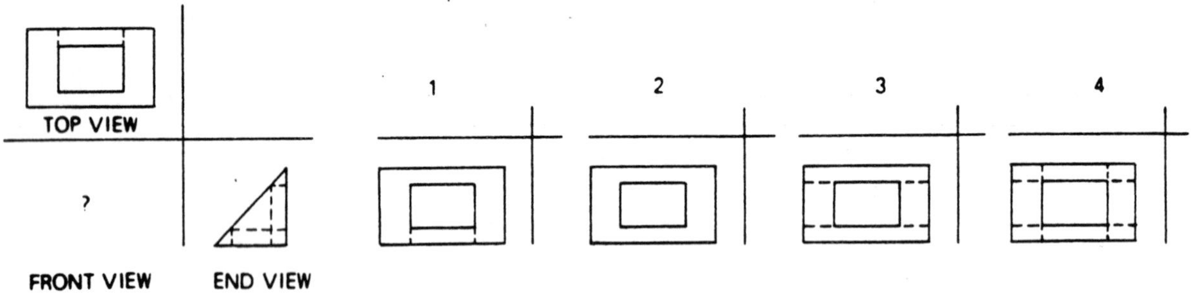

TEST 2

For questions **16** through **30** you are to examine the four INTERIOR angles and rank each in terms of degrees from SMALL TO LARGE. Choose the alternative that has the correct ranking.

EXAMPLE: (Do not mark these on the answer sheet)

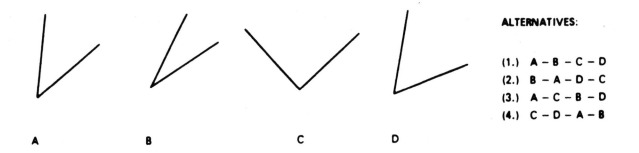

ALTERNATIVES:

(1.) A – B – C – D
(2.) B – A – D – C
(3.) A – C – B – D
(4.) C – D – A – B

The correct ranking of the angles from small to large is B – A – D – C; therefore, alternative (2) is correct. Now, proceed to the questions marking the correct alternative on your answer sheet.

16.

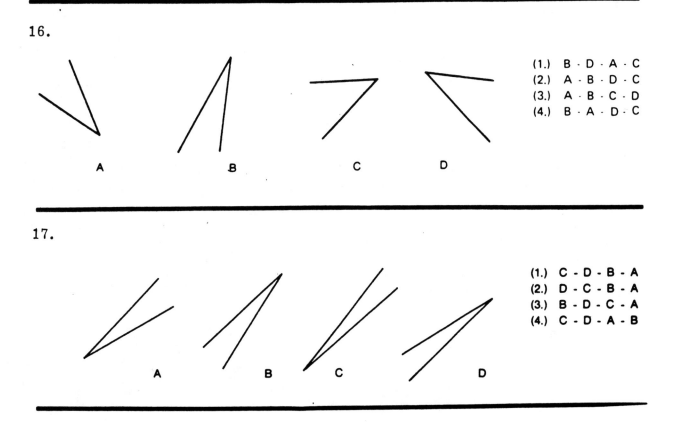

(1.) B - D - A - C
(2.) A - B - D - C
(3.) A - B - C - D
(4.) B - A - D - C

17.

(1.) C - D - B - A
(2.) D - C - B - A
(3.) B - D - C - A
(4.) C - D - A - B

18.

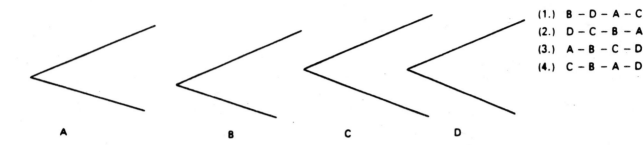

A   B   C   D

(1.) B – D – A – C
(2.) D – C – B – A
(3.) A – B – C – D
(4.) C – B – A – D

19.

A   B   C   D

(1.) D - B - A - C
(2.) B - D - A - C
(3.) B - D - C - A
(4.) D - B - C - A

20.

A   B   C   D

(1.) C - D - B - A
(2.) D - C - B - A
(3.) B - D - C - A
(4.) C - D - A - B

21.

A   B   C   D

(1.) A–C–D–B
(2.) C–A–B–D
(3.) A–C–B–D
(4.) C–A–D–B

22.

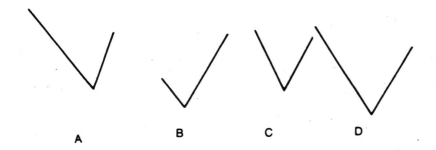

(1.) C - A - B - D
(2.) A - C - B - D
(3.) C - A - D - B
(4.) A - C - D - B

23.

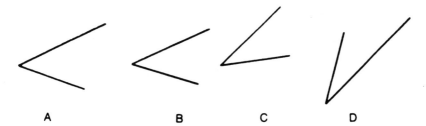

(1.) C — D — A — B
(2.) D — C — A — B
(3.) C — D — B — A
(4.) D — C — B — A

24.

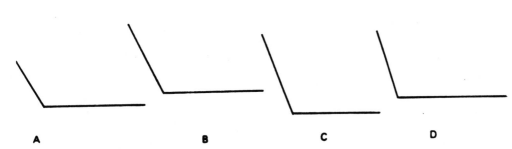

(1.) C - D - B - A
(2.) D - C - B - A
(3.) B - D - C - A
(4.) C - D - A - B

25.

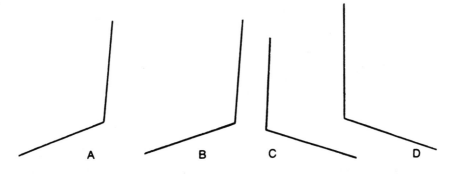

(1.) C - D - B - A
(2.) D - C - B - A
(3.) B - D - C - A
(4.) C - D - A - B

26.

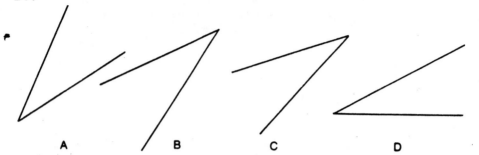

A   B   C   D

(1.) C · B · D · A
(2.) D · C · B · A
(3.) C · D · A · B
(4.) D · A · C · B

27.

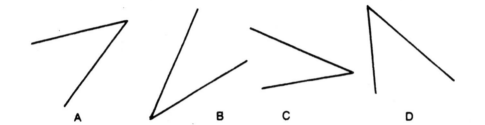

A   B   C   D

(1.) C · A · D · B
(2.) A · C · D · B
(3.) A · C · B · D
(4.) C · B · A · D

28.

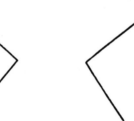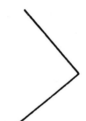

A   B   C   D

(1.) D – A – B – C
(2.) A – D – C – B
(3.) D – A – C – B
(4.) A – D – B – C

29.

A   B   C   D

(1.) B – A – C – D
(2.) B – A – D – C
(3.) A – B – C – D
(4.) B – D – C – A

30.

 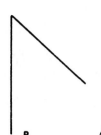  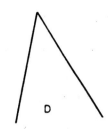

A   B   C   D

(1.) C - A - D - B
(2.) A - C - D - B
(3.) A - B - C - D
(4.) C - A - B - D

TEST 3

For questions **31** through **48**

This visualization test consists of a number of items similar to the sample below. A three-dimensional object is shown at the left. This is followed by outlines of five apertures or openings.

In each item the task is exactly the same. *First*, you are to imagine how the object looks from *all* directions (rather than from a single direction as shown). *Then*, pick from the five apertures outlined, the opening through which the object could pass directly if the proper side were inserted first. *Finally*, mark on your answer sheet (after the number of the item) the letter corresponding to the answer you have chosen.

Here are the rules:

1. Prior to passing through the aperture, the irregular solid object may be turned in any direction. It may be started through the aperture on a side not shown.

2. Once the object is started through the aperture, it may not be twisted or turned. It must pass completely through the opening. The opening is always the exact shape of the appropriate external outline of the object.

.3. Both objects and apertures are drawn to the same scale. Thus it is possible for an opening to be the correct shape but too small for the object. In all cases, however, differences are large enough to judge by eye.

4. There are no irregularities in any hidden portion of the object. However, if the figure has symmetric indentations, the hidden portion is symmetric with the part shown.

5. For each object there is only one correct aperture.

EXAMPLE: (Do not mark these on the answer sheet)

The correct answer is 3 since the object would pass through this aperture if the side at the left were introduced first.

12

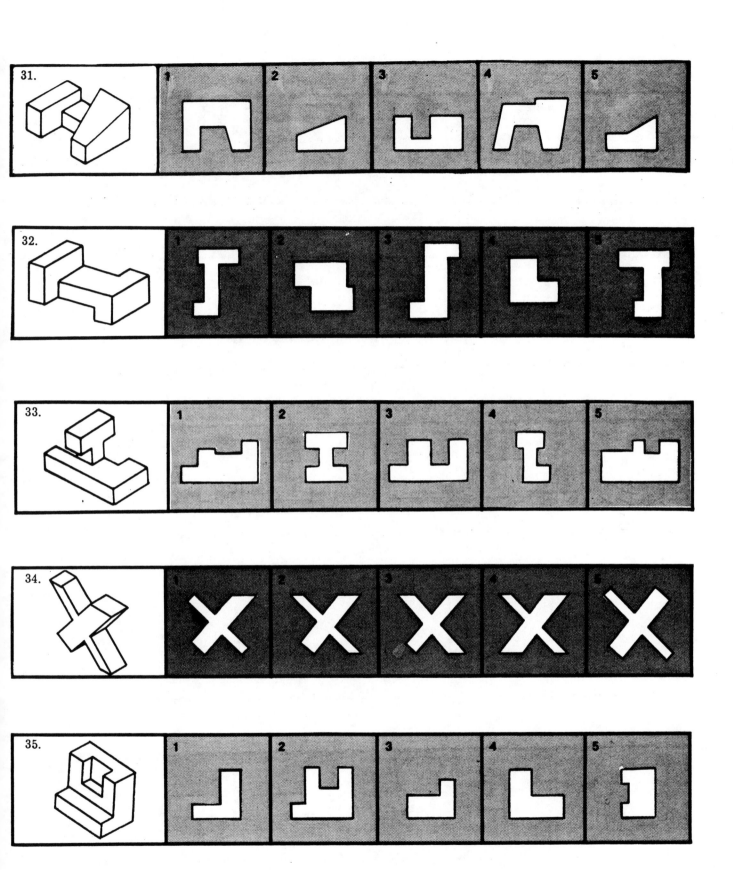

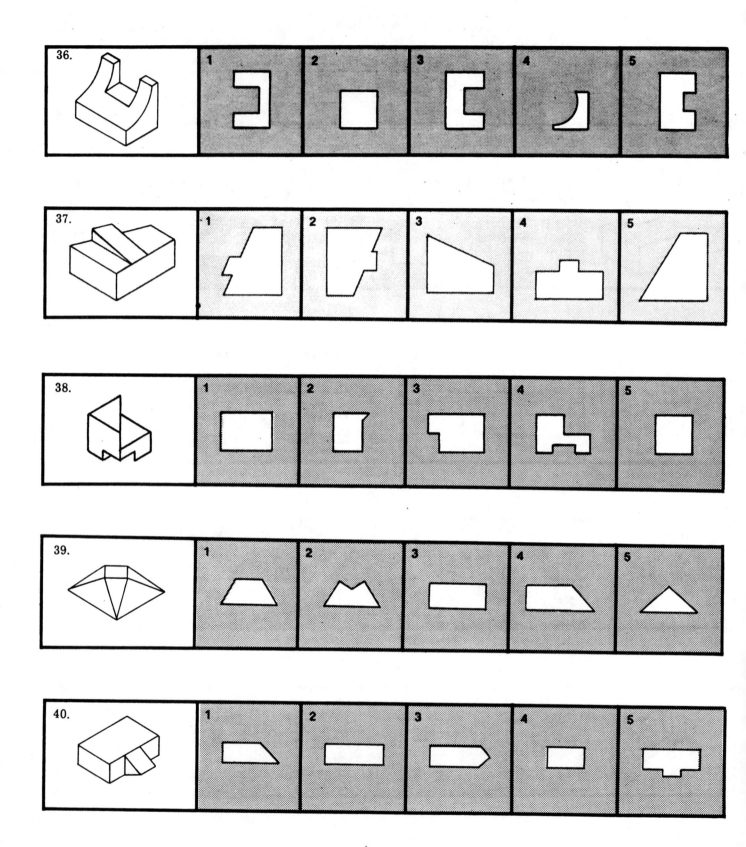

14

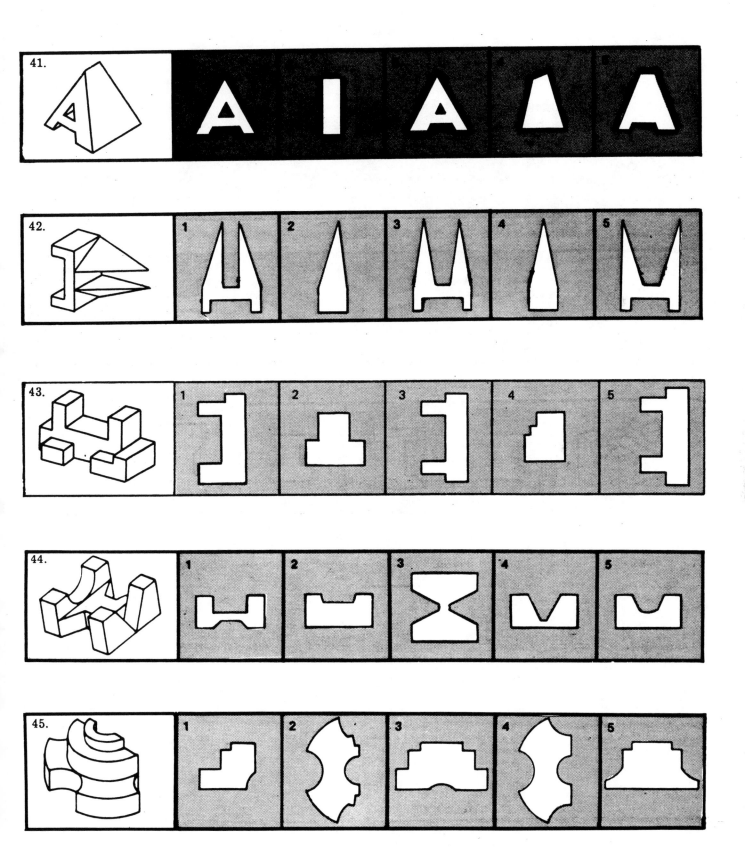

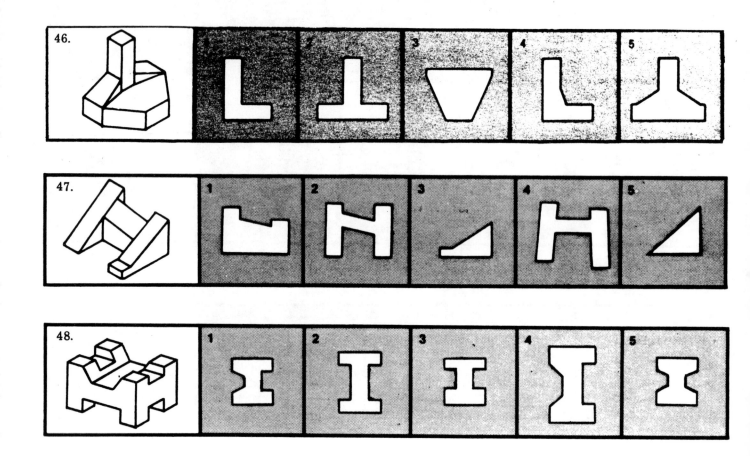

TEST 4

Each group of cubes has been made by cementing together cubes of the same size. After being cemented together, each group was PAINTED ON ALL EXPOSED SIDES EXCEPT THE BOTTOM ON WHICH IT IS RESTING.

For questions 49 through 60 you are to examine each figure closely and then determine HOW MANY CUBES have:

one of their exposed sides painted.
two of their exposed sides painted.
three of their exposed sides painted.
four of their exposed sides painted.
five of their exposed sides painted.

Note: There are no problems for which the answer zero (0) is a correct answer.

Example: (Do not mark these on the answer sheet)

PROBLEM Z   **ANSWERS:**

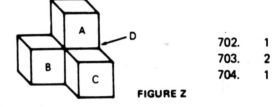

In Figure Z how many cubes have

702. two of their exposed sides painted?
703. four of their exposed sides painted?
704. five of their exposed sides painted?

702.   1
703.   2
704.   1

FIGURE Z

Now, proceed to the questions. Mark on your answer sheet the number of cubes that have the different number of exposed sides painted. Remember, after being cemented together, each group was PAINTED ON ALL EXPOSED SIDES EXCEPT THE BOTTOM.

___

PROBLEM A

In Figure A how many cubes have

49. two of their exposed sides painted?
50. three of their exposed sides painted?

FIGURE A

17

PROBLEM B

In Figure B how many cubes have

51. two of their exposed sides painted?
52. three of their exposed sides painted?
53. four of their exposed sides painted?

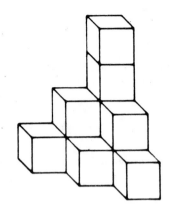

FIGURE B

PROBLEM C

In Figure C how many cubes have

54. two of their exposed sides painted?
55. three of their exposed sides painted?

FIGURE C

PROBLEM D

In Figure D how many cubes have

56. two of their exposed sides painted?
57. four of their exposed sides painted?

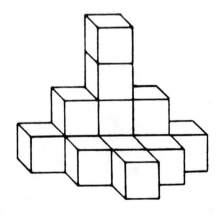

FIGURE D

PROBLEM E

In Figure E how many cubes have

58. two of their exposed sides painted?
59. three of their exposed sides painted?
60. four of their exposed sides painted?

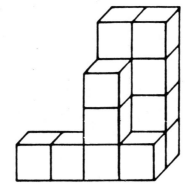

FIGURE E

KEYS (CORRECT ANSWERS)

TEST 1		TEST 2		TEST 3		TEST 4	
1.	3	16.	4	31.	1	49.	1
2.	1	17.	1	32.	3	50.	4
3.	2	18.	3	33.	2	51.	2
4.	4	19.	1	34.	2	52.	1
5.	3	20.	2	35.	3	53.	5
6.	2	21.	1	36.	3	54.	3
7.	4	22.	3	37.	3	55.	5
8.	3	23.	4	38.	5	56.	1
9.	4	24.	2	39.	1	57.	6
10.	3	25.	1	40.	2	58.	4
11.	3	26.	2	41.	3	59.	5
12.	2	27.	4	42.	1	60.	4
13.	3	28.	4	43.	5		
14.	4	29.	2	44.	5		
15.	1	30.	2	45.	4		
				46.	4		
				47.	1		
				48.	4		

ANSWER SHEET

TEST NO. ____________ PART ________ TITLE OF POSITION ______________________________
(AS GIVEN IN EXAMINATION ANNOUNCEMENT - INCLUDE OPTION, IF ANY)

PLACE OF EXAMINATION ______________________ (CITY OR TOWN) ______________________ (STATE) DATE ____________

RATING

USE THE SPECIAL PENCIL. MAKE GLOSSY BLACK MARKS.

1 A B C D E	26 A B C D E	51 A B C D E	76 A B C D E	101 A B C D E
2 A B C D E	27 A B C D E	52 A B C D E	77 A B C D E	102 A B C D E
3 A B C D E	28 A B C D E	53 A B C D E	78 A B C D E	103 A B C D E
4 A B C D E	29 A B C D E	54 A B C D E	79 A B C D E	104 A B C D E
5 A B C D E	30 A B C D E	55 A B C D E	80 A B C D E	105 A B C D E
6 A B C D E	31 A B C D E	56 A B C D E	81 A B C D E	106 A B C D E
7 A B C D E	32 A B C D E	57 A B C D E	82 A B C D E	107 A B C D E
8 A B C D E	33 A B C D E	58 A B C D E	83 A B C D E	108 A B C D E
9 A B C D E	34 A B C D E	59 A B C D E	84 A B C D E	109 A B C D E
10 A B C D E	35 A B C D E	60 A B C D E	85 A B C D E	110 A B C D E

Make only ONE mark for each answer. Additional and stray marks may be counted as mistakes. In making corrections, erase errors COMPLETELY.

11 A B C D E	36 A B C D E	61 A B C D E	86 A B C D E	111 A B C D E
12 A B C D E	37 A B C D E	62 A B C D E	87 A B C D E	112 A B C D E
13 A B C D E	38 A B C D E	63 A B C D E	88 A B C D E	113 A B C D E
14 A B C D E	39 A B C D E	64 A B C D E	89 A B C D E	114 A B C D E
15 A B C D E	40 A B C D E	65 A B C D E	90 A B C D E	115 A B C D E
16 A B C D E	41 A B C D E	66 A B C D E	91 A B C D E	116 A B C D E
17 A B C D E	42 A B C D E	67 A B C D E	92 A B C D E	117 A B C D E
18 A B C D E	43 A B C D E	68 A B C D E	93 A B C D E	118 A B C D E
19 A B C D E	44 A B C D E	69 A B C D E	94 A B C D E	119 A B C D E
20 A B C D E	45 A B C D E	70 A B C D E	95 A B C D E	120 A B C D E
21 A B C D E	46 A B C D E	71 A B C D E	96 A B C D E	121 A B C D E
22 A B C D E	47 A B C D E	72 A B C D E	97 A B C D E	122 A B C D E
23 A B C D E	48 A B C D E	73 A B C D E	98 A B C D E	123 A B C D E
24 A B C D E	49 A B C D E	74 A B C D E	99 A B C D E	124 A B C D E
25 A B C D E	50 A B C D E	75 A B C D E	100 A B C D E	125 A B C D E

ABSTRACT REASONING

CLASSIFICATION INVENTORY SECTION
INCOMPLETE PATTERNS(NINE FIGURES)

The tests of incomplete patterns that follow consist of items which involve the visualization of nine figures arranged in sequence.

An incomplete pattern only is given. The candidate is to select from the five-lettered choices the correct figure for the last or ninth space.

DIRECTIONS: Each item in this test consists of an incomplete pattern. The complete pattern would be made up of nine figures arranged in sequence. The candidate is to determine the correct figure for the last or ninth space from the five-lettered choices given.

SAMPLE QUESTIONS AND EXPLANATIONS

QUESTIONS

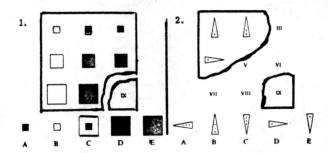

EXPLANATIONS: In question 1 notice how the figures change as they go across each row of the pattern. They become darker. As they go down, the figures become larger. Therefore, the CORRECT figure for space IX is large and dark. Answer choice D is the CORRECT answer.

In question 2 the figures acquire more dots as they go across the top row. As they go down, the point of the figure is rotated a quarter of a turn to the right. Therefore, the CORRECT figure for space IX has three dots and its point is directed toward the bottom of the page. Answer choice C is the CORRECT answer.

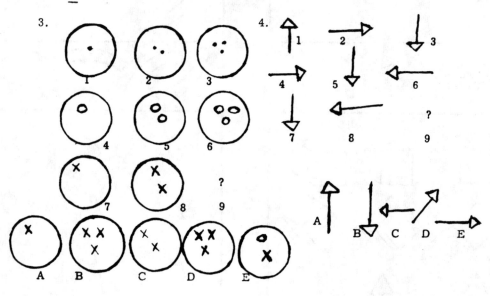

3. The correct answer is D. Each of the rows of circles has, exclusively, a number of ., o, or x's in ascending order. (Note that B is incorrect since the circle is larger than the given circles.)

4. The correct answer is A. Note that in row 1, two of the arrows (1, 2) are turned to the right, and one (3) is turned to the left. In row two, one of the arrows (4) is turned to the right, and two (5, 6) are turned to the left. In row three, two arrows are turned to the left (7, 8). Therefore, one arrow (9) must be turned to the right in a similar way (answer A).

TESTS IN INCOMPLETE PATTERNS
TEST 1

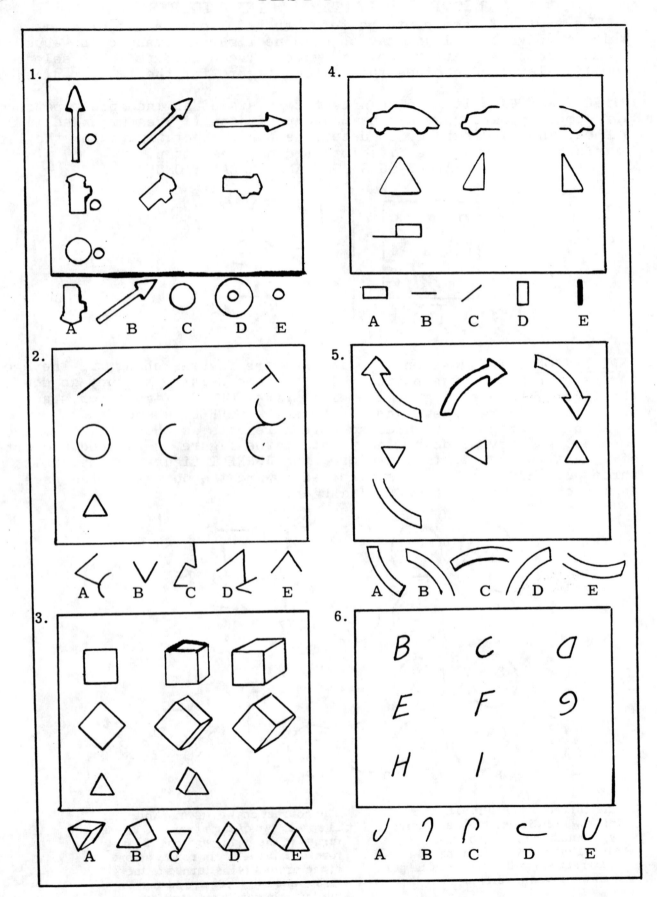

TEST 2

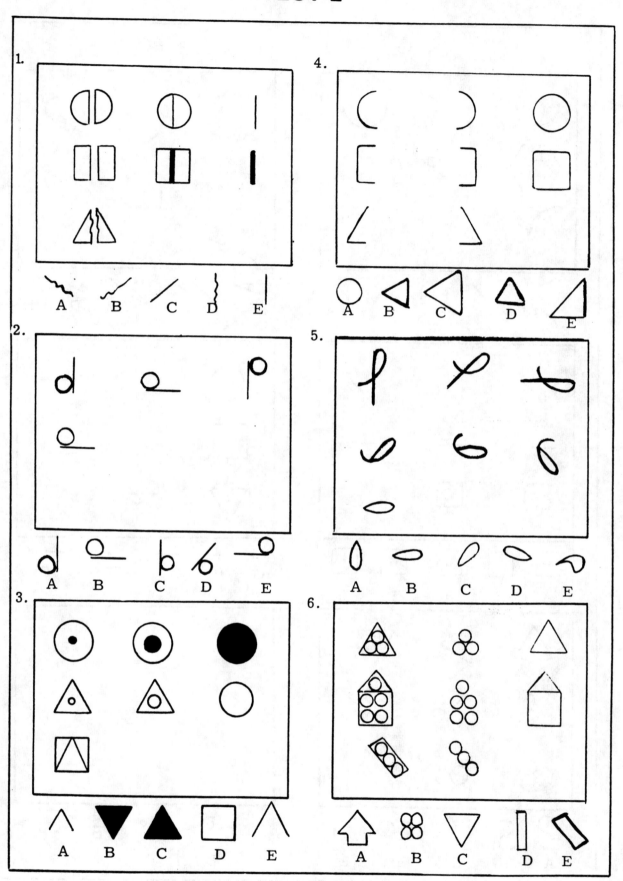

3

TEST 3

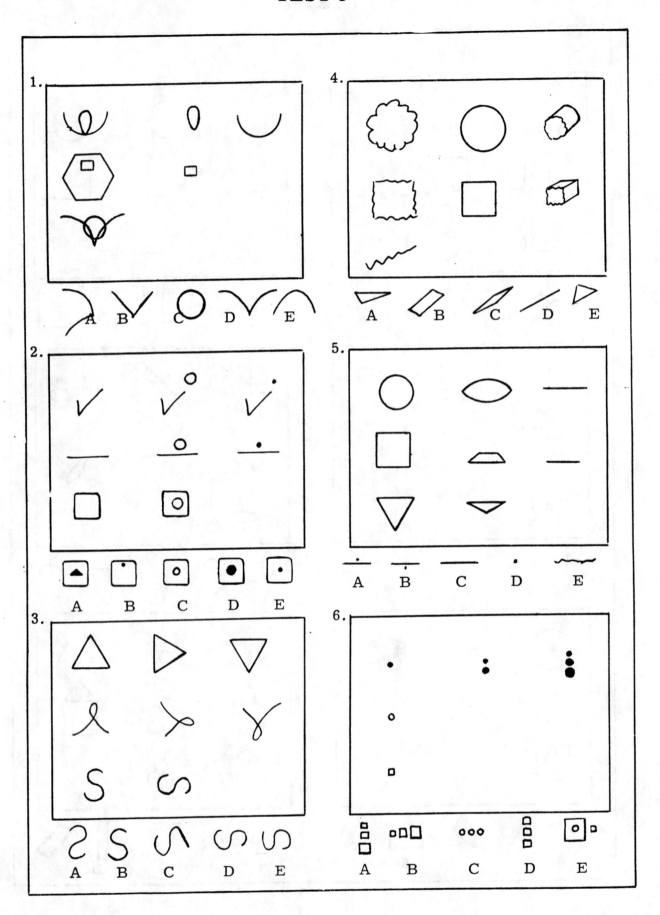

4

TEST 4

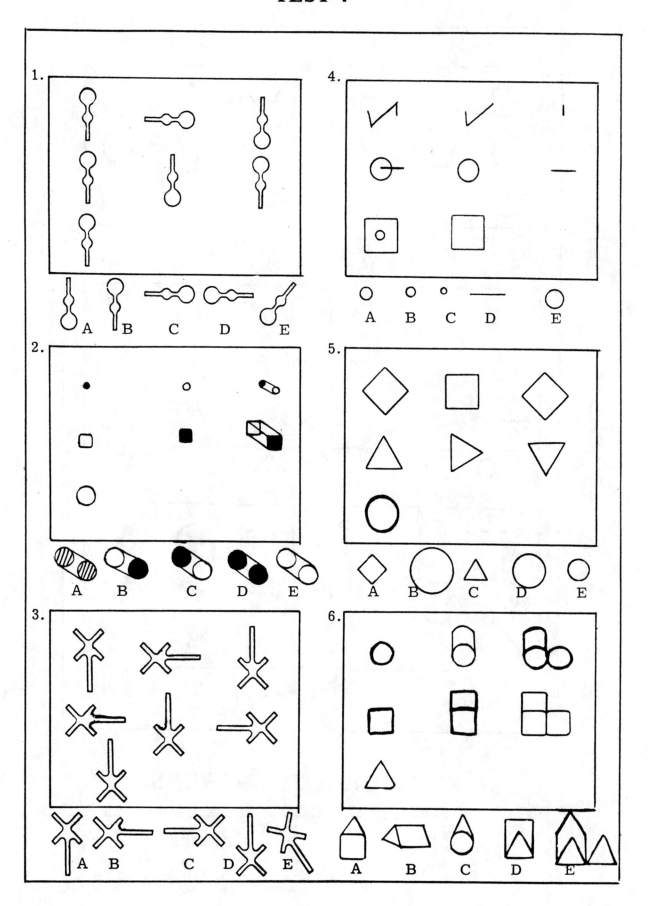

TEST 5

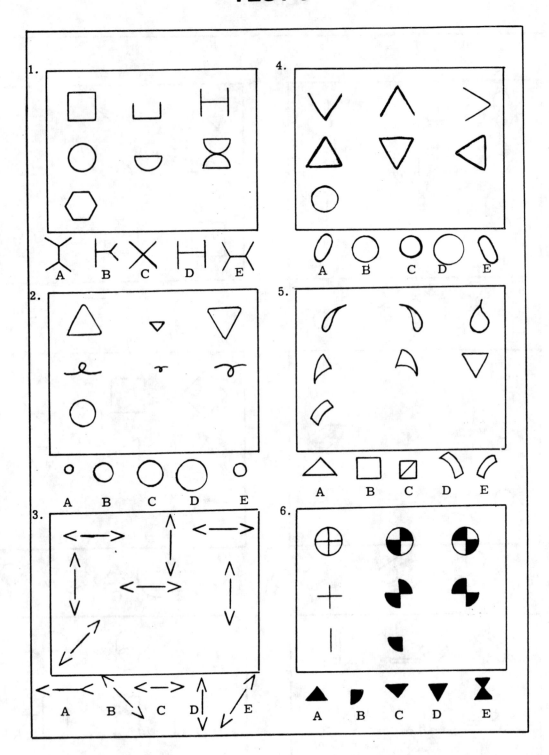

KEY (CORRECT ANSWERS)

TEST 1		TEST 2		TEST 3		TEST 4		TEST 5	
1.	C	1.	D	1.	D	1.	A	1.	E
2.	C	2.	A	2.	E	2.	B	2.	C
3.	E	3.	A	3.	B	3.	A	3.	B
4.	A	4.	C	4.	C	4.	B	4.	B
5.	B	5.	A	5.	C	5.	D	5.	B
6.	C	6.	E	6.	A	6.	E	6.	B

PATTERN ANALYSIS (RIGHT SIDE ELEVATION)

SAMPLE QUESTION

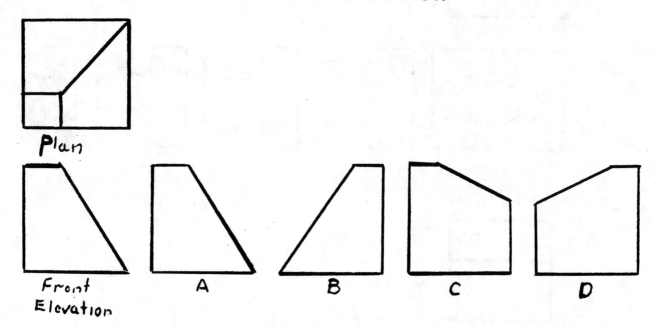

In the sample shown above, which figure *CORRECTLY* represents the right side elevation?

    1. A   2. B   3. C   4. D

The *CORRECT* answer is 1.

TEST 1

Questions 1-5.

DIRECTIONS: In questions 1 through 5 which follow, the plan and front elevation of an object are shown on the left, and on the right are shown four figures one of which, and ONLY one, represents the right side elevation. Mark on your answer sheet the number which represents the right side elevation.
               1. A   2. B   3. C   4. D

7

1.

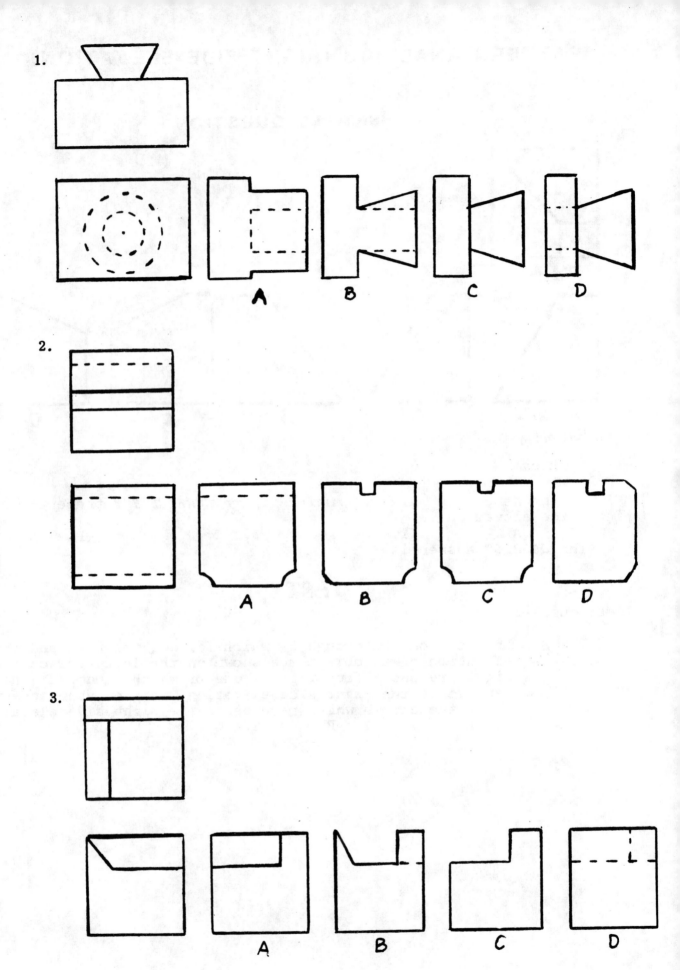

2.

3.

4.

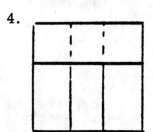

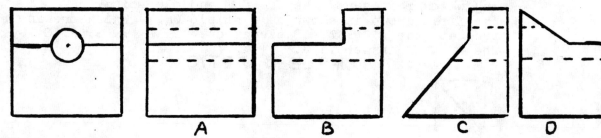

5.

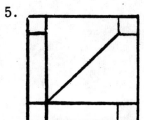

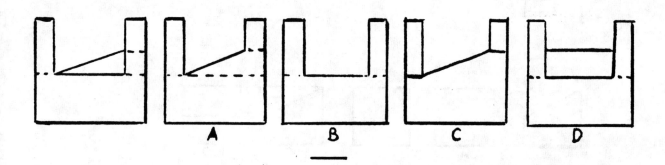

KEY (CORRECT ANSWERS)

1.	4
2.	3
3.	3
4.	2
5.	2

PATTERN ANALYSIS (END ELEVATION)

Questions 1-5.

DIRECTIONS: In each of the following groups of drawings the top view and
front elevation of an object are shown at the left. At the
right are four drawings, one of which represents the end elevation of the object as seen from the right. Select the drawing which represents the CORRECT end elevation.
The first group is shown as a sample ONLY. Which drawing represents the CORRECT end elevation? 1. A 2. B 3. C 4. D
The CORRECT answer is 3.

SAMPLE QUESTION

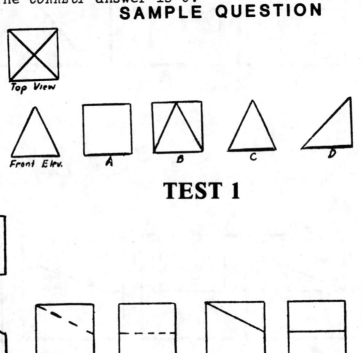

TEST 1

1.

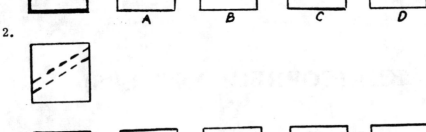

2.

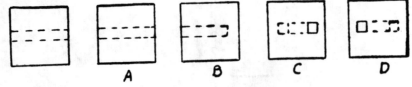

3.

4.

 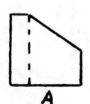  

A   B   C   D

5.

  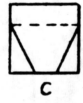 

A   B   C   D

KEY (CORRECT ANSWERS)

1.   4
2.   3
3.   2
4.   1
5.   1

11

PATTERN ANALYSIS (RIGHT SIDE VIEW)

TEST 1

Questions 1-5.

DIRECTIONS: In each of questions 1 to 5 inclusive, two views of an object are given. Of the views labelled A, B, C, and D, select the one that *CORRECTLY* represents the right side view of each object.
Which view represents the right side view? 1. A   2. B   3. C   4. D

1.

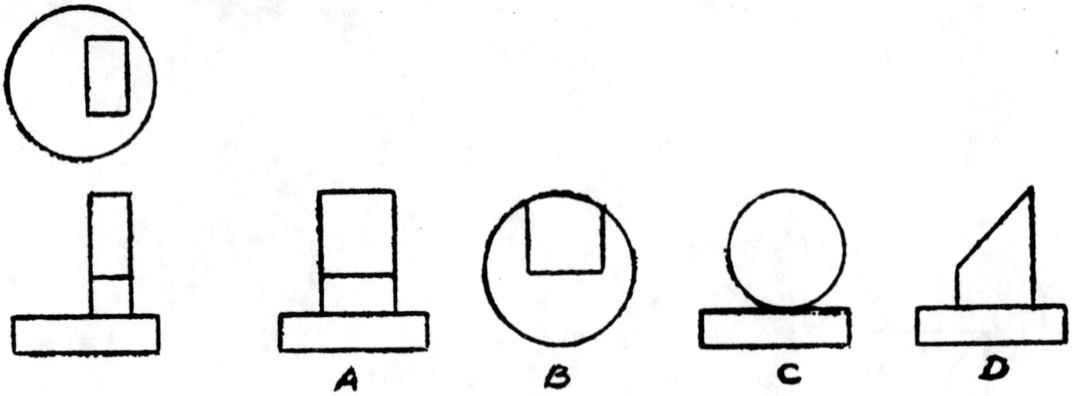

A   B   C   D

2.

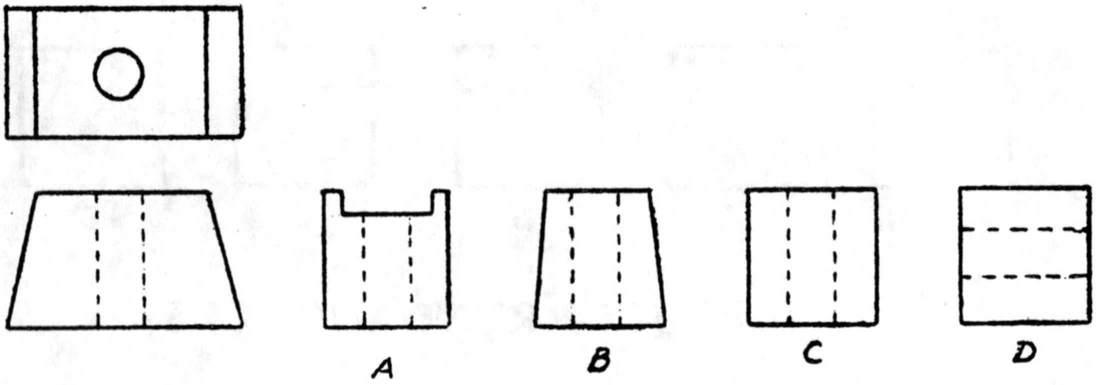

A   B   C   D

3.

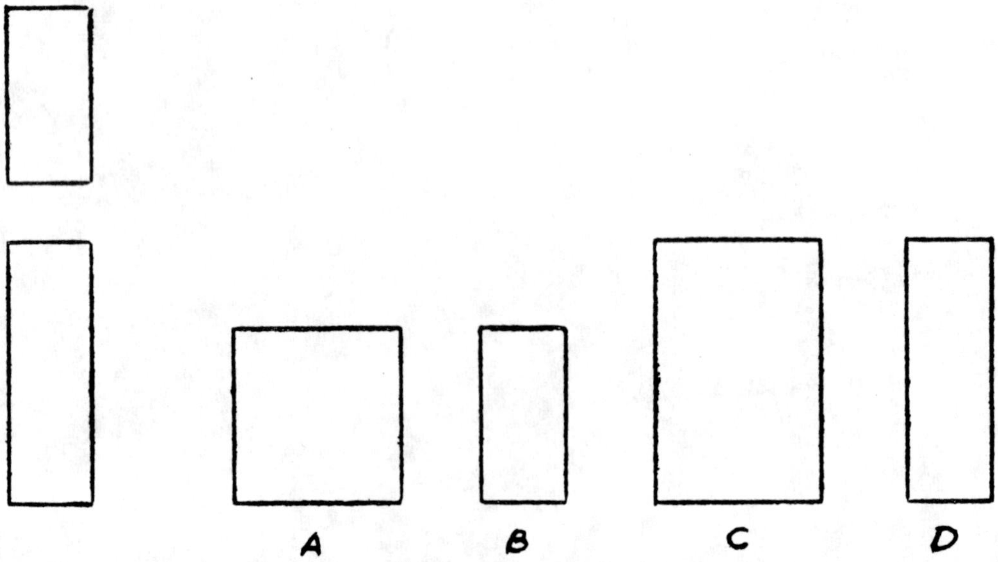

A   B   C   D

4.

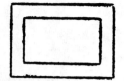

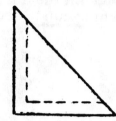 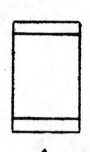 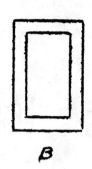 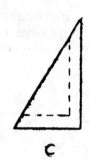 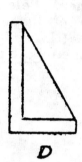

A   B   C   D

5.

   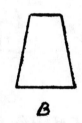 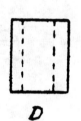

A   B   C   D

KEY (CORRECT ANSWERS)

1.	4
2.	3
3.	3
4.	2
5.	2

SOLID FIGURE TURNING

Questions 1-3.

The following questions represent figures made up of cubes or other forms glued together. Select the ONE of the four figures lettered A, B, C, D, which is the figure at the left turned in a different position and mark the correct space on the answer sheet. (Note: You are permitted to turn <u>over</u> the figures, to turn them <u>around</u>, and to turn them <u>both</u> over and around.)

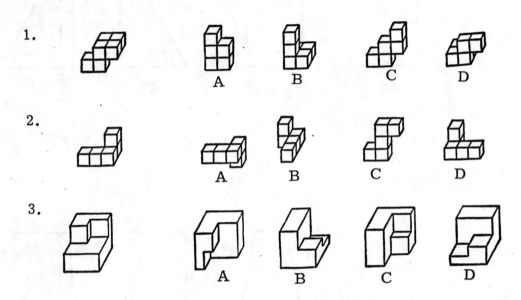

1.   A   B   C   D

2.   A   B   C   D

3.   A   B   C   D

TOUCHING CUBES

Questions 4-7.

Questions 4 and 5 are based on the group of touching cubes at the left, and questions 6 and 7 on the group at the right.

All the cubes are exactly the same size, and there are only enough hidden cubes to support the ones you can see. The question number is on a cube in the group. You are to find how many cubes in that group touch the numbered cube. Note: A cube is considered to touch the numbered cube if ANY part, EVEN A CORNER, touches. Mark the answer sheet to show how many cubes touch the numbered cube by blackening space

    A if the answer is 1 or 6 or 11 cubes
    B if the answer is 2 or 7 or 12 cubes
    C if the answer is 3 or 8 or 13 cubes
    D if the answer is 4 or 9 or 14 cubes
    E if the answer is 5 **or** 10 or 15 cubes

 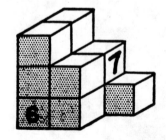

14

CUBE TURNING

Questions 8-9

In each of the following questions, the drawing at the left represents a cube. There is a different design on each of the six faces of the cube. At the right are four other drawings of cubes lettered A, B, C, and D.

Select the ONE of the four which is actually the cube on the left turned to a different position and blacken the appropriate space on the answer sheet. (Note: The cube at the left may have been turned over, it may have been turned around, or it may have been turned both over and around, and faces not seen in the drawing on the left may have become visible.)

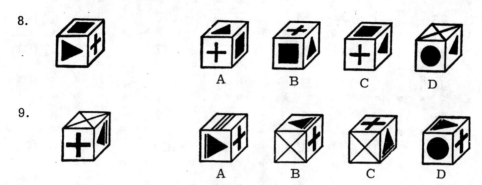

8.

    A   B   C   D

9.

    A   B   C   D

CUBE COUNTING

Questions 10-15.

In each of the following questions, count the number of boxes or cubes represented in the drawing and blacken the appropriate space on the answer sheet.

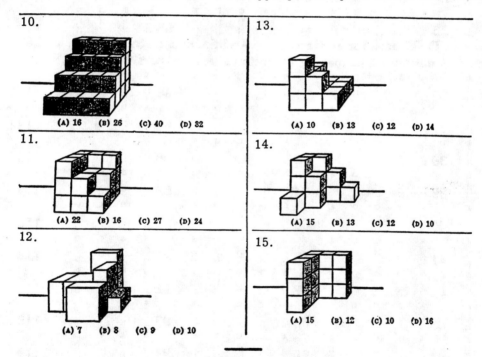

10.

(A) 16   (B) 26   (C) 40   (D) 32

13.

(A) 10   (B) 13   (C) 12   (D) 14

11.

(A) 22   (B) 16   (C) 27   (D) 24

14.

(A) 15   (B) 13   (C) 12   (D) 10

12.

(A) 7   (B) 8   (C) 9   (D) 10

15.

(A) 15   (B) 12   (C) 10   (D) 16

KEY (CORRECT ANSWERS)

1.	D	6.	B(7)	11.	A
2.	B	7.	E(10)	12.	B
3.	D	8.	B	13.	D
4.	C(3)	9.	A	14.	A
5.	A(6)	10.	C	15.	A

ANSWER SHEET

TEST NO. _____ PART _____ TITLE OF POSITION _____

(AS GIVEN IN EXAMINATION ANNOUNCEMENT - INCLUDE OPTION, IF ANY)

PLACE OF EXAMINATION _____ DATE _____

(CITY OR TOWN)   (STATE)

RATING

USE THE SPECIAL PENCIL.   MAKE GLOSSY BLACK MARKS.

	A B C D E		A B C D E		A B C D E		A B C D E		A B C D E
1	⋮⋮⋮⋮⋮	26	⋮⋮⋮⋮⋮	51	⋮⋮⋮⋮⋮	76	⋮⋮⋮⋮⋮	101	⋮⋮⋮⋮⋮
2	⋮⋮⋮⋮⋮	27	⋮⋮⋮⋮⋮	52	⋮⋮⋮⋮⋮	77	⋮⋮⋮⋮⋮	102	⋮⋮⋮⋮⋮
3	⋮⋮⋮⋮⋮	28	⋮⋮⋮⋮⋮	53	⋮⋮⋮⋮⋮	78	⋮⋮⋮⋮⋮	103	⋮⋮⋮⋮⋮
4	⋮⋮⋮⋮⋮	29	⋮⋮⋮⋮⋮	54	⋮⋮⋮⋮⋮	79	⋮⋮⋮⋮⋮	104	⋮⋮⋮⋮⋮
5	⋮⋮⋮⋮⋮	30	⋮⋮⋮⋮⋮	55	⋮⋮⋮⋮⋮	80	⋮⋮⋮⋮⋮	105	⋮⋮⋮⋮⋮
6	⋮⋮⋮⋮⋮	31	⋮⋮⋮⋮⋮	56	⋮⋮⋮⋮⋮	81	⋮⋮⋮⋮⋮	106	⋮⋮⋮⋮⋮
7	⋮⋮⋮⋮⋮	32	⋮⋮⋮⋮⋮	57	⋮⋮⋮⋮⋮	82	⋮⋮⋮⋮⋮	107	⋮⋮⋮⋮⋮
8	⋮⋮⋮⋮⋮	33	⋮⋮⋮⋮⋮	58	⋮⋮⋮⋮⋮	83	⋮⋮⋮⋮⋮	108	⋮⋮⋮⋮⋮
9	⋮⋮⋮⋮⋮	34	⋮⋮⋮⋮⋮	59	⋮⋮⋮⋮⋮	84	⋮⋮⋮⋮⋮	109	⋮⋮⋮⋮⋮
10	⋮⋮⋮⋮⋮	35	⋮⋮⋮⋮⋮	60	⋮⋮⋮⋮⋮	85	⋮⋮⋮⋮⋮	110	⋮⋮⋮⋮⋮

Make only ONE mark for each answer.   Additional and stray marks may be counted as mistakes.   In making corrections, erase errors COMPLETELY.

	A B C D E		A B C D E		A B C D E		A B C D E		A B C D E
11	⋮⋮⋮⋮⋮	36	⋮⋮⋮⋮⋮	61	⋮⋮⋮⋮⋮	86	⋮⋮⋮⋮⋮	111	⋮⋮⋮⋮⋮
12	⋮⋮⋮⋮⋮	37	⋮⋮⋮⋮⋮	62	⋮⋮⋮⋮⋮	87	⋮⋮⋮⋮⋮	112	⋮⋮⋮⋮⋮
13	⋮⋮⋮⋮⋮	38	⋮⋮⋮⋮⋮	63	⋮⋮⋮⋮⋮	88	⋮⋮⋮⋮⋮	113	⋮⋮⋮⋮⋮
14	⋮⋮⋮⋮⋮	39	⋮⋮⋮⋮⋮	64	⋮⋮⋮⋮⋮	89	⋮⋮⋮⋮⋮	114	⋮⋮⋮⋮⋮
15	⋮⋮⋮⋮⋮	40	⋮⋮⋮⋮⋮	65	⋮⋮⋮⋮⋮	90	⋮⋮⋮⋮⋮	115	⋮⋮⋮⋮⋮
16	⋮⋮⋮⋮⋮	41	⋮⋮⋮⋮⋮	66	⋮⋮⋮⋮⋮	91	⋮⋮⋮⋮⋮	116	⋮⋮⋮⋮⋮
17	⋮⋮⋮⋮⋮	42	⋮⋮⋮⋮⋮	67	⋮⋮⋮⋮⋮	92	⋮⋮⋮⋮⋮	117	⋮⋮⋮⋮⋮
18	⋮⋮⋮⋮⋮	43	⋮⋮⋮⋮⋮	68	⋮⋮⋮⋮⋮	93	⋮⋮⋮⋮⋮	118	⋮⋮⋮⋮⋮
19	⋮⋮⋮⋮⋮	44	⋮⋮⋮⋮⋮	69	⋮⋮⋮⋮⋮	94	⋮⋮⋮⋮⋮	119	⋮⋮⋮⋮⋮
20	⋮⋮⋮⋮⋮	45	⋮⋮⋮⋮⋮	70	⋮⋮⋮⋮⋮	95	⋮⋮⋮⋮⋮	120	⋮⋮⋮⋮⋮
21	⋮⋮⋮⋮⋮	46	⋮⋮⋮⋮⋮	71	⋮⋮⋮⋮⋮	96	⋮⋮⋮⋮⋮	121	⋮⋮⋮⋮⋮
22	⋮⋮⋮⋮⋮	47	⋮⋮⋮⋮⋮	72	⋮⋮⋮⋮⋮	97	⋮⋮⋮⋮⋮	122	⋮⋮⋮⋮⋮
23	⋮⋮⋮⋮⋮	48	⋮⋮⋮⋮⋮	73	⋮⋮⋮⋮⋮	98	⋮⋮⋮⋮⋮	123	⋮⋮⋮⋮⋮
24	⋮⋮⋮⋮⋮	49	⋮⋮⋮⋮⋮	74	⋮⋮⋮⋮⋮	99	⋮⋮⋮⋮⋮	124	⋮⋮⋮⋮⋮
25	⋮⋮⋮⋮⋮	50	⋮⋮⋮⋮⋮	75	⋮⋮⋮⋮⋮	100	⋮⋮⋮⋮⋮	125	⋮⋮⋮⋮⋮